PERSUASION
AND
POWER

PERSUASION
AND
POWER

The Art of Strategic Communication

James P. Farwell

Foreword by John J. Hamre

Georgetown University Press
Washington, DC

Library of Congress Cataloging-in-Publication Data

Farwell, James P.
  Persuasion and power : the art of strategic communication / by James P. Farwell ; foreword by John J. Hamre.
     p. cm.
  Includes bibliographical references and index.
  ISBN 978-1-58901-942-3 (pbk. : alk. paper)
  1. Communication in politics. 2. Communication in international relations.
I. Title.
  JA85.F37 2012
  320.01'4—dc23   2012007819

⊗ This book is printed on acid-free paper meeting the requirements of the American National Standard for Permanence in Paper for Printed Library Materials.

15 14 13 12   9 8 7 6 5 4 3 2   First printing

This is dedicated to four exceptional colonels from whose wisdom I have learned much:

Colonel Al Bynum, USAF (Ret)

Colonel Paul Huxhold, USMC (Ret)

Colonel Stephen Padgett, OBE, British Army

Colonel Sandy Wade, OBE, British Army

Contents

Foreword

The late Senator Russell Long once told a story, making fun of his own experience. It seems that two different cities in Louisiana were competing for a federal project. A delegation from each city contacted his office asking for his special help to sway the process in their favor. Senator Long's scheduling secretary became confused, not realizing there were competing delegations. She arranged for both city delegations to meet with Senator Long at precisely the same time. Senator Long walked into the meeting, and, realizing the peril in the situation, drew upon his vast reservoir of humor: "Look here, friends. If you want me to agree with you, you are going to have to come in here separately."

This rather simple story contains vast wisdom for our age. We live in a time when it is no longer possible to take two different positions to a problem, thinking they will never be exposed to reconciliation over time. There was perhaps a time when differing messages could be offered to different audiences to no ill effect. This is no longer the case. In an era of global and near-instantaneous communications, there is no practical way to segment different themes to one's motives or actions.

Democratic governments have an inherent problem: they need to undertake some activities of state in secrecy. But democracies ultimately have to take all matters to the public for open debate. Private, secret actions may represent an initiative of an administration, but they do not represent a commitment of the nation until they are forged through public debate into a national consensus. The so-called WikiLeak controversy in 2010 was illuminating. Tens of thousands of secret cables were suddenly released to newspapers for public display. Importantly, there were no disconnects between secret policy and public debate. Certainly, there were important details in the secret cables, and sometimes salacious details that would be embarrassing when exposed to the public. But there was no fundamental disconnect in our secret diplomacy and our public debate about national intents and purposes. The WikiLeaks incident demonstrated a fundamental integrity in American democracy, where our secret diplomacy was fully faithful to our democracy.

So now we consider the role of strategic communication. The demands of our democratic idealism and the imperative of the age of communication immediacy dictate the same course. There can be no fraudulent strategic communication of our national policies or purposes. Clever, good public relations cannot compensate for flawed policy. Good policy is the foundation for good public diplomacy. James Farwell's book is a timely, insightful examination into the concepts of strategic communication, and how people have thought about and applied its principles from antiquity to the present.

In recent years America has drifted into an irritating habit of lecturing the world about what an inspirational country it is. Our national character is to consider America a unique nation, either privileged in its history or destined by greater powers to be an exception. There is no question that America has been inspirational to people around the world. But America is not welcomed when it lectures to everyone else about how inspirational it is. And in recent years, claims of exceptionalism have been severely diminished by behavior. The recent recession proved enormously corrosive to our claims of competency as world leaders in business, finance, and governance. How the country runs its own domestic polity is the most fundamental strategic communication it offers to the world. No amount of artful messaging can alter observable reality. Strategic communication, therefore, must be fundamentally grounded in the daily business of government.

While strategic communication cannot depart from the fundamental reality of governance, we do live in a time when truth can be distorted by manipulation. We live in a time where the Internet has provided vast new reservoirs of information that cannot be validated through traditional structures. Few news organizations can now afford the robust editorial staffs and disciplined editorial processes that once validated news as "true." Fraudulent news channels can be made to appear just as authoritative as honest ones. The opportunities for disinformation have exploded dramatically, presenting challenges to managers of institutions—whether they are universities, corporations, or governments.

Strategic communication for a democracy is ultimately an exercise in helping others ascertain the truth about our real intents and purposes as a nation. Strategic communication should not be the government equivalent of clever advertising. Communicating a clear, consistent, and truthful message is the foundation of effective governance.

John J. Hamre
President and CEO
Center for Strategic and International Studies

Acknowledgments

This book is possible only with the incisive, insightful criticism, support, suggestions, and input from a large group of gifted individuals who have tremendous backgrounds and expertise in the subjects that this book covers. Many of them engaged in extensive discussions and generously provided their time to help ensure accuracy, clarity, and relevance.

I am deeply indebted to the extraordinary and gracious generosity of Patricia Kushlis for reviewing and editing the manuscript before submission. Matt Armstrong is a tremendous friend and colleague who shared his insights and expertise gained from long years of dealing with topics that this book embraces. My close friend and often partner in political campaigns, Joe Gaylord, constantly reviewed key sections and was a great help. Ron Faucheux and Chris Stewart, both top Washington pollsters, offered important contributions. Col. Stephen Padgett and Col. (Ret) Al Bynum provided vital help in examining aspects that affect the military. Jack Guy, Dan Kuehl, Ted Tzavellas, Ambassador Brian Carlson, Ambassador Gil Robinson, Doug Schoen, Ed Goeas, Herb Friedman, Glen Bolger, Scott Straus, Brent Scowcroft, Marvin Weinbaum, Sandy Wade, Col.Paul Huxhold (Ret), Jerry Renne, Stan Schrager, Glen Ayers, Amy Zalman, Ayesha Jalal, Shuja Nawaz, Maj. Gen. (Ret) David Scott, Lt. Gen/Amb. (Ret) Dell Dailey, Christopher Paul, Trita Parsi, Doug Waller, Virgil Scudder, Rich Galen, Celinda Lake, Christopher Lamb, Joseph Meissner, Joe Duffey, Shimon Naveh, Eric Michael, Julian Wheatley, John Maddox, Steve Tatham, Herb Lin, Farhad Cacard, Carina Tertsakian, and my longtime editor, Jim Wade, helped make this book significantly better with their criticisms of the manuscript in its different stages, and their many insights and suggestions. I am indebted to the encouragement and support that Don Jacobs at Georgetown University Press provided.

Steven Luckert, principal curator at the United States Holocaust Memorial Museum, and other staff at the museum were notably helpful in examining the issue of propaganda and helping to find posters, artwork, and illustrations.

Chapter 15 is adapted from James P. Farwell, "Jihadi Video in the 'War of Ideas,'" in *Survival: Global Politics and Strategy*, vol. 52, no. 6, December 2010–January 2011, 127–50.

Abbreviations

AMISOM	African Union Mission in Somalia
ANWR	Arctic National Wildlife Refuge
AQAP	Al-Qaeda in the Arabian Peninsula
CAAT	Counterinsurgency Advisory and Assistance Team
CDR	Coalition pour la defense de la republique
CFA	Committee for a Free Asia
CIA	Central Intelligence Agency
CID	Criminal Investigation Division
CIDE	Centro de Investigacion y Docencia Economicas
CIIR	Center for International Issues Research
CJTF-7	Combined Joint Task Force-7
COI	Coordination of Information
COIN	Counterinsurgency
CSCC	Center for Strategic Counterterrorism Communications
ECA	Bureau of Educational and Cultural Affairs
ECOWAS	Economic Community of West African States
EZLN	Zapatista National Liberation Army
FARC	Fuerzas Armadas Revolucionarias de Colombia
FIS	Foreign Information Service
FLN	Algerian National Liberation Front
HRCP	Human Rights Commission of Pakistan
ICTR	International Criminal Tribunal for Rwanda
IED	improvised explosive device
IIP	Office of International Information Programs
IO	information operations
IPI	International Public Information
ISAF	International Security Assistance Force
ISI	Inter-Services Intelligence
MAS	Movement towards Socialism
MISO	Military Information Support Operations

MRND	Mouvement revolutionaire national pour le developpement
NATO	North American Treaty Organization
NCFE	National Committee for a Free Europe
NSC	National Security Council
OCB	Operations Coordinating Board
OSI	Office of Strategic Influence
OSS	Office of Strategic Services
OWI	Office of War Information
PATCO	Professional Air Traffic Controllers Organization
PCA	Production Code Administration
PNSR	Project for National Security Reform
PSB	Psychological Strategy Board
PSUV	Partido Socialista Unido de Venezuela
PSYOP	psychological operations
RFA	Radio Free Asia
RFE	Radio Free Europe
RINO	Republican In Name Only
RL	Radio Liberty
RPF	Rwandan Patriotic Front
RTLM	Radio Television Libre des Mille Collines
RUF	Revolutionary United Front
SIPSA	senior information policy and strategy adviser
SMM	Southern Mobility Movement
TARP	Troubled Asset Relief Program
UNAMIR	United Nations Assistance Mission for Rwanda
USIA	United States Information Agency
VOA	Voice of America

INTRODUCTION

THIS BOOK IS ABOUT THE ART OF STRATEGIC COMMUNICATION, HOW IT IS used, where, and why. It examines how people have thought about the notion through the ages and applied its principles, and what lessons for today we can learn from past experience. Technology evolves, but the strategic approaches that people have used over the centuries bear striking similarities. Mark Twain wrote that history doesn't repeat itself; it rhymes. For example, modern election campaign pins echo the way Julius Caesar used coins to build awareness and communicate his power. Barack Obama's approach to social media employed twenty-first-century technology using the Internet, but the strategic thinking in reaching social networks resembled Martin Luther's approach to the Reformation through the use of pamphlets and his translation of the Bible, which reached out to opinion leaders who then passed on the message orally to even greater numbers of people.[1] Venezuelan president Hugo Chavez may philosophically identify with Simon Bolivar, but his approach to dealing with the news media by forcing newspapers and television stations to toe the line is closer to Napoleon's mindset.

Strategic communication has spawned many definitions. Some view it as a process for engaging or understanding key audiences through activities such as information operations, public affairs, and public diplomacy. The US Department of Defense tends to treat it in that light. This book focuses upon the art of strategic communication. What are its elements? How are its principles applied? It's helpful to describe the way the US government delineates forms of communication that may qualify as strategic communication, but concrete examples seem to offer a clearer appreciation than theory. After examining definitions or descriptions of how the US government (notably the Department of Defense and Department of State) view forms of communication, the book consciously adopts an anecdotal technique to illustrate and explain this art. The scope of this book extends beyond the notion of strategic communication that the US government employs. It also challenges the view that the Pentagon should avoid characterizing its activities as aimed at influence—a view that has unfortunately drawn adherents after an absurd turf war that took place in the Pentagon in 2002. The debate over whether the Pentagon should influence or merely inform certainly exists regarding public affairs, but the debate has spilled over into other areas of the Department of Defense. Yet the fact is that the art of strategic communication specifically aims to influence behavior. This book asserts that while respecting truth, influencing behavior is an appropriate and necessary activity for the Department.

The Declaration of Independence

The Declaration of Independence illustrates strategic communication more vividly than abstract theory does. In justifying a claim for independence from Britain by the thirteen colonies, the Declaration proclaimed a natural equality among people as a guiding principle for government. The document's objective was to arouse support abroad, especially in France, for the revolution.

The Declaration is rooted in values manifest in certain "self-evident" truths: "That all men are created equal, that they are endowed by their Creator with certain inalienable rights, that among these are life, liberty and the pursuit of happiness. That to secure these rights, governments are instituted among men, deriving their just powers from the consent of the governed." There follows an indictment of the king of Great Britain for seeking to establish "an absolute tyranny over these states," and ignoring or abusing human rights. It also snubs Parliament, the real power in Great Britain, sending another message equally important to the authors. This was not lost on the members of Parliament.

Matt Armstrong, the former executive director of the US Advisory Commission on Public Diplomacy, rightly observes that the Declaration "stands as one of history's great examples of strategic communication."[2] Through its eloquent language and by the bold action it takes in issuing it, the document seeks to influence the attitudes and opinions of domestic and foreign audiences. It provides a platform to unite people, and it pronounces facts and ideas around which they can mobilize and identify.

Although it draws squarely upon ideas from John Locke and the English Enlightenment, politically, the Declaration broke new ground in its intent to actually form a new nation rooted in its stated values. The Declaration registers its claim for a new nation, as journalist Henry Fairlie acutely observes, "not for a sovereign or for a church, not in the name of a god or of a king, but for an idea."[3] Truth that is self-evident, he notes, cannot be proven; it is an idea. The idea was for a nation founded in the belief of human equality, endowed by their

Creator with certain rights, for *each* American. Rights proceed from the higher moral order ordained by God, not human fiat. God grants power that we loan to government through "the consent of the governed."

In other nations liberty was not a natural right bestowed by God, but the product of political concessions made to particular groups to resolve specific tensions.[4] The English Revolution curtailed powers of the monarchy and was not concerned with equality. The French Revolution, Fairlie points out, "was concerned with man as an abstraction but not with men as individuals," while the Russian Revolution "was not concerned with liberty."[5]

The Declaration provided an intellectual core for the Revolution, aroused support among Colonials, and, critically, struck a strong responsive chord among supporters of the Enlightenment in France. Historian Jonathan Dull emphasizes that the Declaration "was largely a foreign-policy statement; without it, America hardly could appeal for foreign assistance against the great army gathering to attack New York and the navy blockading its ports."[6]

Benjamin Franklin's astute diplomacy, and prodding by the Marquis de Lafayette, helped encourage the French—who were also looking for an opportunity to extract revenge upon England for its loss in the Seven Years War—to provide decisive support for the American Revolution.[7] A "contest that had been precipitated by folly was conducted with stupidity," James Breck Perkins observes in a book written a century ago but that is replete with insight. In elegant prose he argues that while without France, the Revolution might not have prevailed: "It was entirely possible that the struggle begun in 1775 should have ended in disaster, and the history and development of the United States been different."[8]

The Declaration shines brightly as the epitome of American strategic communication. It was a carefully drawn, well-thought-through document that identified its target audiences and used the power of language and ideas to influence attitudes and opinions. It shaped behavior decisively. The Declaration offers a dramatic example of an art that is too often little understood and awkwardly employed.

What Is Strategic Communication?

Official and unofficial definitions in defense circles are all over the board, divided between process, capability, expected effects, and the art of strategic communication. The Pentagon defines strategic communication as "focused United States Government efforts to understand and engage key audiences to create, strengthen, or preserve conditions favorable for the advancement of United States Government interests, policies, and objectives through the use of coordinated programs, plans, themes, messages, and products synchronized with the actions of all instruments of national power."[9]

The term strategic communication, as used today in the US military, originated in 2002 in the office of then–Brig. Gen. Jack Catton at the Pentagon. Catton worked with three other people, Ted Tzavellas, Rhett Hernandez (currently a major general), and Lt. Col. (ret) Jeff Lau, to hammer out a term that everyone working on communication would be willing to use as a means to inform and influence key audiences. Ted Tzavellas was the senior information policy and strategy adviser (SIPSA) to the Joint Staff, deputy director of global operations. Tzavellas explains: "At its inception, Strategic Communication was simply intended to bring practitioners of Public Affairs, Public Diplomacy, Information Operations, et al. to the same table for them to independently pursue what they were each skilled at doing, but to do so under a harmony of interests and with knowledge of each other's activities. Public affairs had used the term 'strategic communications'—plural—but limited the meaning of that term to informing, not influencing."[10]

A retired senior military public affairs official points out, "Department of Defense people often view strategic communication as a process rather than a capability or the art of communicating strategically."[11] The concepts are different. The process is to create consistency in message and purpose and to avoid information fratricide—what in politics is called cross-pressuring the message. Consistency is achieved by getting every stakeholder at the strategic or operational level at the table.[12] Moving everyone in the same direction, obviously, can prove more challenging.

Political leaders are less interested in definitions, capability, or process in communication. They think in terms of political communication, not strategic communication. It's a vital distinction. Government officials may debate the meaning of strategic communication, who employs it, when, and how. But policy is made by political figures who generally think about communication in different terms. Joe Gaylord, the true strategic architect of the Republican successful takeover of the US House of Representatives in 1994, and for whom the Association of Political Consultants bestowed the honor of "Campaign Manager of the Year," defines political communication as "any communication, by word or deeds, that helps to execute a strategy or tactic to achieve a desired result in influencing attitudes, opinions, or behavior of targeted audiences." Kevin McCarty, who served as the director for global outreach on the National Security Council, adds that strategic communication includes "managing the information environment to shape attitudes and behaviors."[13] His view applies to national security and to the commercial world.

In this book I define strategic communication as the use of words, actions, images, or symbols to influence the attitudes and opinions of target audiences to shape their behavior in order to advance interests or policies, or to achieve objectives. For the military, which employs a notion of "operational design," it includes creating conditions that define a desired end-state.[14] That definition guides most political, corporate, and issue management campaigns, at home and abroad.[15] Some branches of the military talk about it in terms of influencing emotions, reasoning, and motives, but political professionals and corporate communication experts believe that those are what influence attitudes and opinions. Reason persuades, emotion motivates.

There is an added nuance in thinking about "influence." Ed Goeas, a top US pollster, draws a distinction between the notion of influencing attitudes and opinion and molding them: "Influence means to have an effect on the direction of thinking. It relates to shaping behavior. In politics, it is important to understand that one also 'molds' attitudes and opinions. Mold means to shape the thought itself. You can influence people to think more conservatively, but that does not necessarily mold them to conservative philosophy. It is a nuance that represents a step towards influence."[16]

Strategic communication has acquired talismanic status in national security discourse. Merely defining it is insufficient. One also has to consider, what does it embrace? Do propaganda, psychological operations, military information support (MISO), information operations, public affairs, or public diplomacy qualify as strategic communication? If not, what distinctions might be drawn? What are its elements? How do people employ it to promote national strategy, or operationally for strategy or tactics? Where have its principles been well or badly applied? Do the definitions matter operationally in the field or do people ignore them in the interest of getting things done? Official and unofficial efforts—none successful—within US government circles to define the notion abound.[17]

Cutting across that debate is the issue of who can engage in strategic communication globally. At the Department of State, the secretary speaks for the department. The assistant secretary for public affairs, the departmental spokesperson, or someone properly designated by the secretary is an official communicator. Abroad, the ambassador acts as chief spokesperson, but normally designates the public affairs counselor, public affairs officer, information officer, or press attaché to speak for the embassy. Broadly, the government uses public diplomacy to engage, inform, and influence foreign audiences, and through such clearly identifiable communication, advances US interests.

At the Department of Defense, the secretary speaks for the department and speaks through the assistant secretary of defense for public affairs or other designated spokespeople. In the field, different commands operate principally through commanders or their designated spokespeople. It influences foreign

audiences through psychological operations units (renamed military information support) and public affairs units. The units are kept separate and distinct,
although that distinction does not always function smoothly in a modern,
global media environment. Matt Armstrong notes that "the Pentagon's social
media policy allows individual soldiers to communicate by Twitter or e-mail on
their own behalf, but not officially." He points out that this "poses a significant
challenge to the military, which has to operate in a 24/7 global environment."[18]

Definitions can muddle operational reality in the information environment. In the field, lines can get blurred. This book argues that strategic communication subsumes many communication activities that some may consider
distinct.

How This Book Is Organized

Strategic communication is a broad notion and applies in many dimensions. The
interest here is its use for political and national security issues. This book's focus
is broader than US government discourse. It looks at the notion historically and
today, and from the perspective of different nations, cultures, and societies.

Part I reviews different concepts and definitions employed by the Departments of Defense and State to understand how they view different forms of
engagement. This book argues that psychological operations (in the military,
renamed military information support operations), propaganda, information
operations, and public affairs generally constitute different forms of strategic
communication. Definitions and concepts often bump up against one another.
The US government has an important, compelling interest in maintaining a
reputation for honesty, candor, and integrity. Its credibility depends upon that.
Unfortunately, a combination of ambiguity in definition, an unnecessary fear
of the term psychological operations (PSYOP) and the use of verbal gimmicks
to distance the United States from it, and inconsistencies between theory and
practice make the government appear hypocritical and create a problem it
strives to avoid. While different forms of communication may qualify as strategic communication, the distinctions are important. Each is directed at different
audiences; each is governed by different considerations.

Part II examines the elements of the art of strategic communication. This
book is not a litany of every example of strategic communication, but key historical examples uncover comparisons that offer lessons for today in thinking
about content of the notion. Part III analyzes campaigns of influence and how
strategic communication is employed to execute them. It draws on historical
and contemporary examples to suggest lessons for today. Part IV examines how
television and radio can be used as weapons for strategic communication. Part V

offers recommendations to improve strategic communication by the US government. Not all are new—but bear advocacy.

I aim for this book to help policy and decision makers, action officers, and those who deal with communication to ask hard questions about when, where, and how they can apply the principles of strategic communication to inform and influence audiences to achieve defined objectives.

PART I

The Forms of Strategic Communication

CHAPTER 1

Psychological Operations

THE TRAP THAT THE US GOVERNMENT, AND ESPECIALLY THE DEPARTMENT of Defense, has put itself into in its approach to defining forms of communication is notable in its queasy attitude toward psychological operations (PSYOP). Several points are relevant. First, PSYOP is a form of strategic communication aimed at foreign audiences. It is carried out through the use of words, actions, images, or symbols. It aims to mold or shape public opinion in order to influence behavior. Second, the government's current tendency to treat PSYOP as a ticking bomb that could blast its reputation for honesty, integrity, and credibility is unnecessary—although unless properly conceived, monitored, controlled, and exercised, it could backfire. Worse, its efforts to disassociate PSYOP from propaganda, as the Defense Department defines that term, make it look hypocritical. The effect is to create the problem the US government seeks to avoid.

There is a need for a pragmatic, consistent approach to defining PSYOP that differentiates it clearly from propaganda, which in the modern world is viewed pejoratively as an effort to lie, trick, deceive, or manipulate. Although the terms have been used interchangeably, drawing the distinction makes sense. Protecting US credibility in communication merits obvious priority to preserve the government's flexibility in acting to leverage its power, as well as to avoid tainting strategic communication that the United States employs. Experience shows that this goal is easily achievable.

What Are Psychological Operations?

The Defense Department defines PSYOP as "planned operations to convey selected information and indicators to foreign audiences to influence their emotions, motives, objective reasoning, and ultimately the behavior of foreign governments, organizations, groups, and individuals. The purpose of psychological operations is to induce or reinforce foreign attitudes and behavior favorable to the originator's objectives."[1]

For some, the term had, as Col. (ret) Alfred H. Paddock Jr., former director for psychological operations in the Office of Secretary of Defense put it, "a nefarious connotation."[2] Some equate psychological operations with lies and deception. In response, in June 2010 the Pentagon rebranded the term and now calls it Military Information Support Operations (MISO). The definition of MISO employs the same language that defines PSYOP; only the name has been changed. Indeed, many in the military continue to use the term PSYOP colloquially to mean action aimed at demoralizing the enemy. In this book I use the term PSYOP, with the understanding that the Department of Defense has renamed it.[3]

As PSYOP expert Joe Meissner, editor of *Perspectives* and the *Daily Front Post* publications directed to the PSYOP community points out, "MISO is not a good name for what we do. It does not describe our work, nor does it limit our work by its words of Military Information Support Operations. The term is both overinclusive and underinclusive."[4] It encompasses activities that public affairs or public information officers do. You can be certain they would object to any suggestion that their activities comprise MISOs. MISO is too narrow a term. Those who are engaged in psychological operations understand that PSYOP is conducted to support other military operations. But it can also be the main activity, not just a supporting activity. On this count, as well, critics argue that the term MISO is unsatisfactory.

Meissner criticizes the words "military information" as unclear. "What does 'military information' mean?" he asks. "Does this mean only information on military topics? What about social, economic, and cultural information? Must MISO personnel all be military—or merely have a military goal and perspective? The notion of PSYOP has no such limitations."[5]

A competing school of thought views the transformation of PSYOP into MISO as a way to broaden, not narrow, the notion. PSYOP (MISO) units were extremely helpful in the New Orleans area in the aftermath of Katrina, providing support to civilian relief efforts. Many concluded that the military's considerable talents and expertise in this area could be applied more broadly. The term MISO is gaining adherents in many quarters.

Britain's Approach

Britain resolved the debate over a name change to MISO in favor of PSYOP. Commander Steve Tatham, a senior officer in Britain's influence development organization, notes that in 1999 the 15 (UK) PsyOps group, which had been established in 1996, announced that it would change its name to the Information Support Group. The name change was brought about because of the perception that Psyops was a pejorative term, somehow associated with brainwashing and mind-bending. "However," Tatham points out, "the name lasted less than three years and in 2002 it was changed back to PsyOps. In that intervening period the group had been plagued by three problems as a direct result of the change: The British army had presumed that it now possessed no PsyOps capability and the group was written out of routine exercises and, worse, inclusion in operations; second, NATO had decided not to change its name and fellow NATO members were unhappy; finally, the group became plagued by phone calls and e-mails from around the UK armed forces for requests to help fix IT and computer problems!"[6]

He adds: "In 2010, when the US changed from PsyOps to MISO the MoD convened a meeting to discuss whether the UK should follow suit. In almost undue haste there was widespread agreement amongst various senior officers that this was a good idea until the Commanding Officer of 15 (UK) PsyOps Group was finally asked to comment. After relaying the group's history the matter was quickly closed and the meeting adjourned; the UK would not be changing its name anytime soon."[7]

PSYOP Is Strategic Communication

Aimed at influencing and shaping the behavior of foreign audiences through words, actions, images, or symbols, PSYOP qualifies as strategic communication. The Defense Department acknowledges that PSYOP's mission is to influence perceptions and the subsequent behavior of audiences, although it cautions against confusing "psychological impact with PSYOP." Actions "such as strikes or shows of force have psychological impact but they are not PSYOP [MISO] unless their primary purpose is to influence the perceptions and behavior of a TA [target audience]."[8] In short, the test for whether an action is PSYOP is intent. If it's PSYOP, it is strategic communication.

Christopher Lamb of the National Defense University distinguishes PSYOP from other forms of influence communication. He states: "PSYOP supports military operations and aims to modify behavior directly. Toward that end it will use emotion as well as reason; it employs truth but selectively; it will omit facts and on occasion, may mislead the audience. It is inherently biased and the interests of the target audience are incidental compared to the objective of supporting military operations.[9] Public diplomacy is directed at foreign publics. It seeks to modify perceptions indirectly by presenting issues from the US government point of view. In terms of techniques it appeals to reason and only subtly and infrequently to emotions. Relevant facts may be omitted, but Public Diplomacy never seeks consciously to mislead, lie or deceive. Public Affairs attempts to influence by creating a better informed public. In addition to emphasizing accuracy, Public Affairs officers take care to avoid omitting facts critical to a story even if they are inconvenient, although once disclosed, they are presented in ways that are favorable to US interests if possible."[10]

The issue over whether PSYOP should mislead has engendered controversy. Many argue that because it is advocating a message, it is selective about the facts it uses and its presentation, aimed squarely at persuasion and influence, is inherently biased. The extent to which it may properly mislead is unresolved. The notion of "misleading" is also subjective. Is it misleading to influence an audience to oppose an enemy by characterizing the enemy in very strong, negative terms? Suppose we call an opposition a gang of murderers. Or criminals masquerading as political leaders, interested merely in gaining power and lining their pockets. Others may view those forces very differently. What is appropriate? The answer depends upon one's perspective.

Joseph Meissner argues that this is why "truth is the best PSYOP. Truth should be the guideline. It is the key to maintaining credibility."[11] Meissner raises an important point. People will accept disagreement with your point of view. But credibility is irretrievably lost once they cease to trust because they feel you are lying or misleading them. Political campaigns offer a cogent analogy. The *first thing* consultants do when assessing communications from opponents is to identify any misstatements or distortions of fact, misleading assertions, untruths, or lies. That affords a basis for discrediting the opponent with either of two simple messages about what the opponent has stated. First, ask a target audience: If they would mislead you on this, can we trust them on anything else? Second, declare to a target audience: Some people will say or do anything to win (or, advance their own self-interests), at your expense.

Effective PSYOP requires a more careful, measured, and nuanced approach than it may at first appear. Truth *is* an ally, but the truth communicated must resonate as plausible to an audience. Meissner notes wryly that one of the ironies about PSYOP is that on occasion the truth is not accepted: "In World War I, a piece was put out showing German POW's eating eggs, to show they were well treated. Unfortunately, the Germans, who had limited access to such food, found that not at all believable."[12]

Such concerns help frame the anxiety over psychological operations and the related notion of propaganda (discussed in the next chapter) and are understandable, but misguided. Historically, the US government has recognized that both notions are neutral in content. Whether good or bad, prudent or imprudent, it depends upon the context in which the tools are employed, the character of the message, and how PSYOP or propaganda is used. We have always tried to influence foreign target audiences, from the time of the Declaration of Independence. A key issue, especially today, is whether communications that are employed to exert influence are factual, accurate, or consciously misleading. That issue is entwined in whether people perceive that statements are truthful.

Truth is an essential quality to the credibility of any communication. PSYOP's mission is not, it bears noting, to serve the best interests of a target audience. As Christopher Lamb has observed, "PSYOP may provide information that is helpful to a target audience, but fundamentally it exists to further the interests of our military personnel and their endeavors, not those of the target audience."[13] He notes as well that "this is why PSYOP is ethically suspect in public affairs [PA] and public diplomacy [PD] circles," where it is viewed with suspicion. But the history and use of PSYOP suggests that PA and PD concerns are overstated.

The Historical Context

The legendary Office of Strategic Services (OSS), which existed between 1942 and 1945, offers a good starting point to examine the evolution of US official thinking on psychological operations and propaganda. OSS's chief, Bill Donovan, believed them to be powerful weapons, and he drew no distinction between the two. Both tactics employ words, actions, images, or symbols to mold or shape attitudes and opinions in order to influence audience behavior. Both qualify as strategic communication.

Donovan was impressed by the British Special Operations Executive, which integrated intelligence activity, special operations, and psychological warfare.[14] He persuaded Roosevelt to adopt the approach of the Special Operations Executive. In 1941, the president established the office of Coordination of Information (COI) under Donovan's leadership. From the start, a heated debate broke out over what strategies and tactics were appropriate for the United States. This debate continues today. The pivotal issues include how closely US government communication should stick to the truth, and whether the source of communication should be disclosed or attributable.

On one side stood New Deal supporter and playwright Robert Sherwood, a personal friend of Roosevelt and head of the Foreign Information Service (FIS) unit within COI. Sherwood supported psychological operations—which he, too, thought of as propaganda—for democratic education. He considered neither term pejorative. Sherwood hoped to mobilize Americans by contrasting good American values with the evil of the Nazis. But he believed that all communications should be true and attributable. Today, Sherwood's view is called "white" strategic communication.[15] White communication acknowledges US government communication as emanating from US official sources.

Sherwood disdained "black" or "gray" propaganda—covert communication that could be untrue and whose source was unattributable or unattributed.[16] Donovan favored both. He saw the Nazis as a tough foe whose defeat required brass knuckles. For Donovan, what counted was winning, not how you won. Deception struck him as fair game. He embraced black propaganda that concealed the true source and could appear to come from a party hostile to the United States, as well as gray propaganda in which the true source, such as the US government, is not revealed. Gray propaganda may have no attribution or come from a nonofficial source.

Neither Sherwood nor Donovan gave ground, and Roosevelt tended to like having things both ways. He gave each man his own turf. On June 11, 1942, he transferred Sherwood and his FIS to the Office of War Information (OWI). He dissolved COI, formed the OSS, and installed Donovan in charge. OSS engaged in intelligence, espionage, propaganda, and various forms of direct action and special operations. OWI communication was directed at US audiences. OSS focused on external audiences, such as South America, where turf battles with Nelson Rockefeller and J. Edgar Hoover shut Donovan out, and the Pacific, from which Douglas MacArthur excluded OSS. (The organization did operate in Southeast Asia and China, although in 1944 MacArthur created his own psychological warfare branch that dropped over 400 million leaflets and secured the surrender of 20,000 Japanese troops.[17])

Donovan was determined to subvert enemy morale, and his efforts were adventurous. The OSS operation named the "League of Lonely German Women" epitomized the organization's deviousness. Interviews with German POWs had revealed emotional concerns that their women back home were having affairs. The OSS exploited these fears (which American broadcast media also found in soldiers posted to Iraq in the 2003 war, who shared the same concerns about girlfriends at home finding other men and the impact that had in increasing personal stress). Apparently that stress is common to soldiers no matter the war or who they're fighting for. OSS leaflets dropped over German soldiers bore the drawing of a heart with a key inside. The leaflets advised German soldiers to cut out the heart symbol and display it at home during leave, where German girls who saw it would lavish them with sexual attentions. Many German POWs were found in possession of League leaflets and pins.[18]

Donovan biographer Doug Waller admired the OSS's ingenuity and imagination. "In Donovan's day," Waller says, "psychological operations were fairly crude. They could be heavy-handed. His London station spread rumors that senior Nazis had gone into hiding. They faked German mailbags and stuffed them with poison-pen letters whose addresses were copied from prewar German phone directories. The sacks were air-dropped in the hope that civilians would provide them to postmen for delivery. Some ideas worked better than others. Spreading rumors that German soldiers were freezing at the Russian front while Hitler stayed warm and cozy at Berchtesgaden made sense. Other ideas were silly, such as one suggesting that photos of succulent meals be dropped over the German public to make them go crazy with hunger. The point of these operations was to sway the attitudes and opinions of German soldiers and civilians to stop fighting. Donovan was a true pioneer in such operations and demonstrated the breadth and scope of what was possible."[19]

Donovan conducted his operations under a broad charter. The OSS Supporting Committee prepared a basic estimate of psychological warfare that endorsed subversion, propaganda, and intelligence as essential for executing PSYOP.[20] PSYOP operations in the OSS proved very effective.[21] General Dwight Eisenhower created a separate psychological warfare division for Western Europe that defined PSYOP as "the dissemination of propaganda designed to undermine the enemy's will to resist, demoralize his forces, and sustain the morale of our supporters."[22] Eisenhower became a strong proponent for PSYOP.

While Roosevelt appreciated the OSS, Harry Truman had no use for it, nor for Donovan's proposal to turn it into a central intelligence agency once the war ended. On October 1, 1945, Truman disbanded the OSS. Still, three months later he created the Central Intelligence Group, which later became the Central Intelligence Agency (CIA). The CIA received authority to conduct covert psychological operations, although its priority was intelligence collection. Prodded by diplomats like George Kennan, Truman supported the use of propaganda and psychological operations. Kennan and others worried that the Soviets would win over public opinion in Europe and argued for the use of propaganda to counter their efforts. Truman agreed and authorized the CIA to engage in covert propaganda against the Soviet Union. He created the Office of Policy Coordination attached to the CIA that could conduct operations.

Radio Free Europe (RFE) and Radio Liberty (RL) broadcast to Eastern Europe and Russia. In 1951, Truman created the Psychological Strategy Board (PSB) to unify and coordinate US activity. The State Department did not agree with its perspective and showed verve and effectiveness in obstructing it. It failed to mobilize the national security bureaucracy behind a coordinated effort, rendering its efforts ineffective.[23] The lesson is that forging and executing a coherent, coordinated policy of psychological operations or propaganda requires hands-on attention from a president. Truman's attention was focused elsewhere. Opposition to psychological warfare from the State Department stymied its use during his administration; that Truman preferred to use the department as a lead agency for national security policies magnified the problem.[24]

The country finally got such a president in Dwight Eisenhower. His experience in World War II had persuaded him that psychological warfare was effective. On becoming Army Chief of Staff, he argued that the War Department should retain the capability to conduct psychological operations. In his view, "practical, political, and moral grounds" required the United States to undertake psychological operations.[25] His position drew few supporters, as most military considered PSYOP a civilian function. Things changed when he became president.

Even as a candidate, Eisenhower had made clear his strong support for psychological warfare. During a famous speech delivered in October 1952, he advised his San Francisco audience: "Don't be afraid of that term just because it's a five-dollar, five-syllable word."[26] Once elected president, Eisenhower was able to act on his views. He appointed C. D. Jackson, a career propagandist, as his chief advisor on psychological strategy and made him a speechwriter.[27]

He created the Committee on Information Activities, headed by New York businessman William Jackson, to study what was needed to defeat the Soviets. Kenneth Osgood, who wrote a penetrating study of Eisenhower's approach to propaganda and psychological operations as part of a "total war" strategy, notes that C. D. Jackson was the brainchild of the committee. Osgood vanquishes the myth that Eisenhower was a passive executive: his objective was to defeat Communism, not coexist with it.

As historian Stephen Ambrose has done in pointing out Eisenhower's assertiveness in his decisive rejection of recommendations among key national security advisors to employ nuclear weapons, Osgood and Fred I. Greenstein dismiss the charge that Eisenhower was disengaged on this issue.[28] Ike vigorously asserted leadership in devising, monitoring, and pushing this strategy, and did not flinch from overruling Secretary of State Foster Dulles or anyone else who harbored criticism of it.[29] His long army career had provided him a deep understanding of how military staffs functioned and what it took to make things work. "No one in his cabinet," a later study of his decision-making process concluded, "would challenge his national security policymaking approaches."[30]

The Jackson Committee concluded that psychological operations were integral to diplomatic, economic, and military strategy. It argued that while people resented being told what to think, it was important to provide them the information they desired.[31] A committee report concluded that "the art of persuasion is to give him what he wants so truthfully and so skillfully as to influence his thinking in the process."[32] Endorsing propaganda, the committee argued that "men and women throughout the world on both sides of the Iron

Curtain must come to believe that what we are and what we stand for in the world is consistent with their own aspirations."[33]

A key element was presenting a positive picture of the conditions of freedom and happiness for human beings.[34] Significantly, although convinced that propaganda was a key weapon for winning the Cold War, the Committee felt strongly about the need for truth in communication, declaring that "to be effective, [propaganda] must be dependable, convincing, and truthful."[35]

Some have perceived Eisenhower as favoring a modus vivendi with the Communists. Actually, his real instinct was to beat them by winning hearts and minds and challenging the appeal of Communism at home and abroad. Eisenhower felt passionately about this, and supported campaigns that targeted Americans and foreigners in a global contest for public opinion. He agreed with the Jackson Committee. He set up the Operations Coordinating Board (OCB) to handle psychological warfare planning, replacing Truman's ineffective psychological strategy board (PSB). Osgood observes that it developed plans of action and put them into action.

To ensure that the White House itself could enforce a unified approach to strategic communication across the government, Eisenhower established the OCB under his authority to operationalize plans. He was not about to allow other departments or agencies to undercut his commitment to conducting effective psychological warfare against the Soviets.

The OCB served as one of two primary structural components of Eisenhower's national security system that functioned under the control of the National Security Council (NSC). The NSC served as the central policymaking forum, where Eisenhower chaired the weekly NSC Planning Board and the Operations Coordinating Board meetings. The Planning Board prepared papers that served as the basis for discussion at the weekly meetings of the NSC members. Presidential decisions were "then conveyed to the departments and agencies via the Operations Coordinating Board, which monitored implementation of presidential decisions."[36] Eisenhower also consulted a circle of close advisers as part of his decision making. The effect ensured his control and supervision and placed strategic communication for psychological warfare under White House direction. In Eisenhower's scheme, propaganda and psychological operations were merely one aspect of a broader effort in which words had to be matched by deeds. He instituted a comprehensive, integrated approach to driving America's message that the West offered a better life and future than the Communists. Eisenhower had the experience and ability to make the system work. With the exception of President George H. W. Bush, no other president since that time has enjoyed equal success in forming a coherent communication strategy for national security, but Bush did not centralize communications the way Eisenhower had done.[37]

Eisenhower used several organizations, including the Defense Department and the CIA, to influence world opinion.[38] In 1953, he established the United States Information Agency (USIA), whose efforts targeted audiences outside the Iron Curtain, although the USIA also used the Voice of America (VOA) to broadcast radio messages through it as well.[39] Eisenhower ensured that USIA reported to the president through the National Security Council.[40] He approved clandestine deals between USIA and media outlets and permitted information to be disseminated on a nonattributable basis, acting as if it were a news organization. Despite USIA's aura as a news agency, it was an instrument of propaganda. USIA's Voice of America and the CIA-run Radio Free Europe/Radio Liberation (later Radio Liberty) helped enable USIA's mission. USIA also employed grey propaganda tactics that used third parties not identified or attributable to the United States, such as front organizations or private individuals.

Broadcasting was a vital tool that Eisenhower used for propaganda. By 1958, there were also USIA officers at the US mission in Poland, although they had had to officially "resign" from USIA and be "hired" by State for the duration of that assignment.[41]

Eisenhower insisted that communication be truthful to boost respect and trust. His team found that positive messages worked better than ones that attacked the Soviets, who worked hard to position themselves as champions of peace and coexistence. He endorsed a message of "Faith and Vision," expressing the themes of "humanity," "right of self-determination," and the need for "disarmament" and the peaceful use of nuclear energy.[42] It was a message of hope and opportunity. That approach and theme has been echoed in modern US political campaigns. Although his message evoked skepticism among Muslims, President George W. Bush attempted the same in waging what he described as the War on Terror, which contrasted a future of freedom, hope, security, and prosperity offered by the West against one of poverty, fear, violence, and repression offered by al-Qaeda.[43] The Eisenhower administration, Osgood remarks, "camouflaged its propaganda through its overt and covert strategies."[44] The lesson, as we think about PSYOP or propaganda today, is that until recently it was not only sanctioned but central to US strategic thinking about how to advance American interests and policies.

Tragically, USIA was disbanded in 1999 as part of a political deal cut between Secretary of State Madeleine Albright and Senator Jesse Helms, who viewed it as a way to make government smaller. USIA's broadcasting functions were transferred to the Broadcasting Board of Governors, and its other functions moved to the newly created Under Secretary of State for Public Affairs and Public Diplomacy at the Department of State. Most USIA employees were slotted into the Bureau of Educational and Cultural Affairs (ECA) and Office of International Information Programs (IIP). Others were sent to support regional and functional bureaus. It was an imprudent decision. USIA was an excellent agency that drew talented individuals and carried out its mission effectively. Neither the Department of State nor any other part of the government has matched USIA's impact or effectiveness in communicating US points of view or the relevant information that supports it. Christopher Paul contends that the decision destroyed the organization's coherence and unity of purpose.[45] He echoes the view expressed by the Heritage Foundation that breaking up USIA forced creative, independent-minded operators "into the lumbering, rigid State Department bureaucracy" that sent unqualified officers to fill public diplomacy jobs. The vacuum created has not been successfully filled.[46]

Eisenhower's view that PSYOP should respect the truth represented a sharp departure from Donovan's philosophy and defined an ethos that set the stage for today's employment of psychological operations. A review of more recent examples bears that out.

Grenada to Afghanistan

PSYOP has proved its value over time, and the empirical experience of the United States in conducting such operations should counter concerns that the US government achieves its goals through deception or lies.[47] Key case histories show that the United States has proven adept at executing smart, well-targeted psychological operations that were culturally attuned, clearly messaged, and politically savvy in supporting military efforts, and respected the intelligence of foreign audiences to whom they were targeted.

During the Korean War, Gen. Matthew B. Ridgeway, the commander in chief of United Nations' forces, saw psychological operations as useful and made no bones about calling them propaganda. Ridgeway avidly supported PSYOP, especially the use of flyers and loudspeakers against the North Koreans. He considered it "the cheapest form of warfare."[48] The policy guidance for American PSYOP was concise and savvy. Units were to speak from a UN, and not US, point of view; treat the conflict as aggression, not civil war; attack Communism and its visible effects on everyday life rather than in ideological terms; and focus on concrete subjects with a bearing on Korea. After the Chinese entered the war, objectives were refined to include weakening the resistance of North Korean troops, telling North Koreans the truth about the war, and bolstering the morale of South Koreans. They were politically on-target and appropriately summarized the key themes and messages that UN forces needed to drive.[49]

The Psywar Division approved radio and loudspeaker scripts in Chinese and Korean done by university-educated writers in Seoul, although the work drew criticism as being too sophisticated for uneducated Chinese and North Korean peasants.[50] The leaflets were more successful. They stressed themes of the "Happy POW," "good soldier—bad leaders," "surrender and you will be well-treated," "we can crush you," and nostalgia for family back home. Military historian Stanley Sandler concluded that "at no time before or since has the Army fielded such effective printed propaganda."[51]

Sandler notes that "Army psychological warriors cleverly worked on latent Chinese anti-Russian feeling, harping on the brutal Soviet 'liberation' of Manchuria in 1945 and proclaiming that 'Stalin will fight to the last Korean.'"[52] A third of the total prisoner of war population polled by the United Nations said that propaganda leaflets caused them to surrender.[53] In his book on the Korean War, Sandler points out that surrender leaflets were "the most used to the extent that many Communist soldiers came to believe that they *had* to have one to surrender unharmed."[54] PSYOP did, he concludes, "make a difference, particularly when directed at the so-called 'marginal man,' the Communist soldier who was already discouraged, perhaps in trouble with his NCOs, homesick, and worried."[55]

Even in Operation Urgent Fury (1983) in Grenada, an operation that has been sharply criticized for poor planning, psychological operations performed well and brought credit to the military.[56] Maurice Bishop had staged a coup in 1979 against the legitimate government. In 1983, Bishop was murdered and his place taken by the Marxist Deputy Prime Minister Bernard Coard, who invited the Cuban military into the country. President Ronald Reagan refused to countenance a Communist buildup on the island. In the wake of Bishop's murder, there were also concerns for the safety of six hundred American medical students studying there. Reagan moved quickly to depose Coard and restore democracy. During the operation—some of the more colorful incidents were dramatized by Clint Eastwood in the film *Heartbreak Ridge*—4th PSYOP Group loudspeaker teams proved effective in persuading enemy troops to surrender, while specialized leaflets projected the image that the operation was a combined Caribbean and not merely a US operation. It deployed a 50-kilowatt transmitter, "Spice Island Radio," to broadcast news and entertainment and keep islanders informed and calm, while Navy SEALs disabled the island's commercial AM transmitter.[57]

Operation Just Cause in Panama (1989) employed loudspeaker teams to convince Panamanian Defense Force units to surrender, telling them they had fought with honor and could honorably cease resistance.[58] Another PSYOP team took over Panama's most popular TV station and broadcast prepackaged materials that helped calm the civilian population.[59] "Ma Bell" missions used Special Forces to phone Panamanian defense force commanders. Using Spanish speakers, they told the Panamanian commanders to put all weapons in an arms room, line up their men on the parade field, and surrender to US forces that would arrive. The operation produced 2,000 surrenders without loss of any Americans.[60]

Assured Response in Liberia (2003) was a brilliantly successful operation in which the United States provided support for the military forces of the Economic Community of West African States (ECOWAS) to restore calm in the wake of the civil war that led to the removal of Charles Taylor as president. The conflict exploited thousands of child soldiers on both sides. As civilian casualties mounted, the security situation collapsed. President George W. Bush authorized the deployment of a 5,000-member force from the US Army Southern European Task Force that set up a joint task force to support ECOWAS.

The United States helped assure calm among the frightened civilian population by conducting aggressive information operations with PSYOP units. As Lt. Col. Thomas Collins notes in his commentary on the operation, the information operations working group developed plans and produced products to coordinate with the country team. The products "were critical to gaining public support" and "shaping the environment for the arrival of UN Forces."[61] Products included public service announcements, radio broadcasts, leaflets, and newspaper advertisements. The PSYOP operations were well conceived and executed. The posters and leaflets were clear and to the point, delivering an articulate message that the forces were peacekeepers on a humanitarian mission to provide relief, security, and protection.

One poster pictured a tough, gun-toting US Marine with his palm raised, advising that US Marines "have temporarily secured this area to allow humanitarian assistance to arrive" and warned people "not to interfere." A leaflet pictured African military and declared that "the multinational interim forces are well trained and equipped peacekeepers. Follow the instructions of the peacekeepers to help restore safety and security." Another pictured marines and a hovering helicopter and stated that "US Forces Are Near. They Are Ready to Provide Assistance if Needed." Billboards proclaimed that the United States and the UN were there just to help.[62]

Other leaflets, retired Sgt. Maj. Herbert Friedman reports, "held out a carrot and a stick. On one side they showed massive food stock issued to the people, on the other side they would show armed troops, military vehicles or aircraft." Another warned that marines would use deadly force to protect the embassy.[63] The psychological operations were effective in helping to restore calm and end violence.

The Nobil Anvil operation in Kosovo (1999) deployed PSYOP units to communicate the truth about what the Serbian authorities had been doing and to counter Serbian propaganda that twisted the facts. A multimedia campaign using leaflets, handbills, posters, radio, and television informed Serbs about Slobodan Milosevic's campaign of mass murder, systematic rape, and forced evacuation, and "served as a source of information and hope for the Kosovo refugees in Albania and Macedonia." Over 100 million leaflets were dropped, and radio and television spots blanketed Belgrade and northern Yugoslavia, Kosovo, and southern Serbia with "Allied Voice and Television."[64] These were precursors to the 2003 war in Iraq and the 2001 war in Afghanistan, where PSYOP has proven invaluable rather than a cause for deep-rooted anxiety.

One of the efforts for psychological operations in support of our military took place in 1991 during Operations Desert Shield and Desert Storm. The president asked Gen. H. Norman Schwarzkopf to prepare to eject Saddam Hussein's troops from Kuwait. Schwarzkopf's PSYOP chief, Col. Tommy Norman, advised the general that US Central Command should plan a strategic communication plan that would integrate the efforts of all government agencies. Schwarzkopf submitted a plan to Chairman of the Joint Chiefs of Staff General Colin Powell. Powell forwarded the plan to the Department of State and other relevant parties, and in cooperation with the Defense Department, coordinated an approach to the invasion that included the placement of experienced operators in key Arab capitals to inform and educate the Arab public as to the rationale for the action that the United States intended to take. As US forces bombarded Iraqi formations in Kuwait, messages were sent to Iraqi soldiers that specified how and under what circumstances they should surrender. The strategy worked beyond all expectations, with Iraqi units even surrendering to US press people. It was a remarkable demonstration of what well-planned and executed PSYOP could achieve.

During Operation Iraqi Freedom in 2003, the tactic was different. More than 40 million leaflets were dropped before the war commenced, urging citizens to ignore Saddam Hussein's order and to surrender. Although surveys could not prove causation, a postoperational review led by National Defense University distinguished research fellow Christopher Lamb found that the leaflets may have influenced the surrender of many Iraqi soldiers. Direct tactics such as using loudspeakers to call Iraqi insurgents hiding among women and children cowards caused some to emerge to fight more directly. Instructions broadcast from helicopters to Iraqi soldiers on Faylaka Island ordering them to surrender during the first Iraqi War, Desert Storm, caused their surrender. Ninety-eight percent of POWs captured had seen or possessed PSYOP leaflets imploring their surrender.[65]

Operation Enduring Freedom in Afghanistan employed a PSYOP plan to "shift the debate from Islam to terrorism and to counter adversarial propaganda, discourage interference with humanitarian affairs activities, support objectives against state and non-state supporters and sponsors of terrorism and disrupt support for and relationships of terrorist organizations."[66] Once Kabul fell, PSYOP units helped support US diplomatic efforts and bolstered Hamid Karzai's credibility at the time.[67]

The issue is intent. Still, psychological operations are strategic communication. One understands the conceptual reluctance about their use, but their utility and relevance remains well proven. Not every psychological operation produces the desired results. Mistakes are made. During Desert Storm, a leaflet that meant to assure Iraqi soldiers that the United States did not want them to come back "dead or crippled" was mistranslated to assert the opposite.[68] Leeds University professor Phil Taylor pointed out that a *Superman* comic book that depicted Superman saving two children from mines was a mistake, as it encouraged children to walk into minefields in the hope that Superman would save them, and then reported that the comic had been withdrawn.[69] Psychological warfare historian Herb Friedman investigated further and reported that it was neither withdrawn nor motivated any children to walk into minefields.[70] The point is, one has to be very careful about the content included in PSYOP pieces.

In Afghanistan, a leaflet depicting the dove, a symbol of peace, was mistaken by some Afghans to be a certificate that entitled them to a free meal from coalition forces.[71] An Iraqi family whose photograph appeared on a leaflet asked for a million dollars for use of their image, loss of privacy, and personal risk for appearing to help Americans.[72] Marine Corps University professor Pauletta Otis has pointed to a leaflet dropped in Iraq bearing the image of an evil eye, apparently intended to apprise insurgents that the United States was watching. The leaflet failed to factor in cultural considerations; Iraqis found it offensive.[73] In Afghanistan, Americans dropped soccer balls inscribed with a Saudi Arabian flag and the Shuhada (declaration of faith) written on it: "There is no God but Allah, and Muhammad is his Messenger." Friedman notes the blunder: "Some Muslims felt that kicking the holy statement was heresy."[74] The lesson is that no operation is foolproof. No less clear is that the mistakes were unintentional and not aimed at deceiving, which is the critical point in addressing those who fear the notion of psychological operations: successful PSYOP requires the hand of those with strong linguistic skills, cultural awareness, and strategic sensitivity.

The issues don't always just affect what we tell the enemy. When former pro football star Pat Tillman joined the Army Rangers after September 11, he was killed in Afghanistan. Although the communication concerning his death was more an issue of public affairs, his death was treated, in Joseph Meissner's words, "as a heroic act and the event was used to make the case that our efforts in Afghanistan were for a valiant cause."[75] In reality Tillman—a courageous American who gave up a lucrative career on the gridiron to serve his country— proved to be the victim of a tragic accident that can happen in any war: He lost his life to friendly fire. Tillman's mother refused to be mollified by the story that the military put out, digging through a mountain of heavily redacted official documents to reveal inconsistencies that forced the government to set the record straight.[76] Comments Meissner: "It hurt American credibility. We would have been far better off getting the facts out—and getting ahead of the story by getting them out first, and quickly. That would have bolstered, not damaged, our credibility. The lesson is that effective, credible communication requires respecting the facts and truth in these situations."[77]

A RAND Corporation study of PSYOP in Afghanistan identified a series of challenges that such activity needs to address now or in future conflicts.[78] These include ensuring that information operations officers are well integrated with operations centers to assure that they have good knowledge of activities taking place and planned, and that information operations are integrated with all activities within a command. "Ground troops," it noted, "cannot rely on higher echelons to perform some PSYOP functions," and centralizing press releases, radio broadcasts, and relations with the Afghan media at the brigade level can be counterproductive. The study embraces the concept that "every soldier should be a communication platform," in order to capitalize on "the value of face-to-face activity and using host nation capabilities."

The study points as well to the need to establish close coordination between information operations and public affairs and to integrate their activities more closely.[79] Indeed, the 2003 *Information Operations Roadmap* recommended closer coordination between Defense Department Public Affairs and other US government agencies, notably the State Department Office of Public Diplomacy and Public Affairs, noting that DoD Public Affairs and PSYOP capabilities should support public diplomacy.[80] The roadmap emphasized that PSYOP "may be employed to support U.S. public diplomacy as part of approved theater security cooperation guidelines."[81]

Calling for new initiatives to revise information operations doctrine and a new multimedia strategy, RAND's Afghanistan study identified a series of organizational challenges that affected information operations and psychological operations, including lack of standardized information operations (IO) and PSYOP integration with operations; long response times and coordination–process delays; conflicting IO, PSYOP, and public affairs functions; failure to exploit the informal, oral Afghan communication system; and a general lack of measures of effectiveness.[82]

Concerns that the United States should be vigorous in protecting its credibility and upholding a reputation for honesty and integrity are vital. That is why the military has instituted a series of protocols to ensure that PSYOPs carry out and respect the process that respect national objectives, the president's strategic intent, and the commander's intent; or for nonmilitary projects or cases where the military is providing support, that of parties with the responsibility for decision making.

The military has generally shown prudence in planning and executing psychological operations, but they are not perfect. They are constantly striving to improve their concept and execution. Forward-thinking studies such as that led by Christopher Lamb reflect efforts to uncover issues that highlight the need for improvements. Some people in the media and elsewhere do worry that both the term and substance of "psychological operations" connote deception or lying. By intent, design, and execution, US government psychological operations make a conscious effort to avoid both traps, respect the truth, and preserve credibility, and that applies to the State Department as well as the Pentagon. In a later chapter we'll see how the State Department planned and executed one of the most significant and effective psychological operations in history, the Marshall Plan.

The concerns do not justify flinching from conducting such operations, calling them PSYOP, or criticizing a strategic communication because it bears that name or carries overtones of such an operation. Indeed, rebranding PSYOP as MISO on the theory that it sounds more innocuous is precisely the kind of action more likely to arouse rather than allay suspicion.

Influencing Foreign, Not Domestic Audiences

It bears noting that PSYOP and MISO operations must aim to influence *foreign* target audiences. The closest language to an explicit prohibition is this wording in congressional authorizations for defense: "Funds available to the Department of Defense may not be obligated or expended for publicity or propaganda purposes within the United States not otherwise specifically authorized by law."[83] The department is prohibited from using PSYOP or MISO on the American public, except in limited circumstances such as providing interagency support to other US government agencies. Such activities range from providing public information for humanitarian assistance and dealing with disasters like hurricanes, to assisting with drug interdiction. These require specific deployment-and-execution orders from the secretary of defense, who shares with the president the legal authority to conduct PSYOP. That procedure ensures strict control and accountability.

Information Operations

PSYOP/MISO is a form of information operations, even as a debate has raged as to what "information operations" means. Planners and practitioners are too often unclear on the terms. As one senior retired military public affairs officer said, "Were it me, I'd eliminate the term information operations from discourse. It produces too much ambiguity. Too many people use the term when they mean public affairs or MISO/PSYOP." The confusion this public affairs officer identifies is reflected in poor planning and poor execution of both communication and actions. We need to clarify the meaning of information operations and its components.

On January 25, 2011, Secretary of Defense Robert Gates issued a memorandum that tried to clarify the definition and use of IO.[84] The memo redefined information operations, shifting the emphasis from core capabilities to integration. He stated: "The new definition will be 'the integrated employment, during military operations, of information-related capabilities in concern with other lines of operation to influence, disrupt, corrupt, or usurp the decision making of adversaries and potential adversaries while protecting our own."[85]

The memo made clear that the prior definition led to too much emphasis on core capabilities and confused the distinction between these and IO as an integrating staff function. The secretary's action provided far greater flexibility in enabling the Pentagon to conduct influence activities.

In the same memo, Secretary Gates formally designated the undersecretary of defense (policy) and the assistant secretary of defense for public affairs (ASD/PA) as the co-leads for strategic communication in the department to ensure that policymaking and communication planning will be "better integrated." He designated the Global Engagement Strategy Coordination Committee to serve as the department's central coordinating body for strategic communication. Dan Kuehl, a professor of information operations at the National Defense University who provided input into the secretary's definition of IO, believes we must think beyond IO as purely a coordinating activity and view it substantively.

"In some situations," he says, "IO ought to be the key *supported* activity, rather than the *supporting* activity. Kinetic activity—dropping bombs or firing missiles—is not necessarily the lead tactic that leads to success in an operation." Kuehl explains, "When we think of information operations, one should think about it in two different dimensions. First is the technical aspect. That embraces electronic warfare, computer network operations, television—any technology used to communicate information. It's the technology employed to achieve communication objectives. That has been true since the day of the

Guttenberg printing press. The second dimension entails influencing attitudes and opinions to shape behavior."

He points out that IO must be understood in the context of the information environment: "We use technology for information connectivity to deliver information content that has a cognitive effect. Thinking about information operations in this light is important, because you can measure and quantify all three of those factors." In short, Kuehl sees IO as an aspect of strategic communication and a direct tool for influencing behavior.

Matt Armstrong echoes this view: "IO is and should be treated as part of the communication spectrum, but where in the spectrum is unclear. Some influence actions are for small audiences, such as decision makers and planners, while others are for larger audiences, such as troops and civilians. All actions and words communicate, mutually reinforcing each other, or undermining. So, what is IO and where does it sit? It depends on how the tactics, techniques, and procedures are separated."[86] Armstrong is correct. His notion brings IO squarely within the ambit of strategic communication.

Christopher Paul offers the following judgment. He contends that "virtually all information operations in contemporary operations are psychological operations."[87] That may be too broad. Electronic warfare and computer network operations, cyberwar, do not necessarily qualify as MISO/PSYOP. One army information operations officer may be closer to the mark: "IO not only involves influence, but also the ability to disrupt command and control systems, infrastructure, vehicles, and machinery in a way that can be analogous to kinetic effects. Kinetics, obviously, are different from PSYOP, although disrupting command and control certainly influences decision making and information gathering."

One challenge these different views about IO raise is explaining who besides a commander and those to whom he assigns the job of conducting an influence operation has the authority to do so. Certainly, those conducting PSYOP/MISO and public affairs act under prescribed authorities. But who else has the authority to act? Some had argued that categorizing IO into five categories—electronic warfare, computer network operations, PSYOP, military deception, and operational security—assured that each activity came with its own set of authorities that governed who could do what, when, and under what circumstances. Others, like Armstrong, contend—and this author concurs—that can lead to confusion, overlapping authority, and unproductive debates over definitions.

Where has broadening the notion of IO left us? It puts more emphasis upon the instruction that a commander gives, based upon his own authority. Commanders must ask: What are my objectives and resources, and how will I use my resources to achieve these objectives? The fact is, one does not need to own capabilities in order to build and execute a plan that uses them. Their use simply has to fall within a commander's authority.

Col. (ret) Jack Guy, an expert on information operations who in 2010 worked as a senior IO adviser on the Counter-Insurgency Advisory & Assistance Team (CAAT) for International Security Assistance Force (ISAF) in Kabul, argues that "the key for troops is to understand the commander's intent. That allows the staff to plan operations that focus on the perceptions and behaviors of a target foreign audience that need to be changed. While MISO forces play a key role in that endeavor, in today's environment, everything that we say or do in a theatre of operations affects perception and behavior. This makes it imperative that those in charge of information operations have to be able to coordinate the message from the top to the bottom and the bottom to the top. It has to be a two-way street. They also need—and in places like Afghanistan this is a challenge—to develop a more reliable system of measures of effectiveness so that we actually know what works or doesn't, where, and why. We have to get much better than that."[88]

The bottom line is that information operations embraces the broader Pentagon notion of strategic communication as a process to the extent that they entail influence activity, but not necessarily as they affect kinetic activity. One understands why the term has led to vigorous debates and different views within the Pentagon. Christopher Lamb argues that IO be treated as a core military competency with five core capabilities (and several supporting capabilities) that are increasingly interdependent.[89] He suggests creating a corps of professionals composed of planners and capability specialists who understand all five disciplines (electronic warfare, PSYOP, computer network operations, military deception, and operational security) to provide combatant commanders with experts who can integrate information operations into contingency plans. In Lamb's view, information operations should be a core military competency, like air, ground, sea, and special operations, to enable decision superiority. Military information operations built for battlefield conditions intersect with national-level strategic communications primarily when one of the five core IO capabilities, PSYOP, takes content guidance from the national strategic communications plan. The IO roadmap that he embraces was at one time Pentagon policy, and it is a commonsense approach that the Pentagon should revisit and act upon.

CHAPTER 2

Propaganda: The Resonance of Emotion

Historians Garth S. Jowett and Victoria O'Donnell have pointed out the use in ancient times of "the equivalent of modern-day propaganda techniques to communicate the purported majesty and supernatural powers of rulers and priests." They cite symbols such as dazzling costumes, insignia, and monuments as techniques used to persuade audiences, and to Alexander's practice of arranging marriages between his officers and Persian noblewomen.[1]

Most credit Pope Gregory XV with coining the term in 1622. Concerned by the spread of Protestantism, he established a committee of cardinals within the Roman Curia called the Congregatio de Propaganda Fide (Congregation for Propagating the Faith). His goal was to regiment and enforce religious orthodoxy in Church doctrine among priests who embarked upon evangelical missions to the New World and other places.[2] In his introduction to the book by the eminent students of propaganda, as well as being the nephew of Sigmund Freud, Mark Crispin Miller wrote that propaganda was associated with Catholicism well into the nineteenth century.[3] Even in those times, the term was pejorative.

That holds even more true today. Labeling a communication as propaganda destroys its credibility. People and the media in the United States and abroad are culturally attuned to treating propaganda as inherently misleading or as an outright lie. The media is on the lookout for any government action that smacks of manipulation. Often, there is a rebuttable presumption that *anything* a government says requires close examination, as if it evidences a potential crime scene. In this era people have grown skeptical about what governments do and how they do it—and what they say to justify or explain their actions.

The Scholars' Views

A closer look at the notion reveals a more complicated and nuanced picture. Some people view propaganda more harshly than others. Harold Lasswell, famous for his pithy descriptions of politics ("politics is who gets what, when, and how") and communication ("who says what, in which channel, to whom, and with what effect"), called propaganda "the management of collective attitudes by the manipulation of significant symbols. The word attitude is taken to mean a tendency to act according to certain methods of valuation."[4] The key word is "manipulation." Laswell does not argue that it is inherently evil.

Daniel Lerner tried to put Lasswell's obtuse definition into plain English: "When communication seeks to persuade—that is, when it operates as propaganda—it manipulates symbols to shape attitudes that will condition (facilitate or constrain) the future behavior of its 'targets.'"[5] He goes on to say that "propaganda is the distinctive instrument which manipulates only the symbols by which people think, feel, believe; it works with threats and promises to affect people's hopes and fears. It shapes human aspirations as to what should happen and human expectations of what will happen."[6]

Leeds University professor Phil Taylor was interested in how propaganda differed from psychological operations. He argued that in wartime, "propaganda is a process designed to persuade people to fight. Psychological warfare, on the other hand, is propaganda designed to persuade the opposition *not* to fight."[7] Taylor believed that because it persuaded people to lay down arms instead of fighting and dying, stigmatizing propaganda was "a serious obstacle to our understanding of the propaganda process."[8] Taylor thought that propaganda could be good or evil, and that the key question was *intent*. "Propaganda," he argued, "uses communication to convey a message, an idea, or an ideology that is designed to serve the self-interests of the person or persons doing the communicating."[9]

Jowett and O'Donnell echo Taylor: "Propaganda is the deliberate and systematic attempt to shape perceptions, manipulate cognitions, and direct behavior to achieve a response that furthers the desired intent of the propagandist."[10] Both sets of definitions bring propaganda within the ambit of strategic communication and psychological operations and accept that it can be rooted in truth and communicate truth.

Edward Bernays, among the most renowned scholars of propaganda, viewed propaganda as a "wholesome word" of "honorable parentage": "Propaganda becomes vicious and reprehensible only when its authors consciously and deliberately disseminate what they know to be lies, or when they aim at efforts which they know to be prejudicial to the common good."[11]

Other scholars take a darker view. George Orwell was blunt: "All propaganda is lies, even when one is telling the truth."[12] The current *Oxford Dictionaries OnLine* definition echoes Orwell: "Propaganda. *Chiefly derogatory* [original emphasis] information, especially of a biased or misleading nature, used to promote a particular political cause or point of view." This definition includes "the dissemination of such information as a political strategy."[13]

Steven Luckert and Susan Bachrach of the US Holocaust Memorial Museum echo that view, defining propaganda as "the dissemination of information, whether truthful, partially truthful, or blatantly false, that aims to shape public opinion and behavior. Propaganda simplifies complicated issues or ideology for mass consumption as always biased, and is geared to achieving a particular end."[14]

Scholar Randal Marlin believes propaganda is about suppressing rational, informed judgment: "Propaganda = The organized attempt through communication to affect belief or action or inculcate attitudes in a large audience in ways that circumvent or suppress an individual's adequately informed, rational, reflective judgment."[15]

The Pentagon View

The Department of Defense comes down hard on the negative connotation. It defines propaganda as "any form of *adversary* communication, especially of a *biased or misleading nature* [emphasis added], designed to influence the opinions, emotions, attitudes, or behavior of any group in order to benefit the sponsor, either directly or indirectly."[16]

One can understand why the government distances itself from propaganda. Still, this view creates serious challenges. It will always face a cynical, questioning 24/7 media environment that increasingly is colored by social media. But this definition limits flexibility, constrains action, and opens US communication to charges of contradiction, tolerance for deception, and outright hypocrisy when the definition is compared to that for PSYOP. Other problems with the way public affairs is generally viewed within government add further constraints and complications.

One starts by comparing the definitions for propaganda and PSYOP. Which category a communication falls into depends on who is communicating. In essence, propaganda is seen as what the *enemy* does, whereas PSYOP is what *we* do. The implication is that propaganda entails deception by the enemy, but the phrase "*especially of* biased or misleading" communications renders that a description, not a requirement. In essence, the definition implies that the enemy lies but we tell the truth. The distinction is neat but disingenuous in the use of language and as one reviews American history; it places the United States in the position of appearing to wink at the use of PSYOP as a tool through which it can put out biased or misleading communication—in short, lies.

As with PSYOP, propaganda qualifies as strategic communication. Both tools of communication seek to shape target audience behavior by molding and influencing their attitudes and opinions. But labeling strategic communication as propaganda triggers explicit and implicit constraints as policymakers and action officers strive to protect their credibility. In the past there was more realism. The definition needs revision—or perhaps, for the faint of heart, omission from the Pentagon dictionary entirely, accompanied by an explanation if queried that the US government does not tarnish its communication by use of the term. Should we retain the definition, consistency with PSYOP and MISO suggests calling propaganda a neutral term that may apply to our communications as well as to an adversary's, while asserting that US communications will always aim to be truthful.

Although his recommendation was not accepted, former Deputy Principal Assistant Secretary of Defense for Public Affairs Robert T. Hastings offered an excellent definition of propaganda that directly addressed the problem with the current definition: "Propaganda. 1. The systematic propagation of information, ideas, or rumors reflecting the views and interests of those advocating a doctrine or cause, deliberately spread for the purpose of helping or injuring an institution, movement, or person. 2. The material disseminated as part of such an effort. Propaganda is designed for political effect and selects information with little concern for truth or context. In common usage, 'propaganda' implies misrepresentation, disinformation, and the creation of ambiguity through omission of critical details. Communication activities designed to educate, persuade, or influence do not, by themselves, constitute propaganda."[17]

Hastings recognized that the current definition was "overly broad" and that it was important "to protect reasonable and truthful efforts to persuade and influence from being misinterpreted or misrepresented as propaganda." His comments are on the mark. It separates propaganda from PSYOP, and it affirms the critical importance of requiring US strategic communication to respect the need for truth and place communication into context (excluding activity such as military deception). That would ensure vital flexibility. It bears stressing: Truth is our ally. It enables us to counter adversaries who cry foul, as they habitually do. Failure to respect truth in strategic communication—whether it is propaganda or PSYOP—can lead to political, diplomatic, or military calamity.

That approach would bring the definition of propaganda back, as Taylor correctly argued it should be, to the issue of intent. One acknowledges that propaganda as well as psychological operations aims to serve the self-interests of the communicator.

The Lessons of History

In analyzing the role of propaganda in US government attitudes or actions, it's well to understand that propaganda has enjoyed a long tradition in the

United States. In 1898, J. Stuart Blackton and Albert E. Smith produced *Tearing Down the Spanish Flag*, a pseudodocumentary depicting a US army attack in Havana. It was complete hokum. War had been declared, but no shots had been fired. That didn't prevent thousands of people sitting in vaudeville houses from cheering Americans on to victory.[18]

As World War I broke out, President Woodrow Wilson appointed journalist George Creel to head the United States Committee on Public Information. It sponsored paintings, posters, cartoons, and sculptures. Over 75,000 public speakers—called "Four Minute Men" for the length of their presentations—as well as artists, writers, and filmmakers, were mobilized.[19] Compub was created as a government news agency to distribute propaganda postured as new information presented as news to the public around the world.[20] Newsreel footage of the war was faked; much of it was restaged after battles had already been fought.[21] President Wilson's speeches were translated and transmitted globally within twenty-four hours, establishing him, as historian Kenneth Osgood put it, as *"the* spokesperson for the allies."[22]

Creel was proud of his committee's work but later realized that the term propaganda had become pejorative and associated with the enemy. In his post-war report he wrote that "we strove for the maintenance of our own morale and the Allied morale by every process of simulation; every possible expedient was employed to break through the barrage of lies that kept the people of the Central Powers in darkness and delusion; we sought the friendship and support of the neutral nations by continuous presentation of facts. We did not call it· propaganda, for that word, in German hands, had come to be associated with deceit and corruption."[23]

He also insisted that Americans fought lies with truth: "Our effort was educational and informative throughout, for we had such confidence in our case as to feel that no other argument was needed than the simple, straightforward presentation of facts."[24]

Creel's remarks are facile but they gloss over the fact that every act that his Committee engaged in was to influence audiences, notably at home, and not to inform. It was excellent propaganda and effective. But it was propaganda, not news, and its aim was to persuade people that the US cause during the war was right and just and stood for democracy, and defended America against a ruthless foe. But after the war people decided the US government had distorted the truth, and thus began a strong reaction against the notion of propaganda.[25] The wounded came home and prompted questions as to whether the price of war had been worth it. Films depicting the war graphically began to appear in the mid-1920s.

A single book written by Erich Maria Remarque and the film made from it by Lewis Milestone crystallized opinion: *All Quiet on the Western Front*. Both the book and the movie offered a savage meditation on the futility and brutality of war, telling the story of German schoolteacher Paul Baumer, who joins the army and finds himself locked in the middle of a savage conflict characterized by random death or injury. Returning home on leave, he discovers that his hometown has become for him a strange land to which he can no longer connect. He returns to the front lines, where his friends lose their lives, and eventually, just before the armistice is declared, he loses his own at the hands of a sniper. Remarque wrote about a generation of men destroyed by the world. They lose their youth, get cut off from family, and become beholden to officers oblivious to how the frightening war is affecting their men. The book and the film are about disillusionment, alienation, and loss of hope. They resonated powerfully with audiences and helped shape the political climate in the postwar years.

That did not prevent the United States from embracing propaganda during the Second World War. It bears stressing that psychological operations and propaganda were viewed as the same thing. Robert Sherwood's key point was that it respect truth. OSS chief Bill Donovan employed it without such scruples.

On the home front, notably central to US war propaganda was the collaboration between the government and Hollywood; the government also produced films. Excellent books have been written about this topic.[26] Critical here is the US government's explicit endorsement of propaganda and a recognition that cinema offered a uniquely powerful tool.[27] George Marshall thought cinema so crucial as a vehicle for laying out a compelling rationale for fighting the Nazis that he personally supervised the production of seven films in a series called *Why We Fight*. All were directed by Frank Capra, renowned for the popular films *Mr. Smith Goes to Washington* and *Arsenic and Old Lace*.

The first film in the series, *Prelude to War*, offers insight into Marshall's mindset. It is out-and-out propaganda. Its message is about defending democracy rooted in the four freedoms: the freedom of speech, freedom of religion, freedom from want, and freedom from fear. Called "the greatest gangster film ever made," it employs the technique of "mash-up" familiar to today's Internet users.[28] Stylistically, it integrates footage from German propaganda with images that depict a free society of faith to define the stakes and explain why we must fight and win. A documentary flavor heightens the impact. The glamorous German Leni Riefenstahl may be celebrated as the genius of film propaganda, but Capra was by far the better filmmaker. Capra's seven films are blunt and compelling. They are heavy-handed by today's standards, and lack the subtle sophistication of contemporary storytelling and modern film technology. But they are very good.

In Hollywood, the United States levied pressure through the Production Code Administration (PCA) and the Office of War Information (OWI). Both had real leverage. Absent a PCA seal, no studio would distribute a film, thereby effectively killing it. The OWI created an office under Elmer Davis to liaise with Hollywood. Davis and his team believed strongly in propaganda, and their philosophy was to insert ideas into mass entertainment. "That meant," cinema historians Clayton Koppes and Gregory Black write, "an emphasis on understanding the issues of the war—as OWI interpreted them. When asked what OWI's strategy would be, Davis replied simply, 'to tell the truth.'"[29]

Their experience highlights the challenge of strategic communication by government agencies. Truth shines differently among the eyes of different beholders. In Davis's era, people held diverse notions about the "nature of American right, and what American might should accomplish."[30] Henry Luce and Vice President Henry Wallace exemplified this divide. Writing months before Pearl Harbor, Luce penned a *Life* magazine editorial titled "The American Century" to decry isolationism. He tied America's future to defeating Hitler. Failure would lead to "the organized domination of tyrants" and the "end of constitutional democracy."[31] He declared that "we are in a war to defend and even to promote, encourage, and incite so-called democratic principles throughout the world."[32] His views would resonate with many of today's political conservatives.

In 1942, the left-leaning Wallace delivered his speech "The Century of the Common Man," which espoused different priorities.[33] He did see the war as "a fight between a slave world and a free world." But for Wallace, New Deal social justice was the key goal. Davis and his colleagues at OWI shared Wallace's social philosophy, and the pressure they exerted upon Hollywood reflected that orientation.

Davis pushed for films that expressed egalitarian, populist values. Movies that paid homage to the British class system were disdained. OWI wanted to show that Britain was evolving toward equality. I can offer no defense for Britain's social structure here, but it's troubling that government officials were so eager to refashion reality—and to use official authority to recreate it in their own vision. It is precisely such caprice that gives contemporary observers heartburn when they consider the implications of permitting bureaucratic control or influence over attitudes and opinions. A government consists of its people, and people have opinions. Consciously or not, neutrality is not a natural state of affairs.

OWI was no blushing violet in expressing its opinions. When Warner Brothers Studio released *Princess O'Rourke*, OWI objected to the storyline, in which the president busied himself with marrying off an heiress to a royal throne with the consent of the government. Comedy that celebrated extravagance was out. Many in today's populist world might find it easy to wave away such objections to such frivolity, although this author finds OWI's arrogance hard to sanction. Even on OWI's own terms, its passion for equality had limits. When issues like race relations cropped up in scripts, characters who embodied the problem were written out—moral scruples about *that* social injustice easily tossed. One should not be surprised that a poll taken in Harlem after Pearl Harbor revealed the startling figure that 49% believed that they would be no worse off should Japan win, and 18% thought that life would improve.[34]

There is a lesson. Even where government officials in good faith believe they are merely informing and telling their version of the truth, judgments remain personal, selective, and subjective. As Phil Taylor wisely observed, propaganda "does not operate in a vacuum divorced from social or political realities. It is an essential means by which leaders attempt to gain public support for—or avoid opposition to—their policies."[35] New Deal officials took as their mission to *inform* audiences of the truth. Like Sherwood, OWI believed that communication of truth would mobilize war support. They believed that they were informing. Even so, their selection and presentation of facts and truth as they saw it were actions of influence. That holds true for any effort by public affairs officials to inform, and it affects, as we shall see, how well the US government's view on public affairs functions.

As we saw in the previous chapter, Gen. Matthew Ridgeway saw nothing wrong with either psychological operations or propaganda, drawing no distinction between the two. President Truman embraced propaganda, mounting a Campaign for Truth, and eagerly embraced propaganda directed at foreign audiences. Radio Free Europe and Radio Liberation/Radio Liberty mounted a Crusade for Freedom. They labeled their broadcasts as objective news and information, but employed "both private and public rhetorics that are representative of the dominant motives, means, and symbolic manipulations" typical of Cold War communication.[36] The Crusade for Freedom campaign spanned fifteen years, from 1950 to 1965, through four US presidential administrations. The National Committee for a Free Europe (NCFE) was formed on May 27, 1949, and the Committee for a Free Asia (CFA) was formed on March 12, 1951. Radio Free Asia (RFA) chose as its symbol a wooden Asian bell with the slogan "Let Freedom Ring." They conducted live broadcasts to discredit Communism.[37] This clandestine campaign—clearly considered propaganda—drew active support from millions of Americans.

Eisenhower believed in the power and necessity of propaganda. So, when does propaganda become inherently a bad thing? That the public deems it pejorative may be no more than perception, and that alone may justify avoiding action that enables it to be labeled as propaganda. But for decades the US government and top leaders embraced the notion of propaganda as not only beneficial but necessary for the protection of US vital interests.

Where does one draw the line? Is it where communicators engage in deception that advances their own interests, knowing that it may harm audiences? Donovan would gleefully agree that the OSS did precisely that. He justified it on the theory that his means not only justified the ends, but that achieving the end mandated the means. Bernays would argue that where the authors of a communication *know* that it is prejudicial to the common good, it is propaganda and therefore correctly deemed pejorative. Then what of the Nazis and the Soviets? Until the latter stages of Nazi and Communist rule, many actually believed their twisted ideologies. Did that render their propaganda pejorative? Retired Foreign Service officer Patricia Kushlis notes that by "1978, few Soviets, including government officials with whom I dealt, believed in Communism. They could see the system was failing and had lost their faith in it."[38] That's valid, but at what point, then, does propaganda and strategic communication become unacceptable and ineffective, and justify being pejorative?

The issue is not easily resolved. For example, how should one characterize the George W. Bush administration's May 2003 Iraq victory celebration held aboard the aircraft carrier USS *Abraham*? Critic Mark Danner feels that it would have been "quite familiar to the great propagandists of the last century," and compares it to Leni Riefenstahl's *Triumph of the Will*.[39] The event was grand, with an S-EB Viking landed on deck to kick off a carefully choreographed ceremony beneath a towering banner that proclaimed "Mission Accomplished."

Bush and his team believed that their handiwork in Iraq—and especially removing Saddam Hussein from power—merited the celebration.[40] The event aimed for maximum impact to bolster Bush's political credibility and unite Americans around the Iraq war. Was that wrong? Danner is entitled to his criticism, but in judging the ethics of what took place, the real issue is whether the Bush team honestly believed victory had been achieved. Their optimism over Iraq proved to be premature, but they judged unfolding events in Baghdad more positively. The Bush team used the event to congratulate themselves and salute the military. Danner denounces it as a conscious fraud in which the power of the presidency was exerted to create a misleading image of success for the benefit of election cameras.[41] Whether you agree with Danner or Bush, one point seems uncontestable: the event was propaganda and met all the requirements for strategic communication. The lesson is familiar: How you judge propaganda depends upon your perspective.

The field of propaganda is well studied. Until recently, the US government felt no shame in using the term. PSYOP or MISO has generally been labeled by scholars more properly as propaganda. As propaganda has become pejorative, there's good reason to call it something else, or at least redefine the term. What's clear is that denying that we engage in anything that could be considered propaganda, except by artificially categorizing it as activity engaged in solely by our enemies, makes the US government look hypocritical. At a minimum, Deputy Principal Assistant Secretary of Defense Robert Hastings' response offered a plausible way out of this bog. The issue needs to be revisited, and either Hastings' definition or a similar one needs to be adopted.

Prohibitions against Influencing Domestic Audiences

What about strategic communication that aims to influence American audiences? That debate often arises in arguments over propaganda as it affects who in the US government can do what. The White House may engage in propaganda—although they wouldn't pin that label on their political communication—at will. The Departments of State and Defense, the intelligence community, and other parts of the US government are prohibited from engaging in communication that seeks to influence Americans. Such efforts are viewed as propaganda. As a political body, of course, the White House is free to engage in it, although one might wince at the exploitation of our military to serve as a prop for the show. The Bush team's response would be that in their view, the mission had in fact been accomplished, in which case the White House had every right to crow about it. Who is correct depends on how you feel about the Bush White House and its perception of what it had achieved.

This debate is a sidebar to whether propaganda is strategic communication. In 1948 Congress enacted the US Information and Educational Exchange Act, known as Smith-Mundt.[42] The act empowered the State Department to engage with foreign audiences. But this was the dawn of the Cold War struggle for minds and wills, and some in Congress worried about the stigma of propaganda, accusing the State Department of being "drones, the loafers, and the incompetents."[43] A second concern was raised by people like Congressman Eugene Cox, who believed the State Department was "chock full of Reds."[44] To reduce the stigma of propaganda and to address the concerns, the State Department was authorized to engage with foreign but not domestic audiences. It may do so through broadcast, face-to-face contacts, educational or cultural exchanges (which also engage American audiences), publications, and other forms of contact. The department considers most of that public diplomacy, not strategic communication. One should note that the department engages with the US press corps every day in public affairs.

Smith-Mundt erected a firewall as to Voice of America (VOA) activities. It allows VOA to influence foreign audiences. Except for the journal *Problems of Communism*, it prohibited the State Department from disseminating within the United States any informational (as opposed to educational, technical, or cultural) materials intended for foreign audiences.[45] Patricia Kushlis notes that the department also published the *English Teaching Forum*, a quarterly journal distributed to teachers of English as a foreign or second language that had nothing to do with anti-Communist communication.[46]

The legislation imposed three other key restrictions: The department was to engage in information activities only to supplement private efforts; it could not acquire a monopoly on broadcast or other channels of communication; and it was required to invite private sector leaders to review and advise the State Department's information activities. The third oversight on such activities was implemented through the formation of what is today called the Advisory Commission on Public Diplomacy.

Senator J. William Fulbright succeeded in amending the law in 1972. His amendment enabled the State Department to ignore the act for cultural and education exchanges, but toughened up the original language by banning the dissemination to the American public of any "information about the United States, its people, and its policies" aimed at foreign audiences. An exception to that ban authorized the department to make such material available for examination to the media, academics, and Congress.[47]

In 1985, Senator Edward Zorinsky tightened it further. Zorinsky worried that the US Information Agency could be used as a mechanism for government propaganda, and in his view, that's how the Communists operated. The Soviet Union used propaganda and fear to control the Russian people. Zorinsky acted to ensure that no US government agency could do the same. He passed a prohibition that barred USIA from using funds to influence public opinion in the United States or from distributing USIA materials prepared for foreign audiences.[48] Zorinsky declared that "the American taxpayer certainly does not need or want his tax dollars used to support US government propaganda directed at him or her."[49]

The Defense Department rules prohibit efforts to influence domestic audiences. Public affairs can communicate with Americans, but as its brief is to inform and not influence, technically public affairs is legally on safe ground. As discussed below, however, in practice its behavior does not always respect that distinction.[50] Legally, MISO or PSYOP must be targeted toward foreign audiences.[51]

Where does the debate on Smith-Mundt stand today? Its provisions clash with the realities of the 24/7 global media environment. Satellite television and the Internet broadcast and report on Pentagon and State Department press conferences and statements, and these reach American audiences. Anyone today can download a VOA transcript from the Internet, just as in days gone by, people with shortwave radios can listen to VOA broadcasts. The dichotomy is that official US government entities that conduct public diplomacy, including the International Information Programs Office of the State Department and the Broadcasting Board of Governors, are prohibited from making such statements available to Americans—yet they are also available to Americans through State's Bureau of Public Affairs.

This produces odd consequences. When NATO, Johns Hopkins University, and Harvard University tried to show a 2008 Voice of America documentary film on Afghanistan's poppy harvest to US audiences, for example, the law blocked VOA from providing it—though any interested citizen could easily download the program from YouTube. How ridiculous is that result?

In 2009, scholar and reformer Matt Armstrong organized a symposium to discuss the Smith-Mundt Act. Distinguished journalists, flag officers, and both active duty and former State Department officials convened. It turned out that people held diverse views. Former Foreign Service officer Barry Zorthian argued that the act did not impede public diplomacy, at least in practice, while former Under Secretary of State James Glassman felt that it relieved the State Department from the burden of talking to domestic audiences.

Critics argued for ignoring the act, a view that sat poorly with the military, "who view laws as granting permission for what they can do."[52] From the cross-benches, Marc Lynch, author of an illuminating book on Arab satellite media, argued that the firewall *does* have merit, while conceding that it could be strengthened in a "more creative and innovative way" to adapt the act to the modern era.[53]

The Smith-Mundt symposium's final report concluded that the "firewall does more than limit American access to information generated by their tax dollars. It taints overseas broadcasting."[54] Armstrong declared: "Parties abroad know that what we are telling them we can't tell the American public. It raises questions as to the integrity of our foreign messages. Inevitably, people will ask: if the American people can't legally listen to it, why should we trust it?"[55] Karen De Young, the senior *Washington Post* diplomatic reporter, concurred with the need to provide Americans access, while sensibly insisting upon a requirement for transparency "to let Americans know what is being said in their name."[56]

What to do about Smith-Mundt is not cut-and-dried. Glassman's objection rests upon a slender reed. If the State Department wants to avoid dealing with an issue it can do so easily, whether or not legal constraints choke off action. As it happens, the department takes a proactive view on public affairs. Its statements advance administration agendas—a classic definition of influence activity. Indeed, State public affairs provides official texts and transcripts to domestic and foreign audiences and places them on a web page that anyone can access.

Ignoring the law, as some suggest, is absurd. But Lynch raises a valid point that some limits on communicating with domestic publics do make sense. The presidency is a bully pulpit. The executive branch rightly possesses clear authority to assert its policies. It will capitalize on every venue possible to drive themes and messages. Today, where presidents wield enormous power to leverage influence, the firewall makes sense, if reasonably applied.

What solution is workable, given that communication from any US government party carried over the Internet may be seen by American audiences? Is it realistic to expect that Americans would not be influenced by them? Today's fast-moving politics render geographical boundaries of states increasingly less relevant. The global impact of the Internet and the dynamics of 24/7 global media are increasing. Diasporas are spreading. These factors should help frame what reforms are needed to bring Smith-Mundt into the current era. The act should apply a test rooted in intent, good faith, and transparency. Legal restrictions should not bar government parties from redistributing within the United States what the US government disseminates abroad and clearly labels as US communication. The State Department should also forge an efficient process to enable it to redistribute its information at home.

Patricia Kushlis makes the point that "ensuring clarity and understanding of State Department messages requires placing the distribution of messages to foreign audiences into a different context than those distributed to Americans. That is where Public Affairs and the Bureau of International Information Programs have different missions. PA deals with domestic audiences. IIP deals with foreign audiences."

The process should appropriately balance the interests of transparency and the need to communicate with the interests in steering as clear as possible from partisan domestic propaganda. The issue affects American strategic communication to the extent that it affects who has the authority to say or do what. The fact that communications reach and influence an American audience at home limits the authority of the military to act. Who can do what, when, where, and how is important for understanding the art of strategic communication. But the debate over Smith-Mundt does not alter the key relevant consideration here. Any communication that influences a public, foreign or domestic, qualifies as strategic communication.

CHAPTER 3

Public Affairs: Concept versus Reality

Abu Ghraib threw a roundhouse punch to US credibility in Iraq. Taking responsibility, Secretary of Defense Donald Rumsfeld offered to resign.[1] Abu Ghraib offers a good case for reviewing the Pentagon's philosophy that public affairs should inform, not influence. The answer is that in crisis, necessity trumps doctrine. The military moved aggressively to protect American interests: They executed a savvy campaign of influence that got out in front of the story, moved to control it, defined the narrative, and drove home specific themes and messages. Some military personnel might argue that they were merely informing—but don't believe it.

The Abu Ghraib detention facility is a prison located twenty miles west of Baghdad. Brig. Gen. Janis Karpinski was commanding. The senior commander for coalition forces in Iraq was Lt. Gen. Ricardo S. Sanchez. Soldiers of the 372nd Military Police Company (320th MP Battalion), attached to the 800th MP Brigade, had primary operational supervision of the prisoners. These were under-strength reserve components units, not active duty. Members of the 205th Military Intelligence Brigade conducted interrogations there.[2]

In October 2003, Specialist (E-4) Joseph M. Darby, an MP, visited Abu Ghraib. He was shown a photo of a naked prisoner chained to his cell, arms above his head. On January 13, 2004, he made a report to the military's Criminal Investigation Division (CID) that included a CD with photos. CID opened a criminal investigation.[3]

Two days later, the military announced a criminal investigation. Shortly after, seventeen US soldiers were suspended pending the outcome of the investigation. Maj. Gen. Antonio Taguba led an investigation and reported in March that guards had placed bags over the heads of detainees, threatened them with rape, used dogs as intimidation, and broke chemical lights and poured phosphoric liquid on detainees, while grinning male and female American soldiers looked on.[4] The abuses shocked the world and undercut the hard work by coalition authorities to drive a positive message about US involvement in Iraq.[5]

Carol Downing and Patricia Swann identified five specific press strategies that the White House and the military employed to contain the damage: preemption, commiseration, disassociation, shock, and rectification.[6] Each aimed to influence attitudes and opinion and defuse controversy about the US presence in Iraq, the US military, and administration policy.

Preemption seeks to get out in front of a story, control it, and defuse controversy before serious damage is inflicted or to limit the amount of damage that might be suffered. It also recognizes that media stories exist today in "one universal *digital medium*" in which radio, television, and print media are converging into "one digital expression."[7] The impact of that singularity is far-ranging. Social media such as blogs, Facebook, Twitter, and YouTube are supplanting traditional media of newspapers, radio, and television by empowering individuals to shape the discourse over emerging events in unprecedented ways, within single media cycles that can last less than twelve hours before the public appetite for a single episode is sated.

The coalition's senior public affairs officer, Brig. Gen. Mark Kimmit, took the lead. At a March 20 press conference, he disclosed what had happened and said that *60 Minutes II* planned to broadcast a story. It was a difficult press conference; the press peppered him with tough questions. But the shock and disclosure won attention. Getting the media's attention is step one in getting a story out. Invoking a strategy of disassociation, Kimmit declared Abu Ghraib an aberration and gave assurances that the United States would treat prisoners with dignity.

On April 30, President George W. Bush denounced the abuses at a press conference: "Yes, I shared a deep disgust that those prisoners were treated the way they were treated. Their treatment does not reflect the nature of the American people. That's not the way we do things in America."[8] He commiserated with the prisoners—although, in an error of judgment, failed to apologize to the Iraqis. He disassociated the behavior at Abu Ghraib from what he deemed acceptable. Employing a strategy of rectification, he promised that justice would be done.

Donald Rumsfeld, State Department spokesman Richard Boucher, Maj. Gen. Geoffrey Miller (commander of US-run prisons in Iraq), and Kimmit all echoed the president's message in their own television interviews, statements, and press conferences.[9] They maintained tight message discipline. They drove a campaign message that the United States stood for the right values and was helping, not hurting, the Iraqis. In August, the Department of Defense issued a public affairs guidance.[10] The guidance prescribed the campaign theme that the "army is committed to ensuring all soldiers live up to the army values and the laws of land warfare regardless of the environment or circumstance."

The guidance further defined campaign messages: The army investigation would "go where the facts lead." The incident was caused by "misconduct by a small group of soldiers and civilians," "lack of discipline" by leaders and soldiers of the 205th MI Brigade, and "failure of leadership by multiple echelons" within the Combined Joint Task Force-7 (CJTF-7). The messages limited the scope of abuse, denounced them as counter to US Army values, and stressed that soldiers were operating in "a complex and dangerous environment," a fact that "should not blind us to the noble conduct of the vast majority of our soldiers."

Was that approach consistent with Pentagon rules that govern the conduct of public affairs? Pentagon public affairs doctrine holds that the military should *inform but not influence:*

> PA capabilities are related to IO, but PA is not an IO discipline or PSYOP tool. PA activities contribute to IO by providing truthful, accurate and timely information, using approved DOD PAG to keep the public informed about the military's missions and operations, countering adversary propaganda, deterring adversary actions, and maintaining trust and confidence of the US population, and our friends and allies. PA activities affect, and are affected by, PSYOP, and are planned and executed in coordination with PSYOP planning and operations. PA must be aware of the practice of PSYOP, but should have no role in planning or executing these operations.[11]

In the case of Abu Ghraib, public affairs was instructed to "inform and educate our internal and external audiences." But was the campaign to defuse controversy on Abu Ghraib merely informing and educating? Or did the military produce a message of influence? One insider amusedly described the Pentagon's actions as "*actively* informing." The label does not change the substance: It was influence.

Rumsfeld's acting assistant secretary for public affairs, Lawrence Di Rita, castigated editorial writers for criticizing the conduct of the military and implying that Abu Ghraib was anything except a rare and tragic aberration. Was that stating a fact or influencing? Understandably, Di Rita was driving a message; he was influencing. From his perspective, perhaps he believed that all he was doing was getting out the facts, but anyone who thinks he intended to avoid getting out the Pentagon's viewpoint is being unrealistic. The administration grasped instantly the damage that the story could do to its policy and US credibility in Iraq. The handling of Abu Ghraib shows that in crisis, operationally, policymakers and action officers are going to act as they think best.

Indeed, critics like Helle Dale and Stephen Johnson of the conservative Heritage Foundation charged that the administration "chose press agentry over two-way communication" and opted for "publicity management—issuing news releases, checking camera angles, and keeping spokesmen on message."[12] They criticized the Bush administration for failing to "reveal bad news as quickly and completely as possible." They felt that military and civilian public affairs officers proved ill-prepared to talk about the problems at coalition-controlled prisons. All that is part of the discourse. The issue here is not how well the Pentagon or the president handled the Abu Ghraib controversy; it's whether their strategy and actions were to inform or influence. Plainly—and correctly—a strategy for influence won out.

Similarly, the Pentagon treated the rescue of Private Jessica Lynch as an event worthy of a James Bond movie. Pentagon public affairs presented the story as the heroic rescue by Special Forces in a dangerous situation of a helpless and much abused victim who had fought gallantly to avoid capture by the Iraqis who took her captive and abused her. In reality, she was injured when her Humvee crashed, her gun jammed with sand so she couldn't use it, and Iraqi doctors and nurses treated her well. She was in no danger at the time Special Forces stormed the hospital where she was recovering. The military's handling of the case clearly went beyond informing. It communicated a strong message extolling the heroism of a female soldier—later awarded the Bronze Star—and her rescuers.[13]

Were perceptions of the facts presented as the story broke accurate? Was the military's handling of the matter reasonable? That debate lies in another venue. As often occurs, initial reports did not prove accurate, and Lynch herself later dismissed any notion that she had been a hero. The point is that public affairs will—and, in my view, should—fully respect the truth as it is understood, but use it actively to drive narratives favorable to our actions that influence the media and their audiences. In this case, the story backfired when the truth came out. Lynch's story is a case study that vindicates the wisdom of the approach that Kevin Mc-Carty and other members of the National Security Council team adopted in developing a narrative for capitalizing on the surge, which aligned facts and narrative: Make the case, and do it by sticking to the truth as you know it.

There is no consistency to the Pentagon's posture as to whether public affairs should only inform and not influence. Politics often drives its behavior. In 2001, Rumsfeld and his undersecretary for policy, Douglas J. Feith, wisely set up an Office of Strategic Influence (OSI) under Brig. Gen. Simon P. Worden. Its mission was to engage in strategic communication to counter violent extremists and their ideology, coordinate information-related work of the Defense Department, and to represent policy's views with other parts of the government. Feith keenly observed that neither the Pentagon's public affairs office nor the State Department's public diplomacy office "was equipped to promote initiatives to fight jihadist ideology."[14]

But the secretary's public affairs team, led by Torie Clarke, viewed OSI as a challenge to their own turf. Clarke objected that the design of OSI, which ostensibly could provide policy guidance to public affairs officers, risked damaging the credibility of her team. Feith and others worked to allay the concern, but Clarke viewed this as a political battle over turf, not ideas. OSI found itself ruthlessly attacked in the name of protecting the Pentagon's integrity and credibility. News reports written by *New York Times* reporters Eric Schmitt and James Dao were followed in short order by a request made to Rumsfeld from the Senate Armed Services Committee to refute the allegations. The result was an internal review within the Department of Defense. The review produced a report that found no instance that corroborated the *New York Times*'s inaccurate reporting.

One informed observer recounted: "Rumsfeld's Assistant Secretary for Public Affairs, Torie Clarke, hated the idea of setting up a Pentagon office to carry the battle to the enemy using strategic communication."[15] The furor produced a poster child for bad journalism in *New York Times* reporters Eric Schmitt and James Dao.[16] Schmitt has done top-flight reporting on Pakistan and other national security topics, and in 2011 coauthored a fine book on counterterrorism, but this controversy dimmed his star.[17] Reporters Schmitt and Dao quoted an unnamed senior Pentagon official who charged that OSI intended to conduct covert operations that went "from the blackest of black programs to the whitest of white." In short, the story went, OSI planned to disseminate lies.

OSI actually intended to use truth, not lies, in its mission to drive messages that supported the US position of discrediting and marginalizing violent decisions. Instead of quashing Clarke, Secretary Rumsfeld shut down OSI. The decision was tragic. Public affairs consolidated its power, but its parochial victory cost the military and the US government. The White House and the Department of State were reluctant to engage on their own in drafting a strategic information campaign of the type that Dwight Eisenhower would have eagerly initiated. The controversy hamstrung efforts to conduct strategic communication against violent terrorists and locked officials in an unresolved debate over what the Pentagon should or should not do about engaging in it. The effect was chilling. Skeptics have complained that Rumsfeld sidestepped controversy. A strong personality with an incisive mind—on full display in his press conferences and his 2011 memoir—he looked for innovations. Why he declined to shut down the efforts of public affairs to eliminate OSI remains puzzling.

The State Department takes a somewhat different approach. The undersecretary of state for public diplomacy and public affairs has tended to take a more active approach in advocating for US policies and serves as the chief spokesperson for the department. In US embassies, says Patricia Kushlis, who has served as a Foreign Service officer and writes a respected blog about public diplomacy, "only a few officers are designated to speak for the US government on the record to the news media. They are the Ambassador (or the Deputy Ambassador/Head of Mission in his or her absence); the Public Affairs Officer; and the Information Officer. State has good reasons for not wanting most of its officers to be quoted on the record. There is just too much chance of miscommunication. That is equally true for people from other agencies assigned to missions abroad."[18]

The Reality of Smart Public Affairs

Smart public affairs *is* about influence. Professionals in politics and the corporate world know that you do not talk to the press simply to answer their questions to inform but not influence. Success comes when you articulate policies clearly, define a credible rationale that supports them, and project compelling themes and messages. Mobil Corporation's legendary communication counselor, Herb Schmertz, rightly observed that in dealing with the media, achieving a goal requires that you specify exactly what you want.[19] You need to define a debate on *your* terms, in language that drives your message.

US domestic politics well illustrates that principle. Should we drill in Alaska? Proponents say that we should drill in a tiny portion of real estate called ANWR—a neutral-sounding way to define the debate. Opponents talk about protecting the Arctic National Wildlife Refuge as emotionally more resonant.

Savvy public affairs entails strategic judgments about timing, surprise, and documentation, and it affects the way a case is put together and presented, the understanding of how discourse is unfolding, and whether and how to confront damaging or beneficial rumors. Schmertz advised that parties disclose their thought processes, not just conclusions, and never presume that opponents or spectators necessarily share one's assumptions.[20] One should never fail to set the record straight when an adversary misstates a fact. Political campaigns take pains to do that, whether the offending party is an opponent or the media. They reach out beyond reporters to producers, publishers, and editors. That raises major issues for public affairs doctrine: What constitutes correcting the record? Is the action taken informing or influencing?

Experts like Schmertz and Virgil Scudder, one of the nation's top media trainers whose work focuses on Fortune 100 executives, advocate confronting the media when it distorts the views or facts. It's catechism among political consultants that you hit back, quickly and hard, when the press twists the story.

The strategic goal is get out your message. Make clear to the media that you won't let them get away with incomplete information, inaccuracies, or distortions.

These considerations are vital to effective public affairs and extend beyond informing. They entail strategic thinking to influence. Failing to see public affairs as influence activity misconstrues the role played by the press. Here's reality: Reporters are employees of commercial news organizations that exist to turn a profit; they are not public service organizations. ABC News is part of its company's entertainment division. Schmertz observes that "reporters are not surrogates of the public."[21] We have, he notes, lots of surrogates. They are called elected officials.

The sword swings in two directions. Is it realistic to presume that the selection of information a public affairs officer communicates lacks subjectivity? Virgil Scudder's view is widely shared among corporate communication experts and political consultants. He places public affairs squarely within the ambit of strategic communication. Smart public affairs *always* seeks to influence, if for no other reason than to bolster credibility.

Scudder declares: "You *never, ever* talk to the media just to satisfy their curiosity. Public affairs—media relations—is absolutely about influence. The first and crucial question you ask before talking to the press is: What do I want the reader, viewer, or listener to take away from my interview? The press wants a story. Your job in giving an interview or holding a press conference is to satisfy their questions, clarify any misperceptions, help them write the story that *you want them to write*, and through the media, influence the attitudes and opinions of their audiences."[22] For an interview, Scudder says, "it's essential that the topic or topics be agreed upon by the reporter or producer and the interviewee *in advance*. That not only results in a more focused and interesting interview but it gives the newsmaker the ability to bring the discussion back on track if the interviewer wanders afield." An experienced reporter will also steer the questions in other directions. It's up to the government spokesperson to stay on message.

Scudder cites what happened to former Senator Bob Dole to illustrate his point. An adroit political leader, Dole wrote an interesting memoir and appeared on NBC's *Today Show* to plug it. Instead of driving a message about the book, he let Katie Couric pepper him with questions about tobacco industry contributions.

In another example, Scudder cites an appearance on *Meet the Press* by the former head of General Motors, Fritz Henderson, soon after the White House turned down GM's initial restructuring plan in 2009. Says Scudder, "rather than use the moment as an opportunity to demonstrate his quick response to the unexpected turndown and outline a vision for the carmaker's future, he simply gave vague responses to host David Gregory's questions, responses that were devoid of thought and, clearly, of preparation. He made unsupported claims that he and his team would turn General Motors around, boasting: 'We'll get this job done; you just watch us.'" Scudder says: "Had he taken early and positive control of the interview, providing solid information and detail, everybody would have won: GM, Gregory, and the public."[23] Henderson was fired soon after this debacle.

Scudder also offers this more recent example: "In January 2010 Pennsylvania Governor Ed Rendell self-destructed on *60 Minutes* when Leslie Stahl kept trying to get a straight answer as to whether the proliferation of gambling in his state was not having the by-product of creating new gamblers and destroying lives. Rendell kept dodging the question and repeating that people are going to gamble somewhere and the issue was simply whether Pennsylvania or New Jersey would get the substantial tax revenues that gambling would provide." It was a blow-off answer. When Stahl would not accept it, Rendell exploded, calling Stahl and her producers "simpletons" and "idiots."[24]

"Journalists want newsmakers to speak from their own perspective and give their views," Scudder says. "But, they also expect newsmakers to give an honest and truthful response to a question before proceeding to their own agendas. That's a reasonable expectation. Failure to meet a question head on—and to drive a desired message clearly and forcefully—is a sure way to lose credibility, both with the journalist and the public."[25] There is a long-standing rule coaching political and industry leaders: They can ask any question they want; you can answer any question *you* want. The two best practitioners of this rule are Newt Gingrich and Rev. Jesse Jackson.

Celinda Lake is a top national pollster whose clients include Vice President Joe Biden. Lake says that "talking to the media without developing a clear objective about what response you want from their audiences is asking not just for trouble but catastrophe. A lot of the time, the press that covers a story is not clear in their own minds as to what angle they are looking for. Public affairs is about providing the information that shapes and defines both the press angle and the take-away you desire from engaging with the press."[26]

Current officials, employees, and contractors who work with the US government avoid speaking for the record. But almost all who were interviewed for this book agree that holding press conferences to merely inform and not influence is unrealistic. Communications expert Rich Galen, whom the Bush White House specially dispatched to Iraq to help ensure rational, commonsense communication, explains the fears held by many public affairs officers and why their concerns are misplaced:

A lot of it probably originated with the loss of credibility that the United States military suffered during the Vietnam War. Press conferences put out rosy information that many reporters knew was not only inaccurate but deliberately misleading. That spurred the growth of a culture in which public affairs officers believed that even the appearance of trying to use media engagements to influence audiences would open up the US government to loss of credibility.

The concern is understandable but misplaced. The press respects transparency and truth. They make judgments about the reliability of the people they talk to, whether it's a public affairs officer, diplomat, flag officer, politician, or other sources.

They understand influence and the media. They recognize that any engagement entails a value judgment by both parties as to what information is divulged or exchanged. They're adept at figuring out who's leveling with them and who's lying, deceiving, or being manipulative. In political circles, we cut across the lanes that in the Pentagon separate strategic communication from PSYOP, Information Operations, and public affairs. In civilian life, in everything from Presidential to City Council campaigns we move between those disciplines and we do it seamlessly in using the press strategically. The press knows the game and how to play it. It's unfortunate that government officials tie themselves up in knots over distinctions in definitions that govern what they can say, and how they say it, that lead to absurd results and undercut our ability to drive themes and messages.[27]

Galen is a complete professional. Journalists echo his judgment. As a senior correspondent for *Time* magazine, Doug Waller dealt with government public affairs officers regularly. As a reporter, he found that the distinction between a public affairs, public diplomacy, psychological operations, or information operations officer was "largely meaningless and irrelevant. I always assumed, no matter who I was talking to, that they were providing me information to drive a specific set of messages and a particular agenda. The idea that they intended merely to inform and not influence is ridiculous. Any reporter will treat information received from a government official, no matter who that person works for, with some degree of skepticism. Responsible reporters always exercise diligence to check out the facts. The government would do better to recognize that, move forward, and tell us their story. Our job is to report and evaluate it."[28]

How should the Defense Department reconcile its view of public affairs and strategic communication? Some in the department have qualified the view that public affairs should inform but not influence by embracing the somewhat ambiguous notions of "actively inform" or "inform with intent." That's a step toward recognizing the reality of public affairs. A strong dose of realism would help. Some, like Maj. John J. Garcia, have suggested that the answer is to ensure close coordination between information operations (including psychological operations for influence) and public affairs so that they coordinate closely and speak with one, consistent voice.[29] In some cases that approach can work, but it is a bureaucratic response to communication. The United States is blessed with the finest military in the world. But its approach to information strategy—which at heart deals with political communication—often is too compartmentalized. Politics is too fluid. The military needs more flexibility in approaching strategic communication, information operations, MISO, public affairs, and the ways in which they are integrated. Public affairs should retain the sole jurisdiction to determine who engages with the media. Done properly, it is about influence. It is strategic communication. Other nations, political figures, and corporations recognize that and act accordingly. They are being realistic.

CHAPTER 4

Public Diplomacy

The Voice of America carried Neil Armstrong's words "One small step for man, one giant leap for mankind." Certain US embassy diplomats may contact the French newspaper to seek correction or clarification of a story printed, or to give a speech to a trade association. The State Department often sponsors leading scholars or experts from think tanks to engage with audiences on the campuses of universities in other countries. The State Department has set up cultural and information centers, although after the Cold War it destroyed many of them. It also runs American Corners, a miniversion of the cultural centers. It sponsors two-way exchange programs such as the Fulbright and Congress-Bundestag Youth Exchange Programs, which it runs in cooperation with other governments.

The secretary of state and other State Department emissaries engage constantly with foreign government representatives to forge partnerships to prevent, deter, or mediate conflict. Their subordinates engage with one another on political, economic, consular, and commercial matters, as well as other topics. In March 2011, Hillary Clinton visited Egypt after demonstrators forced President Hosni Mubarak from office. She met with military powers and—while not greeted by a friendly reception from youth demonstrators who felt she had been too hesitant to side with their cause—journeyed to Tahrir Square to meet with everyday Egyptians.[1] In Iraq, Ambassador Ryan Crocker engaged with high-ranking members of Iraq's government to communicate US views on American interests about how to defeat a violent extremist insurgency. It was a two-way dialogue that involved listening as much as talking, responding as much as initiating.[2] It helped immeasurably that Crocker is fluent in Arabic.

Public diplomacy embraces strategic communication, although not every act of diplomacy qualifies as such. People have offered different definitions of what public diplomacy embraces.

The planning group for integration of the US Information Agency into the Department of State has a concise definition: "Public diplomacy seeks to promote the national interest of the United States through understanding, informing and influencing foreign audiences."[3] The planning group distinguishes public diplomacy from public affairs using a narrow definition of the scope of public affairs that focuses its mission on domestic audiences—an unrealistic approach in today's 24/7 global environment: "Public Affairs is the provision of information to the public, press and other institutions concerning the goals, policies and activities of the US Government. Public affairs seeks to foster understanding of these goals through dialogue with individual citizens and other groups and institutions, and domestic and international media. However, the thrust of public affairs is to inform the domestic audience."[4]

USIA defined public diplomacy this way: "Public diplomacy seeks to promote the national interest and the national security of the United States through understanding, informing, and influencing foreign publics and broadening dialogue between American institutions and their citizens abroad."[5]

Judith McHale served as President Barack Obama's undersecretary for public diplomacy and public affairs until June 2011. The website of the office states that the mission of American public diplomacy is "to support the achievement of US foreign policy goals and objectives, advance national interests, and enhance national security by informing and influencing foreign publics and by expanding and strengthening the relationship between the people and government of the United States and citizens of the rest of the world."[6]

The Public Diplomacy Council describes public diplomacy as "a tool in the diplomat's briefcase, a process in the foreign policy community" that "impels diplomats and other practitioners to listen, to understand, and to engage before acting. As products, public diplomacy takes the form of actions (programs, activities, products, and deeds) and messages (ideas themes, words, and values)."[7]

The Department of Defense defines public diplomacy broadly as:

1. Those overt international public information activities of the United States Government designed to promote United States foreign policy objectives by seeking to understand, inform, and influence foreign audiences and opinion makers, and by broadening the dialogue between American citizens and institutions and their counterparts abroad.

2. In peacebuilding, civilian agency efforts to promote an understanding of the reconstruction efforts, rule of law, and civic responsibility through public affairs and international public diplomacy operations. Its objective is to promote and sustain consent for peacebuilding both within the host nation and externally in the region and in the larger international community.[8]

Public diplomacy is a relatively recent term. Dean Edmund Guillon of the Fletcher School of Law and Diplomacy at Tufts University is credited with coining it in 1965.[9] The Public Diplomacy Alumni Association points out that people differ in their views as to whether or not public diplomacy and propaganda are similar. The renowned journalist Edward R. Murrow and other USIA proponents argued that USIA programs were factual and truthful, and thus could not be considered propaganda. The problem, as we've seen, is that propaganda is not tied to lies, although some propaganda is untruthful, and one person's notion of what is fact or truth may be seen as the expression of bias or prejudice by another.

Ambassador Brian Carlson explains that "what State Department people mean when they refer to public diplomacy is in fact often strategic communication. I prefer the USIA's definition of public diplomacy." He continues: "That definition is explicit in stating that public diplomacy entails influencing foreign publics. What's important about the definition is that action aims to advance national goals and interest. We're not doing education exchanges just because we favor education. We do it because it advances US interests. That's the purpose. The other three aspects are understanding, informing, and influence. Those are important because to influence an audience, you need to understand it. There is no such thing as one-way communication. It's about dialogue. Informing is an important aspect of the dialogue. All of it aims ultimately to influence target audiences. In that view, public diplomacy, as a rule, should be considered strategic communication."[10]

The former head of USIA and former Assistant Secretary of State Joseph L. Duffey agrees with Brian Carlson: "Public diplomacy is about explaining America to the world—to our would-be friends as well as our adversaries. It is about influence. And that is strategic communication. Today, the world is transparent. People can see what others are saying in the media and over the Internet. During the Cold War, our communication was about 'winning hearts and minds.' In today's world, we need to move beyond that, to explain America, its values, its ideals, and how our politics functions. That is crucial in advancing our agendas and policies."[11]

Matt Armstrong reports that "after the Second World War ended, foreign service officers generally believed that public diplomacy meant engagement with foreign governments, not foreign publics, audiences, or opinion leaders."[12] Current thinking tends to support a broader view that public diplomacy engages all of them. While not every form of public diplomacy qualifies as strategic communication, the fact is that even though some Foreign Service officers shy away from the notion, much of what our diplomats do in their engagements does constitute strategic communication.

In practice, the Department of Defense does not adhere strictly to its doctrines for MISO of PSYOP, public affairs, and even, to a degree, information operations. But they have them. The State Department lacks a specific doctrine, with the concepts of strategic communication and public diplomacy meaning whatever its current leaders say they mean. Consider the "Shared Values" campaign mounted between October 2002 and January 2003 by Under Secretary of State for Public Diplomacy and Public Affairs Charlotte Beers. A former commercial ad executive with J. Walter Thompson, Beers was known for her work in advertising Uncle Ben's rice.

For the State Department she commissioned a $15 million campaign based upon five spots produced by the McCann-Erickson ad agency to combat anti-American sentiment. Her rationale was that Americans and Muslims around the world share many core values—faith, family, learning. Opinion testing revealed that Muslims did not realize that. The ads aimed to foster dialogue and engagement to close the gap between Muslims and non-Muslims. The ads boasted outstanding production values; as filmmaking, they were first-rate.[13] Each ad featured a prosperous American Muslim: a baker, doctor, firefighter, journalist, or teacher. Each communicated a message about American tolerance, opportunity, and personal and religious freedom.

Beers characterized the ads as short-form mini-documentaries. She insisted that Shared Values was not an advertising campaign. That conclusion rested on the argument that the ads were in-depth, unscripted, on-camera interviews with American Muslims in which participants spoke in their own words, without compensation. Her argument was preposterous. They were ads and comprised an ad campaign. Although they were filmed on a significantly higher budget, the ads were created in the same way that testimonials for political campaign advertising for issues or candidates are produced. They shared a common theme, message, and style. Focus group testing had strongly suggested that what American Muslims told Muslims in other Muslim nations could positively influence their attitudes and opinions.

The campaign resonated poorly: Target audiences did not find the message believable. They did not address what concerned most Muslims around the world about American policies. The spots ran only in Pakistan, Malaysia, Indonesia, and Kuwait. Networks like al-Jazeera refused to broadcast the ads, depriving them of access to key audiences. Research conducted by the Pew Research Center for the People and the Press found that anti-American attitudes rose rather than declined during the period that the ads were broadcast.[14] An assessment of the campaign's effectiveness by Alice Kendrick and Jami A. Fullerton found that the campaign was not credible.[15] Others criticized the ads as recruiting posters for immigration to the United States, which was not readily granting visas. This too undercut the credibility of the campaign.

In fairness to Beers, it appears that the test employed focus or dial group testing. Many political consultants (this author included) challenge the reliability of such tests in measuring ads. Mall tests such as those developed by Douglas E. Schoen and Mark Penn have been shown to be the only truly reliable way to measure the effectiveness of television advertising. In a mall test, an individual enters a private booth or area, watches an ad, and provides responses. This method avoids the groupthink of focus groups. Schoen points out that "the problem with focus group or dial group testing, or the variations of that approach that entail interviewing groups of people, is that they produce reactions that are meaningless out of the context of a real world test or simulated setting. The only way to test spots and obtain reliable information is to use what we call 'mall tests,' which enable individuals to judge a spot without being swayed by group-think."[16]

What matters here is not what result the campaign achieved. It's that in the name of public diplomacy, Beers mounted a classic political campaign while calling it public diplomacy and denying it was an advertising campaign. Even if considered purely public diplomacy, it qualified as strategic communication. Realistically, it was also propaganda. The State Department was well within its right to mount a campaign—and smart campaigns do work. But denying the true nature of the Shared Values campaign clouds the meaning of public diplomacy. Public diplomacy is, and should be, treated as a broad term that enables the Department of State to engage effectively with foreign governments and other foreign audiences. State only undercuts itself if, as Beers did, it shies away from the idea that it engages in strategic communication or advertising campaigns that advance our interests, agendas, and policies.

President Bill Clinton attempted to put the State Department into a posture in which it could take action through an International Public Information (IPI) system to influence foreign audiences in support of US foreign policy and to counteract propaganda by enemies of the United States.[17] In theory, the group consisted of top officials from the Defense, State, Justice, and Treasury departments, along with the Central Intelligence Agency and FBI. Under President George W. Bush, the group ceased to function. President Barack Obama's administration has established a new Center for Strategic Counterterrorism Communications to counter violent extremism. It is tapping into top talent from within and outside the government. It will be interesting to see if it is provided the resources to maximize its potential. One issue likely to crop up is that the center's work clearly includes psychological operations. Patricia Kushlis notes that "some people will question whether State should engage in that type of activity."[18]

Public Diplomacy Is Not an Information Operation

Public diplomacy may qualify as strategic communication, depending upon the activity and the circumstances. It is not an information operation. More precisely, it is not a psychological operation. Rachel Greenspan has aptly summarized what public diplomacy does as targeting countries and audiences to explain US policy to governments and populations, with the goal of increasing support for US policies and providing news and information—but her description of MISO and PSYOP is too narrow.[19] A psychological operation focuses on carrying out missions addressing specific issues, is more often short-term, focuses on a particular target region or audience, and prizes classification or secrecy. Public diplomacy builds long-term relationships and addresses an entire country or region, and entails open and public conduct. Public diplomacy fosters dialogue, with the process of sending and receiving to promote understanding. That may also hold true for strategic communication; hence, one may qualify as the other. Psychological operations prize secrecy. Public diplomacy, Greenspan emphasizes, more often takes place in public view.

Greenspan offers important insights, although it's worth noting that public diplomacy may well be carried on in strict confidence. Cultural agreements negotiated with the Soviets were done behind the scenes. In mediating an end to conflict in Lebanon in 1982, after Ariel Sharon led an Israeli invasion into the country, the American diplomat who conducted negotiations for the United States, Philip Habib, told the press he was answering no questions from the press with his wry wit: "You know me by now, it's a silent movie."[20]

Psychological operations and public diplomacy may be short-term or long-term. Decades of support have been provided through military information support teams to the US Embassy in Colombia to assist in that nation's long war against the guerilla group Fuerzas Armadas Revolucionarias de Colombia (FARC). These teams work globally by, with, and through US embassies around the world. One might also differ from Greenspan's suggestion that psychological operations seek to influence a narrow set of targeted foreign audiences. It may—but it may also address an entire country or region. In Cambodia, the United States conducted demining operations. PSYOP forces conducted training of the Royal Thai Army PSYOP forces in building nationwide landmine awareness, with an entire foreign public as the audience. Militarily, "shock and awe" was both a kinetic and a psychological operation. The post–World War II Marshall Plan focused on the publics of a group of nations.

Equally, there is a strong view that State Department public diplomacy efforts should coordinate with the military to capitalize on the strengths that a cross-government approach can bring. Retired Army Colonel Glenn Ayers served as the military assistant to Secretary of Defense Donald Rumsfeld and Deputy Secretary of Defense Paul Wolfowitz, and is an expert in psychological operations. He observes that "long-term US government strategic communication mandates that State and Defense work as a team. The value of that was well reflected in the close cooperation in Iraq that transpired between US Ambassadors to Iraq John Negroponte, Zalmay Khalilzad, Ryan Crocker, and their successors and their military counterparts including Generals William Casey and David Petraeus. The US African Command builds on that experience. Although the commander is a military officer, his deputy is a diplomat. It is a sophisticated and far-sighted approach to the pursuit of US interests. The fact is, civilians ought to take the lead on public diplomacy, but in military theaters of conflict or insecure environments, the support that the military provides to public diplomacy is vital to success."[21] That view echoes a studied position adopted not long ago by the Project for National Security Reform (PNSR).[22] PNSR aroused controversy, but that idea made plenty of sense.

PART II

Words, Images and Symbols, and Deeds

CHAPTER 5

Words

WORDS—LANGUAGE—ARE AN OBVIOUS CURRENCY FOR STRATEGIC COMMUNI-
cation. This book offers no litany of every book, manifesto, declaration, publication, speech, or statement that qualifies. Nicholas J. Cull, David Culbert, and
David Welch have written a fine encyclopedia of propaganda from 1500 to the
present day that provides a good overview; all of the examples represent strategic
communication.[1] Words do not necessarily stand alone. They may serve as lyrics
to music, copy for an ad, or an element in the performing arts. What's striking is
that the *thinking* behind strategic communication echoes from age to age.

The language in which ideas are expressed is critical to defining a cause or
strategy, and sets forth the story, plot, and narrative that underlies a strategy
as well as its themes and messages. In American politics, the language used to
define the controversy is central to the bitter, emotional battle over abortion.
Those opposed to it characterize themselves as "pro-life." Their cause is to protect the life and safety of the unborn, and they view the battle as practical as
well as moral and theological. They consider abortion to be murder. Those who
support the right to abortion (and there are delineations in the levels of support) characterize themselves as "pro-choice." They view the battle as an issue
over who makes this personal decision—the mother (and possibly her physi-
cian or husband)—and hardly see themselves as embracing murder.

In Republican primary contests, calling an opponent "too liberal" communicates that the opponent is not really a Republican. Indeed, conservatives invoke
a derogatory name for such persons: RINO (Republican In Name Only). By
2012, litmus tests on social issues, spending, and taxes had reached the point that
candidates—all of them clearly conservative by any reasonable standard—were
questioning the conservative bona fides of competitors, because the notion of
"conservative" represented for many base Republican voters a make-or-break test
in judging whether a candidate echoed their values and ideas.

The most dramatic dichotomy in the use of language to define a cause may
involve the ongoing dispute between Israelis and Palestinians. Israelis call suicide

attackers "homicide bombers," whereas Palestinians refer to them as "resistance operations." Israelis have employed different language to describe their preemptive attacks. They call their raids "eliminations." Palestinians call them "assassinations." Israelis consider the attackers to be "terrorists," whereas Palestinians call them "martyrs." The West Bank and Gaza are "disputed territories" for the Israelis, but to Palestinians, they are the "occupied territories."[2] Each side sees themselves as the victims and the others as the aggressors.[3]

Until his death, the American-turned-al-Qaeda spokesman Anwar al-Awlaki, ensconced in Yemen with al-Qaeda in the Arabian Peninsula (AQAP), had made himself a visible antagonist against the United States. The United States has a simple name to characterize him: "terrorist." Al-Awlaki saw himself and his cohorts differently, invoking morality and religion to justify his position while denouncing the United States as corrupt for embracing homosexuality at home while pursuing a global strategy "to control the world's valuables and resources and treating people unjustly and stealing their rights."[4]

Al-Awlaki echoed al-Qaeda leader Ayman al-Zawahiri, whose rhetoric has denounced "apostate" regimes like Egypt's as corrupt for deviating from Islam. Egypt, he pronounced, was "nonreligious" and riddled with "corruption of creed, political corruption, economic and financial corruption, and moral and social corruption."[5] Zawahiri's argument for al-Qaeda is more complex, but the organization's strategic communication invoking the notion of corruption to embrace secularity and its lack of values, morals, or creed, as well as other forms of corruption, supports its rationale as a righteous organization. It is politically savvy. Al-Qaeda does not see itself as a terrorist organization, although in the United States it is seen as a death cult whose violent tactics constitute terrorism.

A Chinese proverb holds that "the beginning of wisdom is calling things by their right name." Words have an impact on attitudes and opinions that people hold. As David Green of Hofstra University rightly has observed, "changing how the public labels categories changes the associations those labels invoke in people's minds, which in turn changes their attitudes towards what is being described."[6] The power of language in strategic communication is very broad. Concrete examples illuminate the notion better than theory. It's well to start with antiquity, in an era that predates publishing.

Ancient civilizations used language powerfully. In his *History of Rome* (*Ab Urbe Condita*), Titus Livius trumpeted the founding of the city. Describing the arrival into Italy of Aeneas and the city's rise, the work appealed to Roman patriotism.[7] The Behistun Inscription from 515 BC celebrated Darius I. Situated on the side of Mount Behistun in Iran, it is enormous (over 25 yards long and 16 yards high) and inscribed in Old Persian, Elamite, and Babylonian. A biography of Darius, it magnifies his achievements, including restoration for the people of his Kingdom, temples, pasture lands, and houses. Indians of the Maurya Empire offered up *The Arthashastra*, written in India by a member of the Maurya Empire. It endorses strategies and tactics that inspire comparison to Machiavelli's *The Prince*. Authorship is attributed to Chanakya (350–283 BC), a scholar who served as prime minister of the Maurya Empire. The text endorses deceit, trickery, torture, and other nefarious activities as legitimate means to gain and hold power.[8]

Ancient Greece is fertile territory for understanding the use of language in strategic communication. Phil Taylor cites the use of disinformation—a splendid example of psychological operations—by the Athenians against Xerxes to dissuade the Persians from deploying certain Greek allies at Salamis. They sent messages that cast doubt upon their allies' loyalty.[9] Such thinking is often integral to military planning. In World War II, for example, Operation Fortitude served as the codename for operations used to trick Germans into believing that the allied invasion of Europe would occur in the Pas de Calais or Norway rather than Normandy. Although more narrowly classified as military deception, the operation employed the principles of strategic communication as well.

The Greeks were as imaginative as any modern practitioner. Thucydides records the famous petition of the Corinthians to the Spartans hoping to entice them—which they did successfully—into war with the Athenians, arguing that the aggressive, imperialistic ambitions of Athens threatened Spartan security. It would be correct, they declared, "in saying that it is their nature neither to enjoy peace themselves nor to allow it to other men."[10] It was a direct attack on the Athenian character. They invoked prejudice, suspicion, and fear to arouse the Spartans to war.

Speeches

Pericles's rousing funeral oration to the citizens of Athens for those killed in war with the Spartans stands as a reminder for why language has such power.[11] The war between these two great alliances had inflicted plenty of suffering. A devastating plague that would soon take Pericles's own life inflicted still more. His oration came at a poignant moment. Yale University scholar Donald Kagan has assessed Pericles as an individual, a citizen, and a leader.[12] Pericles had foreseen that Athens might suffer horrible setbacks and urged Athenians to maintain stout hearts.[13] In his oration he celebrates the greatness of Athens, summoning them to greatness through a vision rooted in achievement. He invokes the memory of ancestors. He celebrates Athens for its democracy and respect for excellence. He exhorts his fellow citizens to live up to what their ancestors achieved.[14] Pericles, Kagan pronounces—citing Thucydides—understood that a statesman had "to know what must be done and to be able to explain it."[15]

New York Times columnist William Safire collected some of the great speeches in history delivered with the intent of influencing audiences.[16] They succeeded. Consider the following examples.

Winston Churchill's address to the House of Commons on June 9, 1940, galvanized England to defeat the Nazis. Technically, the speech demonstrates how repetition—"We shall fight on the seas and the oceans . . . we shall fight on the beaches . . . we shall fight on the landing grounds"—can ramp up emotional intensity.[17] Abraham Lincoln's Gettysburg Address is as inspiring as it was brief.[18] Franklin Roosevelt's First Inaugural speech, remembered for his stirring proclamation that "the only thing we have to fear is fear itself," is literary.[19] Hitler mesmerized Germans through his demagogic speeches. He practiced gestures and inflection, honing his style for maximum impact. His status as a figure of evil does not detract from the fact that he was an effective speaker. Martin Luther King Jr.'s eloquent address at the March on Washington on August 28, 1963, also used repetition, and was a key event in the civil rights revolution. It is said that a picture is worth a thousand words. That may be true, but King's words accomplished what only the eloquent use of language can achieve. He skillfully expressed and encapsulated the spirit of a revolution for dignity, hope, and the dream for equality in a land in which people "will not be judged by the color of their skin but by the content of their character."

John F. Kennedy's speech in Berlin was arguably his most moving and powerful, but his First Inaugural speech set the tone for a new generation of leadership.[20] The speech is also historically significant for a separate reason: Kennedy altered expectations for what voters sought in leaders, at least in style. That change was not necessarily positive. Many voters began to judge candidates on their looks or attire, and their ability to deliver a pithy soundbite, rather than simply the substance of their views. Today, standing in the well of the US House of Representatives as members stream past, moving inside the chamber to cast their votes, is telling. Nearly all the men wear dark suits, red "power" ties, and conservative shirts. It feels as if their barbers trained at the same institute. Most are perfectly coifed. This is the norm in most state legislatures as well.

What does that mean for strategic communication? People tend to believe that attractive people are smarter and better. A handsome, well-groomed candidate, and especially a tall person, has an edge in an election, other critical factors being about equal. It skews the way we choose elected officials. Abraham Lincoln's rough-hewn appearance would have faced tough criticism in today's media environment. This scrutiny has it consequences. The contrast between Kennedy's urbane style and Lyndon Johnson's earthy, slow-drawl Texan manner was among the things that made Johnson feel deeply insecure.[21] In his mind, the media and the world thought of Kennedy as hewn from King Arthur's Round Table while pegging him as tacky, poorly educated, and surrounded by men less able than Kennedy had attracted. It affected how he saw the world.[22] Lady Bird Johnson's press secretary, Liz Carpenter, had a name for Beltway media types who held that belief—as she felt a lot of them did: Yankee Hicks. She might have added that while Southerners may talk slow, they think fast.

One cannot minimize star power, especially when combined with genuine talent. President Ronald Reagan exuded both. Never was that more apparent than during his 1984 speech at the ceremony commemorating the fortieth anniversary of the Normandy Invasion. It paid tribute to the courage of heroes. Always one to capitalize on important events to articulate broader meaning, Reagan hammered home an important policy point for Europe: Freedom requires strength, and the Atlantic alliance needed to stand firm against the repression and threat to freedom posed by Communism.[23] His staff work was not always perfect, however. His visit to the Bitburg Cemetery in Germany, where Nazis are buried, sent an unintended message of insensitivity. This example illustrates that strategic communication can be a delicate art.

Style helps, but reliance upon it is dangerous. As president, Barack Obama's rhetoric has often seemed detached, however well written it may be. Sadly, it deflects attention from the fact—whatever one feels about his ideas—that he has a high intellect and enjoys analyzing issues, although one gets the impression that he is not an especially natural politician. He can deliver a formal speech with teleprompters splendidly, yet he often feels ungrounded. Compare Obama to Winston Churchill, Franklin Roosevelt, Ronald Reagan, and Bill Clinton. Eloquence did not obstruct them from using language that connected them emotionally and intellectually to audiences. Obama's speeches as president lack that connection. He fared better during his 2008 campaign; his speech at the Iowa Jefferson-Jackson dinner prior to the Iowa caucuses, for example, was stunning. But campaigning is one thing and governing is another. The flowery rhetoric that moves a campaign audience wears thin quickly after an election as one struggles to make government work.

Obama's vice president, Joe Biden, has a populist, blunt-talking style that resonates. Critics may call him bombastic, but he's consistently prepared on the issues and he has guts, despite a knack sometimes for making bloopers (which, to his credit, Biden is able to laugh at). He won election to the US Senate for Delaware at age thirty with a campaign that had little money. His sister Valerie Biden Owens and other family members managed the campaign, which developed an innovative tabloid that trumpeted Biden's fights against corruption and insider corporate interests. Effective print communication combined with a strong face-to-face grassroots campaign carried him to overcome a thirty-point deficit to upset Senator J. Caleb Boggs.

As a senator, Biden rode the train every day between Washington and Wilmington. His populist appeal, underscored by sticking close to his constituents, helped drive his strategic communication and the messages that he was one politician who remembered the people who elected him while never giving up and never caving in on tough issues. Not surprisingly, Biden was a respected and popular senator. He earned a reputation for an even hand and getting tough on crime, and as chairman of the Foreign Relations Committee, he assembled an able team that accentuated his own natural interest—national security. Pollster and consultant Celinda Lake knows and has worked with Biden. In her view, "he understands the importance of strategic communication. One of his gifts, given his strong interest in the complexities of foreign affairs, is his ability to express his views plainly and persuasively."[24] As vice president, his skills as a negotiator have been evident. While Obama drew fire from conservatives and liberals for poor strategic communication and a failure to assert himself, Biden proved very effective in working with Republican Senator Mitch McConnell to avoid a catastrophic debt default in 2011.

In Bob Woodward's account of Obama's Afghanistan decision making, the vice president comes across as one of the best-prepared participants in the debates, despite the fact that Obama and Gen. David Petraeus disagreed with his conclusions.[25] Still, the thrust of Biden's argument, that capturing or killing Taliban leaders was more likely to produce results than a counterinsurgency campaign rooted in winning hearts and minds, has proven central to the refinements that Petraeus has made to Gen. Stanley McChrystal's strategy. When the issue of extending the Bush tax cuts for two years divided Congress, it was Biden's ability to communicate and negotiate that helped produce a compromise that achieved success. Biden is a natural who intuitively understands strategic communication. His gusto may produce mistakes, but his successes are no accident.

Among Republicans, former Speaker Newt Gingrich, former Governor Sarah Palin, and former Governor Mike Huckabee have demonstrated powerfully what gifted communicators can achieve. Gingrich's ability to combine reasoned intellectual arguments, wit, and concrete metaphors—comparing Federal Express's ability to track packages to the ability to identify the location of illegal immigrants, for example—make him a compelling speaker.[26] Sarah Palin arguably did more political damage to the credibility of Barack Obama's health care legislation with voters than most other opponents combined with two words: death panels.[27] Mike Huckabee's mastery of communication is marked by a style that combines warmth and colorful oratory with a bias for action that infuses his words with credibility. There is no way to separate the important confluence of words with deeds in asserting political leadership. Huckabee combines wit, a willingness to cross partisan lines, and a strong pastor's conscience for social justice that won him strong support, even as a conservative Republican, among African Americans. That combination gives him credibility. It's not surprising that after the 2008 presidential campaign he moved successfully into radio and television broadcasting as a popular national commentator. All three are brilliantly gifted strategic communicators. They possess that rarest of political gifts: the power to employ language to shape or transform political course. One may agree or disagree with their points of view, but it's hard to dispute their talent for making a point through the use of compelling language.

The power of speech in the Arab world is remarkable. Its culture respects language and oratory. Journalist Neil MacFarquhar observed that when Jordanians went on the rampage, attacking buses, police stations, and other government institutions, it took "just one nationally televised speech from King Hussein to still the riots, such was his command of Arabic."[28]

People who have the ability to move audiences through the power of speech include prominent US adversaries. Henry Kissinger has aptly observed that by nature, revolutionaries are "powerful and single-minded personalities" who rely for their success "on charisma and on an ability to mobilize resentment and to capitalize on the psychological weakness of adversaries in decline."[29] He was writing about Mao Zedong, but the words also suited Fidel Castro. William Safire has insightfully pointed to a brilliant speech delivered by Fidel Castro in 1953.[30] By training a lawyer, Castro led a successful revolution that imposed a brutal, repressive regime in Cuba. Years earlier, he stood on the dock after an armed attack on the Moncada Barracks had failed, while leading a revolution against Fulgencio Batista. It's worth noting that before Castro subjugated Cubans to his own tyranny, the regime he was battling against was headed by a president who tortured and killed dissidents and had their bodies "dumped in fields, with their eyes gouged out or their crushed testicles stuffed in their mouths."[31] He sounds more like Thomas Paine than the Communist tyrant who became infamous for seven-hour tirades to the subjects of a police state. It's worth quoting a paragraph from his concise, passionate indictment of Fulgencio Batista's dictatorship:

> Moncada Barracks were turned into a workshop of torture and death. Some shameful individuals turned their uniforms into butchers' aprons. The walls were splattered with blood. The bullets embedded in the wall were encrusted with bits of skin, brains, and human hair, the grisly reminders of the rifle shots fired full in the face. The grass around the

barracks was dark and sticky with human blood. The criminal hands that are guiding the destiny of Cuba [have] written for the prisoners at the entrance of that den of death the very inscription of Hell: "Forsake all hope . . ."

We are Cubans and to be Cuban implies a duty; not to fulfill that duty is a crime, is treason. We are proud of the history of our country; we learned it in school and have grown up hearing of freedom, justice, and human rights. . . . We were taught that for the guidance of Cuba's free citizens, the Apostle wrote in his book *The Golden Age*: "The man who abides by unjust laws and permits any man to trample and mistreat the country in which he was born is not an honourable man."[32]

Americans are often perplexed by why some of its adversaries achieve iconic status among their own citizens. Castro's powerful eloquence is a striking illustration of brilliant strategic communication that can stir the soul and help to shape the destiny of a revolution.

Manifestos, Statements, Reports, Media Appearances

Julius Caesar justified brutal Roman action against the Germanic tribes during the savage Gallic Wars from 58 to 50 BC on the rationale that his adversaries were barbarians whose "greatest glory" was to "lay waste" to the land around them.[33] Historian and Caesar biographer Adrian Goldsworthy offers a somewhat more nuanced view: "Caesar presented his fight against the Germans as necessary to defend Rome, its people, its allies and interests against foreign intruders who posed a future threat and had posed a real threat in the past."[34]

It was a little like demonizing Saddam Hussein, although achieved with more finessse: the world was better off without them. Goldsworthy points out that there was a tradition for generals to write commentaries about their victories. Their writing was propaganda. But Caesar displayed subtlety and savvy that eluded most of his colleagues. Caesar "wrote for a political purpose, to build up his reputation as a great servant of the Republic and show that he deserved his pre-eminence."[35] But the writing was adroit. It was not self-aggrandizing, as competitors like Pompey were in their commentaries. Caesar "avoided emotion. He talked about being the commander, making big decisions, staying close to the front line. He avoids talking about himself. Instead, he allows the reader to *imagine* his heroism, which added to the power of his storytelling. He was an excellent orator. His writing was clear, concrete, and often read aloud at dinners or small gatherings. He had exceptional gifts as a strategic communicator."[36]

The period following Caesar's death in 44 BC was rich in manifestos, pamphlets, and lampoons by which Octavius, Antony, Pompey, and others conducted propaganda campaigns to win support.[37] Political leaders in later centuries and up to the present day have echoed their thinking.

The development of the printing press emerged center stage in politics with the German Reformation, a rebellion against the Roman Church hierarchy, its grip on doctrine, and its corruption.[38] Invented around 1450, printing presses existed in cities across Europe by 1500. Mark U. Edwards Jr. examined Protestant and Catholic four- to eight-page pamphlets produced by the thousands during its early years. The Reformation, he concludes, "saw the first major, self-conscious attempt to use the recently invented printing press to shape and channel a mass movement. The printing press allowed Evangelical publicists to do what had been previously impossible, quickly and effectively reach a large audience with a message intended to change Christianity."[39]

Martin Luther launched what would today be considered a full-scale media campaign. He used the printing press to disseminate his messages about redefining Christianity. Luther and his allies published twenty percent of the thousands of pamphlets published between 1500 and 1530—an output that overwhelmed Catholic opponents and proved a major cause of the German Reformation. The pamphlets were cheap, easy to transport, and easy to read. The printing press enabled him to "broadcast subversive messages" and communicate quickly with influential people and activists who had a relatively coordinated program to transmit their views orally, through conversation, or preaching.[40]

What Luther did centuries ago was the equivalent of what we see in today's political print campaigns, although modern campaigns use direct mail and the Internet. For example, in Barack Obama's brilliant 2008 campaign, his campaign manager, David Plouffe, describes how the campaign used Internet communication to identify and recruit volunteers and to drive themes and messages. It operated on the same principle that Luther employed.[41] By May 2008, the campaign had generated over 13,000 affiliated websites. No campaign in history has even approached that.

In seventeenth-century England, people communicated in many ways. The literate read books, newspapers, and pamphlets. The less literate depended upon single sheets of paper printed with a ballad, rhyme news, or woodcuts that were called broadsides. For the illiterate, there were sermons, ballads, official proclamations, and riots.[42] The first printing press arrived at Westminster Abbey in 1474. At first, printing was expensive; by the 1620s costs had come down, enabling the revolutionary spirits that led to civil war twenty years later. Pamphlets sold on street corners or in print shops were common.[43] Jason

Peacey has skillfully dissected the centrality of print and propaganda in British politics during the seventeenth century.[44]

Pamphlets circulated widely before and during the American Revolution. Thomas Paine was perhaps the most renowned, and his work made an impact. In *Common Sense*, he argued that the real issue for colonists was freedom, not taxes. That became the theme in the war for independence. In *The American Crisis*, written during the darker days of the conflict to boost flagging morale, he uttered his famous declaration: "These are the times that try men's souls."

Both sides during the American Revolutionary War used proclamations, leaflets, pamphlets, and other statements to subvert one another's morale or inspire defections. In 1774, the Continental Congress used the "Address to the Inhabitants of the Province of Quebec" to kick off an intensive, long-term campaign of influence to disrupt the fragile alliance of French Canadians to Britain. It unsettled the British enough that they tried to seal off the province from American agitators and propaganda.[45]

China, Vietnam, and other harbors for authoritarian repression are no less sensitive today as they move to filter or control access to the Internet.[46] China's control is the most pervasive in the world, prompting widespread complaints about clampdowns on freedom of expression and the right to privacy in a system that seeks to legally control all content transmitted over the Internet. The current approach merely enhances China's long-standing practice. Viewers will never forget CBS anchorman Dan Rather's anger in 1989 as Chinese authorities pulled the plug on his broadcast from Tiananmen Square in an attempt to quash media coverage of their suppression. In 2011, Egyptian thugs aligned with President Hosni Mubarak actively sought out and beat up foreign journalists covering protests by hundreds of thousands of antigovernment demonstrators in central Cairo's Tahrir Square. In Libya, the harsh treatment of foreign journalists by Gaddafi until his overthrow in 2011 was aimed squarely at suppressing unfavorable coverage.[47] The same point applies to the George W. Bush administration's cynical treatment of al-Jazeera in 2003, which it viewed as hostile to US policy.[48]

During the revolution, Thomas Jefferson drafted a resolution passed by Congress that offered land grants to Hessian mercenaries who deserted. Americans spread the message through leaflets disguised as tobacco packets that were distributed to the Hessians. Over the course of the war, American propaganda prompted over 5,000 Hessian desertions among the 30,000 who fought. Not surprisingly, Benjamin Franklin proved a master of both black and white propaganda. His exploits included faking an issue of the *Boston Independent* that contained false stories of British scalp hunting.[49] During World War II, Bill

Donovan's OSS would repeat the tactic, fabricating the newspaper *Das Neue Deutschland*, ostensibly an anti-Nazi political group, for distribution to German troops.[50]

Johns Hopkins professor David A. Bell remarks on how Napoleon's supporters "delighted in his unique, even idiosyncratic qualities."[51] Newspapers, broadsheets, art, and print were most efficient during that era in getting out a message. Some suggest that Napoleon's favorite literary form was the novel. Bell contends that he saw himself as a character in a novel, and that his novelistic sensibility, "his ability to make a spectacle of his inmost original self," helps explain his ability to forge bonds with his army and countrymen. He posed as different characters: peacemaker, protector of the arts, and warrior, above all. Napoleon is fascinating because his genius, like his arrogance and ultimate political blindness, was so overwhelming.

When it came to selling himself and his achievements, truth was no virtue in Napoleon's pantheon of values. He did not hesitate to exaggerate feats and minimize losses. Historian Philip Dwyer characterizes his Italian campaign as "a war of representation" that constructed a "narrative of their adventures in Italy, adventures he and the troops shared in common. His victories were amplified, the troops' morale was given a boost, and a bond between the commander-in-chief and his men was created in the process. He was not only enhancing the heroism of his men, as a reflection of his own image as a hero, he was also demonstrating accomplishments as commander-in-chief."[52]

He understood how to use strategic communication to politically exploit his achievements. As Dwyer notes, he understood the power of the press. He presented himself as being in control of events and his men at the center of the action. The newspapers picked up on his narrative that in Italy he was "breaking the chains of slavery and liberating the people."[53] There was a demand for engravings of Napoleon, and what counted to many was what he represented.[54] His propaganda campaigns were well thought out and communicated the narrative that events had unfolded according to Napoleon's strategy. Dwyer observes that these shaped the legend of a young general overcoming the odds, whose strength he did not flinch from exaggerating. He drove home his message through successive letters to the directory that governed France and that were reprinted in newspapers. He sent flags taken from the enemy and dispatched generals to bring back trophies and offer a public address that extolled his achievements.[55] His sense of how to use strategic communication to mold and shape public opinion was superb. It enabled him to mask setbacks and maximize the impact of success.

The Communist Manifesto, written in 1848 by Karl Marx and Friedrich Engels, testifies to the power of nineteenth-century political manuscripts.[56] It summoned the working class-to-class struggle against the powers of old Europe and the bourgeoisie class that had accumulated the wealth and exploited the proletariat for manual labor and cheap wages. It characterized the Communists as their champions, calling upon them to rebel against existing social conditions and forcibly overthrow the ruling classes. It galvanized revolutions and widely influenced political thought.

Manifestos have long been a staple of European politics. The British political parties continue to use them as the intellectual basis for their election campaigns. Those manifestos matter. They set forth policies that the party leaderships respect. European political groups, including the European Peoples' Party, the Party of European Socialists, the United Green Parties of Europe, the Alliance of Liberals and Democrats for Europe, the Independence/Democracy Group, Fianna Fail, Fine Gael, the Labour Party, and Sinn Fein define their ideas through plans and manifestos.[57] In the United States, the Republican and Democratic parties expend a lot of energy in developing party platforms, but presidential campaigns chart their own courses, sometimes to the chagrin of party activists.

Manifestos have also influenced global politics and modern US presidential campaigns. Arthur Schlesinger Jr. wrote a number of them targeted to Democrats. His eloquent, influential tract in 1960, *Kennedy or Nixon: Does It Make any Difference?* focused on the razor-thin presidential race.[58] "A lot of liberal and Adlai Stevenson Democrats," says Ron Faucheux, who is a historian of American elections, "doubted whether Kennedy was really a liberal and whether who won the election really mattered. Robert F. Kennedy's investigation into labor unions, the Kennedy family ties to Senator Joe McCarthy, and JFK's father, Joseph Kennedy, made them uneasy. Schlesinger realized the election would be close. His manifesto was extremely influential in mobilizing the intellectual left on behalf of Kennedy."[59]

Schlesinger began with a direct assault on Nixon's character, whose interests, skills, and motivations he took pains to distinguish from those of Kennedy.[60] He sought to discredit Nixon and vanquish among influential people any feeling that the candidates were equally acceptable. He dismissed Nixon as an opportunist, "a characteristic figure of the Eisenhower period—concerned with externals rather than substance, indifferent to the merits of issues, generally satisfied with things as they are." He stated that Nixon was unique in his failure to identify with substantive positions on issues. He was a pure opportunist, unworthy of the Oval Office: "More serious political personalities," he judged, "stand for something. Nixon is, in his way, a serious political personality; yet he stands for almost nothing." Schlesinger disliked Barry Goldwater too, but at least he felt that Goldwater stood for ideas—although he felt compelled to acknowledge his belief that Nixon would make a better president than the Arizona senator. Nixon stood for himself, with no sense of history; a man who "lacks taste."[61]

Kennedy, he wrote, "stands for a new epoch in American politics. . . . He understands that our nation must awaken from the Eisenhower trance and get on the march again." Kennedy, we are assured, "cares about the reality of issues," and "his intelligence is devoted to searching for answers rooted in specific policies, as a leader who has a sense of history must."[62]

His critics argue that Schlesinger's thesis was hogwash—that whatever Nixon's flaws, Kennedy proved ineffective as an executive and that his personal life left much to be desired. They argue that Eisenhower fostered prosperity and made the nation more secure. A major point that Kennedy harped on, the so-called missile gap with the Soviet Union, proved to be a myth. Still, for the 1960 campaign, Kennedy felt new and fresh, and the manifesto helped drive his message among its targeted audiences. In Theodore Sorensen, Arthur Schlesinger, and others, Kennedy's legacy has been staunchly defended. Biographer Robert Caro has shown how politically adroit Kennedy proved to be in securing the 1960 Democratic nomination through a combination of smart strategy, talented strategists, his father's money, a cool political head, and brilliant strategic communication. His gift for communication shines through especially brightly in his splendid use of wit in debating Lyndon Johnson at the convention before the Texas delegation, in which he defused hostility and punctured any illusions Johnson may have held about Kennedy's formidability.[63] Caro is highly impressed by Kennedy's political skills. As a public presence, he is undoubtedly correct.

But as Caro himself notes, he had neither skill nor success at passing a legislative program. His praise of Kennedy in foreign policy is heavily defended by his admirers and sharply criticized by others. For example, Kennedy's most vaunted success, handling the Cuban Missile Crisis, was apparently thanks to the imagination and prudence of his CIA director, John McCone, who came up with the idea of a blockade, then persuaded Dwight Eisenhower—with whom Kennedy consulted on the crisis—and Robert Kennedy to support the idea. To Kennedy's immense credit, he maintained an open, objective mind and showed an ability during the crisis to seek, recognize, and heed sound counsel.[64]

Journalists like Henry Fairlie and Frederick Kempe have challenged the Kennedy image as hype.[65] Relevant here is the impact of Schlesinger's strategic communication. Among his target audiences, it was substantial.

Schlesinger published his manifesto as a small book. In today's media environment it would be uploaded onto the Internet and probably accompanied by a mass blogging campaign. More recently, Egyptian demonstrators who toppled Mubarak cited Gene Sharp's manifesto on the use of nonviolence for its influence on their strategic thinking.[66] Whatever channels of communication are used, manifestos can make a difference.

Napoleon, again, set the standard for an effective leader who understood the power of strategic communication. He actively influenced French cultural activity to advance his agendas. Like the OSS's Bill Donovan, he considered propaganda a weapon of war. Napoleon required authors to submit two copies of every book, play, poster, or lecture for prior censorship while cultivating the "image of soldier-emperor." Freedom of the press was unwelcome. "If I had a free press," Napoleon said, "I wouldn't last more than three months."[67] He limited the number of newspapers that could publish, thereby controlling the press and using it to advance his agendas.[68] Like modern political leaders, he also wrote newspaper columns.

The British countered Napoleon's propaganda with a campaign to discredit the French leader among his fellow citizens. Their campaign eventually extended across Europe into Russia. Historian Simon Burrows notes that they funded pamphlets and sponsored newspaper and periodical publications. They denounced Bonaparte as a tyrant, a threat to Europe, and generally despicable. The British targeted official elites, such as office holders, churchmen, and the military; the politically active literate public who influenced policy; and to a lesser extent the general public, which did not participate in public policy debates.[69]

That segmentation of target audiences held true in France one hundred and fifty years later, when the civil war in Algeria prompted fierce debate over the use of torture by the French army. That debate took place mainly among elites and influentials but not the general public.[70] By contrast, in the United States, the debate over Vietnam embroiled officials, influentials, the military, and the general public.

Politics knows no formula. In Mexico, the Zapatista National Liberation Army (EZLN) managed to transform itself during the 1990s from a Marxist guerilla organization with limited credibility into a social movement with strong international support and credibility that dramatically affected the options and actions of the Mexican government.[71] The Zapatistas used the Internet and urged media to focus international attention on their grievances, arouse support, and forge solidarity, helping to bring about a settlement. Setting aside violence was important. But by turning to language as a key tool of strategic communication, the Zapatistas rebranded themselves and circumvented the might of the Mexican military with an effective communication campaign.[72] Between 1994 and 1998, they put the Mexican government on the defensive as the country evolved from an authoritarian to a more open system.

Jihadi websites have served as a primary tool through which violent Islamists—defined as Muslims who seek to overthrow governments by violent means in order to impose upon a country a new government that conforms to their interpretation of what the Qu'ran requires—have used the Internet to spread ideas and create links, as well as to identify, recruit, and mobilize supporters. Although some websites use sophisticated graphics and video, the core messages are communicated in words, not images. Until imprudently abolished, the Department of Defense–funded Center for International Issues Research (CIIR) in Washington tracked many of these websites in real time, on an open source basis.

Eric Michael was the program manager for CIIR. The insights that CIIR drew from its analysis of those websites is revealing. He reports that the "epiphany for us was when we were looking at a photograph on the front page of *The Washington Post* in October 2003 of an armed adversary in Fallujah. One of our analysts pointed out that the person was not Iraqi. She identified him as Chechen. We dug and discovered there was a group of Chechens, wearing what we considered identifiable uniforms, helping the insurgents there. It was significant because we were able to conclude that in Iraq, we were fighting a revolution, not battling against just terrorists. That raised the question as to what narrative was driving the participation by the Chechens and other adversaries in Iraq. The answer was belief. And belief comes from words."[73]

Michael continues: "Every time we looked at an extremist website, we generally found three things that their narratives tried to convey: first, the legitimacy of their actions. That was rooted in both the religion and culture of Islam. Second, invitations to join the extremists financially as insurgents or as supporters. There was a way to support the revolution simply by saying certain prayers in the safety of your kitchen. We asked: what were they saying to recruit? Third, what arguments did they use to discredit their adversaries? These were invaluable to recognize and understand, because in passing it to military in the field, it provided a basis for countering their efforts. What was also striking about the extremist propaganda was how similar, despite the extensive references to their interpretation of Islamic teaching, their rhetoric often was to Soviet-era propaganda. All of this was conveyed through their use of language. For these parties, language was the currency of strategic communication. They did use images, but that came much later, in 2004 and 2005, as they built Western-style presentations after forming their electronic websites. The foundation of extremist websites lies in the use of words. Words stand at the core of their use of the Internet. And belief comes from words, especially in Islam."[74]

CIIR's work was unique in the information it was able to pass on to the military. The decision to terminate its operation as a key political appointee shifted budget priorities was unfortunate. While most militant radical Islamist websites conveyed propaganda, CIIR also passed on terrorist postings that detailed vital instructions on how snipers and improvised explosive devices (IEDs) could kill American troops. The information helped the military counter insurgency tactics. American political campaigns combine deeds, images, symbols, and language, but every aspect of them starts with developing a credible rationale for a cause or candidacy, a narrative, and the themes and messages that emanate from them. That is about language. Election campaigns around the world are no different. No matter how powerful the images and symbols or the actions taken, promoting a political idea or advancing a cause requires a clear recognition that language offers a unique power to influence target audiences.

Books

Campaign biographies, histories, and books—set aside most self-help books, investigative reporting, philosophy, history, or journalism—that explicitly aim to influence opinion on issues or build an image of gravitas are strategic communication.

Modern British political leaders after Winston Churchill are not known often for their books. Harold Macmillan, Tony Blair, Margaret Thatcher, and John Major wrote memoirs—after they left office, not to win one.[75] Their books represented strategic communication to bolster their images and the judgments of history rendered upon their performance in office.

In the United States, it has become common for modern American candidates for president to publish books, sometimes with the assistance of ghost writers. They vary in scope from personal reflections, such as Barack Obama's two books and Bob Dole's memoir, to extended campaign brochures.[76] The strategic message of books written for campaigns is that the authors are thoughtful, visionary, and have the intellectual stature to be taken seriously. Such books are transactional politics, not literary pursuits. Former Vice President Al Gore's book on climate warming also pushes his ideas on an issue.[77] Richard Nixon and Jimmy Carter used substantive analysis in their postpresidential books to advocate for their ideas and to communicate relevance.[78]

In France, publishing books seems de rigueur for political leaders. Charles De Gaulle unnerved the French military establishment in *Towards a Modern Army*, published in 1937, in which he argued for a new approach to military tactics that stressed fire and maneuver. The French ignored him, but the Germans put his innovative thinking to good use in their blitzkrieg tactics to overrun Poland, France, and most of Europe. De Gaulle's memoirs are elegant and insightful.[79] The prolific Francois Mitterrand wrote both nonfiction and novels. Prime Minister Dominique de Villepin was proud of his poetry and nonfiction.[80] Both competitors in the last French presidential election, Nicolas Sarkozy and Segolene Royal, have published clearly written, substantive books.[81] French politicians seem more genuinely interested in their literary ability than their American counterparts, and their ability and interest in writing and publishing is an element of what French voters expect of their leaders by way of judging their gravitas.

Books can be used strategically to define a political posture. In China, Mao's *Little Red Book*—more properly, *The Quotations of Chairman Mao*, edited by Lin Bao—became a cultural icon as a way of understanding his thinking. Lin declared in his foreword to the second edition that its purpose was "to help the broad masses learn from Mao Tse-tung's thought more effectively. . . . Once Mao Tse-tung's thought is grasped by the broad masses, it becomes an inexhaustible source of strength and a spiritual atom bomb of infinite power."[82]

Michael Crichton's novel *State of Fear* challenged the views of those warning about global warming.[83] Whatever the merits of that debate, Crichton made no bones about its purpose: to use popular entertainment to influence attitudes and opinions on the issue. A best-selling author like Crichton can be influential.

During World War II, Pulitzer Prize–winning writer John Steinbeck wrote a novel called *The Moon Is Down*.[84] Steinbeck was working with the Office of Strategic Services at the time, and he wrote the book as propaganda to encourage the resistance movement. The book worried the Nazis to the extent that mere possession of a copy merited an automatic death sentence.[85] Highly inventive, Steinbeck was an active presence. Some ideas he proposed were more actionable than others. Bill Donovan's biographer, Doug Waller, says that "Steinbeck sent Donovan a number of interesting ideas for OSS operations. One was to airdrop tiny grenades over occupied countries so that kids could toss them from rooftops at German soldiers. Donovan ignored this suggestion."[86]

Poetry and Songs

Virgil, Horace, Ovid, and Propertius used poetry to advocate political messages in Augustan Rome.[87] Neil Faulkner points out that the Romans were masters of spin. In the *Aeneid*, he observes, Virgil wrote a famous passage in which "the achievements of the Greeks are acknowledged, but their need of Roman government asserted."[88] Brian Croke shows that the Byzantine emperor Anastasius I, who reigned as emperor of the Eastern Roman Empire from 591 to 518 AD, used poetry from several panegyrists to celebrate his military victory over the Isaurians and his sparing of the defeated. It was a message about power that compared him to the Roman general Pompey.[89]

The Crusades fostered the notion of chivalry, giving rise to epic poems like *The Song of Roland* that extolled combat as a noble cause through which men could prove themselves.[90] Is it strategic communication? That's arguable—there's no evidence the unknown author *intended* for the poem, meant for oral recitation rather than reading, to influence the attitudes or opinions of people, although that may have been the effect. Some believe it that does.

In 1681, John Dryden wrote *Absalom and Architopel* specifically to bolster the childless (and thus heirless) King Charles II of England.[91] Opponents worried that he would allow his Catholic brother James to succeed him, a cause for war in Anglican England. Dryden was both poet laureate to the king and his royal historiographer. A political satire written in heroic couplets, his poem is an allegory. It uses Absalom's rebellion against King David to discuss the Monmouth Rebellion, the Popish Plot, and the Exclusion Crisis, all related to the succession issue. Dryden mocked Protestants, priests, and even the king, although the king himself may have been the one who persuaded Dryden to write it.[92]

In the twentieth century, as the Germans waged war in 1914, poems written by E. E. Cummings, Witter Bynner, Ford Madox Ford, and various Russian, Italian, and Scandinavian poets for propaganda became part of the war effort.[93] John F. Kennedy quoted Robert Frost to communicate that he was erudite. Poetry is no longer generally a part of modern Western politics.

Poetry is integral to Islamic politics, however, where poetry and dreams play a vital role in political discourse and perception. Historian Philip Hitti states that "modern audiences in Baghdad, Damascus and Cairo can be stirred to the highest degree by the recital of poems only vaguely comprehended and by the delivery of orations in the classical tongue, though it be only partially understood."[94] Dreams offer a way through which Muslims can experience mystical revelation and are seen, as Michael Valhos has pointed out, as a message from God. Muslims take dream interpretation seriously in a way that few in the West may appreciate. Al-Qaeda's success in conducting a suicide attack against the USS *Cole* prompted Osama bin Laden to celebrate his success with a poem:

> A destroyer: even the brave fear its might.
> It inspires horror in the harbour and in the open sea.
> She sails into the waves
> Flanked by arrogance, haughtiness and false power.
> To her doom she moves slowly
> A dinghy awaits her, riding the waves.[95]

Dreams play a role in this discourse. After the attacks on the Twin Towers, bin Laden tells the Shaykh in a well-known video: "He told me a year ago, 'I saw in a dream, we were playing a soccer game against the Americans. When our team showed up in the field, they were all pilots. . . . Abd Raham al Gahmri said he saw a vision, before the operation, a plane crashed into a tall building." At his son's wedding the following month, he recited a poem celebrating the action. The lesson is that different cultures use language in different ways to elicit emotional responses from audiences and to shape attitudes and opinions. An American politician who communicated to his or her constituency in verse would be laughed off the stage. Bin Laden was a murderer and the leader of a death cult, but he was also an icon to his followers.

The Taliban are no less vigorous in their use of poetry and songs to appeal to the Islamic and patriotic sentiments of their audiences. Poets and singers denounce the Crusader occupation of Afghanistan. Songs performed a cappella by male singers (musical instruments are viewed as not Islamic by groups like the Taliban) fit melodies of well-known and traditional Afghan songs, and appeal to religious and patriotic feeling. Taliban leader Mullah Mohammad Omar has called upon poets to enshrine Taliban achievements in poetry. Shahamat, the Taliban's official website, offers sections for poetry and songs, which resonate among many youth.[96] Dawlat Khan told the *Kashmir Monitor*: "I have a five-year-old son who doesn't listen to music, but he asks me to play the Taliban songs for him and he sings along with them." They are stored on Khan's mobile phone. Passed from hand to hand, the songs capture the popular imagination in ways that overt appeals from the Karzai government and the Taliban otherwise fail to do.[97]

Ironically, though it is now embracing modern technology, during its last period in power the Taliban banned television and songs, although unaccompanied songs about Islamic themes or Afghan patriotism were encouraged. Phones that support video film clips of Taliban attacks and audio formats lend themselves to Taliban propaganda. As an anecdotal measure of their impact, one Afghan National Army soldier has stated that he keeps material like this on his phone on the theory that it might save him if captured. "Besides," he said, "there's nothing bad about these songs. They are all songs about the country, and Islamic poems. We too are children of the country and we are Muslims. So we listen to them."[98] Songs represent a powerful method of strategic communication to touch people at the grassroots, and stopping their dissemination has proven extremely difficult. Afghan political experts like Abdul Basir argue that the songs and videos "constitute a major factor in favor of a Taliban victory."[99] Basir may yet be proven incorrect, but his comment reflects some of the sentiment in that country.

Arabs who stand for reform and democracy have been equally vigorous in their use of poetry or song. In the 2010–2011 upheavals in Tunisia, Balti, Tunisia's best-known rapper and a founding father of hip-hop music (a wildly popular form of entertainment in North Africa), helped to fuel the revolution. His recording "Zine el Abadine Ben Ali and the 40 Thieves" zapped the former president for corruption. Singer Hamada Ben Amor, nicknamed "El General," composed "Mr. President Your People Are Dying." The piece went viral and police slammed the performer into prison. Eight days after the release of the song, Amor went free and the president was in flight from his country.[100]

In the Balkans during the 1990s, Joseph Nye has reported, the dissident radio station B-92 in Belgrade played Public Enemy's lyric "Our freedom of speech is freedom or death—we got to fight the powers that be."[101] It became a political anthem.

Comic Art

Political cartoons played important roles in political discourse in the eighteenth century and continue to help shape discourse today. William Hogarth and James Gillray cartoons in the eighteenth and nineteenth centuries pushed incisive political messages. In the nineteenth century, Honoré Daumier commented on social and political issues through savage satires. Popular, irreverent, and humorous editorial cartoons are familiar in the West and have been for two hundred years. They are no less popular in places like the Middle East.[102]

J. G. Lewin and P. J. Huff have shown how widely political cartoons were used during the American Civil War to influence opinion on all sides.[103] *Harper's Weekly* mocked Jefferson Davis as the Confederacy reeled from the sting of the Northern blockade of Southern ports.[104] It portrayed Gen. George B. McClellan as squeezing the life out of the Confederacy like a snake.[105] *Punch* jibed Abraham Lincoln as caught between demands for more soldiers and more money to finance the war.[106] *Leslie's Illustrated* castigated Lincoln when it appeared he might distance himself from the issue of slavery.[107]

In modern times, comics continue to play a key role. President Gamal Abdel Nasser used comic books like *Jamid 'Abd al-Nasir*, composed by J. M. Ruffieux and Muhammad Nu'man al-Dhakiri and Salma al-Dhakiri, to create an image as a superhero in images to which everyday people could relate. The images dwell on key events that evoke Nasser as a leader who identifies with Egypt through "communion with the people," and who shares their tragedies and triumphs. The comic drives a strong ideological message about Nasser's role as the direct representative of Egyptians and his exploitation in Europe by an antidemocratic right.[108]

Although better known for his children's books like *The Cat in the Hat* and *How the Grinch Stole Christmas*, Theodor Seuss Geisel—better known as Dr. Seuss—made his living as a political cartoonist.[109] In World War II, Walt Disney mobilized Donald Duck to the cause of US victory.[110] In Britain, David Low created the character of Colonel Blimp to satirize the British establishment of his day. Pat Oliphant and Herbert Block earned fame for their award-winning editorial cartoons.[111] By definition, these works all intend to influence attitudes and opinions.

Fredrik Stromberg has well illustrated the rich diversity of comics by propaganda in the Second World War, the Cold War, the 2003 Iraq War, and for social issues. Stromberg points out that the comics are the most widely read section of newspapers. "They catch the eye," he says, "and keep the reader enthralled. The intimate combination of words and pictures is one explanation." In his view, the "iconic, simplified way in which many comics display their images is inherent in the way we view the world and thus speaks very directly to the reader."[112]

Today, a new generation of graphic novelists targeting adults has begun to use the form to examine America's relationship with the rest of the world. They affirm the power of graphic images in comic form to advance ideas.[113] In Iraq, the Coalition Provisional Authority commissioned comic books from The Lincoln Group, a controversial firm (which has since changed its name) to drive its narratives. The firm denied that it was engaged in propaganda but admitted that its work aimed to influence.[114] The more its executives talked, the deeper the hole they dug for themselves. It was clear that the work aimed to influence; it was strategic communication.[115] Planting fake news stories was imprudent. Conducting influence operations (presuming they were properly authorized), the work was competent, satisfied governing legal authority, and worked strategically, and was nothing to be defensive about. Knowledgeable critics eviscerated the Pentagon for "singularly questionable" efforts to influence foreign audiences.[116]

Words matter, and for effective strategic communication, they matter a lot.

CHAPTER 6

Images and Symbols

IMAGES AND SYMBOLS CAN ACHIEVE HUGE IMPACT IN COMMUNICATING narratives, themes, and messages. In a thoughtful essay, art historian Jutta Held contended that the political effect of a work of art depends upon its context in a political culture. That gives a symbol meaning about values, beliefs, attitudes, and opinions. The effect "depends upon the political forces active at the time, as well as the particular meaning the work is given through its political use."[1] She has a point, but politics is more complicated and nuanced. Symbols matter especially for identity politics, and in today's world, identity motivates political activity. It enables people to forge bonds, share a sense of cause, and rally around common values. Symbols can provide points of reference that ground a campaign. They can help express identity.

Joe Gaylord observes that "who you include in campaign photographs and how they are presented is often a function of identity politics. Ideally, symbols say a lot without using words what a campaign is all about. When Dylan Glenn, a dynamic African American, stood for the Republican Party nomination for Congress in Georgia, we knew it was important to show that he related well to all age groups. All images that the campaign projected in commercials and print photography showed him relating well with young and old age groups. Campaign bumper stickers that include a tractor emphasize that the candidate understands rural America."[2]

Ron Faucheux points out that "politicians and political causes often invoke symbols to communicate messages that they prefer to avoid expressing with words."[3] Faucheux is on target. Years ago, Georgia Governor Lester Maddox handed out or sold red pickaxe handles to customers at his Pickrick restaurant, as a symbol of his segregationist views. He made his point about his political philosophy without having to say much. Ironically, as governor, he proved more tolerant than anyone expected, although years later, he lost an effort to secure a state pension when State Rep. Billy McKinney displayed an axe handle to fellow legislators as a reminder that Maddox had obstructed racial progress.

Symbols may also serve as positive shorthand for a message. The Romans marched under the banner SPQR—the Senate and People of Rome. The official signature of the Roman Republic, it expressed the Republic's philosophy that authority flowed from the people. American flag lapel pins concisely express pride in the United States as a nation in American politics. Stamping products provided by USAID as originating in the United States—which the agency is sometimes criticized for doing insufficiently—is a way of communicating our humanitarianism to those who we help. The Christian symbol of the cross conveys religious meaning and communicates belief. In American politics, evangelical Christians often demonstrate publicly their belief by attaching the outline of a small fish to the back of their car.

History offers many examples of images or symbols to communicate strategically.

The Diversity of Symbols

The Romans, Persians, and Indians of the Maurya Empire issued coins to publicize military victories.[4] One sees the modern equivalent in political campaign buttons and lapel pins, which raise visibility of parties, candidates, or campaigns. The duplication of use may not be exact, but the political mindsets rhyme. Paul Zanker remarks that the Romans adopted Hellenistic art and found that it "provided military victors with an impressive medium in which to express their assertions of military power." By that, he means the totality of images: "works of art, buildings, poetic imagery, religious ritual, clothing, state ceremony, the emperor's conduct and forms of social intercourse."[5] Zanker shows that the Romans in the age of Augustus had a finely developed sense of how to use political imagery strategically to communicate Rome's "imperial mythology," rooted in Hellenistic culture.

Julius Caesar understood propaganda and used it to advance his interests. His triumphant processions, full of pomp, served as a demonstration of power.[6] Adolf Hitler thought about communicating mass support, his power, and his status as führer in a comparable way with Nazi torchlight parades. In a sense they were a version of "shock and awe," the nickname for the doctrine of "rapid dominance" to affect the will, understanding, and perception of an adversary that gained prominence during the bombing of Baghdad in 2003.[7] Hadrian's Wall was not defensive. It provided, in archeologist and *Military Times* editor Neil Faulkner's words, a "symbolic statement of Roman grandeur."[8] The Pharaohs built the pyramids and the Sphinx. A ticker-tape parade in New York after the 1991 Desert Storm victory was a modern equivalent of Caesar's procession and was meant to symbolize American strength, power, and success.

Attire can be used as a form of strategic communication. Historian Akbar S. Ahmed contends that the way Muhammad Ali Jinnah of Pakistan dressed in national attire became an important symbol, arguing that it conveys the image of a fundamentalist leader.[9] Historian Ayesha Jalal, who offers a compelling case that Jinnah was a secularist who believed in a moderate interpretation of Islam, says his dress was to help forge a Muslim identity (but not a fundamentalist one).[10] There's a corollary precept in politics that politicians should not be photographed wearing funny hats or doing physically unexpected things, but the application is not universal. In the 1988 presidential campaign, Democratic nominee Michael Dukakis looked ridiculous standing in the turret of a tank, his hand on a machine gun, wearing a helmet with his name tag emblazoned upon the front (despite the fact that he had never served in the military). It did significant damage to his credibility. On the other hand, Prime Minister Margaret Thatcher, who was known as the Iron Lady, was filmed in a tank used in commercials aired during the 1987 British general election. One's instinctive reaction in this case was not to laugh—it was to get out of her way.

The British experience in Northern Ireland demonstrates that attire can have an emotional impact. British Colonel Stephen Padgett served on the ground there. "In Northern Ireland," he says, "the importance of the messages communicated by the presence, profile, and posture of troops on patrol was well understood. Thus, responsibility for deciding whether, when, and where troops dressed in helmets or in berets and wore camouflage paint or not usually was retained at senior levels. Often, the policy was dictated by brigade commanders. They understood that, depending upon the ground realities, showing up in a neighbourhood in full battle regalia could be helpful or destructive."[11]

In American politics, politicians have grown convinced that they need to dress like working people in order to communicate a common touch. Candidates for Congress, the Senate, even the presidency are decked out in sport clothes. Mitt Romney declined to wear a tie for his announcement declaring his candidacy for president in 1996. Lamar Alexander turned a red plaid shirt into a symbol for his populist campaign, which flopped. Actor Fred Thompson motored around Tennessee in his populist campaign for the US Senate, which won. All of which goes to show that in politics, at least, voters tend to look beyond attire in judging the character, personality, and ideas of candidates.

Bill Clinton and his staff embraced the concept of casual Fridays, while Ronald Reagan and George W. Bush insisted that men entering the Oval Office wear a coat and tie out of respect for the office. The significance of attire differed considerably between Clinton and his Republican counterparts.

In Iraq and Afghanistan, attire has mattered in the strategic communication of coalition forces. Active-duty military personnel report that while Kevlar vests offer good protection against bullets, they can send a message of insensitivity—although as former Commander of British Forces in Afghanistan Col. Stephen Padgett notes, "people may make cultural allowances to accommodate the fact that our soldiers come from different backgrounds. On the other hand, when we ask them to take more professional responsibility in fighting the Taliban, they become skeptical unless appropriate equipment including protective gear to get the job done is worn."[12]

Dictators can be as adept at using symbols as democrats. In Syria, President Bashar al-Assad and his cronies rule their nation as a ruthless mafia. When peaceful dissent emerged, they shunned political settlement and launched a bloody repression. Their brutality has slaughtered innocent children and turned efforts by United Nations mediators into a tragic exercise in futility.[13]

Yet unlike Saddam Hussein, whom most Iraqis despised, al-Assad's regime has retained a strong base of support among a quarter of the population, including his Alawite community, the Syrian Baath Party, Syrian Christians, Druze, and Kurds, as well as business interests in Damascus and Aleppo.[14] Alawites hold most of the officer and NCO positions in the military, which is a part of the Baath Party. These elements greatly fear a regime collapse. Baathists remember the "de-Baathification" that transpired in Iraq. It has served as a pointed warning.[15] Buoyed by that reality, al-Assad has acted ruthlessly to crush dissent. Arguably, his forces have killed thousands of civilians.[16]

Yet despite unrelenting use of automatic weapons and tanks, al-Assad has been conscious of his own strategic communication. The regime has used symbols to show support, distributing baseball caps, shirts, and flags adorned with his face, while billboards depict him surrounded by pink hearts. In the past, he has capitalized upon his stylish, beautiful-born wife Asma, who at one point was advised on media imaging by a well-known British public relations firm.[17] During the early period of the Syrian uprising in 2011, she tried to burnish the family image by securing a feature on herself in *Vogue* magazine, which proclaimed her to be a "rose in a desert."[18]

President al-Assad's strategic communication represents an anything-goes campaign to assert himself as an icon for national identity opposed to foreign and Islamist miscreants who commit violence. His message has been that the violence is perpetrated by Saudi Arabia and Qatar, in league with al-Qaeda. Essentially he's playing to fears among non-Sunnis that a Sunni-dominated State would repress their rights and opportunities.

The Guardian reported initially that al-Assad's campaign was surprisingly effective.[19] Events in 2012 have cast a dark shadow, however. Assad may or may not hang onto power. At this writing, a collapse does not appear imminent, but history teaches that should they collapse, strong authoritarian regimes fall fast.

A key lesson is that regime violence constitutes its own form of strategic communication, generating media coverage that discredits and trumps slick public relations that tries to mute its savagery. It is a lesson authoritarian regimes rarely comprehend. Their instinctive response most often is to repress dissent rather than to ameliorate or resolve it through peaceful means. The lesson is that the use of symbols and images to bolster political support matters as much in authoritarian as in democratic societies.

Colors

Colors can rouse passions, forge bonds, and provide a rallying point. They provide simple, concrete images or symbols that people can recognize and invoke. As journalist Jeremy Singer-Vine observes, they can be catchy—a quality helpful for political recruitment and mobilization.[20]

The red, white, and blue of the French Revolution certainly roused passions. Symbols have encapsulated many modern grassroots uprisings, too. In 1974, the Portuguese ended a forty-year dictatorship with a bloodless Carnation Revolution.[21] In 1989, the Czech rebellion against Soviet rule called itself the Velvet Revolution. During the 2004 presidential campaign in the Ukraine, supporters of Viktor Yuschenko turned his campaign color, orange, into a symbol of defiance against massive voter intimidation and fraud sponsored by his Russian-backed opponent, Viktor Yanukovych, who rigged the vote. They forced a new election and prevailed. In 2009, Iranian opponents of President Mahmoud Ahmadinejad created a green movement symbolizing the prophet Muhammad, who wore a green cloak and turban. Muslims used green banners on battlefields, and the Muslim flag is green. For many, the color symbolizes nature and life.[22]

In 2005, citizens fed up with the corruption of Kyrgystan President Askar Akayev rose up and overthrew him. Anxious to pin the right label on things, the media variously called it the Pink Revolution, then the Lemon Revolution, followed by the Daffodil Revolution.[23] Akayev himself branded it the Tulip Revolution.[24] The name stuck, matching the use by Georgians of a rose as the symbol for their 2003 revolution.[25] Dissidents in Moldova apparently were planning a Grape Revolution.[26] Further east, disgruntled Thai launched the Silk Revolution.[27] In 2011, Tunisians sent strongman Zine El Abidine Ben Ali packing after three decades of iron-fist control, chasing him out in a Jasmine Revolution. The anti-Hezbollah and Syrian response in Lebanon is a nation of cedar trees. Former Prime Minister Rafik Hariri's assassination in 2004 triggered a Cedars Revolution. In 2006, the democratic opposition in Belarus wore denim as part of a silent protest for democracy in 2006. The media dubbed it a Jeans or Denim Revolution, a reference to the color blue.[28]

These grassroots movements have produced mixed results. In the Ukraine, Kyrgystan, and Georgia, respites from old authoritarians had given way by 2011 to new authoritarian rule. The Belarus protests went nowhere. But as a matter of strategic communication, the symbols dissidents invoked facilitated their ability to unite and act.

Color can be potent. Hugo Chavez wore a red beret in leading a coup against the administration of Venezuelan President Carlos Andres Perez. It struck a potent rallying note several years later when he was elected president and has served as a keynote for his Bolivarian Revolution. Adolph Hitler and the Nazis understood the impact that color has as well, especially when integrated with other symbols and actions. The diabolically evil nature of the Third Reich should not obscure the value of understanding their skill at propaganda.

The impact of the bright red field emblazoned with a white disc and black swastika on Nazi banners is far greater when seen in person than in photographs or film. What the Nazis referred to as propaganda marches—perhaps influenced by Julius Caesar—were carefully designed to impress audiences, stir emotion, and mobilize action. Albert Speer, Hitler's architect, created cathedrals of light to enshroud stages. Color banners, well-shined jackboots, formations of marching, uniformed supporters, the beat of drums, rousing music like the Horst Wessel song or the Badenweiler march, and symbols of an eagle—different ministries used different variations—heightened the drama. Crowd participation generated high energy. Everyone had a role; everyone could participate. They followed Hitler, but they were also meant to feel part of the panorama, not simply bystanders. Steven Luckert, curator for the permanent exhibition at the United States Holocaust Memorial Museum, which has staged a brilliant exhibition of Nazi propaganda, notes that "the Nazis were incredibly innovative and imaginative."

"Enthralled by ancient German myths, theatre, and music—especially Wagner—Hitler and Goebbels had a remarkable gift for moving mass audiences," Luckert says.[29] "They had an intuitive understanding of the power of color. They chose red, black, and white, the colors of imperial Germany, but anchored the flag in the swastika, an ancient symbol that became the emblem for Hitler's twisted ideology. It was identified with the 'Aryan' civilization of India, whom they equated with 'Nordic" or 'German-blood peoples.'[30] Above all, there was Hitler himself. He was a mesmerizing speaker who honed his skills brilliantly. His ideas were not original. He plagiarized them from demagogues like Karl Lueger, the anti-Semitic mayor of Vienna, whose followers called him Fuhrer (leader) and used the Heil (hail) as a greeting. Other ideas were routine rhetoric espoused by lots of right-wing nationalists. Where Hitler stood apart was his own extraordinary skill as a communicator."

Hitler learned the power of propaganda from his experiences in World War I. He admired Britain's propaganda campaign as "psychologically sound." In *Mein Kampf,* he wrote that it prepared "the individual soldiers for the terrors of war . . . while on the other hand it increased his rage and hatred against the vile enemy." He blamed these efforts partially for Germany's defeat.[31] In his rise to power and his rule, he spared no effort to employ propaganda, which notably targeted youth—for Nazi leadership was young, and saw youth as the key to its future—and to arouse a spirit of fortitude and resilience. Historian Anthony Rhodes notes that Josef Goebbels found truth in these communications to be irrelevant. "Historical truth," Goebbels declared, "may be discovered by a professor of history. *We* however are serving historical necessity."[32] Nazi propaganda might have been rooted in facts, but it communicated messages that served the regime's political agenda, no matter how misleading or false.

The Third Reich was creative in getting out its message. It distributed medals imprinted with the Nazi eagle and knights in armor to commemorate the 1936 Olympics. Posters and murals glorified women clasping children to their bosoms for protection. Hitler was majestically costumed as a knight in shining armor in the famous Hubert Lanzinger portrait *The Standard Bearer*—a leader of destiny bringing Germany to a future of hope and glory. Hermann Otto Hoyer's remarkable painting *In the Beginning Was the Word* has reminded some viewers of *The Last Supper* in its portrayal of a mesmerizing Fuhrer appealing to a broad cross-section of Germans.[33] The paintings depicted German men as physically fit, uniformed, handsome blonde Aryans, their expressions beaming with pride and confidence. Postage stamps extolled athletic champions, technology, and State power. Other propaganda exposed the darkly sinister underbelly of Nazi rule. Posters dehumanized Jews, portraying them with distorted features and malicious expressions, figures of greed ready to betray the Fatherland. Allied pilots and troops fared no better: They were depicted as monsters and gangsters. One poster depicted Winston Churchill holding a tommy gun in the tradition of a Chicago mobster.

Film director Leni Riefenstahl made the ponderous 1935 film *Triumph of the Will* to communicate the message that Germany supported Hitler. British historian Richard Overy reports that the "systematic adulation" of Hitler—as well as Stalin—"was a defining feature of both dictatorships and was understood to be so at the time." His plain attire, suggesting no need for pomp for this man of the people, and well-rehearsed theatrical speeches, marked by his particular way of gesturing, portrayed him, Overy says, as "the Chosen One."[34] Hitler's approach offers an example of dictator style itself as strategic communication. His vast palatial office where he received guests was an element of that strategy: "The theatrical effect was acute—intimate and intimidating at one and the same time. . . . Hitler was one of the people but at the same time he was more than one of the people." It was no accident that his speeches were built around the theme that Hitler was Germany, and Germany was Hitler. Hitler's cult of personality grew deep roots. As late as 1967, a poll revealed that one-third of Germans believed that Hitler would have ranked among Germany's greatest statesmen but for the war.[35]

Hailed as a classic, Riefenstahl's film is full of symbolism that evoked an emotional response. To a modern sensibility it shows off her superb eye, but as cinema, it's a snore. Her two-part *Olympia*, about the 1936 Olympics, is better and more striking. Too long and emotionally cold, *Triumph of the Will* records repetitive mass rallies, meetings of the faithful, and torchlight parades starring a cast of thousands of perfectly coifed Aryans. The Nazis staged their formations and movements specifically for her thirty cameras. What's most striking about Hitler's speeches are his gestures. His rhetoric itself is curiously empty; he says nothing memorable. The women and children smile, mesmerized by their Fuhrer. The men are dour. Hitler lacked the upbeat charisma that's typical of great—including evil—politicians. He was too consumed by his messianic complex of self-importance and his twisted obsessions.

Symbols also helped drive the French Revolution. The conical Phrygian hat, its front pulled forward, had served in antiquity as a symbol of freedom. During the French Revolution it was worn as a symbol of equality. The fasces (a bundle of wooden sticks with an axe blade emerging from its center) emerged from the revolution as a symbol of fraternity. The female figure of Marianne—always depicted wearing a Phrygian cap—symbolizes liberty and reason. (The hat can be seen in the seal of the United States Senate.) Nothing better symbolizes the heroism of this nation's soldiers than the classic sculpture that stands as a tribute to the courage of marines at Iwo Jima. The iconic photograph of a US astronaut standing on the craters of the moon in front of the American flag remains, four decades later, a stirring testament to a resilient American spirit and our fearless focus on using technology, imagination, and innovation to create a better tomorrow.

The Significance of Architecture

Hadrian, Napoleon, Hitler, and other rulers have used architecture to communicate power and their usefulness to their publics. Gaining power is one thing; keeping it usually requires impressing the people with the ability to exercise power and exert authority, as well as demonstrating that leadership of a particular figure is beneficial. Architecture is concrete. You can see it, touch it, and actually use it. It is a great way to strategically communicate.

Napoleon imprinted the letter "N" all over Paris as a sign of power. Today, he'd probably try to trademark the letter. Greek and Roman amphitheaters provided forums for ceremonies or meetings. Middle Ages churches were gathering places for meetings, concerts, and sermons.[36] Public baths, public squares, fountains, and courthouses communicate effective leadership that serves the people. Seventeenth-century Dutch architecture and painting communicated that society's confidence, power, and optimism—useful messages for a global trading nation.[37]

Hitler planned a new capital, designed by Albert Speer, to be called Germania, as a symbol of Aryan supremacy. Italian Prime Minister Benito Mussolini's office at the Palazzo Venezia in Rome and Hitler's Chancellery in Berlin were, in journalist Peter York's description, gestures of scale.[38] The personalities of the two dictators were very different. Hitler was a madman with surprising personal idiosyncrasies, whereas Mussolini was more like Junta leaders Juan Peron or Augusto Pinochet, and prided himself on his masculinity. He was athletic, liked to bare his chest, and used his office for sexual trysts.

Both dictators used art, architecture, and taste in style to communicate power and demand for loyalty, respect, and obedience. Their offices bore striking similarities. They were grand, spacious, stark. Both contained massive furniture. Immense portraits of the men hung on the walls. Both offices conveyed "an operatic quality" to express power and authority.[39]

They hardly stood alone. When it came to using architecture and pomp to signal an impression, "president for life" of the Central African Republic Jean-Bédel Bokassa starred in his own pantheon. Self-appointed as emperor, he saw Napoleon as his role model. His 1977 coronation employed Parisian stage designers, jewelers, and couturiers. Napoleonic eagles and laurel wreaths abounded. Bokassa's coronation illustrates an important lesson in strategic communication: putting on the Ritz with a $22 million blowout is no guarantee of success. Nobody who mattered to Bokassa showed up for the event.[40] Wearied by his behavior—Bokassa inferred that, like his grandfather, he was a cannibal—the French sent in five hundred troops and tossed him out in favor of a different despot, David Dacko, in a coup code-named Operation Barrucada. Bokassa's fall helped take down the pompous French President Valery Giscard d'Estaing, who had famously hailed Bokassa as "my relative."[41]

Al-Qaeda's attack on the Twin Towers at New York's World Trade Center represents the corollary: They were targeted precisely because they were seen as icons. In a broader context, great architecture of a nation has always communicated a sense of its confidence. That has been true from Rome to Holland, whose architecture reflected confidence in its mercantile prosperity, to countries today.[42] China used the 2008 Olympics to unveil several stunning masterworks of architecture: the Beijing National Stadium, the National Swimming Center, the National Grand Theatre, and the Beijing International Airport. These joined imaginative achievements like the CCTV building. The strategic message for this coming-out party was clear: China was the twenty-first century rising global power, a nation that was confident, optimistic, and strong.[43] The Oriental Crown (China Pavilion) for the 2010 World Expo in Shanghai designed by He Jing, the Canton Tower in Guangzhou built for the opening of the sixteenth annual Asian Games in November 2010, and the remarkable new Opera House in Guangzhou designed by Zaha Hadid echo that confidence and China's emerging sense of its regional and international status as a superpower. One can see China's confidence in its selection of Hadid and other foreign architects to design their new buildings. There is intelligent State purpose behind the support provided to such bold architecture.

Looking ahead, one can anticipate a similar outpouring of confidence in India, probably starting in Mumbai. Britain is viewed by some as pessimistic and struggling, but the country's hosting of the 2012 Olympics represents, at one level, nothing less than a move to achieve—and clearly signal—its revitalization. One might argue that any country can construct interesting new buildings. That may be true, but what stands out today are cases where a nation like China makes a strategic decision to use exceptional and grand architecture to make a statement about where it stands in the world. It is a sophisticated, powerful way to strategically communicate confidence and strengthen national identity and optimism.

The Power of Art

Louis XIV understood that a painting could be used to strategically communicate power and authority. The major details of his portrait from the workshop of Hyacinthe Riguad that hangs in the Getty Museum illustrate this goal. The king is depicted in ceremonial robes, an elegant stance, and with a haughty expression that proclaims his regal status. The purpose of the painting was to glorify the monarchy.[44] To his right, we see his crown. Everything this king did—from the elaborate etiquette that governed his Royal Court at Versailles to his patronage of the arts—underscored his position as the Sun King.

Among the most famous examples of art as strategic communication—and unabashedly propaganda—is Jacques-Louis David's *Oath of the Horatii* (1785). The painting was inspired by a story by Titus-Livius about combat among three Horatii and three Curiatti brothers during the 669 BC war between Rome and Alba. A Curiatti sister, Sabina, was married to one of the Horatii, and Camilla, a sister of a Horatii, was engaged to one of the Curiatti. In the painting, the father of the Horatii exhorts his sons to fight, ignoring the weeping women seated behind him. The painting is a metaphor for discipline, sacrifice, and patriotism, which David ennobled. The brothers take an oath to defeat their enemies or die. The painting served as a manifesto for neoclassicism and proclaimed a new moral order.[45]

David also painted the iconic portrait *Napoleon Crossing the Alps*. He painted five versions. It depicts a dynamic, young Bonaparte wearing the uniform of a general with a gold-trimmed bicorne, sitting astride a magnificent white stallion that is rearing up on its hind legs. A large, red cloak billows in a fierce wind. It portrayed Napoleon not only as he saw himself, but as many French saw him. The painting is about power, portraying Napoleon as a leader whom destiny has fated to greatness. It was the sort of thing that helped arouse support and enthusiasm. Napoleon also made effective use of engravings by Carl Vernet, especially after major battles. These appeared in newspapers and broadsheets, glorifying himself and his exploits, to promote his image and to promote the narrative of a heroic general. He was happy to conjure up the image of a modern Caesar. Vernet's engraving depicting the entry of the French into Milan evoked Roman triumphal parades.[46]

After Ferdinand VII was restored to the Spanish throne in 1814, Goya's *Third of May, 1808: The Execution of the Defenders of Madrid* dramatized Spanish nationalism.[47] Depicting the execution by a French firing squad of Spanish rebels, its drama, directness, intensity, approach to illumination of subject, modern conception, and original composition and emotion produce a uniquely powerful homage to the May 1808 rebellion and a denunciation of inhumanity. Goya's work included eighty-five prints called *The Disasters of War*, recording brutalities committed during Spain's battle for independence from France.[48]

In the twentieth century, no painting has sent a stronger political message in its time than Pablo Picasso's 1937 *Guernica*. This was an era before people could watch CNN or check the Internet, and the greatest day-to-day emotion was fear. People were not certain what was happening or what the future held. Many artists and intellectuals rallied against fascism—and therefore painting and plays became a form of strategic communication. These artists painted, created banners and floats, and took part in demonstrations.[49] The opening of Jean Giraudox's play, *The Trojan War Will Not Happen*, a metaphor that used the Trojan War to express the inevitability of a new war in Europe, was a major political event.[50] Although to modern audiences the play comes across as turgid despite the author's reputation for stylistic elegance, with a few amusing scenes, in its time it created a stir.

Painting influenced opinions. Hoping to generate international support, the left-wing Popular Front government commissioned Picasso's masterpiece for the Spanish pavilion at the International Exhibition held in Paris in 1937. Rendered in black, white, and gray, *Guernica* is a uniquely compelling denunciation of German and Italian bombing that slaughtered innocent civilians and animals and destroyed buildings. This masterpiece won champions for the view that avant-gardism could be used to make a political statements.[51] Ironically, Picasso later drew heavy criticism for his refusal to leave Paris once the Nazis occupied it.

Works of artists like Picasso and Andre Fougeron, and writers like Andre Malraux, galvanized support against fascism.[52] Juta Held argues that their voices helped establish a consensus that fighting fascism in Spain was standing up for freedom, and associated that fight in France and Spain with nationalist values. She has a point: they did raise consciousness.

What they did not do is change the political outcome in France or Spain. The inept Popular Front in Spain failed to establish order at home before the outbreak of the civil war, or to gain needed international support to defeat Francisco Franco's right-wing forces. Communists clamored for Leon Blum's French Popular Front government to provide help. The radicals resisted, and the right was unsympathetic. Eventually, France sent a few arms to the republic under the French policy of "loose non-intervention," but France sat on the sidelines.[53] In Britain George Orwell, W. H. Auden, and others championed the Republican cause. But Britain stayed neutral. Its ambassador to Spain, Sir Henry Chilton, admired the right-wing nationalists.[54]

Conventional wisdom in many quarters romanticizes the Republic. For once, as historian Antony Beevor remarks, it was the losers and not the victors wrote the history.[55] Still, politics exists in different shades of gray, not black and white. The left was politically dysfunctional and divided. It aligned itself with Joseph Stalin and invited in Soviet Communist advisors who channeled resources to Communists. That orientation was unlikely to win enthusiastic converts in France and Britain, whose active support the Republicans desperately required. Beevor's penetrating history of the civil war confirms the brutality of both sides, the Red Terror and the White; Fascist violence was more extensive, savage, and systematic. Final pushes by Franco in 1939 overran Catalonia, Madrid, and Valencia to secure victory.

The Nazis and Italian fascists understood the power of art and employed it widely. As propaganda and strategic communication, they had a knack for concise and powerful messages. They were easy to grasp, and they worked. The United States and her allies displayed their own powerhouse talent with posters created by artists like Henry Koerner, Norman Rockwell, John Atherton, Glenn Grohe, and McKnight Kauffer. Viktor Deni, Boris Efimov, and the Kukriniksy art collective excoriated the Nazis as brutes and boosted morale for Russia.

Oil paintings today lack the same political impact in a digital age that they had in the past. Poster art is a different story. It is visible and plays a role in shaping emotions as well as attitudes and opinions in most countries. Iran's autocrats use murals and posters to give legitimacy to the 1979 Revolution and the leadership, while the dissident Green Movement that challenged them in 2009 has developed their own creative posters featuring a green tongue, green hands, green doves in a cage, and a hand with two fingers raised in a V—a green bird perched atop one—asking, "where is my vote?"

Posters are a mainstay of US political campaigns as well. In 2008, street artist Shepard Fairey's multitoned "Hope" poster for President Barack Obama, based on Associated Press Manny Garcia's photograph, became iconic. It was also challenged by the AP for copyright infringement, and cross-claims were filed in court. The litigation was settled as the Iowa caucuses rolled into high gear.[56] Fairey's poster shows why great art can top a world-class photograph. It splendidly captured the modern tone that Obama's campaign adroitly projected. Obama argued that he stood for hope as well as change that people could believe in. The theme meant everything and nothing—and it worked liked a charm.

CHAPTER 7

Deeds

Sᴛʀᴀᴛᴇɢɪᴄ ᴄᴏᴍᴍᴜɴɪᴄᴀᴛɪᴏɴ ᴄᴀɴ ʙᴇ ᴀꜱ ᴍᴜᴄʜ ᴀʙᴏᴜᴛ ᴀᴄᴛɪᴏɴ ᴀꜱ ᴀʙᴏᴜᴛ ʟᴀɴ-guage, images, or symbols. The British Field Manual is explicit: "The presence, profile and posture (the 3 Ps) of commanders and troops in contact with a local populace will send specific messages that will either undermine or engender support."[1] Col. Stephen Padgett, who served as the United Kingdom defense attaché to Afghanistan and commanded British forces there in 2005 and 2006, notes that "while effective SC requires a clear political intent for any operation, the actions, good or bad, of those at the bottom of the chain matter. Politicians can say what they please, but 'strategic corporals,' the boots on the ground, can have a huge impact on the perceptions of audiences."[2]

How does placing the military in charge of a government change the definition or the principles that govern effective communication? The core principles of strategic communication apply for both forms of government. Examples illustrate how deeds are used by the military to communicate strategically.

Sierra Leone

By 2000, ten years of civil strife had devastated the once-rich country. The army was corrupt and generally viewed as hardened criminals in uniform. Worse were the Revolutionary United Front (RUF) rebels, who exploited child soldiers, committed atrocities, murdered thousands of civilians, and used the diamond trade to finance its malevolence. Foreign mercenaries were active. The UN had lost its mandate, and the country was in meltdown. Although it scrambled dates and events, and even in one shot used a plane operated by the notorious Russian weapons merchant Victor Bout, the movie *Blood Diamond* conveyed some sense of the RUF's perversity.[3] Eventually, the British intervened with 1,000 troops to restore stability.[4] As an element of strategic communication, the Brits employed helicopters over the capital to communicate

the point that they meant business. It was simple but effective. Small actions
can create large effects.

Afghanistan

The impact of using weapons to make a political point varies. During a tense
period in 2005, Padgett notes, "an angry crowd of 1,000 to 2,000 Afghans surrounded a NATO outpost in the north of Afghanistan held by a contingent of
30–40 Norwegian soldiers. The crowd threw stones, fired small arms and occasional RPG at and into the compound. Later, vehicles were used to ram the gates
and the crowd broke through the perimeter. The beleaguered contingent feared
for their lives."[5]

He goes on to say that "no reinforcements on the ground were available.
A couple of NATO fast jets were sent from Kabul to overfly the crowd in an
attempt to deter it from further aggression. The low-level passes had no effect
whatsoever. The jets were given authority to fire rockets into waste ground
beyond the crowd. There was a spectacular fireworks display, but no deterrent
effect was achieved. The Afghans correctly grasped that NATO lacked the will
to employ such a blunt instrument as an air strike on a large, mixed crowd on
the edge of an urban area. This was despite the widely known fact that US and
UK aircraft responded reasonably often at that time to insurgents ambushing
US forces in the south (pre-handover of that sector by US to NATO). The
situation, and NATO's reputation, were saved at the last moment by the arrival
of a company of vigorous British soldiers, hastily dispatched by C130 from
Kabul."[6]

Somalia

The case of Somalia offers dramatic lessons in the potential and limits of strategic communication. After President George H.W. Bush left office, UN General
Secretary Boutros Boutros-Ghali prodded the UN into a new mission in Somalia, UNOSOM II, focused on nation building.[7] An effort conceived to feed
the hungry wound up as a dragnet, and it had huge ramifications as the players
figured out their strategic communication. Somali warload General Mohamed
Farrah Hassan Aidid whipped up nationalism and clan pride. The special representative to Boutros-Ghali in Somalia, retired US Navy Admiral Jonathan
Howe, was on the same page as the secretary-general. He put a $25,000 price
on Aidid's head, ordered his arrest, and assembled Task Force Ranger, which
included Rangers and members of the Delta Force, to hunt him down.[8]

That led to the events of October 3, 1993, which Mark Bowden wrote about in *Blackhawk Down*.[9] Militarily, the command deemed the operation a success despite the casualties, but criticism of US intelligence and tactics has been harsh.[10] Politically, and as strategic communication, it was a debacle. Blackhawks became a symbol of the vulnerability of modern weaponry against low-tech firepower. Chris Stewart of Gallup, an avid student and practitioner of strategic communication, believes that "the tactics employed in UNOSOM 1 by US Marines avoided civilian casualties and proved more resonant than the heavy firepower employed by Task Force Ranger. The real challenge, however, lay in the strategy, which dictated the heavy use of firepower. As it was, in chasing after Aidid, American soldiers had the worst of it in being compelled to go after Aidid with insufficient firepower to achieve mission success."[11] A very senior US military officer who was involved in the action has said privately that the biggest mistake was forgetting that the mission was about apprehending Aidid and allowing it to expand its original, intended scope. Once that happened, operations were destined to run into trouble, for which additional firepower was not the solution.

The downing of the Blackhawks illustrates key lessons for campaigns that involve a combination of information strategy and kinetic activity. The use of the Blackhawks was an information strategy that backfired when the helicopters were shot down. Their appearance shaped the battlefield—and their demise did as well. Tactics used effectively to achieve one goal may backfire as the situation evolves, the roles of troops change, and strategic objectives shift. Using troops trained for combat to conduct police work can be treacherous.[12] An excellent analysis by Richard Shultz and Andrew Dew shows how ill-judged communication can inadvertently turn adversaries into political heroes.[13] Treating Farrah Aidid as an outlaw when his Machiavellian qualities were well accepted by Somali culture only made him more powerful.

In a book full of vivid lessons about strategic communication, Naval War College strategic studies expert Jonathan Stevenson insightfully identified another trap that shows why with strategic communications it pays to look before you leap. As Aidid turned Somalia into a live-fire simulation of the postapocalypse, Stevenson says, Howe decided to disarm the Somalis. The Somali response sounded like the National Rifle Association on Second Amendment rights. "My gun is to protect myself, my family and my property," Stevenson quotes one person.[14] Lines like that will draw a standing ovation at a C-PAC convention. It gave pause to Howe's team as well. Needless to say, the disarmament effort alienated Somalis.

Liberia

Is adept political communication solely reserved for civilian politicians? Not at all. Liberia shows what can be achieved when savvy commanders devise and successfully execute a strong plan for strategic communication that uses words and actions. During the 1990s, civil war plagued Liberia, leaving 200,000 dead before a shaky peace agreement was mediated in 1996. Things came unglued when Charles Taylor's National Patriotic Party won a 1997 election victory. Rebels from Liberians United for Reconciliation and Democracy tried to oust Taylor. Thousands more died while others were left homeless and starving.[15] In June 2003, a UN-backed war crimes court indicted Taylor for arming and training rebels connected to Sierre Leone's RUF in exchange for diamonds. The United States joined a United Nations effort to prevent a bloodbath in Monrovia, where 250,000 helpless civilians slept in the streets and child soldiers dressed in camouflage bearing AK-47s posed a terrifying threat.

The United States relied on persuasion rather than force in order to secure the capital for humanitarian relief. An American Joint Task Force supported the Economic Community of West African States (ECOWAS) led by Nigeria and seven regional nations. Success required strong persuasive tactics, rooted in a clear understanding of what the key players wanted. That limited violence helped get Liberians to support the peace process. The story, well told by Col. Bair A. Ross Jr., shows strategic communication succeeds when it respects the realities on the ground.[16] A few hundred US troops coordinated closely with a regional African force that was better suited to provide stability. Joint visibility in downtown Monrovia sent a powerful strategic message not to mess with them. A strong US joint task force commander ensured coordination among Americans and the UN, empowered African troops, used economy of force, and made sure that objectives were clearly defined. That's what strategic communication at its best is all about in successful campaigns of influence.

Egypt

In 2011, the Egyptian army provided a clear illustration of how military fiat can prove decisive. A 1952 military coup led by Col. Gamal Abdel Nasser formed the modern Egyptian state. But over his long tenure, President Hosni Mubarak maintained control through his police and security apparatus. The army prided itself as a professional institution that remained above the political fray, although it exerted pressure behind the scenes.[17] Extensive commercial interests invested the military with a stake in who controlled political power well beyond its interests in security. As Mubarak became an octogenarian, the military was inevitably destined to assert its voice—if only as a veto—on his succession.

By 2011, Egyptians had grown alienated from the corrupt and ineffective government. They took to the streets to demand change. Mubarak's political fortunes disintegrated, and chaos threatened the country. It was the army's forceful strategic communication that eased Mubarak out of the picture, stabilized the situation, and set the way for a peaceful transition.

Pressure from the April 6 Movement, We Are All Khaled Said, the Muslim Brotherhood, and broadcasts by al-Jazeera all contributed to the end of Mubarak's reign. The combination of cellular communication and satellite television provided real-time information that mobilized demonstrators, enabled them to understand how events were unfolding, and provided informed communication. At one point the government cut off Internet and cellular links for a few days, which had no effect in stifling protests—and may well have intensified them. Like many politicians who wield too much power for too long, Mubarak had lost touch with political reality. Prodded by pressure from the Obama administration to use restraint—a move made possible by close personal relationships between high-ranking officers in the two nations' militaries—the Egyptian army sought to avoid a violent revolution. Realizing that Mubarak had put his head into the sand, the military took matters into its own hands.

The eighteen-member Supreme Council of the Armed Forces announced that it had gone into "permanent session." Such action is associated with putting itself on a war footing. It issued a missive titled "Communiqué Number 1"— a tactic that in Arab cultures often signals that a coup has taken place. The communiqué consciously omitted any mention of Mubarak or Vice President Omar Suleiman. That sent the message that the army was calling the shots. Television stations broadcast images that reinforced this message. Defense minister and military commander-in-chief field marshal Mohamed Hussein Tantawi was seen chairing a solemn meeting of two dozen flag officers, at which Mubarak and Suleiman were absent. The army was making clear that it would decide for itself where it stood, and that it would ignore Mubarak or Suleiman's directions.[18] The strategy worked, and Mubarak was eventually forced out.

Demonstrators in Cairo heard the message. Significantly, they did not disperse immediately afterward but returned to Tahrir Square in Cairo again and again to communicate their serious intent to bring about democratic change. They protested against including any members of Mubarak's National Democratic Party in a new regime. Soon enough, NDP's headquarters was torched, many of its key figures were tossed behind bars, and both of Mubarak's sons, Gamal and Alaa, were detained; Mubarak himself avoided prison only by checking into a hospital.[19] That did not prevent the government from putting them on trial. Egypt's Supreme Administrative Court then ordered the dissolution of the NDP.[20] The term "power to the people" took on real meaning in this case. Their own strategic communication capitalized on social media—notably Facebook—and orderly, mass displays of visible resolve through street demonstrations.[21] It resonated with the military, whose power still counted.[22]

Within two weeks, the military-led provisional authority announced plans for new elections, although the provisional prime minister, General Ahmad Shafiq, was viewed as a Mubarak kingpin. Whether it will succeed in maintaining its grip on power and realizing its goal of avoiding real regime change is unclear at this writing. The parliamentary elections held in the fall of 2011 produced an overwhelming victory for Islamist and Muslim Brotherhood candidates. The presidential election surprised many observers, proving, apparently, to be a free and fair election—Egypt's first—pitting four major contenders against one another in a very close, unpredictable contest.[23] In a second surprise, Ahmed Shafiq, who had been viewed as a long shot, made the runoff against the Muslim Brotherhood's candidate, Mohammed Morsi.[24]

The Egyptian military's actions show that simple, direct strategic communication by military with power and credibility can quickly and drastically change the political equation in a country. No matter who prevails, the extent of power to be exercised by the new president remains unclear.

China

In January 2011, China unveiled its J-20 stealth fighter jet during a visit by US Secretary of Defense Robert Gates. The action surprised some observers. Gates acknowledged that China was moving ahead with new technology faster than US intelligence had estimated. The unveiling and its timing were taken as a show of strength.[25] In a different vein, in 2003, the United States moved assets to support its invasion of Iraq. It had a longtime commitment to maintaining a strong air force deterrence to deal with potential crises with North Korea or China. In 2003, the United States moved forces that historically were dedicated to the Pacific theater to deter aggression by China or North Korea. In order to compensate for that, the US stationed bomber and fighter aircraft in Guam as a signal that its commitment in the Pacific would not be diluted.

Rwanda

Strategic communication can be used for good or evil. The final part of this book offers a case study to show how, in strategic communication, radio can be used as a weapon. Chris Stewart's work for Gallup has covered Africa. He recounts: "When the Hutu leadership communicated through the 'magic box' (Radio Mille Collines) that a national duty existed to clean the country of 'Tutsi cockroaches,' it triggered genocide."[26]

The Hutus recognized the power of strategic communication. They knew that it cut both ways and went to great lengths to get their message out while—like the Soviets—they also used violence or fear to suppress narratives from any source that contradicted it. They confiscated cellphones from journalists and banned travel to the region. "News" from the combat zone was passed to selected journalists as "exclusives" by military minders, or presented at press briefings organized by military commanders. The strategies worked so well that President Paul Kagame boasted that they had "invented a new way of doing things."[27]

Radios stolen from the UN were used to pass coded messages between different regions of the country. During that debacle, the Rwanda military monitored NGO communications transmitted without encryption to extract information passed by aid workers to each other about the location of refugees fleeing the Rwandan troops. Rwandans used that to track down and kill their adversaries.[28] (See chapter 16 for a more detailed discussion of Rwanda.)

The Power of Personal Presence

On June 2, 1979, Pope John Paul II shook forever the foundations of Poland's Communist regime through a nine-day return home that commenced with his arrival at Okecie military airport, where he fell to his knees and kissed the ground. The emotions aroused among enormous crowds that the pope drew are hard to capture in words. His trip was designed to be—and was—a turning point in Polish politics.[29]

In their documentary *Nine Days That Changed the World*, produced and hosted by Newt and Callista Gingrich, a broad range of experts including the pope's biographer, George Weigel, attest to the remarkable impact that the pope's visit—carefully planned, timed, and thought through in consultation with President Ronald Reagan—achieved in inspiring fresh hope and new determination among Poles in shaking off the iron grip in which they had been held by Polish Communist dictators and their Soviet masters. His message, former Speaker Gingrich has said, was that "freedom is based on faith and a message that says no government can come between you and your God."[30] His trip facilitated the founding of Solidarity, the Soviet bloc's first independent trade union, and helped set the stage for collapse of the country's dictatorship.

Communicating a Commander's Intent

Military commanders employ strategic communication internally to ensure that their organizations are cohesive and that people understand their intent. One reason Gen. David H. Petraeus is so effective is that he uses strategic communication skillfully in his internal communication. Good strategic communication is as much about informing and influencing your own organization as it is about informing and influencing the target audience. Petraeus takes pains to ensure that his entire command understands his goals, his thinking, and what he wants them to achieve. When he gives an interview to the *New York Times* or *60 Minutes*, his own officers and many troops read or watch it closely—perhaps more closely than the enemy does. Call it commander's intent or call it strategic communication; ensuring that your own people understand and implement your intent—your communication strategy— enables a commander to more effectively influence external target audiences through information strategies. Certainly, one lessens the chances of crossfire and confusion.

During the American Revolution, George Washington enhanced his own effectiveness by taking steps to communicate with his troops. General orders provided news to bolster morale and maintain discipline. Historian Carl Berger reports that Washington used casual conversations to start rumors in order to achieve effects. He had such a commanding presence that his appearance alone roused the troops.[31]

Strategic Alliances

The Roman Emperor Constantine the Great was a ruthless but effective ruler. He founded Constantinople, but he also murdered his wife, his son, and many friends when he thought it suited his interests. Scholars like H. A. Drake contend that his conversion to Christianity was genuine, but politically, Constantine recognized too that Christian support was a powerful factor in that culture, and that a successful ruler required it to assure political stability. He ended the persecution of Christians and communicated imperial favor by appointing them to positions in government. In 312 AD, he ordered his men to fight as Christians. Christian bishops immediately threw their support to the Emperor, and used preaching and sermons to influence the public.[32]

Strategic Positioning with Other States

In 444–443 BC, citizens of Sybaris relocated to Greece and established a colony at Thurii, in southern Italy. In need of inhabitants, they asked Sparta and Athens to send colonists. Robert Kagan records that Athens responded by sending messengers across Greece advertising for settlers to create a Pan-Hellenic city. The idea was an innovation. Athens explicitly took no action to exert dominance over Thurii, and it remained outside of the Athenian Empire's sphere of influence. Kagan sees the action of Athens—led by Pericles—as a diplomatic signal that it had "no imperial ambitions in the west and would pursue a policy of peaceful panhellism." It represented a significant effort to maintain stable, peaceful relations with Sparta.[33] In today's world, the United States is extremely careful about how it deals with Taiwan, balancing American interests in maintaining strong economic and political ties to that democracy with its interest in forging a stable relationship with China, which declines to recognize Taiwan's status as an independent state. In classic examples of strategic communication, the United States calibrates its statements and actions to maintain that balance.

Surges

At the time that the United States launched the surge in Iraq in 2007, the strategic situation on the ground had grown tenuous. Secretary Rumsfeld believed that by the spring of 2006 al-Qaeda had seized the initiative, and he and his team recognized that the coalition strategy needed to be adjusted.[34] An alliance with Sunnis in western Iraq, the Sons of Iraq (also called the Awakening Movement), helped change the dynamics on the ground.[35] Some argued that adding another 30,000 troops would make at best a marginal difference.

The real case for the surge was psychological, in terms of providing a boost for coalition forces and the Iraqi government, and also as a method of strategic communication. At the time there was much debate on whether the United States should draw down its forces and what effect that might have on the Iraqi government's ability to defeat the insurgents. The surge was never conceived as a cure-all; Rumsfeld contends that it coincided with favorable political developments. These included the seating of a new government, the end of a latent Shia rebellion, and Iraq security forces reaching critical points in numbers, equipment, and training. Given doubts that had grown about the war at home, the "true genius of the surge," Rumsfeld concluded, "was the political effect it had in the United States, where the conflict's true center of gravity had migrated."[36] Others add that it helped stabilize Iraq and provided Iraqi political leaders an opportunity to resolve differences on powersharing that would keep Sunnis, Shias, and Kurds invested in postconflict Iraq.[37] It pressured insurgents and helped strengthen security.[38] Combined elements have been required to produce a favorable outcome in Iraq. One aspect of the surge that made a difference was what it strategically communicated about US resolve.

Kevin McCarty suggests that a key challenge that confronted the United States at the time was that ground truth—an improving situation on the ground—was at odds with media perception. The surge itself was strategic communication, but the action succeeded as well as it did because, in his words, "the White House refined its narrative about what the United States was doing and what was really happening. Al-Qaeda had evolved into a bunch of thugs. They were the mafia. They were thieves who killed to maintain power, and everybody who dealt with them knew that. Yet al-Qaeda's media perception and its narrative was about nationalist Muslims fighting against foreign infidels who had invaded Iraq. The truth on the ground and the media perception were two different things. The US strategy was actually working on the ground. The media perception was the opposite. The media was portraying the war as a loss. The US government was mired in a narrative of 'kill-capture'—how our forces were winning militarily and providing security. It was sticking to a theme of violence. That played into al-Qaeda's hands. We said we were trying to stop violence. All al-Qaeda had to do was create an act of violence to discredit that existing narrative."[39]

McCarty continues: "The White House created a new communication strategy to align the narrative with what was actually happening on the ground. The White House made sure it got ahead of the story, getting its story out first. Its narrative portrayed al-Qaeda for what it was: murderers and thugs. We achieved information dominance. On a positive note, we stopped talking about violence and talked about building schools, creating jobs, and building a future. Most critically, we communicated this narrative with an Iraqi face. We wanted the Iraqis to have a stake in what they were doing and to have confidence in their own government. And we needed to draw a contrast between an Iraqi government that was building a secure, prosperous future and an al-Qaeda that offered one rooted in death and destruction."[40]

He adds: "We put out only facts that independent reporters could verify. They did verify them. It was not propaganda. It was just aligning the narrative with the facts. We made no effort to sell anything that was not true or not happening. The media coverage shifted, and suddenly al-Qaeda was portrayed for what it was. The impact was extraordinary. In three months things had been turned around. Al-Qaeda's leaders advised their followers to stop targeting civilians. The media began to cover the conflict on terms that favored the Iraqi government's narrative—its successes on the ground and a strategy that was unfolding as designed."[41]

Honoring Ethnic Groups

Although anything the White House does should be considered classic political communication, events at the White House offer a powerful symbol and a bully pulpit. In 2011, President Obama hosted a traditional Ramadan break-the-fast dinner at the White House. He recognized Muslim survivors of the September 11 terror attacks and thanked Muslims for their service to the country. He reminded Americans that Muslim Americans had responded to attacks on the Twin Towers and that some had died there, and that others served in the military to defend the country. "There is no them and us," he declared. "It's just us." President George W. Bush had hosted similar dinners.[42] The event served as excellent strategic communication to reassure an ethnic group that has felt unfairly besieged that the nation honors them as Americans. PSYOP expert Col. Lawrence Dietz has suggested that the idea could have been made more strongly. The event paid homage to Muslims who died in the attacks, and Dietz sensibly argues that such communication would be stronger if we spent more time also profiling well-respected, pious survivors.[43] The point is that high-level political events serve effectively for persuasive strategic communication that may reach and influence narrow and broad audiences.

Foreign Aid as a Psychological Operation: The Marshall Plan

The European Recovery Program lasted between 1947 and 1951. The initiative owes its name to Secretary of State George Marshall. It was the brainchild of State Department officials, notably Ambassador George F. Kennan and William Clayton. Kennan was Marshall's director of the policy planning staff. On June 5, 1947, Marshall delivered a historic speech at Harvard that laid out the rationale for the program of rebuilding. The war had destroyed Germany's economy, he declared:

> The truth of the matter is that Europe's requirements for the next three or four years of foreign food and other essential products—principally from America—are so much greater than her present ability to pay that she must have substantial additional help or face economic, social, and political deterioration of a very grave character.
>
> The remedy lies in breaking the vicious circle and restoring the confidence of the European people in the economic future of their own countries and of Europe as a whole. The manufacturer and the farmer throughout wide areas must be able and willing to exchange their products for currencies the continuing value of which is not open to question.[44]

The motives of the United States were political as well as humanitarian. Kennan wrote a top secret memorandum (since declassified) that defined Europe's recovery problem from an American viewpoint. Kennan and his colleagues were deeply concerned that Communist propaganda might succeed in attracting the support of Europeans. The challenge was both economic and political, and the Marshall Plan provided the solution. Kennan stated that "any set of events which would substantially restore to people in Western Europe a sense of political security, and of confidence in a future marked by close association with the Western Powers, would itself release extensive recuperative forces in Europe which are today inhibited or paralyzed by political uncertainty. In this sense, *we must recognize that much of the value of a European recovery program will lie not so much in its direct effects, which are difficult to calculate with any degree of accuracy, as in its psychological and political by-products*" [emphasis added].[45]

Kennan made clear that the true purpose of the program—a psychological operation to influence the attitudes and opinions of Europeans to move their loyalty to the United States and Western powers—would remain secret. He emphasized: "To state this [the true intent of the Marshall Plan] publicly, however, would be a self-defeating act." Doing that "would only confuse them and undermine in advance precisely the psychological reaction which we aim to produce."[46] Matt Armstrong contends—and he is correct—that Kennan's plan was to ensure that Europeans "felt empowered and secure," and to cut the ground from beneath Communist propaganda.[47] Kevin McCarty notes that "while Europeans lacked funds to restart their economies, what was even more important in Kennan's view was that we provide that support in a form that restored confidence in those governments, and deterred people from moving their political allegiance towards Communism. The key was not the tactic of how do you help them most efficiently recover economically. It was in the psychological impact of how you provided the aid in order to provide the condition that the United States desired, which was faith in Western democratic government rather than Communism."[48]

In short, for those who worry that psychological operations are cause for concern, one of the most significant, successful, and far-ranging post–World War II programs carried out by the United States was the Marshall Plan.

PART III

Campaigns of Influence

CHAPTER 8

Do Authoritarians Care?

Hﾨ OW MUCH DO AUTHORITARIAN REGIMES CARE ABOUT STRATEGIC COM-
munication when they control the instruments of power and can generally
exert their will through coercion? Most of them care a lot. For starters, they
crave legitimacy. They seek popular sanction for their right to exercise power.
They want to foster and maintain credibility. Even draconian regimes desire
that. No matter how ruthless or violent, politicians (as well as military jun-
tas) do not think of themselves as criminals, thugs, or monsters. In their own
minds, they are patriots and heroes. Forging support within key constituencies
is vital to getting what they want, and popular support matters in influencing
those constituencies. Consider a few examples.

Burma

Since Ne Win, a military commander, seized power in a coup d'état in 1962,
Burma (also known as Myanmar) has held two elections. The first, in 1990,
was nullified, and the head of the winning party, Aung San Suu Kyi, was placed
in house arrest where she remained on and off until 2010, when the second
election was held. This resulted in a sweep for the government-backed party,
the United Solidarity Development Party (USDP). For the remaining time
since the 1962 coup a military junta has ruled Burma; even now, after the elections, the military continues to play a dominant role (albeit in civilian garb) in
the newly elected national and regional assemblies.

The military government has not been hesitant to crush dissent, notably the
student uprisings in 1988 (and earlier) and the protests led by monks during
the so-called Saffron Revolution of 2007. "Despite a reputation for ruthlessness
and corruption," says Burma expert Julian Wheatley, "the junta were certainly
concerned with perceptions of legitimacy as well as popular approval. But they
defined legitimacy first in terms of national unity rather than in terms of elections and democratic or pluralistic institutions that might register the actual

will of the people. National unity required defending the nation against 'external meddling' and preserving traditional culture and social values, or at least, the culture of the dominant ethnic group, the Burmans, who make up about two-thirds of the population of the country."[1]

Shifts between violence and constraint probably reflected factions within the junta and the army, as well as general recognition among the military that popular outrage represented a long-term threat to stability and progress—as well as to themselves. In their own minds, they spoke for the Burmese, and they had a Buddhist perception that they occupied an enlightened kingship. In Wheatley's words, "they felt that they formulated and executed their policies to help the people. Criticism was perceived as the product of sinister foreign influence. They were quite paranoid about foreign media and institutions who they believed were always interfering with domestic politics. Still, they tended to bull ahead regardless of whether the populace agreed with their policies. But actions were taken in the devout hope that the Burmese would acknowledge that such policies were wise and for their own good."[2]

The 2011 elections can be viewed as an attempt to procure legitimacy in the eyes of the international community—not just to the West and the UN, who are unlikely to be impressed, but ASEAN and China, who are more receptive—while still holding onto power within the country. The junta learned the lessons of the previous 1990 election debacle well, engineering the new elections so as to ensure a dominant position for the military (requiring 25% of seats in the new state and regional legislatures to be filled by serving military officers), and excluding Aung San Suu Kyi, leader of the only viable opposition party, from participating on the grounds that she had been married to a foreigner. But "discipline-flourishing democracy" replacing rule by decree that had been in effect since the student-led uprisings of 1988 may at least diffuse some popular discontent and offer the possibility of local or regional input.[3]

Until the 2010 elections, Senior General Than Shwe presided as head of government in what Mary P. Callahan describes as "the most durable incarnation of military rule in history."[4] The army (*tatmadaw* in Burmese) provides the source of power. Its historical prestige is rooted in having driven out Japanese invaders and British colonists and winning independence for the country in 1948. In the years after independence, the army acquired additional moral legitimacy as the defender of the realm in the face of a succession of threats from minority groups, and as a disinterested force for stability in the face of political opportunism. More recently, army leaders have cemented loyalty for its members through privileges that range from special educational and health facilities to business preferences. Somewhat like Pakistan, it is almost a state within a state.

While ensuring a monopoly on power and enriching themselves and their friends through corrupt practices and business dealings, the army views itself as the selfless guardian of the nation, seeking to preserve the union, promote Burmese cultural values, and guide economic progress until the populace is mature enough to take a larger role. As Robert Taylor puts it in a recent book on the Burmese state, the military government argued that they were "holding the state power in trust for the people until conditions were created such that a return to a representative civilian government would be possible and permanent."[5]

Wheatley notes that "the Burmese government is concerned with its legitimacy, both in the eyes of the outside world and its own people. It seeks to buttress this legitimacy in the traditional style of Burmese kings, by supporting the monkhood—the *sangha*—and building or repairing religious edifices; and by undertaking public works, such as bridge and road building. Army officers who perform or acknowledge such good works provide the mainstay of daily newspaper fare."[6]

Not long after the 1988 crisis, all newspapers and books, as well as many prominent billboards, were imprinted with a list of the government's long-term objectives, grouped into four groups of four. The four categories of objectives are political (e.g., national reconsolidation), economic (proper evolution of the market-oriented economic system), and social (uplift of the morale and morality of the entire nation). But they are headed by the four items under the heading of "people's desire," which is in fact what the government decrees that the people desire for their own good. The first of these is "oppose those relying on external elements, acting as stooges, holding negative views," and the last of the four is "crush all internal and external elements as the common enemy." The final item, of course, includes anyone who opposes government policy—a position underscored by Than Shwe's message for this year's Burmese Independence Day, in which he called on the people to make the "correct choices" in the upcoming elections.[7]

The military, Wheatley says, "purges its own ranks from time to time to reign in regional commanders who have become virtual warlords in their domains. Still, in its more deliberative moments, the leadership uses strategic communication vigorously to cast itself as a helmsman, steering the nation around reefs and shoals towards the Promised Land. It takes pains to arouse in Burmese a sense that its policies are wise and taken for their own good, although, as in Pakistan, the military has little faith in their judgment and has no compunction about treating them as 'the common enemy' if they fail to follow the prescribed path."[8]

No matter how tightly the Burmese generals gripped power, by 2012 they recognized that maintaining their power required communicating that some opposition would be tolerated. In November 2010, the military allowed new elections and a transition to a civilian government. The military-backed Union Solidarity and Development Party won about 75 percent of the seats in a new bicameral parliament. Former general and prime minister under the junta, Thein Sein, became president. The military appointed a quarter of the new parliament's members.

In December 2011, the opposition National League for Democracy was allowed to register for parliamentary elections and its leader, Aung San Suu Kyi, who had spent years under house arrest, was permitted to stand in a second by-election held in April 2012. Despite initial complaints about election fraud, she and her party won 43 seats. Although this was a small percentage of the 440 seats, she quickly hailed a new era in Burmese politics.[9] This represented a sea change, with most of the seats now held by civilians.

One potential sign of popular moods may be the sweeping reception that greeted her when she attended the World Economic Forum in Bangkok. Indeed, that the Burmese government allowed her to travel abroad sent a signal for tolerance in an effort to shore up its popular legitimacy and credibility.[10] From Thailand she went on to Europe. Although this would be routine for politicians in most countries, in Burmese politics this represents a major shift by the military, which had previously clamped down on her activities.

The election underscores as well the conclusion that authoritarian regimes do consider their image at home and abroad as part of a broader effort to protect the legitimacy of their power. The ruling junta has calculated that allowing a more open society will enable it to control the aspects of Burmese politics that it most cares about. The interesting question for the future is whether popular desire for change, once unleashed, can be contained.

Saudi Arabia

The royal family that controls the Kingdom of Saudi Arabia emphatically resists challenges to its legitimacy and national stability. It employs a sophisticated program to counter radicalization and to promote the state's official narrative. Key elements include a security strategy implemented by security forces and the community, and an advocacy and advisory strategy rooted in counseling programs and dialogue. The Saudis will kill or otherwise remove extremists who cannot be reconciled to the regime and whose views are deemed radical and deviant. The government also works hard to prevent new recruits from joining violent extremist groups. It takes pains to rehabilitate and care for extremist recruits who can be rehabilitated, while carefully monitoring their activities and holding their families accountable and responsible for their behavior.

Saudi strategic communication mobilizes local and national government. They work with schools, mosques, mass media, social service providers, and nongovernmental organizations to drive its narrative. They mobilize independent third-party religious authorities to bolster credibility. The campaign strategy is integrated with the Saudi concept of *da'wah* (call to faith) as a governmental obligation. This ties into Wahhabi Islam, which stresses loyalty, recognition of authority, and obedience to official leadership.

Two core campaigns drive Saudi Arabia's approach. The counseling campaign (*Al-Munasahah*) persuades detained extremists that unscrupulous individuals have manipulated and misled them into false beliefs. It tells them that violent extremism rests upon a corrupt understanding of Islam and lacks religious justification. The tranquility campaign (*Al-Sakinah*) employs volunteers who engage potential extremists through websites, chat rooms, and forums to curb the spread of radicalization over the Internet.[11] These campaigns espouse the official interpretation of Wahhabi Islam. They discourage those they deem to lack qualifications from offering their own interpretations. The kingdom employs posters, television and film, editorials, books, tapes, and conferences to promote its message, and relies on support from the education and clerical communities. It even mounts comprehensive social engagement that helps people find jobs or spouses, in order to promote regime stability.

North Korea

The Democratic People's Republic of Korea (DPRK), known as North Korea, is a country whose propaganda machine sustains government legitimacy through myths it conjures up. The machine employs strategic communication to great effect. Brian Myers has written about its race-based, paranoid nationalism and a regime whose ideology and worldview "is utterly at odds with the teachings of Marx and Lenin," and far removed from "Confucianism and the show-window doctrine of Juche Thought."[12] It is a nation of self-reliance that revolves around ideas of independence from great powers, military strength, and reliance on the country's natural resources.

Until his death in December 2011, Kim Jong-il maintained legitimacy, credibility, and support through myths that extolled the notion that "the Korean people are too pure blooded, and therefore too virtuous, to survive in this evil world without a great parental leader."[13] The campaigns of influence embraced oral campaigns at party lectures, fake news media, television dramas, war movies, animated cartoons, magazines, novels, dictionaries, textbooks, and wall posters. Myers states that "so significant is the propaganda apparatus that it was one of the few North Korean institutions that did not miss a beat even during the catastrophic famine of the 1990s."[14] He points out that the regime required propaganda to sustain its official myths about North Korean moral purity and military strength and the trepidation that its might engenders among Americans.

Significantly, North Korea's strategic communication has generated sufficiently strong support to make the regime desperate to hold on to it.[15] Crucially, Meyers observes, the failure to understand the regime's worldview—well revealed through its communications and which colors a regime that Meyers believes most resembles pre–World War II Japan—has prompted serious errors in forging realistic strategies in dealing with North Korea. For example, food aid provided by the United States to help the regime through famine was treated by North Korea as supplication, not generosity.

Kim Jong-il was succeeded by his son Kim Jong-un. Now in his late twenties, he was promoted in September 2010 to the rank of four-star general in the People's Army and chaired the military commission of the Workers' Party. His father adopted a military first policy that provided him with a preeminent role. US Secretary of Defense Robert Gates has said that the son "has to earn his stripes with the North Korean military."[16] It remains to be seen how Kim Jong-un's reign will play out, but one can bet that the ruling clique will move to cloak the son in stories and myth that build and strengthen his credibility— unless they get rid of him. But the State wasted no time burnishing the son's credentials. It produced a documentary, *Succeeding Great Work of Military-First Revolution,* that depicted him as an experienced military leader.[17]

Iran

The legitimacy of the Iranian government is wrapped up in the 1979 revolution, and it uses strategic communication to maintain it. Noted Iran expert Trita Parsi points out that "the regime views strategic communication as vital to its survival. Its leaders feel a compelling need to justify their actions as the guardians of the revolution and as champions for Iranian independence against foreign interference. In their own mind, they have legitimacy. They want people to agree in order to neutralize any inclination they may have to question the regime. They also want people to feel that the regime has integrity and does the right things for the right reasons. Ideological coherence is important to their claim for legitimacy."[18]

The regime relies heavily upon mass media—television, newspapers, radio—as well as posters, banners, billboards, speeches, and demonstrations to get out and drive its themes and messages. Parsi also emphasizes the pivotal role that clerics and mosques play: "The Supreme Leader has representatives in every city. He decides who speaks at Friday prayers, what is said, and everything else that happens in the mosque in between. They control the clerical establishment. It is a powerful tool for strategic communication that is incredibly hard for anyone else to compete against or co-opt."[19] As new media—Twitter, Facebook, and other emerging tools of social network mobilization—become accessible to everyday Iranians, the regime has made efforts to block out competing views. It has indicated that it will block Google's gmail service, and it has blocked YouTube, banned rallies, and used force to suppress opposition.[20]

Anyone who doubts whether the regime cares whether people accept its legitimacy need merely look at the controversy that broke out in the wake of the June 2009 presidential race, when President Mahmoud Ahmadinejad was accused of stealing the election. The government pressed its position hard. Still, charges of fraud have opened up cracks within the Islamic leadership between the clerics and the military. These appear to have eroded the power and authority of Supreme Leader Ayatollah Ali Khamanei in favor of the Iranian Revolutionary Guard Corps (IRGC). A shadow has been cast over the regime's legitimacy.[21]

The Green Movement opposition that seeks to oust Ahmadinejad understands strategic communication. Green was the symbol of presidential candidate Mir Hossein Mousavi, and it has become the symbol of change. Participants in mass demonstrations wave banners demanding, "Where is my vote?" Opposition leaders have spoken up at rallies and through social media, forcing the regime into a corner. As Iran's top opposition leader, Mousavi has declared that election fraud has cost the regime its legitimacy.[22] He has warned regime leaders in an open letter: "We will stand firmly in order to preserve this valuable accomplishment [revolution]. Unless we succeed in this, the government will not have any legitimacy. The system and the heritage of the Islamic revolution are the fruits of our 200-year-old struggle against oppression."[23] In a second open letter, presidential candidate Mahdi Karroubi concurred, adding: "I will not recognize the legitimacy of the government which has resulted from this process and will not participate in any of its processes, in any way."[24]

According to Parsi, "the regime has always played on preexisting sentiments in the population against the Shah, the history of foreign interference, and the perception of double standards by the US, in setting forth a narrative that foreign powers abuse the nation. It has been relatively easy for them to play on these ideas. In the past they have been quite successful. Their current problem is that playing on religious tradition and nationalism is a flawed strategy when it now feels compelled to rely upon force to retain power."[25]

President Ahmadinejad and his cronies may have stolen the election, but he cannot afford to acknowledge doing so. He even went to the United Nations to defend himself, insisting that the election was "glorious and fully democratic."[26] Whether the regime's repressive measures backfire and bring about its collapse remains an open question. The fact that its survival depends as much on winning an information war as battles in the streets says much about the need for any authoritarian state to intelligently employ strategic communication.

Ironically, in 2011, Iranian rulers cheered Arabs for sweeping away autocrats like Hosni Mubarak and Zine Al Abidine Ben Ali, whom it labeled as lapdogs to the United States. President Ahmadinejad urged protestors in Cairo to free themselves, sounding almost like Thomas Paine. What he really meant, of course, was that the Iranian government was pleased to see unfriendly regimes toppled, especially those with ties to the United States or Israel. "The arrogant powers will have no place in the Middle East," he snarked, in a haphazard effort to liken the 2011 unrest to Iran's 1979 revolution.[27] Not surprisingly, dissidents to Ahmadinejad who tried to stage their own street protests in Tehran were met with gas and baton charges by security forces.[28] The regime has not flinched from using violence or placing opposition leaders like Mahdi Karroubi under house arrest. (Karroubi had summoned Iranian opposition activists to rally in support of Egyptian pro-democracy demonstrators.[29]) Ahmadinejad was sending a strong strategic message to Iranians that he will use violence to block efforts to topple the regime or remove him from power.

His threat did not deter tens of thousands, however—many wearing green ribbons, the symbol of the opposition Green Movement—from marching in the streets during 2011. They chanted "Death to the Dictator."[30]

CHAPTER 9

Is Success about Leadership or Communication?

Is success or failure a matter of political leadership or effective strategic communication? Or is it both? Many separate the two, but successful leadership usually requires the ability to conduct effective strategic communication.

Egypt

Hosni Mubarak ruled his nation for three decades after President Anwar Sadat's assassination. His fellow Arab leader, Zine El Abidine Ben Ali, ran a tight-fisted regime in Tunisia. When waves of demonstrators hit the streets in 2011, the Tunisian leader fled to Saudi Arabia and promptly suffered a stroke.[1] Egyptians followed suit with their own protests to demand Mubarak's exit. Mubarak stood his ground, but clumsily. Looking twenty years younger with his hair died black, the eighty-two-year-old strongman took to the airwaves with a videotaped speech announcing that he had sacked his cabinet, and promised reform.[2] Like the former Tunisian leader, isolation paralyzed and blinded his political faculties.

Apparently, he hoped that his security forces could intimidate the protestors into dispersing. He misjudged the situation badly. His goons were willing to use their fists, but the army and most police were not. The police retreated.[3] Prideful of its self-appointed role as protector of the nation, the army—apparently pressured from behind the scenes by the US military—refused to fire on demonstrators. In powerful illustrations of strategic communication, they took measured action that helped maintain calm while deciding what posture to take. Mubarak continued to stonewall as insiders and his citizens clamored for his resignation.

Everything about the way Mubarak handled himself was a fiasco as strategic communication. He failed to confront political realities on the ground; he failed to articulate clearly or intelligently his intentions or expectations; he was ambivalent. All of this undercut his already weak position, and he took no steps to bolster his credibility. By videotaping his statement, he may have thought that he would ensure a smooth delivery—but what came across was a canned response from an eighty-two-year-old with his hair dyed to make him appear younger. Claiming the mantle of reform, he appointed a vice president—a tepid gesture. Worse, the person he selected, Omar Suleiman, was a much despised security official. Dispatching thugs to beat up demonstrators and the press communicated fear and provoked a more intense backlash. By choking off free elections and failing to provide good governance, Mubarak had lost most of his credibility at home. His ill-conceived strategic communication and clumsy leadership drained what was left. His final departure was ignominious. Instead of ensuring his personal security, he left in disgrace and remains vulnerable to being held to account by angry Egyptians.

United States

Barack Obama won a stunning landslide victory in 2008. His campaign had been ignited by an inspiring speech delivered at the Iowa Jefferson-Jackson Dinner in Des Moines in 2008. Yet once in office, voters delivered him—quoting his word—a "shellacking" in the 2010 midterm elections, when Republicans won control of the House of Representatives. Had the GOP nominated stronger candidates in Nevada, Delaware, Colorado, and perhaps California, the Republicans might have ended up with fifty Senate seats. The GOP might have seized control had Senator Joe Lieberman, who had endorsed John McCain, then switched parties. Lieberman had resisted efforts, but the fact is that McCain had fully intended to place him on the ticket as his running mate, backing off only when it became clear that an unsympathetic Republican convention would have refused to nominate him.[4] We'll never know if Lieberman might have switched, but the possibility cannot be excluded.

The US Lesson

A forceful Obama admirer, Frank Rich of *The New York Times*, rightly observed that he won through the power of "his ability to communicate a compelling narrative."[5] The Jefferson-Jackson Day speech defined him as a candidate of hope and change; his Iowa victory was no fluke.[6] Obama and his team outorganized, out-spent, out-thought, and out-campaigned Hillary Clinton. They had superior communication.

Obama's able campaign manager David Plouffe expressed consternation when she refused to drop out once it became clear to him, at least, that Obama had a lock on the Democratic nomination.[7] Hillary Clinton viewed things differently. She got her act together and finally articulated a compelling message. The dynamics shifted. She won the popular vote in Texas, Ohio, and the major primaries that followed. The argument she posed was simple: her experience made her the stronger general election candidate. Had she gotten her campaign in order ninety days earlier, she might have been the one waking up in the Lincoln bedroom as president.

Gaining power is tough enough, but its exercise is an art form. Obama has impressive rhetorical skills, but during his first two years as president he was buffeted by rough seas. He appeared to vacillate on health care, leaving it to Senate Majority Leader Harry Reid, House Speaker Nancy Pelosi, and various committee chairpersons to decide the contents of the legislation. It's not clear whether anybody truly understands what the voluminous legislation that emerged actually contains. The British Petroleum oil spill raised doubts about his executive management skills and deeply angered residents of South Louisiana—Republicans, Democrats, and Independents—for the White House failure to devise or execute a coherent, realistic strategic action plan to contain the spill or deal with its consequences. The issue is the ability to communicate a narrative and drive messages that advance Obama's interests, policies, and agenda. Partly his challenges have been about whether he is an effective executive. Putting it mildly, his supporters and critics disagree. His generally ineffective strategic communication has complicated his challenges. Heads of state need both qualities: strong executive leadership and effective strategic communication. At this writing before the election, most view the outcome of the Obama-Romney contest as a toss-up, with no more than 5 to 7 percent of the electorate undecided. But at this writing midway through the election year, while building an impressive campaign organization staffed by high talent and stymied by a flagging economy, most political insiders agree that Obama's strategic communication has faltered, although his supporters believe that his attacks on Governor Mitt Romney's record as a private equity executive and his refusal, as of July 2012, to release his tax returns are gaining traction. Romney has fired back, defending his record and vigorously attacking the president's.

Despite his challenges, some, like journalist James Fallows, argue that Obama is a president who learns fast and if reelected may well prove much more effective at strategic communication in a second term.[8]

John Maddox is an experienced consultant to political candidates and large corporations in America. He observes that "governing requires providing a vision that is reassuring, but effective leadership requires the practical application of ideas. Otherwise competing interests will gridlock you."[9] Obama stalwarts like columnist Frank Rich have ascribed the president's difficulties to a failure to "find a theme" and a "consistent, clear message" that is "arresting to the majority of Americans who still like him and are desperate for him to succeed."[10] This perspective casts Obama's problems as poor communication. Rich has a point, but the failure to communicate is a familiar refrain for executive mishap. There is usually more to it than that.

Obama critics charge that Obama has spread himself too thin across a broad agenda and has failed to mobilize voters behind his policies. They point as well to the fact that Obama inherited an economic crisis bequeathed him by the Bush administration. Indeed, in 2001, as Bush took office, the budget was balanced and the Congressional Budget Office was forecasting annual surpluses indefinitely.[11] The financial meltdown that broke in September 2008 was helped along in no small measure from ill-judged Republican action in supporting the Gramm-Leach-Bliley Act of 1999 that repealed the Glass-Steagall Act. The Gramm-Leach-Bliley Act allowed commercial and investment banks to merge, and permitted banks to take on riskier investments in mortgages.[12] It proved a monumental failure of regulation.[13]

The Obama team took pride in its economic achievements. In its view, their action had averted an imminent collapse of global financial markets. Yet their strategic communication made politically costly mistakes. The Obama team failed to curb what the public viewed as excessive executive compensation for financial institutions that accepted government loans. On the other hand, the $700 billion in authorized Troubled Asset Relief Program (TARP) loans—$245 billion was actually invested—to banks proved a huge success. It stabilized institutions and, by March 2011, repayments had exceeded the amounts loaned. Indeed, estimates were that TARP would turn a $20 billion profit.[14] Inexplicably, the White House did a poor job of communicating this success story, providing an opening for Republicans to dominate political discourse with talk about unemployment figures and criticism of Obama's stimulus package.

From the start, Republicans contended that Obama's ideas were too left wing. Obama had expressed hope for compromise, but Republicans did not find him compromising. For their part, distrustful Democrats viewed Republicans as interested mainly in unseating the president. In terms of his communication, Obama came across as cavalier to voters as the health care debate grew more acrimonious.

Obama's posture to the GOP was basically, "I won this election and you didn't." Aided by huge majorities in both houses of Congress, he passed health care reform, reforms to curb what he considered to be Wall Street excesses, anti-predatory credit card laws, and, with key Republican support, the new Strategic Arms Reduction Treaty (New START), which was signed in April 2010 and entered into force in February 2011.[15] He repealed Don't Ask, Don't Tell. One might challenge his philosophy—and few voters doubted that he had brought change. But in judging his strategic communication, as the smoke cleared from election battles most voters felt that he had failed to make a persuasive case for that change. In the 2010 midterm elections, they dealt Democrats a brutal setback.

Obama and the Democrats allowed Republicans and their allies to define him and them rather than defining themselves. That is always a recipe for political catastrophe. Republicans dubbed his health care reform "Obamacare." Labeling the legislation health care reform was misleading, they argued, calling it instead a poverty program to redistribute wealth. They branded him a socialist, charging that he was spending America into bankruptcy. Relentlessly, focused Republican strategic communication drew blood. Galvanized by conservatives who dubbed themselves members of the Tea Party, and supported by outside independent expenditure advertising, they talked about cleaning up Washington, controlling spending, and opposing new taxes. Only fifteen years before the nation had faced a $1.5 trillion nation debt, and that had seemed like a nightmare—now it was a multitrillion yearly budget deficit.

Obama and his supporters felt strongly that that they had done the right thing. They *believed*. Yet they mounted a feeble defense as Republicans unleashed unrelenting criticism. It felt as if Democrats had run from their own record. Whatever the flaws in the health care plan, key elements—notably on aspects of insurance reform—could have been used to mount a defense and go on the offense. There had been plenty of legislative achievements. Some Republicans disliked the new financial regulations in Obama's Dodd-Frank Wall Street Reform and Consumer Protection Act.[16] But the provisions aimed to correct problems that a Republican Congress had created in repealing Glass-Steagall. Democrats could have capitalized on what it meant, but instead they went punting. They allowed Tea Party Republicans to demonize them and barely fought back. The Democrats' 2010 midterm defeat represented a stunning failure by Obama and his political party of strategic communication. How could that have happened?

Partly, it was challenges that would have daunted any president. As Obama's team saw it, they had averted financial meltdown. One Obama insider recounted how Hank Paulson, Bush's Treasury secretary, was so rattled as the crisis deepened that he rushed to the bathroom and threw up. Critics blasted Paulson for allowing Lehman Brothers to fail, spurring a loss of confidence in financial markets and accelerating matters to a breaking point. Obama supporters believed that Bush bore responsibility for a catastrophe but had left it for Obama to deal with.

The merits of the argument lie elsewhere. Important here is that Obama failed to strategically communicate the conclusion that he had stabilized the nation's financial crisis. In the meantime, unemployment and the rising debt became top concerns. In 2010, many voters worried that the administration had failed to effectively address the problem. Was that an issue of leadership, or of strategic communication? It is a mixture. Leadership requires forging sound policies and then rousing popular enthusiasm and building political coalitions to support them. Successful political leadership requires skills in policy and communication.

Political fortunes shift. After the 2010 election, Obama temporarily gained surer footing before the debt crisis blew up in his face. He embraced a bipartisan tax compromise that won broad popular support. His rationale for exiting Iraq was that we needed to focus on fighting "the good war" in Afghanistan. On taking office, he found himself boxed in by that position. After much debate, he endorsed Gen. David Petraeus's approach, which is still tough going but at least making some military progress.

In early 2011 Yemen, Bahrain, Syria, and North Africa imploded politically. Obama's performance drew mixed reviews, hurt by a lack of clarity in his strategic communication. He may have been working the diplomatic front hard behind the scenes, but that point never came through well at any time. His ambivalence in stating national intention made him look passive. While Mubarak cratered, some advised Obama to help prop up America's longtime ally and went public with their views, angering Egyptians opposed to Mubarak and making many of them cynical about US policy.

Obama quickly realized that Egyptians were fed up with a repressive regime that choked off democracy and failed to provide good governance. His instincts proved correct as he sided with those demonstrating in the streets for freedom. Even then, his communication failed to present him as a strong leader in clear, forceful, persuasive visual or verbal vocabulary. The issue is not what was on his mind or what transpired in private discussions, but rather the image Obama conveyed in public through his strategic communication. Even in coming down on the side of democracy, that communication was flawed in its lack of clarity.

Support for democracy in Egypt was also contradicted by US support for the monarchy in Bahrain, which plays host to the US Fifth Fleet and is under the protection of Saudi Arabia. Unrest in Bahrain was driven by protests from Shiites, who feel mistreated as second-class citizens. The United States turned mostly a deaf ear to these uprisings. Clearly, the administration felt that American strategic interests mandated standing with the monarchy and Saudi Arabia. Unfortunately, that placed the administration in the posture of looking hypocritical in support for democracy. Strategically, the administration found itself in a no-win situation.

Then Libya exploded. Steven Clemons, new editor-at-large of *The Atlantic*, offered a compelling argument that behind the scenes Obama moved at warp speed to make things happen while managing crises in Egypt, Syria, Yemen, and the Japanese nuclear disaster.[17] His critics lambasted him for holding back, as President Muammar Gaddafi unleashed paid mercenaries to shoot down his own countrymen.[18] It took prodding by French and British leaders and his Secretary of State, Hillary Clinton—perhaps haunted by the failure of her husband to heed her counsel to intervene in Rwanda, where genocide could have been prevented—before the United States supported a United Nations Security Council Resolution to stop Gaddafi from slaughtering Libyans who rose up against his dictatorship.[19]

Whatever posture a head of state adopts publicly, public hesitation can drain credibility—fast. Obama found himself buffeted by pressure from all sides. Unflappability can be seen as strength, but it can easily convey an impression of disengagement or indecisive leadership. The day after the UN acted, he finally showed passion as he warned Gadhafi against committing "atrocities against his people."[20] Others had advised that if he opposed intervention, he could at least target strong communication at the Libyan strongman, his commanders, soldiers, and security forces and warn that they would be held fully accountable and responsible for war crimes against civilians. Indeed, the UN had already referred the matter to the International Criminal Court, and its chief prosecutor, Luis Moreno-Ocampo, had opened an investigation of the Libyan crisis. Obama's delay in publicly expressing himself clearly, forcibly, and consistently drew fire from almost all quarters. First criticized on the right for failing to act, his left flank worried that he was propelling the United States into another foreign war without giving the issue sufficient foresight.

The fact is, Obama had trouble managing his strategic communication for the Libyan narratives. A positive narrative of people rising up to throw out a tyrant dissolved into one about whether the United States was right or wrong, succeeding or failing, in intervening in the internal affairs of another Arab regime. Within two weeks, Libyan rebels were complaining to CNN journalist Anderson Cooper that a paucity of air strikes might be a conspiracy by the West to kill rebels, perhaps in exchange for a deal for Libyan oil.

Ultimately, aided by strong NATO military support, the opposition toppled Gaddafi. That has created the opportunity to articulate a new narrative in which the West is seen as fighting alongside Muslims in supporting, not leading, a quest by Muslims for democratic government. Achieving that may have lasting consequences for how the West is perceived in North Africa and the

Middle East as increasing numbers of citizens in those countries rise up against political systems dominated by repression, patronage, corruption, and lack of hope or opportunity.

Comparing Obama's skills at strategic communication to those of world-class pros like Ronald Reagan and Bill Clinton is enlightening. Famously known as "the great communicator," Reagan was a former movie star and accomplished speaker who more than lived up to his billing. He could play to most audiences, although some Europeans remained skeptical, especially during his first term. He had a common touch. He could be eloquent or earthy, whatever the occasion called for.

Consider Reagan's concise eulogy for the *Challenger* astronauts delivered from the Oval Office.[21] Beautifully written by Peggy Noonan, it captured the heartfelt anguish of a nation while celebrating the heroism of the fallen. He spoke *for* Americans, not *to* them. He expressed what Americans felt. It is a remarkable example of powerful strategic communication in that he was able to express compassion and strength as well as a firm resolution to stay focused on the future even in the face of tragedy. It was nothing less than a testament to the American identity.

Reagan's critics sold him short. This president knew who he was. Politically, he stuck to espousing his core agenda: defeat Communism, reduce the size of government, lower taxes. He did it with grace and style, qualities notably apparent when John Hinckley tried to assassinate him. He projected confidence and optimism—and his strategic communication, led by himself as chief communicator, made the nation more confident and optimistic, despite the fact that during his first term the nation experienced an economic recession.

Broadcast commentator and former House Speaker Tip O'Neill adviser Chris Matthews has wisely observed that Americans like leaders who keep the sun in their faces and the wind at their backs.[22] Reagan's communication projected that image. It translated into political leverage, as his legislative team toiled behind the scenes to identify and mobilize grassroots efforts to influence senators and congressmen to support his proposals.

Bill Clinton was a formidable intellectual who had high touch. Many view him as a force of nature. One GOP leader remarked privately that in Oval Office meetings, Clinton was so persuasive you had to pinch yourself to snap out of the spells he wove. He handled himself with equal dexterity one-on-one and before larger audiences. Like Reagan, he could explain big issues in plain language. After the Oklahoma City bombing, for example, he showed a strong ability to muster the words to inspire a grief-stricken, shocked nation.

Only time will tell whether Obama measures up as a communicator to Reagan or Clinton. It's worth recalling that support for those presidents varied throughout their terms: Reagan faced a liberal Democratic Congress whose views often collided with his, especially during his second term, whereas Clinton was doing fine until the Monica Lewinsky scandal broke. After suffering devastating losses in 2004 comparable to those inflicted on Obama in 2010, Clinton shifted gears. He adopted a brilliant strategy devised by his imaginative, innovative political counselor Dick Morris and top-notch pollster and strategist Doug Schoen. Playing off against the right and the left in politics toward the center, they called it triangulation. It annoyed many liberal Democrats, but it also enabled Clinton to get things done and win an overwhelming reelection.

Reagan and Clinton put strategic communication to work for them. Each was a gifted horse-trader. They focused on a goal and fought tenaciously for it. Their teams understood and effectively used social network mobilization—a category in which Obama's team surprisingly lags. Reagan and Clinton used the bully pulpit to their advantage. Each displayed a disarming sense of humor about themselves and issues. Obama may be amusing and good-natured in private; he delivers set lines at a Gridiron dinner with excellent timing that draws laughs. In 2011, his put-downs of Donald Trump at the White House Correspondents dinner were funny and exposed Trump as a man who liked to throw punches but took them with ill-humor. Still, spontaneous, self-deprecating humor or wit rarely graces Obama's public appearances.

Events enabled his strategic communication to provide a uniquely powerful boost in May 2011 as US Navy Seals launched a successful assault that killed Osama bin Laden in Bilal Town, northeast of Abbottabad, Pakistan.[23] The White House skillfully focused media attention on its narrative of the presidential decision-making process. The narrative acknowledged that there had been some differences in view on whether to proceed with the mission, and some have suggested that at least one key political adviser worried about the consequences of failure.

The White House narrative projected a tough, disciplined president who carefully weighed competing arguments, assessed the options, and concurred with his national security team about taking the risks inherent in the mission. The decision to assassinate bin Laden was gutsy, and the risks were real. No one was certain whether bin Laden was inside the compound. Equally, the narrative communicated the message that Obama had proven savvy in rebuffing prodding by the Taliban and others to release unsightly photographs of a slain bin Laden that al-Qaeda and its allies could use to inflame and recruit.[24]

An unspoken but dramatic distinction between Obama's decision making and that of President Jimmy Carter also emerges from the narrative. The White House stressed that Obama insisted that US forces had every resource needed to succeed, along with his own resolve. By contrast, Carter's failure in 1980 to ask the right questions before giving the go-ahead for Operation Eagle Claw to rescue the Tehran hostages tragically resulted in avoidable failure.[25] Eagle Claw planning contemplated the use of six helicopters to fly into Tehran. Eight Sea Stallions were assigned to the mission. Two never reached the rendezvous point outside the city, code-named Desert One. One helicopter was forced down about an hour and a half into the mission due to rotorblade problems, and the very fine sand through which the helicopters had to travel forced another to return to an aircraft carrier with directional gyro failure.

Six helicopters did reach Desert One, where they met up with several C-130 Hercules transports for refueling. After landing, hydraulic system failure rendered a third helicopter inoperable, leaving only five to complete the operation.[26] At the White House, leaders debated whether to proceed. They accepted the ground commander's recommendation to abort. LTA Chua Lu Fong's examination of the decision making for Eagle Claw concluded that "the finalized plan of the mission impressed upon everyone that six was the absolute minimum." Apparently the mission commander, Colonel Charles Beckwith, took exception to a White House message asking the ground commanders to reconsider and proceed using five helicopters. Fong supports Beckwith's recommendation to stand down.[27]

By all accounts, Beckwith was a tough, smart, courageous, outstanding officer. This book intends no criticism of a fine soldier. But two points stand out in comparing the decision making for Eagle Claw to that for the bin Laden assault. Marine Colonel (later Lt. Gen.) Charles Pitman conducted the final briefing for Eagle Claw to General David C. Jones, chairman of the Joint Chiefs. Jones then briefed the president on the evening before the operation was launched. Pitman pointed out later that while mission planning had called for six helicopters, in fact, five could probably have accomplished the mission (and had been planned as a possible alternative).[28] That point, however, was not disclosed to the president or to General Jones (it was an internal Delta option). Prior to the presidential briefing, General Jones had asked Pitman about the number of choppers required "to take all of the personnel and equipment to town." Pitman reconfirmed that six were planned, if all equipment and personnel were to go to town.

The problem Pitman had lay in the way Jones had phrased the question. Jones wanted to know how many helicopters were necessary to take all of the equipment to Tehran. The answer was six. This was similar to President Obama's statement to make everything necessary for success available. Pitman says, "While we had practiced to go minus equipment not absolutely necessary to accomplish the mission," he believes "we should have taken the increased risk," but makes clear that he could not fault anyone for sticking with the plan.[29] "As you know, we continued to plan for extraction, if necessary, up until the day the hostages came home."[30]

While Carter did not press on the issue of ensuring sufficient firepower and resources, it appears that Obama did. Media reports suggested that the initial planning to get bin Laden contemplated two choppers. Obama insisted on adding two more and that the force be large enough to fight its way out of Pakistan should it encounter hostile local troops or police interference.[31] The plan was to avoid confrontation if possible, but to return fire should it occur. Teams were on standby to bury bin Laden if killed and to interrogate him were he captured alive.[32] It is easy to say in the afterglow of success that Obama's decision was easy, and almost certainly, Americans would have supported any reasonable opportunity to get bin Laden. The diplomatic consequences to a failed operation were also considerable. As it was, despite secreting bin Laden—which many Americans considered a betrayal of trust between the two nations—some Pakistanis complained about breaches of its sovereignty through "an unauthorized unilateral action" that would not be tolerated in the future.[33] Still, other Pakistanis have leveled their fury at the hypocrisy of their own leaders in protecting bin Laden while stating that they were fighting al-Qaeda.[34]

The raid exposed raw realities in Pakistan–US relations. It embarrassed the Pakistani Army and Inter-Services Intelligence (ISI), whom many Pakistanis suddenly viewed as less powerful or competent than imagined. For the first time in memory, its leaders felt compelled to account for the performance of their organizations before a closed session of Parliament. General Lt. Gen. Shuja Pasha, director of ISI, defended the agency's record, arguing that it had paralyzed al-Qaeda before bin Laden's death by shattering its whole network. He nevertheless offered to resign.[35] Still, PML-N leader Nawaz Sharif, whose relations with the army have long been uneasy, issued an unprecedented demand for parliamentary review of the army and intelligence agency budgets.[36] In the meantime, Pakistan Army Chief of Staff Lt. Gen. Asfaq Parvez Kayani issued a stern public warning that Pakistan would not tolerate a repeat of that covert operation.[37]

Two critical glaring mistakes in White House strategic communication dimmed the success of the operation. Inaccurate details came out too quickly about what exactly had happened. Within 48 hours, the White House was forced to retreat from assertions that bin Laden had hidden behind a female shield, and acknowledged that he had been unarmed.[38] Reports were mired in an avoidable discussion over whether or not bin Laden had resisted. Americans overwhelmingly supported his elimination because he was the murderer of tens of thousands of innocent civilians. Taking him alive would have exposed Americans to severe threats of hostage taking and triggered draining legal debates over whether he should be tried by a federal court, a tribunal, or turned over to the International Court of Justice. None of that would have been productive.

Initial reports were not immediately clear as to who had been killed and who else was in the compound with bin Laden beside a son and the two slain couriers.[39] That error had to be corrected. Apparently, the SEAL team encountered him on the third floor. One of his wives rushed the commandos and was shot in the leg.[40] Bin Laden was shot twice, once by each of two SEALs. There were no bodyguards. Initial reports suggested a more intense firefight than actually may have occurred, but bin Laden was killed relatively early in the operation. SEALs spent at least half their time collecting laptops, hard drives, CDs, and paper files.[41]

The lesson for strategic communication is that first reports from chaotic battle situations are usually incomplete and often contain inaccuracies.[42] No matter the temptation or pressure, it's wiser to wait until the facts are received and action assessed to speak out. The White House made an avoidable mistake in speaking too quickly. The discrepancies hurt credibility abroad and with Muslims for whom bin Laden's popularity was diminishing, and whom we should otherwise attract.[43]

The second mistake was revealing operational details. Secretary of Defense Robert Gates expressed grave reservations about the postoperation disclosures. "Frankly a week ago Sunday, in the (White House) situation room, we all agreed that we would not release any operational details from the effort to take out bin Laden," Gates told an audience of marines. Pentagon press secretary Geoff Morell added: "Anonymous sources revealing secret information about the tactics, training and equipment of covert forces put at risk our ability to successfully mount similar missions in the future."[44]

At this writing, just over a year after the attack, the longer-term political impact of the attack on Obama's political fortunes remains to be seen. The president's re-election campaign has made the decision-making process and Obama's firmness in approving a risky operation in the face of divided opinion among his counselors a centerpiece of its argument that he has been a strong president. His opponents have denounced that, arguing that he is politicizing an operation that should remain nonpolitical and seizing too much credit that should be shared with the CIA, Navy SEALs, and former president George W. Bush. Given that the economy is likely to dominate the election, assessing the impact of this strategic communication is not easy. Both sides have been clear and forceful in asserting their cases.[45]

Muhammad Ali Jinnah and Pakistan's Founding

Muhammad Ali Jinnah (known as Quaid-I-Azam, or the Great Leader) and his allies employed smart strategic communication to establish Pakistan by invoking the notion of Islam as a broad notion to unite the people and forge a national identity. Scholar and former Pakistani diplomat Husain Haqqani notes that Jinnah used it "simply as a way of giving a semblance of unity and solidity to his divided Muslim constituents."[46] His leadership reflected uncommon strength of character and power of intellect. He operated in a chaotic political environment beset with raw emotion and rife with violence, and his success was rooted in his character and his skill in using communication.

Pakistan came into being after the Indian National Congress led by Mahatma Gandhi and Jawaharlal Nehru thumbed its nose at a British plea for support against the Japanese. The Muslim League answered the call, recruiting Punjabi and Indian Muslims.[47] After the war, Britain supported their demand for an independent state separate from India. Interestingly, historians like Ayesha Jalal point out that in Jinnah's mind, creating a wholly new nation was not the sole option. Jalal states: "Jinnah felt very strongly about achieving equal status for Muslims. He spoke of Islam, but it was an Islam that was in line with an enlightened, moderate view of Islam. You saw that partly in the way he dressed. His attire became an important symbol of Muslim identity, but it is vital to stress that for Jinnah, Islam was a matter of faith, not something that should be enshrined as state policy or made the basis of an Islamic Republic. He talked the language of Wilsonian democracy. His goal was to ensure that Muslims enjoyed equal treatment with the Hindu and anyone else. Indeed, the hard-core religious conservatives opposed both Jinnah and his Muslim League as too Westernized, too tolerant of other faiths, too moderate."[48]

India's governing Congress was cool to ideas of confederation that accorded a sovereign status to Muslims. Partition became inevitable. British Viceroy Lord Mountbatten of Burma proposed a plan that led to the creation of Pakistan on August 14, 1947. Years before, Choudhary Rahmat Ali had offered a name for the new nation in a 1933 pamphlet: "PAKISTAN—by which we mean the five Northern units of India, via.: *P*unjab, *N*orth-West Frontier Province (*A*fghan Province), *K*ashmir, *S*ind and Baluchi*stan*."[49]

Pakistani nationalists argued that the new Muslim homeland would be a progressive state, because Islam was a modern religion that "brought to perfection the religions of the modern, advanced, scientific West, Judaism and Christianity."[50] Their faith was further informed by notions of pride and honor that called upon individuals to lead honorable lives in accordance with religious and moral principles.[51]

Haqqani observes that Pakistan has been characterized from the first by a duality that stems from insecurity in identity amid perceived external threats from India. Jinnah and his Muslim League worked to establish unity and stability through strategic communication built around an Islamic identity. Jalal says that Jinnah "needed a demand that was specifically ambiguous and imprecise to command general support, something specifically Muslim though unspecific in every other respect. The intentionally obscure cry for a 'Pakistan' was contrived to meet this requirement."[52]

The tactics that Jinnah, the Muslim League, and their allies employed for strategic communication, Jalal says, "focused on speeches and statements published in newspapers, although they also used radio, leaflets, and pamphlets." But, she emphasizes, "One must understand the critical point that is too often obscured. The issue was what kind of Islam they were talking about. What did Islam mean? For Jinnah and his key allies, Islam did not mean going back to an improbable version of Islam that fulfilled somebody's notion of what life was like in the seventh century. That vision had little in common with the radical Salafist thinking that crept into Pakistani discourse about Islam after Zia ul-Haq seized power. His regime marked a significant point of departure, moving the discourse towards a very radical perspective."[53]

Jinnah's approach to strategic communication offers a striking parallel to Barack Obama's approach to themes and messages in 2008. Jinnah employed the notion of a moderate, enlightened Islam, whereas Obama invoked the notions of hope and change. In both cases, their rhetoric was broad. The studied ambiguity was masterful political communication. It enabled and encouraged individuals to fill an empty vessel with their own feelings, emotions, and ideas, while uniting supporters under a common banner. Both men displayed shrewd campaign leadership and outstanding strategic communication.

Jinnah and his allies also worked to calibrate feelings about Islam "so that it serves its nation-building function without de-stabilizing internal politics or relations with Western countries."[54] Haqqani points out that its military and intelligence establishment have developed a close alliance with religious leaders as part of a "strategic commitment to jihadi ideology."[55]

Jinnah's strategy was fraught with political danger. He recognized that he trod a narrow path. At heart stood the question of whether Pakistan was to be secular, and his success in achieving a desired political ambiguity at the time is affirmed by the sharp divisions that remain about whether he actually was a secularist.

Radical Islamists like Hamid Gul insist that Jinnah "wanted an Islamic state."[56] Rafiq Ahmed, the former vice chancellor at Punjab University, concurs: "The Quaid on many occasions had clearly and unambiguously stated that Pakistan would be an Islamic democratic State and Islam would be the ideology of Pakistan. He meant what he said and he said what he meant and he was never equivocal."[57]

Mubarak Ali, former chairman of history at Karachi University, agrees that Jinnah believed in a two-nation theory, but "he believed in using religion for public consumption to achieve his political ends. . . . And Jinnah used Islam as a motivating force to rally Muslims to the cause of Pakistan politically. But the state they aimed to create was to be secular, not a theocracy."[58] Hassan Askari Rizvi, former chairman of the political science department at Punjab University, agrees that Jinnah supported the two-nation theory. He believes that "Jinnah definitely was a secularist who viewed Islam as an instrument of identity formation and political mobilization for the Muslims of South Asia."[59] I. A. Rehman, director of the Human Rights Commission of Pakistan (HRCP), argues that Jinnah "said goodbye to the two-nation theory at the first opportunity," and "was a secularist given the fact that he always adopted a secular approach while dealing with constitutional and legal issues."[60] Imtiaz Alam, the secretary-general of the South Asia Free Media Association, and Rashid Rehman, former daily editor of *The Frontier Post*, also concur that Jinnah was a secularist.

What did Jinnah actually say? Most famously, on August 11, 1947, Jinnah proclaimed to Pakistan's Constituent Assembly: "You are free, free to go to your temples; you are free to go to your mosques or to any other places of worship in this state of Pakistan. You may belong to any religion or caste or creed that has nothing to do with the business of the state."[61]

Haqqani observes that later official accounts of Jinnah's life included "only an edited version of the speech. References to religion having no role in the business of the state were taken out."[62] Jinnah's pronouncements can be read both ways. Two months after the speech, he told civil, naval, military, and air force officers: "We should have a State in which we could live and breathe as free men and which we could develop according to our own lights and culture and where principles of Islamic social justice could find free play."[63] While promoting Islam, the speech makes clear that "we shall continue to protect the life and property of minorities in Pakistan." On February 21, 1948, he told officers of the 5th Heavy Ack Ack and 6th Light Ack Ack Regiments in Malir: "You have to stand guard over the development and maintenance of Islamic democracy, Islamic social justice, and the equality of your manhood in your own native soil."[64]

On the other hand, in February 1948, he declared: "In any case Pakistan is not going to be a theocratic state to be ruled by priests with a divine mission. We have many non-Muslims, Hindus, Christians, and Parsis—but they are all Pakistanis. They will enjoy the same rights and privileges as any other citizens and will play their rightful part in the affairs of Pakistan."[65] On June 14, 1948, he advised the Pakistani Military Staff College: "Never forget that you are the servants of the state. You do not make policy. It is we, the people's representatives, who decide how the country is to be run. Your job is to only obey the decisions of your civilian masters."[66]

Jinnah died in 1948, but his successors continued to invoke Islam as the key symbol for unity and did not flinch to use it constantly in education and propaganda to forge a national identity. It lay at the core of their strategic communication. The lesson to be drawn is that strategic communication rooted in an idea that is powerful enough can move a nation. Along with Urdu and hostility to India, Islam became a cornerstone, Haqqani concludes, of a new national ideology.[67]

Hugo Chavez's Bolivarian Revolution

"Watch every Sunday *Alo Presidente* ("Hello President") with President Hugo Chavez. There will be news, singing, jokes, and entertainment." The promo refers to the live, unscripted, seven-hour weekly television show that Chavez was broadcasting every week from different locations. His fight with cancer has limited his appearances, and at this writing whether he will survive is unclear. But his approach offers interesting lessons in effective strategic communication.

His show has enabled citizens to call and talk directly to their president. Usually wearing red, the color of Bolivarian revolution, and the beret he wore as a soldier, Chavez has broadcast from oil rigs, electrical plants, and a cattle farm. The show is unpredictable. He has used it to scold his mistress, praise Fidel Castro, and call President George W. Bush "Mr. Danger" or "a donkey."[68] In one famous incident, he ordered a general to send ten battalion of troops to the Colombia border after a Colombian bombing raid in Ecuador killed Colombian FARC guerilla leader Paul Reyes.[69]

He uses a portable air conditioner to keep him cool while promoting his social and political agenda. He calls upon quailing ministers—who are required to attend the show—and members of a live audience from the public (especially if they look sleepy), who often dress in red shirts or caps, and rails against the United States. He is a true showman. Journalist Jon Lee Anderson muses that Chavez has "a preacher's deftness with language and an actor's ability to evoke emotions. With a single soliloquy, he comes up with rhymes, breaks into song, riffs on his own words, gets angry, cracks jokes, loops back to where he started."[70]

The lesson that Chavez illustrates is that like any democratically elected leader, even a semi-authoritarian leader—for despite winning elections, that is what Chavez has become—needs to apply the principles of strategic communication to connect emotionally and intellectually with his supporters. Power cannot be taken for granted. Political figures have to work at keeping it, and figures like Chavez, who are natural populists, succeed best when their strategic communication communicates messages of caring, vision, strength, and effectiveness.

Chavez is well read, a passionate nationalist, and—though US policymakers and Venezuelan elites cringe at the notion—an idealist. He exploits cutting-edge technology to employ words, action, images, and symbols for strategic communication. He moved into the Twitter space with a bang. His account, @chavezcandanga, drew 50,000 followers within twenty-four hours of going live, 500,000 within a month, and these days depends upon a staff of two hundred to help him engage with his 1.2 million followers.[71] The use of the word *cadanga* (meaning "daring" or "rebellious") is typical for Chavez.

Chavez has employed every element of strategic communication to define his narrative, themes, and message that he's a man of the people who stands up for fighting corruption, eradicating class division, eliminating racial prejudice, and providing economic equality. He has donated his salary for scholarships, moved to clean up Venezuela's sordid prisons, and dispatched the army to help clean up the *barrios*.[72]

He was born in a mud hut, in the dust-choked village of Sabaneta in *los llanos*, a tropical grassland plan east of the Andes. His mother, Rosa, sold sugar-coated spiders to help make ends meet.[73] Admitted to the military academy, he developed a life-long devotion to Simon Bolivar and graduated near the top of his class. Venezuela is rich in resources, yet a vast gulf exists between the extraordinary wealth of a small elite and the majority of people, who live in abject poverty. Pervasive corruption has riddled the government. Indians have been treated as subhuman. Whether under military or civilian rule, none of the country's political leaders has ever showed much interest in bridging the gulf. Chavez resolved to effect the populist change he believed Bolivar had championed. That passion has enabled him to survive criticism that he has failed to deliver and merely replaced the old regime of corruption with a new one.[74] But his strategic narrative about himself and what he stands for has resonated. "The orality of the Llaneo," biographer Alberto Barrera points out, "is deeply rooted in his personality."[75]

Chavez burst onto the scene in 1992. President Carlos Andres Perez was a grand political warhorse whose free market policies had triggered mass protests against rising consumer prices. The government violently repressed them. Then an army lieutenant colonel, Chavez felt it was time to move. Despite his failure to bring the air force into his scheme, he launched a coup. It nearly succeeded. Perez's own strategic communication played a vital role. Narrowly escaping from his presidential palace, Perez got himself to a television station and broadcast statements that the situation was under control and that he would win. It helped convince Chavez that he was losing and led to his surrender.[76]

Hoping to minimize bloodshed, the army gave him 72 seconds to make a national broadcast to ask his confederates to lay down their arms. Here were two powerful lessons in strategic communication. Allowing Chavez free rein in his remarks was foolish, because it gave him control over the narrative of the coup. The government's interest lay in showing a disheveled, defeated dissident as part of a narrative that trumpeted the victory of democracy over renegade criminals in uniform. Foreign Affairs Minister Ochoa Antich recognized the blunder, noting to Chavez biographer and journalist Bart Jones that authorities let Chavez present himself as "a hero who had risen up against an unjust government that was corrupt."[77] Jones points out that Chavez recalled only too well how poorly Panamanian President Manuel Noriega looked after his capture by Americans: unshaven and wearing a wrinkled t-shirt, the very image of a defeated enemy.[78]

Chavez appeared in his uniform and red beret. He proceeded to wrest control of the narrative and delivered his famous *por ahora* ("for now") speech. He declared that "for now" the coup's objectives could not be obtained, and stated: "Before the country and before you, I accept responsibility for this Bolivarian military movement." Taking responsibility in politics was novel in Venezuela, and his remarks had an explosive impact. His aura of straight talk became— and remains—a hallmark of his strategic communication.

Released from prison by President Rafael Caldera in 1993, Chavez formed the Fifth Republic Movement in 1998. Wearing his red beret, he mounted a whirlwind come-from-behind campaign that clobbered the Yale-educated economist Henrique Salas Romer in a 56 to 40 percent landslide. In 2000, he won reelection, increasing his majority to nearly 60 percent, besting his estranged former political ally Francisco Arias Cardenas in a bitter campaign.[79] In 2006, he easily won a third term against Manuel Rosales.

After a decade in office, many voters find his game wearing thin. Still, Chavez is better at politics than governing: he's an excellent communicator. He speaks the language of the common man. He cracks jokes and sings songs that they relate to. Until his illness, his body language and irreverence communicated a joyous sense of his own individuality. Most Venezuelans are *mestizos*; less than a quarter are white, although for years Venezuela's leaders and its elite have been white. Their contempt for *chavistas* suggests racial overtones.[80] Most citizens are poor and live in shanty towns. Chavez not only talks but *looks like* most Venezuelans, so it is not surprising that many identify with him.

His actions drove a core narrative: He is a man of the people who fights to provide hope and opportunity for the poor; he stands up against imperialist domination by the "empire" (that is, the United States); and he champions the ideals of Simon Bolivar. His tweets are typically ebullient: "What impressive moments we have lived tonight!! We have seen the remains of the Great Bolívar! Our father who is in the earth, the water and the air. . . . You awake every hundred years when the people awaken. I confess that we have cried, we have sworn allegiance."[81]

Bolivar is central to his mindset, although the parallels are dubious. Acclaimed as "the Liberator," Bolivar was a nineteenth-century Venezuelan nationalist, abolitionist, and brilliant military commander who led Bolivia, Colombia, Peru, Ecuador, Panama, and Venezuela to independence from Spain. The patrician Bolivar dreamed of forging a great federation of Hispanic American Republics.[82] Bolivar admired Thomas Jefferson and refused unlimited powers when offered them by the 1825 Peruvian Congress in Lima. While his views on government differed somewhat from those espoused by James Madison, Benjamin Franklin, and Jefferson, he believed in democracy. The Marquis de Lafayette once sent him a gold medallion that praised him as "the Second Washington of the New World."[83] Bolivar may have been a democrat, but he harbored doubts about US influence in South America and was capable of exceptional cruelty. At one point he ordered 1,400 prisoners beheaded.[84]

Actions buttress Chavez's populist rhetoric. He created Bolivarian missions to eradicate illiteracy, improve housing, and establish health care through the construction of free medical clinics for the poor.[85] He formed over 100,000 worker-owned cooperatives. The state has lavished housing and food subsidies on the poor.[86]

While preaching Bolivar, Chavez's approach to strategic communication borrows from Napoleon. Napoleon, as we have seen, saw himself as a character in a novel, ever unfolding and developing. Chavez has been, in biographer Barrera's words, "a myth under construction" who is "writing his biography every day."[87] Like Napoleon, Chavez has aimed to connect himself to symbolic images that evoke patriotism and the idea of a man of destiny. Even in sickness, he has projected the image of a resolute leader who will let no obstacle defeat him.

Chavez has shown the same attitude toward the press. Napoleon wrote articles for newspapers. Chavez prefers to talk on television and the radio. Napoleon famously said that four hostile newspapers are more to be feared than a thousand bayonets—a sentiment to which Chavez would nod vigorously. Like Bonaparte (and for that matter, Vladimir Putin), Chavez shuts down hostile news outlets, encourages self-censorship, intimidates the media, and sponsors friendly outlets.[88] The philosophy recalls another Napoleonic dictate that men are moved by two levers only: fear and self-interest. Until the 2002 coup against him, Venezuela had a relatively free press that was highly critical of Chavez. The failed coup—embraced by the United States—seemed to sharply increase his suspicions about his opponents and his hostility toward the United States. From his viewpoint he had won power through a fair election, and for his opponents to oust him in a coup was outrageous.

Napoleon ruled by decree. Chavez passed the Law of Social Responsibility in Radio and Television, banning messages in the media or over the Internet that "disrespect public authorities" or are aimed at creating "anxiety" in the population.[89] Its impact is felt. Bart Jones points out that the major media was owned by very rich elitists who did everything they could to discredit Chavez.[90] Naturally, he reacted. Venevision used to regularly blast Chavez; today, people refer to it as the Disney Channel. It airs cartoons and canceled a morning show critical of Chavez.[91] Chavez also revoked the license of Radio Caracas Television. Newspapers in Venezuela are private but dependent upon government advertising, so they self-censor.[92] Television and radio stations must clear free broadcast time for Chavez speeches and government advertising.[93] The government uses chains—a practice requiring stations to cede time to government transmissions that chain themselves to broadcast signals. These eat up time and enable Chavez to dominate the media space.

There are pro-government publications and websites. In 2005 he established TeleSUR as a Latin al-Jazeera to compete with CNN en Espanol. He set up a state-funded movie studio, Villa del Cine, that has drawn Hollywood luminaries such as Oliver Stone, Sean Penn, Danny Glover, and Kevin Spacey for wining, dining, and salutations, affirming that in the movie business, it's still money that talks. These actions communicate a clear message that Chavez is in control and that challenging him is difficult or dangerous. Napoleon would recognize the tried-and-true approach of controlling news coverage through ownership.

In the Middle East, the Saudis are not so different, also ensuring favorable coverage by owning news media. The Al-Saud family owns the *Al-Arabiya* satellite television, as well as major pan-Arab newspapers like *Al-Hayat* and *Al-Sharq Al-Awsat*, even though they are edited in London. *Al Jazeera* has evolved into a hard-hitting, professional bastion of broadcast journalism, but you won't see it attack the Emir of Qatar.

Of course, comparisons are dangerous. Napoleon's hubris caused ruinous warfare in Europe and altered the rules of conflict into the modern era of total war, real but dubious achievements.[94] But he transformed France and left a legacy that two centuries later is revered. He established the Napoleonic code that has served as a model for the civil legal system of many nations (and in the United States, of Louisiana). He introduced the metric system. He invented the ambulance service. He inspired the Empire style and promoted major neoclassicists such as Ingres and Jacques-Louis David. He abolished draconian laws that limited the freedom of Jews. His propaganda spread French revolutionary ideas such as democracy and equality, and he restored order to France by stabilizing its economy. He established the system of Grand Ecoles that still educate the French political and economic elites.

Chavez seems likely to bequeath a darker legacy. Rising oil prices have provided him with around $700 billion. He is compelling and entertaining, but critics contend that his record in governing is dismal. The poor in the country remain poor. Yet $50 billion has been given in gifts to other nations in pursuit of empty, grandiose strategic schemes. Inflation hovers at around 30 percent, eroding real household incomes. Rampant murders, kidnappings, and robberies plague neighborhoods.[95] Indeed, Venezuela's crime problem in many ways is as significant as Mexico's, and Chavez has drawn poor marks for his handling of the crisis.[96] Food prices have soared.[97] *The Economist Intelligence Unit* forecasts a poor growth outlook for 2011–15, and concludes that rising government subsidies and transfers won't do much to boost private consumption.[98]

The September 2010 elections for Parliament should have sounded alarms among *chavistas*. Gerrymandering that favored pro-Chavez rural districts helped Chavez's Partido Socialista unido de Venezuela (PSUV) win a majority of 94 out of the 165 seats in the National Assembly.[99] But that was no cause for celebration, as his party lost its two-thirds supermajority needed to make key appointments and reform laws. Ominously, it garnered less than a majority of the total votes cast. With his popularity hovering at about 50 percent, and the opposition divided by internal conflicts, Chavez faces new challenges.[100]

In mid-2011, it was revealed that he suffered from an aggressive cancer, metastatic rhabdomyosarcoma. At this writing, former CBS *Evening News* anchor and longtime journalist Dan Rather has reported that the cancer is terminal and that Chavez is unlikely to survive to the October 7, 2012, election.[101] His death would throw the election outcome into doubt. His forces may try to strong-arm the result through intimidation or election fraud. Still, a key lesson that Chavez's performance teaches is that even adroit strategic communication is often no more effective than the record that a leader amasses in winning popular support.

CHAPTER 10

The Marks of Leadership

Wᴴᴬᵀ ᴅᴏ ᴡᴇ ᴋɴᴏᴡ ᴀʙᴏᴜᴛ ʜᴏᴡ sᴛʀᴀᴛᴇɢɪᴄ ᴄᴏᴍᴍᴜɴɪᴄᴀᴛɪᴏɴ ᴀꜰꜰᴇᴄᴛs ᴛʜᴇ credibility of leaders? In politics, the renowned pollster Richard Wirthlin propounded six criteria that people use in evaluating.

Honesty and Sincerity

Do people like political figures and trust them? In polling, questions about whether people have a favorable or unfavorable opinion about a candidate, party, or organization shed light on this question. Ronald Reagan survived the Iran–Contra scandal because people liked him and believed he was honest and sincere. Bill Clinton got through the Monica Lewinsky debacle because enough voters felt the same way about him. The consideration helped George W. Bush defeat John Kerry in 2004 as well. Whether one agreed with Bush, few doubted that he was sincere about what he was saying.

Do authoritarians care what people think? Yes. They have a thirst to be admired—and, indeed, loved. It is a key element in the eternal quest of authoritarians for legitimacy, and images of dictators as benevolent, protective, and loving patriarchs feature heavily in the propaganda of political monsters from Hitler to Stalin and Mao to Idi Amin.

Track Record of Success

Politicians have a tendency to fall into the trap of believing that voters are happy to reward them with a new office for having done a good job in the past. Actually, the old adage "what have you done for me lately?" is closer to the truth. A track record has one major utility and voters look at track records closely in rendering judgments in this dimension: It can offer proof that a leader can and will deliver on commitments.

Vision for the Future

Vision is what matters most to people. People are motivated by their hopes, fears, and desires. Hope is a function of optimism. Fear is a function of pessimism. Desire relates to both—what they want, and what they want to avoid. Political consultant John Maddox suggests that "desire is really about greed."[1] In politics, it's about showing a target audience where you are, where you want to lead them, how you will get them there, and what it means in terms of satisfying their hopes and dreams while reassuring them about their fears.

American politics offers a telling example. Dick Wirthlin once recounted that during the 1984 presidential campaign, a debate ensued within President Reagan's camp on how to win the election. Astute strategists on each side raised compelling arguments for competing strategies. One camp argued that Reagan should run on his record of success. As president, Jimmy Carter had eroded confidence in the strength of the Oval Office as an institution. Reagan had revitalized confidence and proven that a president can get things done. In their view, that provided a persuasive, credible rationale to support reelection. Wirthlin argued that voters would decide whether to reelect Reagan based upon their assessment of what his first-term achievements meant to them for the future, disagreeing that a track-record rationale would inevitably prevail at the polls.

Wirthlin's view prevailed. It was well manifested in the "Morning in America" television ad. The ad featured powerful images of children raising flags, young men and women on their wedding day, hard-hatted men getting back to work, and people looking vigorous and optimistic. An announcer intoned: "It's morning again in America." The message: President Reagan's leadership had renewed national vitality and provided fresh opportunities for individuals and families to realize their hopes and dreams. It worked as designed. The major theme posed the question: Why would we would ever want to return to past failures?

The precept of looking to the future also applies to other political cultures. Smart political leaders grasp that. The issue goes to the core about what their leadership means to people.

Strength and Integrity

George Bush's 2004 reelection seemed uncertain. A well-conceived campaign led by uber-consultant Karl Rove—a great political strategist—was rooted in the notion that the president was passionate in his convictions and believed in what he was doing. Reagan's political revival after the Iran–Contra scandal owed much to revamping his team and bringing in wise men like former Senator Howard Baker, but just as much to voters' conviction that Reagan was a leader of personal strength and integrity. Franklin Roosevelt and Charles De Gaulle capitalized on similar sentiments while leading their nations through the Great Depression, World War II, and the Algerian civil war, respectively.

Echoing the Values of Those You Represent

This trait is manifest in the agenda a political leader pursues and how it is acted upon. Even knowledgeable people are not usually watching what politicians do every day; they look at broad strokes or specific issues or actions from which they extrapolate larger judgments. People pose basic questions about political leaders: Are they with us or against us? Are they good or bad? Are they one of us or not?

Theodore Roosevelt showed that identifying oneself with values that voters felt strongly about provided a powerful means of ascent in domestic politics. Born to one of the wealthiest families in America, the Harvard-educated New Yorker knew that the path to success lay in portraying himself as a masculine populist. He was a genius at the use of strategic communication to forge that image. In *Imperial Cruise*, a tough-minded reassessment of Roosevelt, historian James Bradley (who also wrote *Flags of Our Fathers*) writes that Roosevelt never allowed himself to be photographed in whites playing tennis. Instead, the press was channeled into photographing him on a horse. Roosevelt presented himself as a frontiersman—although, as Bradley observes, his "frontier life was more soft blankets than barbed wire." Holding a rifle, he posed on artificial grass in a buckskin costume against a painted background. By using this ranchman myth, he ran (unsuccessfully) for mayor of New York as the "Cowboy of the Dakotas." Later, as a Rough Rider in the charge up San Juan Hill, he wore a tailored outfit designed by Brooks Brothers.[2] It worked splendidly for Roosevelt's political career—and in shaping his image for future generations.

Issues can be treacherous to use as yardsticks, because on difficult issues people often stand on both sides of it. In Pakistan, for example, opinion polling demonstrates that citizens as a whole oppose violent extremism, and yet the country was willing to host Osama bin Laden. The attacks that have taken the lives of innocent civilians have intensified that feeling. Yet Pakistanis draw lines as to how they are willing to counter extremists. They are not keen to fight them at the expense of allowing Washington to take action that in their view violates national sovereignty or could, as they see it, open the way to seizure of Pakistan's nuclear weaponry.

In 2011, the US attack on bin Laden's home in the garrison city of Abbottabad, deep inside the borders of the nation, ignited the fury of

Pakistanis. A Pew Global Attitudes Poll found that 63 percent of respondents disapproved of the operation and 55 percent said it was a "bad thing" that the terrorist leader was dead.[3] One should be careful about reading poll data too literally, however. What many were expressing was frustration and anger over the belief that the United States had wrongly violated Pakistani sovereignty. Many Pakistanis felt that the attack placed their military and the elected civilian government in an untenable situation. If they knew about bin Laden's presence, they were complicit. If not, they were incompetent. The Pakistani military seethed with embarrassment as people complained that it was incapable of protecting the nation's borders. When a NATO airstrike in November killed twenty-four Pakistani soldiers, relationships sank to a new low amid suspicions—apparently unfounded but widely discussed and accepted as true in a political culture that breeds conspiracy theory—that the military might stage a coup.[4] At this writing it appears that the military would like to oust President Asif Ali Zardari, whom it views as too pro-American, but, illustrating the complications of politics, fostering such outcomes brings institutions into conflict. Zardari's People's Party has a viable working relationship with the military, which has all the power it needs in areas that interest it, and there is no really viable successor to Zardari. Causing the government to fall is problematic. Zardari's chief rival for power remains Nawaz Sharif, who has an uneasy relationship with the military. The potential new player—currently the most popular political figure in Pakistan, Imran Khan—could emerge to shake up the existing dynamics, but he lacks the political organization necessary to win election as prime minister or president in the country's indirect system of choosing the occupants of both posts.

Many Pakistanis have been willing to challenge religious extremism. Still, most show great sensitivity to issues generated by that nation's harsh blasphemy law. Pakistan's government has been willing to challenge violent Islamists who would like to topple the government and replace it with one that espouses their radical interpretation of Islam. They have shied away from the blasphemy issue, recognizing that attitudes in support of it are firm and that challenging the current law puts their own lives at risk—as the assassinated governor of the Punjab, Salman Taseer, found out.

Other issues can become litmus tests. In the United States, the issues of abortion and same-sex marriage have become windows through which competing sides render judgments as to where politicians stand. In many parts of the Middle East, aligning oneself with Washington can produce pretty much the same impact.

Caring

"I care," say many politicians—as voters yawn or change the channel. In politics, communicating the message that leaders care is about showing that they listen. Actually, no matter the system, they *do* listen, and pretty carefully, although sometimes with the purpose of figuring out who to repress and how to conduct repression most efficiently. But as we've seen in the examples of Burma, Iran, North Korea, and Saudi Arabia, even authoritarian regimes care what their populace thinks and use strategic communication to secure approval. The effort can prove feeble, and failure to secure it will not necessarily effect a change in policy. This is a factor in how people evaluate the credibility of political leaders. No matter the culture, people want to know that their political leaders care, and a core challenge for strategic communication in building or maintaining credibility is to devise narratives, themes, and messages that register that point with target audiences.

CHAPTER 11

Campaigns of Influence

Autocrats may play by different rules than Americans, but their campaigns of influence reveal much about what they believe is important in strategic communication to establish and maintain legitimacy. Princeton scholar Sophie Meunier identifies core objectives for successful information campaigns. In politics, strategic communication seeks "to cement popular identity; rally the populace to gain and consolidate support; scapegoat enemies who impose a failed policy or impede a successful one; and maintain a position of power."[1] It is the means through which one articulates a narrative that defines a credible rationale for a cause, candidacy, or action.

For the military, strategic communication is central in forging information strategies that (1) attack and defeat an adversary's will, (2) influence adversary decision making by persuading them that the price of victory exceeds any benefit, and (3) focus on target audience centers of gravity—decision makers, influential people, and populations—in an area of operations as well as among existing and potential allies.[2]

The military is trained for warfare—what it terms "kinetic operations." But many current and future conflicts require new thinking that moves beyond traditional military action.[3] The centers of gravity have changed, and the role of information strategy has evolved. Those involved in military operations must acquire a clear understanding of the applicable communications strategy to a given operation, although it is only one element of the design. Each person has a role to play in explaining why we are there and how we operate. Information strategies must be fully integrated on an equal basis within kinetic strategies and tactics. Information strategy is about framing issues, defining the stakes, and molding, shaping, and influencing the attitudes and opinions of target audiences to affect their behavior.

CIA director David Petraeus has long argued that the prize in current and future conflicts is increasingly the will, control, and loyalty of populations rather than a tactical military victory or the death of terrorists or insurgents.[4] His approach echoes that of Mao Zedong, who argued that unconditional support of the population is as essential to the combatant as water is to fish. It was critical to the thinking of Roger Trinquier, who viewed revolutionary war as a contest for the political mobilization of a normally inert populace, as well as that of counterinsurgency (COIN) expert Daniel Galula, whose ideas influenced the military's current thinking on counterinsurgency.[5]

Core Precepts That Govern Campaigns of Influence

Successful outcomes for information strategies and strategic communication that comprise a campaign of influence must respect core precepts:

1. Define winning campaign objectives. What is the picture of success?
2. Identify and test the assumptions that make winning the objective plausible, after developing a strategic appreciation of the considerations that make the assumptions relevant.
3. Forge a strategy that enables victory. Strategy prescribes the conditions for achieving objectives (or, for the military, a desired endstate). Strategy may integrate military, political, economic, and diplomatic action.
4. Create a concept of design through which strategy is translated into cohesive, actionable tactics and operations that make the strategy plausible to implement. T. E. Lawrence defined tactics as "the means toward the strategic end, the steps of its staircase."[6]
5. Use strategy and design to properly position a campaign by framing the issues and players, creating a message that resonates, and defining the stakes.
6. Identify and mobilize credible messengers.
7. Identify credible channels of communication.
8. Anticipate responses to messages.
9. Provide effective rebuttals to adversarial responses.
10. Identify metrics to evaluate success or failure.
11. Identify the information baseline from which to measure success or failure.

Centers of Gravity

Any campaign of strategic communication—whether targeted directly against a government, a political group, a conventional or unconventional military force, or a population—should influence centers of gravity. Centers vary depending upon the objectives. There is no formula. Examples of centers of gravity follow.

The Opponent's Will and Its Decision Making

The center of gravity for an enemy in a military situation is whatever enables it to keep on fighting—its *will* and *decision making*. That precept is at least as old as Genghis Khan.[7] In a military situation subverting, undercutting, and destroying the will of an enemy to fight or resist is fundamental.

Will of the Populace

The will of the populace affects its loyalty and support. Influence campaigns that affect whole populations should treat decision makers and influential people— who influence a broader public—as key centers, but the population itself is also a target of influence. The Egyptian military's well-calculated action in clarifying that Mubarak was finished sent a clear signal to the Egyptians who were demonstrating for the president's ouster. Winston Churchill's renowned defiance of the Nazis aroused the will of the British to fight. John F. Kennedy's speech in Berlin was directed at Germans and Americans as well as a global audience, and communicated American resolve to support freedom from oppression.

The shock and awe tactics employed against Saddam Hussein in Iraq aimed to undermine the morale and the will to fight among Saddam's army and regime supporters, as well as the general population. Bin Laden's attack on the United States on September 11, 2001, was directed at the American people, whom he hoped to persuade to force their government to change its policies. Hugo Chavez uses *Alo Presidente* to shore up popular will to back him. In 2008, an obscure individual, Oscar Morales, used Facebook to ignite a million-man march against the Marxist guerilla group FARC. It galvanized the national will and reversed public opinion. Prior to the march, Colombians had faulted the government for failure to prevent kidnappings. Afterward, people rallied behind the government and blamed FARC. The bombing campaign against civilians in Germany during World War II, such as the Dresden bombing, aimed to undercut civilian morale and their will to support the Nazis, and sent a message that civilians would not be spared.

Will of a Government or Party

A target audience may consist of a single government, an individual, or a small group. The mass demonstrations in Cairo were directed against Mubarak, his government, and his army. Other demonstrations that broke out across the Middle East in 2011 were directed toward elites and public officials. As Operation Iraqi Freedom prepared to launch in 2003, efforts to undercut Saddam were targeted at his flag officers. Benazir Bhutto's strategic communication as she prepared to return home to Pakistan in 2007 was aimed at convincing President Pervez Musharraf that he had no choice but to reach an agreement with her, given her popularity and the political strength of the Pakistan People's Party. The British show of strength in Sierra Leone was directed at a powerful but relatively small group of political criminals who were brutalizing the population.

External Decision Makers and Influential People Who Represent the Population of Existing and Potential Coalition Partners

NATO's proactive presence in Afghanistan requires support among European publics. So far they have not sustained that, and it's not clear what the midterm and long-term effects will be. President Obama faced a difficult decision with Afghanistan. Although he backed Gen. Stanley McChrystal and later Gen. David Petraeus, politically he still has to forge a base of popular support from American voters for his decision. Israel's failure to manage media coverage of its actions in Jenin undercut support abroad and damaged Israeli credibility. An even bigger mistake was its mismanagement of the Mavi Mara affair in the summer of 2010, in which Israel intercepted and attacked a ship it contended was bearing weapons and killed twenty people on board. The First Intifada conducted by Palestinians eschewed the use of weapons, neutralizing American opposition and complicating Israel's ability to counter the Intifada.[8] Conversely, action taken against Gadhafi in 2011 became politically possible for President Obama, Prime Minister David Cameron, and President Nicolas Sarkozy only when the Arab League and the United Nations Security Council gave their blessing.

The Will of Domestic Audiences

Authoritarian regimes don't always worry about what their people think about their actions.[9] The problem is that at a certain point, popular frustration can erupt and overthrow a government. North Korean leaders realize that, and it's a key reason they direct such intense strategic communication (i.e., propaganda) at their own people. The 2011 Middle East turmoil offered an apt illustration of what happens when frustrations boils over.

The Soviet Union collapsed for confluent reasons: a militarized command economy that drained more and more from the people, a geriatric leadership (until Gorbachev), the tremendous power of ethnic unrest, the lower price of oil and gas on the world market, and a system that could not keep up with the energy and innovation of free societies. A broken economy and unresponsive government finally alienated enough people, weakened institutions, and drained the will and the requirement to support the system.

The United States pulled out of Vietnam when popular will to support that war weakened sufficiently as to make continued participation politically impossible. Britain was forced to grant India its independence when the Indians showed no willingness to remain under British rule. Donald Rumsfeld has argued that the Iraqi surge had its greatest impact in strengthening the will of Americans to support efforts in that nation.

CHAPTER 12

Defining Winning or Losing

O<small>NE DEFINES WINNING OR A PICTURE OF SUCCESS AS A BENCHMARK FROM</small> which to measure progress and define victory. Metrics are determined by defining the strategic goal. The failure to define clearly what winning meant hampered initial US efforts in Iraq, and the same challenge has bedeviled efforts in Afghanistan. Although Muammar Gaddafi was finally overthrown in Libya, it posed a challenge for the efforts to protect civilian lives as NATO imposed a no-fly zone and launched strikes against Gaddafi's armor and artillery. The failure to define clear objectives helped arouse severe criticism of the US effort in Congress, whose members eventually objected to US participation by executive order as a violation of the War Powers Act. Had the conflict continued, it's entirely plausible that Congress would have cut off funding.

The benchmark for winning can be objective—for example, passing a constitutional amendment or changing a government policy.[1] Moroccan demonstrations in 2011 prompted King Mohammed VI to announce constitutional reforms that include a democratically elected prime minister. He has promised a popular referendum on the reforms to be recommended by a new commission. How the government works out the balance of power between the autocratic king and an elected parliament that holds little power may determine Morocco's political stability. Currently, the constitution enshrines the king as the "defender of the faith" (Islam) and, though modern in style, he wields authoritarian power.[2] Youth movements are demanding real reform.

Winning can be about an election, where the prize is power and legitimacy. In Pakistan, former President Pervez Musharraf and former Prime Minister Benazir Bhutto needed each other as they sought new terms for each office. Musharraf's failure to comprehend that led to his failure to provide adequate security, and to Bhutto's assassination. It came as something of a surprise to him that her death cost him his political career. In 2002, Musharraf had staged a referendum to extend his rule for five years. Officially he garnered 97.7 percent of the votes cast with over a 50 percent turnout, but critics charged fraud.[3]

Musharraf would have won any honest count. Instead, though popular, he squandered an opportunity to establish legitimacy. He wound up isolated and unpopular even before Bhutto's murder. His successor, Asif Ali Zardari, has struggled as president, but no one questions his legitimacy. He won an honest election and his party's strategic communication focused on positioning it and him as the standard-bearers of democracy.

Winning can be about preventing action—for example, deterrence. During the Cuban Missile Crisis, John F. Kennedy established a naval quarantine that signaled to the Soviet Union that the United States would not tolerate nuclear missiles being placed ninety miles from American shores. That produced an objective result: The Soviet Union removed its missiles from Cuba and sent no new nuclear weapons. The United States removed Jupiter missiles based in Turkey as a secret quid pro quo. Leaders from both nations strategically communicated the desire to avert war. The Cold War regime of mutual assured destruction was rooted in clear messages that produced an objective result: Attack by either would be mutually catastrophic.

The 30,000 US troops stationed in South Korea will not impede a North Korean invasion. Their presence is strategic communication, sending the message that such action would trigger conflict with the United States. There is debate as to whether the same end could be achieved by less costly means, but the deterrence effect seems clear.

The formation of the North Atlantic Treaty Organization (NATO) was an act of self-defense and deterrence. Did that intimidate the Soviet Union? Was it too weak to act, or did it simply have no intention of acting? The answer may be one or more of these factors. Certainly, it prompted the Soviet Union to form the Warsaw Pact. The point is that NATO provided strong deterrence and assured stable relations between East and West in Europe. The collapse of the Soviet Union has changed the equation, and NATO has adapted by evolving a new picture of success, pledging to protect the "freedom and security of all its members by political or military means."[4]

This new strategic concept contemplates broad and evolving challenges that may exist outside the borders of NATO members. "What it suggests," says Col. Stephen Padgett, who serves in strategic plans and policy at NATO's Allied Command Transformation Headquarters, "is that while a picture of success today for NATO may seem less obvious than before, NATO's cohesive commitment to collective security, including in the face of emerging threats and challenges, is a real indication of military, political, and diplomatic success. NATO can act but its readiness to do so communicates strategically, can have a deterrent effect and make its members more secure."[5]

Airport security measures have strategically communicated a message of deterrence to potential hijackers. It has not been foolproof and the success is not easily quantifiable. Excellent security and police work have thwarted some efforts—but one can reasonably presume that absent such security, there would have been additional efforts. A picture of success can be subjective. It can merely describe a set of conditions that define a desired end-state that will inevitably change, for in politics, nothing is ever settled. This notion underlies the US military's doctrine of operational design, for which strategic communication is integral.

Does the Nature of the Regime Matter?

Scholars Williamson Murray and Mark Grimsley argue that the nature of the regime affects its ability to define winning. Regime ideology may influence what is plausible. They point to the impact and influence of military and political institutions, and "the ability of the state to mobilize its economic resources, and the individual choices and idiosyncratic behavior of statesmen and military leaders."[6] Whether decisions are made individually, by an insider elite, or by a broader set of influential people, the impact of political and government processes can be crucial.

Does democracy fare better in developing strategies and defining success? We've noticed that Iraq and Afghanistan have proved to be rather less than occasions for celebration. Policymaking in the US government is time-consuming, laborious, and challenging. Competing interagency stakeholders often demand a part in what is said or done. The fights are as often about control of budget as they are about policy, and it is very difficult to get anything done. A president or cabinet secretary must assert their power vigorously to execute policies—and even that is no guarantee of success. Bureaucracies that dislike executive decisions are innovative in resisting them.[7] Britain's smaller government and its parliamentary system arguably produce strategies more easily. The system does not assure superior decisions, but its size and integrated government enable a smoother process for defining objectives.

Religion may influence how a government defines objectives. During the Iran–Iraq War, Iranian leaders did not flinch from sacrificing the lives of thousands of untrained young people. Boys as young as fourteen entered battle as fodder for the enemy, brainwashed by an ideology of martyrdom and accompanied by mullahs who screeched "God is great."[8]

History teaches that Muslims own no monopoly on the use of religion to vindicate strategic decisions or for strategic messaging. "You are engaged in God's service and mine—which is the same thing," Spain's King Philip II reminded his advisers at the end of the sixteenth century. Historian Geoffrey Parker concluded that the "official mind justified difficult political choices on the grounds that they were necessary not only for the interests of Spain but also for the cause of God, and attributed victories to divine intervention and favor, while normally rationalizing defeats and failures either as a divine attempt to test Spain's steadfastness and devotion—thus providing a spur to future sacrifices and endeavors—or else as a punishment for momentary human presumption."[9]

Ancient history? Take a look at former Yugoslavia or Republican politics. North Korean myths take on religious overtones in their reverence for the "Dear Leader" as a parent figure. As the Iron Curtain collapsed and strongmen like Vladimir Putin succeeded the Communists, the Russian Orthodox Church gained prominence that had already begun under Gorbachev. Putin has embraced the Russian Orthodox Church to legitimize his authority, taking a leaf from strategies employed by medieval monarchs who used the blessings secured from the Roman Catholic Church to legitimize theirs. Viktor Yelensky, president of the Ukrainian Association of Religious Freedom, has commented that "the Moscow Patriarchate is devoted to the idea of a Great Russia" and suggested that Patriarch Kirill I sees it as "Putin's church."[10]

There is no formula for defining winning or creating a picture of success; it varies according to design, agenda, policy, ideology, and objective. It is the lynchpin of any strategy. One satisfies expectations and achieves goals where they are known and understood.

CHAPTER 13

Strategy

THE CONCEPT OF STRATEGY, AS WILLIAMSON MURRAY AND MARK GRIMSLEY have astutely recognized, "has proven notoriously difficult to define."[1] The word comes from the Greek word *strategos*, meaning *general*. In ancient Athens, historian Donald Kagan recounts, ten elected generals, or *strategoi*, commanded divisions of the Athenian army, fleets of ships in battle, and filled the key offices of state.[2] These were military men elected for one-year terms. Some, including Cimon and Pericles, became the key political leaders. The concern here is *political strategy*, and notably information strategy that employs strategic communication, and not *kinetic strategy*, as historians and strategists Maj. Gen. John F. Fuller, Carl von Clausewitz, or Thucydides might address it in a military realm, or according to the cultural values that astute analysts like Richard Schultz Jr. and Andrew Dew discuss in analyzing insurgencies and terrorism in Chechnya, Somalia, Afghanistan, or Iraq.[3]

Strategy is a dynamic notion. It requires a strategic appreciation of all of the political, economic, military, and cultural factors that affect the ability to achieve success. No strategy, whether aimed at achieving broad national objectives such as keeping citizens at home and abroad safe from the threat of terrorism, winning a war, or achieving a narrower, more specific objective like passing legislation or winning an election, should be set in stone. Strategy needs to adjust and adapt flexibly and imaginatively to changing circumstances and evolving strategic situations.

Strategy has to be translated into plausible, actionable tactics that, when integrated together, achieve success (or, for the military in its current parlance, that produce conditions necessary to achieve a strategic objective or desired end-state). The military employs a sophisticated concept of operational design to effect that translation. One might presume that a military is more likely to devote the time and resources to conduct in-depth, broad-based inquiry and to develop a strategic appreciation of the considerations that affect whether a strategy will succeed, but the approach applies squarely to the political process and to political communication.

Developing a strong concept of design is vital to strategic communication. The process of developing a design constantly questions and critiques assumptions, observations, beliefs, and conclusions. Evolving challenges that may not have existed or been apparent when the elements of a strategy are first conceived may require reframing or adjusting strategy. Things change, sometimes very rapidly, on political and military battlefields. What may seem to work in theory may prove implausible in practice. The process of design tests whether the tactics selected—or their utilization—will best achieve success. If not, tactics or strategy or both need to be rethought and modified. Priority in that assessment belongs to strategy, not tactics; effective strategic communication and the strategy of which it forms a part must drive tactics, not the other way around. Effective tactics require cohesive, flexible, and adaptive strategy.

Campaign strategist Joe Gaylord, who writes and lectures about these precepts, says that "each step must be satisfied in planning an information campaign and in using strategic communication. Equally, while one can put these down on paper, things change rapidly and unpredictably in any campaign. You need to be agile and opportunistic to be able to adapt to or take advantage of unforeseen developments."[4] The strategy that opens a campaign may differ radically from the one that closes it. This may also prove true for key elements that comprise a strategy, including positioning; the story, plot, narrative, themes, and messages that a strategy employs; the language used; the sequencing and timing of actions; and the targeting of audiences.

Current military thinking tends to view strategy as producing an end-state that reflects a commander's intent. That flows from the view that there is no end to things, although successful strategy will effect changes that create new realities on the ground. There's a parallel in political communication. Former Secretary of State George P. Shultz cogently made the point that in politics nothing is ever settled. Effective strategy needs peripheral vision. It needs to be rooted in a strategic consideration of every factor that can affect whether it succeeds or fails—political, cultural, military, economic. The best strategists possess the rare ability to look over the horizon. Victory does not necessarily end all challenges, though, of course, one must avoid overgeneralizing here. Where the strategic objective is specific—winning an election or passing legislation—one can achieve temporary finality. But there is always a succeeding election, and legislation may not survive the practical aspects of implementation or judicial or political challenge. More often, victory creates new challenges. Victory won must be sustained, and successful strategy must set the stage for future success.

One reason Charles De Gaulle achieved greatness as president of France is that he grasped the longer-term strategic implications of success and was able to forge new strategies to advance French interests that accommodated evolving strategic situations. As a general, he envisioned the significance of mobility and firepower while conservative generals jeered. The German blitzkrieg tactics during World War II vindicated his judgment. As a political leader, he was no less prescient.

By 1960, the French had defeated the Algerian National Liberation Front (FLN), bringing to a conclusion an arduous, bloody conflict that had nearly compromised the heart of French democratic values. De Gaulle recognized that France's hard-earned military victory was politically unsustainable: Either France had to make Algeria a department of France, with Algerians accorded full French citizenship, or provide Algerians the opportunity to gain independence. His strategic communication was clear, forceful, and conveyed strength, and helped enable him to carry out his decision, despite the fact that his judgment caused turmoil and bitter feelings among some French. The episode illustrates the need to forge strategy in multiple frames, and not merely in terms of achieving short-term objectives.

How does strategy differ from tactics? Ron Faucheux is president of a nonpartisan Washington, DC–based polling firm and teaches at the Public Policy Institute at Georgetown University. He describes strategy as "how you position yourself and allocate resources to maximize your strengths and minimize your weaknesses achieving goals. It is a concept. It is a way to win. A tactic, on the other hand, is a tool to implement strategy. It is conduct."[5] It can take different forms, but tactics represent the tools to implement strategy whose deployment is prescribed by the concept of design.

Campaigns require effective strategy, but strategy is only one component.

Lay a Strong Foundation for a Campaign

Communication campaigns require setting a strong foundation. President Ronald Reagan was determined to revitalize the political authority of the presidency. Under President Jimmy Carter, a very smart but ineffective political executive, the office had seemed to diminish. Reagan knew that carrying out his agenda required both strong leadership and an office of the presidency that enjoyed real strength and power.

He understood that the key to achieving that goal was to get results—and then to communicate to the public the fact that results had been attained. As Reagan biographer Lou Cannon says, the "public perception of Reagan's leadership abilities rests in part on his enduring identification with the values of mythic America, a country of the mind in which presidents are necessarily strong leaders. But the perception depended even more on congressional passage of his budget and tax bills in 1981."[6]

Reagan's tough handling of the 1981 Professional Air Traffic Controllers Organization (PATCO) strike also proved that strong presidential leadership worked. When workers walked off the job, the media waited for the inevitable cooling-off period and the usual rounds of negotiations. Reagan had a different idea. He fired the workers and declared the strike over. Voters and insiders got the message. Reagan was not just an actor—he was a president. It set the stage for a successful first term that was the product of Reagan's leadership, supported by an able team that included James Baker, Ed Meese, Michael Deaver, and legislative liaison Ken Duberstein, who proved especially helpful in smoothing relations on Capitol Hill. Reagan had to deal with a Democratic Congress that embraced higher taxes, and he set a foundation for success by reaching out to Democrats such as House Ways and Means Chairman Dan Rostenkowski. He worked cordially with both Republicans and Democrats, and mobilized grassroots support. He used the bully pulpit to rally people. To the chagrin of his critics, he showed an ability for excellent presidential leadership.

Once Bill Clinton recovered his political sea legs after the catastrophic Democratic Party losses in 1994, he pivoted and demonstrated what a politician with real political skills can accomplish. Working closely with Newt Gingrich, he balanced the budget and reformed welfare—significant achievements when one considers today's multitrillion dollar deficits, which critics of George W. Bush contend undid Clinton's efforts. Credit for today's deficits is shared between Clinton, who rejected his Treasury Secretary Robert Rubin's counsel to use budget surpluses to pay down the national debt; Bush, who increased spending (and, say his critics, blew a hole in the budget through tax cuts, an achievement Bush supporters believe was the right decision); and Obama, who also increased spending.[7]

Internationally, Mexican President Felipe Calderon showed courage in taking on the drug cartels. A 2008 survey conducted by Centro de Investigacion y Docencia Economicas (CIDE) revealed that 79 percent of Mexicans viewed drug trafficking and organized crime as the issues of greatest concern.[8] Yet Calderon does not appear to have laid a proper political foundation for a war. Douglas Farah, who coauthored a fine book about the Russian weapons supplier Victor Bout, is a respected expert on counterterrorism, transnational crime, and Mexico's problems in these areas.[9] He points out that part of Calderon's challenge is that Mexicans view the state as corrupt and lacking in legitimacy; they see the state as part of the problem, especially given the long history of its police and military working for the drug cartels.

Strategic communication has been a challenge as well. Says Farah: "Calderon did not lay the foundation for a war. He simply declared one as things got bad. So he made two basic mistakes: he neither gave a clear rationale for why he was doing what he was doing (although that was fairly self-evident). Nor did he make substantive moves that would give people any reason to believe the behavior of his government would be fundamentally different from past, tainted regimes. Calderon did not specifically tell people what the war's objectives would be, or when or under what conditions the military would return to the barracks. All of this has left people without a clear concept of what the plan is or why they should buy into it."[10]

Mexicans seemed taken aback by the ferociousness of the war. By July 2009, even allies within Calderon's own political party were expressing concern that the deployment of 45,000 troops to combat the cartels was too blunt a sword to curb a bloody war that had few, if any, limits.[11] The tough-minded Calderon has stood his ground. Less clear is to what extent the political environment in Mexico will enable Calderon or his successor to maintain the pressure. Calderon's term ends in 2012, and Mexican tradition bars a president from standing for a second term. Few believe his successor will wage war against the cartels as assertively.

Positioning and Narrative

How do you frame the issues, define players, and define the stakes? Successful campaigns of influence require a credible rationale rooted in a narrative for what politicians want to do and why people should support a policy or action.[12] A narrative should define a cause and the stakes—what a policy or action means to an audience. Campaigns and strategic communication should enhance differences that provide an edge while blurring differences on messages that an adversary may use to mobilize their own constituency.

Western and non-Western examples illustrate the point. In 1996, Bill Clinton's strategy drew sharp differences between himself and Republicans on Medicare, Medicaid, education, and the environment to consolidate strength in his base and appeal to women. He blurred differences on taxes, crime, and a balanced budget—traditional GOP issues that had been used to impeach the credibility of Democrats—by mobilizing his base while also wooing Republicans. He achieved that through TV spots attacking Gingrich and Dole that positioned his campaign early on with targeted audiences. In his speeches he talked about how the era of big government was over, and what his pollster Mark Penn characterized as "micro-steps" that, taken as a whole, created a portrait of a centrist: school uniforms, funding for cops on the street, crackdowns on teenage smoking.[13]

In 2008, Obama talked about change to appeal to moderates, new voters, and independents, but used Afghanistan as an antidote to charges that

Democrats were weak-kneed when it came to achieving victory in Iraq. In a ploy that demonstrates the pitfalls of using difficult issues to win an election, during the campaign Obama contended that Afghanistan was the *real* battlefield. For the election it worked. McCain stressed proven strength in leadership and experience, which played to all audiences, and branded himself as a maverick to appeal to independents. He tried to consolidate his own base by portraying Obama as a conventional Democratic liberal, and argued that Obama was inexperienced in order to appeal to a broader audience. The experience issue had worked for Hillary Clinton but it failed for McCain, whose campaign used it poorly. McCain was also hampered by his age, and his Republican Party affiliation didn't help as the financial crisis began to crystalize.[14] The fact is that McCain was leading Obama in the polls until September 15, 2008; it's possible he might have held onto that lead had the crisis not erupted. Once in office, Obama found that Afghanistan presented very complicated, nuanced challenges with no clear or easy solutions.

President George H. W. Bush had discovered that raising taxes cut him off from his base political support within his own party. In part this was a matter of philosophy, as Republicans habitually do not support tax increases. It was also partly because Bush, whose strength was national security, failed to make the case at home for why his tax proposal merited support. It's an excellent example of why big steps in politics require well-thought-out campaigns of influence. As we saw earlier, Ronald Reagan cut taxes after executing a splendid campaign, and Bill Clinton, one of the most talented natural politicians the United States has produced in modern times, knew how to make welfare reform and a balanced budget cut work for him.

Long after she retired, Margaret Thatcher summarized her career to her biographer, Charles Moore, in one word: "Undefeated."[15] The Russian newspaper Tass had long before christened her the "Iron Lady"—a sobriquet given by Yury Gavrilov, a young soldier working as a journalist for the Red Army's Red Star newspaper, after a 1976 speech she made while in opposition.[16] She proudly accepted it.

Although much written about, Thatcher's autobiography well captures her voice, spirit, and resolve, and reveals much about her strategic communication. She had drawn inspiration from William Pitt, the first Earl of Chatham and prime minister during the Seven Years War (1756–63) and again from 1766 to 1768. Chatham, she wrote, had famously remarked: "I know I can save this country and that no one else can." She declared that "if I am honest, I must admit my exhilaration came from a similar inner conviction."[17]

Biographer Hugo Young, witty and skeptical, described the effect of Thatcher's historic election as prime minister as not merely a victory, but "something closer to a transfiguration." It marked, he concluded, "an era in which an ordinary politician, labouring under many disadvantages, grew into an international figure who did some extraordinary things to her country."[18] Confounding skeptics who widely predicted that she would fail, she stood out for her strength and purpose. These qualities were genuine, well-communicated, and defined the strategic communication that was vital to her political achievements.

As prime minister, she made clear from the outset that she would stand and act on principle—from tax reform, control of public spending, exerting British influence to end civil war in Rhodesia, standing up for Britain in the European Union, standing firm against the Soviet Union in foreign policy, and cracking down on trade union abuse. Above all, she was determined to lift Britain. She declared: "I was utterly convinced of one thing: there was no chance of achieving that fundamental change of attitudes which was required to wrench Britain out of decline if people believed that we were prepared to alter course under pressure."[19]

She spoke her iconic line provided by Ronnie Millar for a Brighton Party Conference that defined her narrative and messaging in strategic communication: "To those waiting with bated breath for that favourite media catchphrase, the 'U-turn,' I have only one thing to say. 'You can turn if you want to. The lady's not for turning. I say that not only to you, but to our friends overseas— and also to those who are not our friends.'"[20]

Journalist and scholar Neville Bolt suggests that Thatcher understood two crucial precepts about communication: definition and repetition.[21] Bolt cited a book about renowned international political consultant Scott Miller's firm. Miller makes the point that "to win, politicians need to define who they are, what they stand for, and the stakes in a controversy or an election. Either you define yourself, or your opponents will define you." Thatcher grasped that and took great care to define herself. Repetition does matter. It gives credibility. But one needs to stress: Repetition in language may build awareness for ideas, but matters only if language and actions align. Definition and repetition came easily to her because she had a very strong internal belief system. It's an unusual trait."[22]

For Thatcher, a firm but not especially gifted speaker, her rhetoric counted; her tone, demeanor, attire, bearing, and actions were integral to her strategic communication. When the British armed forces set sail to retake the Faulklands, she declared: "Failure —the possibilities do not exist." When Saddam Hussein invaded Kuwait, she famously advised President George H. W. Bush, "Look, George, this is no time to go wobbly."[23]

No one thought the power that unions had exerted for decades in Britain could be broken. Thatcher proved them wrong, defeating a coal miners' strike, denouncing the miners as "the enemy within" and referring to its action as "the rule of the mob," and repealing legal protections behind which union leaders had hidden.[24]

Thatcher understood the importance of appearance and though no feminist, she was cognizant of the fact that she was a woman. She hired a television producer to help spruce up her appearance. She had her teeth straightened. She abandoned hats as too fussy. And she became, as Moore notes, an elegant power dresser whose most visible symbol of strength was her handbags.[25]

How effective was the image? When a Democratic presidential candidate sat astride a tank, his Republican opponents used the image to provoke laughter, proof that images can be deeply misleading about an individual's character and strength. But that image stuck and contributed to Dukakis's 1988 defeat. In the 1987 elections, the Tories produced a video in which Thatcher was also seen in a tank. The instinctive reaction that image evoked was to get out of her way. For Thatcher, the image reinforced her communication, but it rested upon a solid political foundation driven by words and deeds.

Thatcher's approach to strategic communication echoed that taken by suffragist leader Susan B. Anthony and her close ally Elizabeth Cady Stanton in winning their lifelong battle to assure that women in the United States had the right to vote. Their efforts were the product of a fifty-year close friendship and political partnership. Stanton was a great thinker. Anthony had high intellect but also a brilliant ability to organize, energize, and communicate through her speeches, presentations, and above all, her courageous action that flowed from her ideas. In Stanton's words, "I forged the thunderbolts. She fired them."[26] Perhaps it was no surprise that she earned the nickname "Napoleon" for her ability to galvanize and mobilize.[27]

Anthony was born with the instinct to reform. Throughout her life she felt called to make a better cause. She battled for temperance because sobriety would prevent men from violent abuse of their wives or squandering household income on alcohol. She stood with the abolitionist movement because she knew that slavery was morally wrong.

Prodded by Stanton, the pivotal convention held at the Wesleyan Methodist Chapel in Seneca Falls, New York, produced a masterpiece of strategic communication. Stanton understood that the only way that women could assure fair treatment was by securing the right to vote. Supported by the renowned abolitionist Frederick Douglass, she persuaded the convention to produce a Declaration of Sentiments modeled on the Declaration of Independence.[28]

The wording of the two documents echoes and, in Mark Twain's word, "rhymes." The key distinction lay in the new focus on the rights of women. The Declaration of Independence declares that "all men are created equal."[29]

In our era, "men" in that context has become gender-neutral; it embraces men and women. Not so in the nineteenth century, a thoroughly chauvinist era. As Geoffrey Ward and Ken Burns point out, even in 1920, many and "probably most" Americans "of both sexes believed that differences between men and women equipped them for different life paths and responsibilities."[30]

The Seneca Falls declaration historically declared that "all men and women are created equal," and it excoriated men for depriving women of the "first right of a citizen," the right to elective franchise; for taken-away property rights; the framing of the laws of divorce to assure "the supremacy of man"; the deprivation of women from opportunities for education; and other transgressions.[31]

Reading an article written by journalist Horace Greeley about remarks delivered at the convention by activist Lucy Stone, Anthony found herself moved to take up the cause of women's rights.[32] She and Stanton proved vigorous, resolute champions for the cause of women, at times aligning with abolitionists, at other times, challenging them. When an abused Massachusetts wife sought shelter, Anthony found her sanctuary in New York. Well-known abolitionists like William Lloyd Garrison and Wendell Phillips, who would not have flinched from protecting a fugitive slave, were horrified that Anthony stood her ground. But it was that stout, consistent devotion to principle that lay at the heart of her strategic communication: She had principles and was willing to fight hard for them, no matter who passed a law that expressed contrary rules or values.[33]

Anthony recognized early on that the only way women could gain equal opportunity, earn equal pay, lay claim to rights of inheritance, and stand on a footing equal to men was by gaining the right to vote. She grasped the obvious political link between the battle for racial and gender quality, although debates over whether the Fourteenth and Fifteenth Amendments to the United States Constitution that focused on assuring blacks equal rights and the right to vote, fractured over whether the language should explicitly embrace women.

Anthony and Stanton felt betrayed when abolitionist leaders like Wendell Phillips refused to support equality for women while standing up for male equality. Phillips's battle was to end racial, not gender, discrimination, ignoring the question that Stanton posed: "Do you believe the African race is composed entirely of males?"[34] The pleas of Anthony and Stanton fell upon deaf ears. The political mood of the day was to enfranchise blacks—substantively, black males—not women.

Their fears that failing to assure gender quality would delay its fulfillment proved correct. It took until 1920 to pass the Nineteenth Amendment that guarantees women the right to vote. In the late twentieth century, a new effort to pass a gender-specific equal rights amendment failed.[35]

Anthony's eloquence, discipline, and ability to stay on message propelled her leadership. Its credibility was marked by a career rooted in a fearless fight for the principles she believed in. She put herself on the line time and again. Historian Ann Gordon notes that no reformers rivaled Anthony and Stanton in their tireless pursuit in the 1870s, as they "adapted to the discomforts of strange beds, dirt, sleeping on trains, and schedule that conceded nothing to ill health."[36]

In 1872, Anthony persuaded New York election officials to register her to vote on the basis that they were "citizens" whose rights the Constitution guaranteed, including under the Fourteenth and Fifteenth Amendments, although current law made that illegal.[37] On November 5, she cast a ballot for Ulysses Grant and the Republican ticket.[38] Her actions provoked national response in the press. *The New York Times* hailed her as a hero.[39]

The federal government had other ideas. She was arrested, indicted, and prosecuted for violating a federal law passed in 1870 to keep southern rebels from voting and that prohibited anyone without a lawful right to vote from casting a ballot.[40] She used the government's action as the impetus for touring the country, arguing that "our democratic-republican government is based on the idea of the natural right of every individual member thereof to a voice and vote in making and executing the laws."[41]

The court's nineteenth-century prejudice was evident in its refusal to allow Anthony to take the stand and give testimony. She was convicted and fined $100 but not jailed. She used the court's action as a springboard for taking her case to people nationally. In 1869, she and Stanton formed the National Woman Suffrage Association. An 1890 merger with a group led by Lucy Stone created the National American Woman Suffrage Association.

The lesson that Anthony provides for students of strategic communication is that success lies in developing a story and narrative that defines the stakes, drives a cause, maintains message discipline, and that respects the precept that repetition equals penetration equals impact. Like Thatcher, her willingness to risk everything politically for her principles infused her pronouncements with gravitas and credibility.

Do not sell enemies short—it's a shortcut to losing. In his August 1996 fatwa that declared war against the United States, Osama bin Laden forged a credible rationale for his target audiences. Although wrapped up in his twisted rhetoric about Islam, make no mistake: What bin Laden issued was a political tract that defined a political agenda, not religious doctrine. The road was not easy for him. He desperately sought religious sanction for the attack on the Twin Towers, and he had to search high and low before finding an obscure cleric to issue a fatwa to bless September 11.[42]

Fawaz Gerges points out that until we invaded Iraq in 2003, bin Laden had actually made himself a pariah among most Muslims.[43] Gerges's scholarship shows that al-Qaeda responded to its failure to defeat the "near enemy," or local Arab regimes, by going global against the "far enemy," America—through which it had hoped to establish hegemony in the Arab world, with a global reach and a global solution. Bin Laden offered a rhetorical narrative that resonated with some audiences, but it suffered from the lack of clear, concrete strategic goals.[44]

Bin Laden lodged familiar complaints about how the United States was dividing Muslims, stealing their oil, supporting their tyrants, dominating their politics, occupying their land, helping Israel at the expense of Muslims, killing Muslims, and other actions he considered to be undesirable. He would have expelled non-Muslims from his expansive view of Muslim lands. The debate over his designs lies elsewhere; the point here is that bin Laden's complaints about the United States resonated with the audience he cared about. Open source polling from Pew and other observing organizations makes it clear that bin Laden was becoming discredited.[45] Still, even among those Muslims who disdained bin Laden, polling data have indicated that many agreed with a lot of the core complaints he raised.[46]

Positioning is about story, plot, and narrative. These must set forth a credible rationale that infuses a policy or action with a version of legitimacy. The themes and messages that flow from the rationale are about strategic positioning, and a strong narrative is vital in defining a credible rationale.

A clear, plausible, believable, and persuasive narrative must explain who you are, what you are doing, what your cause is, how you are pursuing it, and what your actions mean for target audiences and how they help them. Successful narratives are about target audiences, not the narrator.

A narrative must define the stakes for each targeted audience and persuade them that actions and objectives provide a desirable, positive outcome for them, while those of adversaries offer undesirable ones.[47] Harvard professor Louise Richardson illustrates this well. She argues that the Achilles heel of terror groups lies in their focus on perceived iniquities in the current system, and the failure to define alternate visions of the societies they wish to create. Offering a credible alternative is critical.

This has been true from Osama bin Laden to Abimael Guzman (of Peru's Shining Path) to Paul Reyes (the former commander of FARC) and Vellupillai Prabhakaran (the former leader of the Tamil Tigers). Some include the late Shamil Basayev (who led the Chechen rebel movement) in this category, but one should note that the Chechens perceive themselves as fighting a war of national liberation against the Russians, as they have for centuries. Their goal is clear: They want a society devoid of Russian overlords. Still, it's worth observing: five terrorists, different continents, differing objectives—yet none were "able to describe the society they are trying to create."[48]

Narratives offer a key tool for subverting or defeating an adversary's will. They do so by providing a comparison that resonates emotionally, and that persuades an enemy that the price of opposition exceeds the benefit of fighting to the point that the will to fight is seriously weakened or destroyed. A key to effective narratives is seizing the moral high ground in the minds of target audiences.[49] Different views exist as to what may be morally justified or even what is required morally, and the global information environment complicates this challenge. A message directed to an audience in one place may be—and likely will be—seen by a wide range of audiences with different views and interests. One can rarely appeal to the moral fabric of all societies at the same time with the same message. The key is to try to avoid being perceived as hypocritical. In political communication, hypocrisy is a cardinal sin and can swiftly destroy credibility.

Still, successful information strategy requires moral authority. One must never assume that audiences will see that you inherently hold the high ground or that others will define it in the same terms that you do. You need to forge and execute information strategies that assert and maintain credibility in ways that strike a responsive chord with foreign audiences. Moral authority helps establish *legitimacy* for actions, while discrediting those of the opposition.

The starting point for building a narrative is the values, attitudes, and opinions of the targeted audience. It must be rooted in situational and cultural awareness. Understand the audience—who you are talking to—and segment them. The key questions are not about your values or desires; they are about *theirs*. What are their hopes and fears—their situation, their political and economic environment, their culture, values, security, and future? Understanding what weaknesses exist that an opposition can exploit to win support among a local population is vital.

Developing a credible narrative requires comprehending the information environment in which it is articulated. That requires accurate intelligence. This means knowing the facts on the ground.[50] Local populations are the key source for these facts. Gaining such information depends on the ability to make them feel secure, and building trust about the legitimacy of your goals and their stake in the outcome.

Language

The right language is critical in framing issues, and different cultures use radically different approaches in articulating a narrative. Americans respect blunt talk, whereas many Arabs perceive direct talk as confrontation. Americans are fact-oriented in putting out messages. Reagan once said that "facts are stubborn things." Arabs, on the other hand, focus heavily on appeals rooted in stories, images, metaphors, and analogies. In a famous post–September 11 video, bin Laden sits in a room on the floor with two shaykhs. The dialogue is metaphorical. Bin Laden says: "And the day will come when the symbols of Islam will rise up and it will be similar to the early days . . . of Al-Ansar. Finally said, if it is the same, like the old days, such as Abu Bakr and Othman and Ali." The video ends, in part, with bin Laden describing a dream: "He told me a year ago, 'I saw in a dream, we were playing a soccer game against the Americans. When our team showed up in the field, they were all pilots. . . . Abd Raham al Gahmri said he saw a vision, before the operation, a plane crashed into a tall building."

The *language* of strategic communication, whether countering or dealing with what a foreign leader says or in reaching target audiences, may spell the difference in whether it succeeds. In Malaysia, British General Sir Gerald Templar helped defeat a Communist insurgency by changing the vocabulary used to identify the rain forest people. Some had referred to them as *Sakai*—slaves. He ordered British troops to call them *Orang ulu*, or "people of the campaign."[51] Then the British rebranded the Malayan Races Liberation Army as the Communist Terrorist Organization. The tactic cut the legs out from under the nationalist appeal of the Reds. Templar understood that defeating the Communists required showing the populace that the Communists, led by Chinese, were neither Malays nor had their interests at heart.[52] It was a fine example of Britain's divide-and-rule policy in action.

The current debate over how to deal with al-Qaeda has shifted under Barack Obama. Discarded is the rhetoric of war on terrorism—why build up bin Laden as a warrior? Al-Qaeda calls its members *mujahidin*, or holy warriors, and those who die are *Shahidden*—martyrs. Why fight holy warriors or martyrs who bring glory and honor to their families? They are better described as murderers who bring disgrace to themselves and their families. There is a word for this: *mufsidoon*—condemned evildoers. Is the United States fighting faithful servants of God or blasphemers who commit *tajdeef*—members of a cult waging *Hirabah* (unholy war)? Why allow al-Qaeda to define the stakes as a trip to paradise where seventy-two virgins await young men with open arms, or a trip to the hell of *Jahannam*, complete with pain and humiliation, rather than honor?

International examples underscore the importance of framing issues and drawing contrasts properly. Advised by a gifted US political team led by Dick Dresner, in 1996 Russia's Boris Yeltsin defeated Communist hack Gennady Zyuganov. British Prime Minister Margaret Thatcher and the Tories clobbered

Neil Kinnock in 1987 by contrasting her strength during the Falklands conflict and her ability to keep unions in check with the Labour Party's weakness at home in failing to preserve social order. In 2008, Senator John McCain won the Republican nomination partly because the campaigns of his opponents failed, however dismal his general election effort. But he merits strong credit for projecting a strong primary campaign that established him as a seasoned, warm, but tough-minded leader. When Hillary Clinton strengthened her campaign, the contrast between her experience and Obama's lack of it helped her win major primaries from Texas and Ohio. George Bush faced tough sledding in 2004, but guided by his brilliant counselor, Karl Rove, the campaign was able to capitalize on Senator John Kerry's statement that "I actually did vote for the $87 billion before I voted against it," to argue that Bush was the stronger leader. As Rove, a national top political strategist, later noted, Kerry's statement—a gaffe uttered when the candidate was exhausted (a lesson for all candidates about campaigning while tired)—was the "gift that kept on giving."[53]

The order in which messages are communicated, to build cumulative impact, is important. Ron Faucheux adds that "the order in which positive and comparative components of the message are presented" is especially vital.[54]

Timing

Timing is about when you do what to achieve maximum impact. Developing a strategy requires keeping in mind practical requirements and limits. You need the capacity and resources to implement a strategy, or it will be useless. You have to expect uncontrollable events to interfere. Democratic campaign consultant Martin Hamburger points to the treacherous undercurrents that flow in any campaign, and offers one key consideration: "Your opposition may surprise you. Outside events over which you have no control may surprise you. Opportunities may open. Circumstances change. You need to be ready to update plans to avoid danger and capitalize on opportunity."[55]

Targeting

What audiences are critical to achieving strategic goals? Targeting segments audiences. It identifies influential people who are indispensable for success, those who can be very helpful for success but are not indispensable, a wider group whose support is desirable, and those whose support may not matter. The identity of these parties and their importance may shift as strategies evolve or are reframed.

Similarly, the composition of target audiences will vary according to the objective. A debate over the validity of a fatwa or a new term in office likely involves winning the support of a different audience from those needed to support a military operation. Strategies consider the strengths and weaknesses of those who can influence the outcome, the strategic environment (taking into account political, military, cultural, geographical, historical, and other concerns), competing interests, resources, themes, messages, and the values, attitudes, and opinions of stakeholders or target audiences.

In strategic communication, one size does not fit all; messages affect different groups differently. Campaigns need to be calibrated to specific audiences. Today they also need to anticipate how the blogosphere affects the political environment, and have the ability to mount and execute an effective one. Messaging and strategy also need to take into account the impact of social media like Twitter and Facebook, which have accelerated the timelines within which one must act or respond.[56] Messages must engage increasingly diverse, active sets of political actors who can affect elections or debates on public issues.

In 2009, bloggers exposed fraud perpetrated on behalf of Vladimir Putin's United Russia party.[57] What Josh Goldstein and Juliana Rotich termed the "networked public sphere" drew local and global attention to violence and election fraud perpetrated by incumbent presidential candidate Mwai Kibaki and his opponent Raila Odinga that afflicted Kenya's 2008 presidential elections. In a prior era, these events might have gone unreported. Modern technology enabled "many-to-many communications (instead of just one-to-many) and the near elimination of the cost of communication."[58] Kenyans used "SMS campaigns to promote violence, blogs to challenge mainstream media narratives, and online campaigns to promote awareness of human rights violations," and when Kenyan authorities declared a ban on live media coverage, they "became a critical part of the national conversation."[59] Former UN Secretary-General Kofi Annan arrived to mediate the bitter disputes that emerged. This process led in February 2008 to a power-sharing agreement and coalition government.[60] Bloggers did not change the outcome of the 2006 presidential race in Mexico won by Felix Calderon over his leftist rival Andres Manuel Lopez Obrador, but they presented new voices in the nation's discourse.[61]

US Senator Scott Brown's 2009 upset victory to win the seat previously held by Senator Edward Kennedy shows how bloggers can turn an election around. "They were not the only reason he won," comments political consultant Joe Gaylord, "but they were a key factor. Their chatter drove people to Brown's website. There they learned about Brown and could make campaign contributions. Day after day, Brown's campaign raised hundreds of thousands of dollars. It was remarkable and astonishing to behold. It funded his campaign, aroused media attention, and excited voter enthusiasm. The combination proved un-stoppable. You had an attractive candidate, a key issue—stopping President Obama's health care initiative—and an active blogosphere that generated mon-ey to fund the campaign and then played a key role in getting out the vote on election day."[62]

Developments in technology affect the ability to develop messaging. A May 2007 US government study found that nearly 30 percent of eighteen-to-twenty-nine-year-olds only use a cell phone and do not have a landline. Glen Bolger, one of the most experienced election pollsters in the United States, says, "That makes it more difficult to poll voters. It affects your ability to get an accurate polling sample and to refine messages and identify and define target audiences."[63] The number has grown since that time. Blog-gers themselves can have an impact, and many criticize the effect because, as political consultant Martin Hamburger puts it, "One worries about the professional standards that some bloggers respect. Some are excellent and make a huge contribution to political discourse. Others lack maturity or discipline and will print any rumor, no matter how unfounded, and that's harmful to the political process."[64] This criticism also, notes Patricia Kush-lis, applies in the mainstream media.[65] Some suggest that it is related to the tendency among many media sources to eliminate the requirement of having two sources to verify an assertion.

Bolger emphasizes that "what really gives blogging political impact and can shift an election dynamic is when the blog message is picked up and amplified by other media."[66] Brown's election and the Kenyan election affirm Bolger's insight.[67] Conversely, getting a story into the media is no assurance that its credibility will stand. When *CBS News* raised questions about Presi-dent George W. Bush's service in the Texas Air National Guard during his reelection campaign, it was bloggers who challenged and picked apart the network's reporting.[68]

The New Democracy party in Greece helped itself in elections some years ago by airing political music videos—a novelty at the time—to appeal to the younger population, who had just been given the right to vote. In 2004, the George W. Bush campaign ginned up turnout by ensuring that in key states there were ballot initiatives on social issues like same-sex marriage that mo-tivated his base among social conservatives. One challenge that beset Barack Obama's efforts on health care has been the failure to identify a consistent, coherent majority base of voter support on a difficult issue. The merits don't matter here. The point is that winning requires that you identify a winning coalition and then match messages to them. Obama did that successfully in 2008 and won the election.

Persuading an Audience That Your Cause Is More Credible

It seems like common sense to persuade your audience that your cause is more credible, but it's astonishing how often political leaders forget that. In the South Korean elections of 1997, Lee Hoi Chang was nominated by the Grand National Party because as chief justice of the Supreme Court, he had a reputation for integrity. His wide support collapsed when it was disclosed that neither of his sons had served in the military. In South Korea that was politically very harmful. Despite the fact that Kim Dae Jung, his leading opponent, also had not served, Lee fell into third place as a former party member, Rhee In-Je, fled the party to form his own and stand as a candidate.

Lee was ready to drop out. A strategy was proposed that would motivate voters to give him a fresh look: They would ask another candidate, Seoul Mayor Cho Soon, to drop out and in effect join Lee's campaign as a running mate. There was no official slot in Korean politics for a running mate, but the president had the power to appoint the prime minister. Although that post had been largely ceremonial, nothing prevented a president from delegating real power to the holder.

The main issue in that election was Korea's economic future. Cho Soon was an American-educated economist and probably the most popular politician in the country, although he lacked the funds and political organization to win the presidency. After first resisting counsel to ask him to run with Lee, the invitation was extended and eventually accepted. As announced at a press conference, within two weeks Lee had doubled his vote, reached a dead heat with Kim Dae Jung, and left Rhee in the political dust. At a critical point, the election came down to who had a plan to save the currency. Kim remained silent. Lee and the Grand National Party presumed that they had momentum and, with Lee's credibility refreshed, were better able to project the strength of character and integrity that South Korea needed. Kim Dae Jung was revered in some Western circles, but at home he was enormously controversial. He started the election with a solid base that he was unlikely to expand, but was also not likely to shrink.

Polling reflected that 72 percent of Koreans would vote for a candidate who offered a plan to save the currency. Lee and his team refused this counsel to put out a ten-point plan. This was garden-variety politics in the United States. Lee's team insisted that solving the economy was a complex job, and they were advised to deal with that nuance after they won the election. First, however, they needed to win. The polling data were cut-and-dried and the candidates were locked in a dead heat.

Having not offered a solution for the currency problem, Kim Dae Jung compounded his problem. All three candidates had agreed to certain accords mediated by US Treasury Secretary Robert Rubin. Kim reneged. Lee had two levers to pull, and either would have assured victory. Confident that he had the momentum and deferring to his academic economics advisers, he held fast, convinced that his momentum and reputation for rectitude would carry him through. He lost in a razor-thin election. His job was simple: persuade Korean voters that he had a more credible rationale for winning. Kim Dae Jung had handed him the opportunity. He passed on it and it cost him—and South Korea—the presidency of a distinguished leader. After losing, he apologized for failing to heed Rubin's counsel, but by then, the votes had been counted.

The lesson: Never presume political support. It has to be garnered by identifying and distinguishing core bases of support and persuading audiences (what political consultants think of as battleground audiences, as their opinions are not fixed and may be changed). And never presume that your message is more resonant than competing messages. You have to drive it and keep driving it.

When the United States went into Iraq in 2003, some people presumed that Iraqis would respond the way the French did when we liberated Paris. They were happy to see Saddam gone, but they were not so happy to see Western forces take control of the country. In a fit of hypocrisy, some who applauded the overthrow of Saddam later moaned about the fact that Western forces had again "humiliated" Arabs. From almost the day he arrived, coalition provisional authority chief Paul Bremer took actions that polarized people. One of the immediate effects of his edicts was to put a lot of ordinary working people out of a job.[69] In tandem with Deputy Secretary of Defense Paul Wolfowitz and former Undersecretary of Defense for Policy Walter Slocombe, Bremer foolishly ignored strong counsel that accurately forecast that disbanding the Iraqi Army—340,000 soldiers who needed jobs to feed their families—would create an unwanted insurgency.[70]

The insurgency led by al-Qaeda was quick to invoke an "us versus them" —Muslims versus infidels, Arabs versus foreigners—argument rooted in religious and cultural differences. It was a cynical ploy, but until Iraqis realized the truth about al-Qaeda—which also included foreign fighters—it had an impact. Al-Qaeda had been nothing in Iraq until after the invasion. The lesson evident in politics applies to military action as well. Defining a credible rationale rooted in a powerful narrative is vital to success, and never presume that you hold the moral high ground, a compelling and credible rationale, or a better one than your adversaries do. Trust has to be earned. Credibility has to be built—and continually strengthened—or it is never achieved; it is lost.

Mobilizing Target Audiences

Persuading target audiences to support a cause is one thing, but mobilizing them to do so actively is different. Winning support is not necessarily sufficient. Motivating target audiences to support a policy or action actively is important. If they won't, the fallback is motivating them to not oppose it. Strategic communication can influence audiences to remain passive or complicit. The best campaigns of influence start by creating, as Faucheux points out, "a demographic profile of the audience."[71] Governments may have census or other data that provide access to this information. It can also be developed through good polling and other research methodology. Knowing the audience is pivotal. Who are they? What do they do? What is their religion? Party affiliation? Employment? Core values? Age? Gender? Family, tribal, or clan status? What issues drive their community, culture, or society? Those are just a few questions that require concrete answers.

No less vital is understanding existing attitudes and opinions on key issues. The answers may come from anecdotal evidence, polling, or focus groups, or the analysis of social discourse heard on the radio, seen on television, or read in posters, newspapers, pamphlets, banners, or other sources.

Identifying the key influences and the ideas or messages most likely to move these individuals enables leaders to identify base support, which is more often fixed, and battleground support, which consists of those who lean or are undecided.

Once those steps are taken, a message grid can be created to evaluate the respective strengths and weaknesses of competing sides. This exercise, which too few political leaders seem to undertake, is critical in understanding message. John Maxwell, one of the smartest and most able political consultants in the United States, originated a now widely used message grid that poses four key questions:

- What do we say about ourselves?
- What do we say about our adversaries?
- What do our adversaries say about themselves?
- What do our adversaries say about us?[72]

The answers need to be compared and contrasted. Then, judgments need to be made as to what messages define a credible rationale and provide a foundation for a strong narrative that supports a cause.

American politics does this as matter of course. The influence of campaign money and special interest politics may be twisting and perverting democracy, but no one can accuse interested parties in this nation of holding their counsel. Audiences are mobilized through social networking, the use of social media (Twitter, Tumblr, e-mail listserves, LinkedIn, cellular text messaging or imaging, Facebook, YouTube), blogging, paid electronic media, and by creating opportunities to drive a message with the news media.

Americans hold no monopoly on the sophisticated application of this precept. In Bolivia, Evo Morales won the presidency and, in 2009, control over the legislative and judicial branches of government. He did this using his political party, the Movement towards Socialism (MAS), to mobilize his key constituencies among *cocaleros* (coca plant growers, whose union he headed) and the indigenous population.

In Colombia, the well-publicized kidnappings of innocent civilians triggered an obscure individual to use Facebook to mobilize a million-person march that achieved national and international resonance. The significance of the event cannot be overstated: It helped to transform attitudes in Colombia against the FARC. Previously, citizens had blamed the government for kidnappings; afterward, FARC shouldered the blame and it facilitated the success that Colombia has had in fighting them.

In southern Somalia, extreme Islamist groups like al-Shabaab and Hizbul Islam recruited and mobilized by using Ethiopia's invasion to play the "us versus them" card, denouncing the Ethiopians as not only foreigners but Christian enemies of Islam (even though Ethiopia is over 40 percent Muslim, a statistic reflected in its army). They may yet topple the transitional federal government, which is holed up in a few blocks of Mogadishu, and whose survival depends on the African Union Mission in Somalia (AMISOM) force comprised of troops from Burundi and Uganda. That message lost resonance once Ethiopia ostensibly withdrew.

Violent Islamist leaders have shifted gears and focused their strategic communication in a series of confluent messages rooted in a combination of intimidation and positive appeal. They argue that war in Somalia is jihad, that Islamists stand for a free and united Somalia, that Muslims will prevail over their enemies (who are US puppets), and that the Somalis welcome them.

"I am a Somali nationalist fighting for a free and united Somalia," said Hizbul Islam leader Sheik Hassan Dahir Aweys, as he called upon all foreigners supporting the Western-backed transitional federal government to leave Somalia.[73] Al-Shabaab leaders like Sheik Mktar Robow abu Mansour and Sheikh Hassan Yakoub Ali have called for Somalis to join with al-Qaeda to form an Islamic state in Somalia and East Africa as part of global jihad.[74]

The efforts of violent extremists to generate support may be undercut—as happened in Iraq—by their harsh violence. In Somalia, they have banned prayer beads as a *bid'a* (new introduction to Islamic ways).[75] In the Bula-Haw district, they banned tree trimming.[76] They have imposed curfews.[77] They have ripped out gold or silver teeth on grounds that artificial teeth are used for fashion and beauty, thus violating their interpretation of Islamic law.[78] They have banned school bells, pronouncing that the bell ring sounds like those of Christian churches.[79] They behead people accused of converting to Christianity.[80] Media reports suggest that the extremists have alienated many adults. Al-Shabaab has responded by recruiting child fighters.[81]

In the long run, it's a strategy that seems likely to fail should a credible alternative to them emerge, although whether this will occur seems highly problematic. There are, however, plenty of reasons to believe that the increasing emphasis among the international community in supporting the regions of Somalia, and in particular those that are relatively peaceful (Somaliland and Puntland and, to a lesser extent, Galmudug), may yet offer an incentive for other less-stable regions to find a peaceful way forward.

Identify and Mobilize Credible Messengers

Even the most popular political leaders benefit from third-party credibility. Arab rulers in places like Saudi Arabia understand this in their mobilization of clerics to validate their actions. Saudi Arabia recognizes that mobilizing clerics known for their independence from the government can be even more effective in counter-radicalization. In 2004, more than two thousand Muslim intellectuals signed a petition calling on the United Nations to outlaw the use of religion to incite violence.[82] The petition urged prohibitions of the broadcasts of "the mad musings of the theologians of terror."[83] In December 2005, King Abdullah II of Jordan convened a conference of two hundred leading Islamic scholars from fifty countries that promulgated the "Three Points of the Amman Message" aimed at discrediting the messages of militant radical Islamic ideology.[84]

Culture can be an important tool in providing third-party channels that shape the political environment. When reporter Patrick Graham asked his Iraqi friend Mohammed why he was fighting against the Americans, Mohammed said he was inspired by Mel Gibson in *Braveheart*.[85]

CHAPTER 14

Tactics

T. E. Lawrence defines tactics as "the means toward the strategic end, the steps of its staircase."[1] He wryly notes that if nine-tenths were certain, the irrational tenth was "like the kingfisher flashing across the pool."[2] Tactics are the specific actions and sequences of actions taken to carry out a strategy. Action taken by Hamad bin Isa al-Khalifa, the King of Bahrain, in declaring martial law sent stick-wielding police and summoned military assistance from Saudi Arabia to crack down on Shiite protestors, which was a tactic to implement a strategy of limiting dissent.[3] Employing the assets of NATO to impose a no-fly zone against Muammar Gaddafi was a tactic to carry out a United Nations–sanctioned strategy for protecting civilians from slaughter.

The civil reconstruction projects in Afghanistan are tactics in Gen. Petraeus's broader strategy of counterinsurgency. The decision by Yemeni Maj. Gen. Ali Mohsen al-Ahmar to position his forces in Sana'a to protect demonstrators against President Ali Abdullah Saleh in 2011 was part of a broader strategy by regime opponents to force the aging president from office. During the Bush years, the "war of ideas" was a strategy to defeat violent extremism, but the specific actions taken to counter violent extremist ideology were tactics. It's an important distinction to make in politics, because most successful political leaders are good tacticians. Few are good strategists.

In civil politics, grassroots mobilization programs to influence legislation are guided by their own strategy, but they are more aptly viewed as tactics in broader strategies. Threats by both sides in Congress to shut down the government unless a budget agreement is reached are tactics used as part of a strategy to implement each party's philosophy and political agenda.

Cabinet shuffles are classic examples of political tactics to deflect criticism, punish opponents, or to refresh political images. Pakistani President Asif Ali Zardari employed the tactic of a cabinet reshuffling to oust Foreign Minister Shah Mehmood Qureshi after Qureshi embarrassed the Zardari government in the Raymond Davis affair.

In France, despite a prior felony conviction for corruption, Alain Juppe is widely regarded by journalists and political insiders as an unusually capable individual. President Nicolas Sarkozy appointed him to replace Foreign Minister Michele Alliot-Marie after his government received criticism for its handling of the 2011 uprising in Tunisia that overthrew the government. Alliot-Marie had stirred up controversy by taking a vacation while antigovernment riots broke out in Tunisia.[4] The tactic was familiar to voters. In 2007, Sarkozy had reshuffled a freshly minted cabinet after Juppe—then the number two official in his cabinet—lost his seat in parliamentary elections. Sarkozy moved to address his political problems by adding women, ethnic minorities, and even members of rival parties to his cabinet.[5] Former British Prime Ministers Gordon Brown and Tony Blair played the same game on different occasions in their governments to shore up credibility and defuse criticism.[6]

Carl von Clausewitz distinguished tactics from strategy. In his view, "tactics is the theory of the use of military forces in combat," while "strategy is the theory of the use of combat for the object of war."[7] Glenn Ayers says that "there are numerous definitions for tactics. Clausewitz was writing in a previous era, but his notions are well regarded today. We spend an enormous time in our service colleges analyzing how his ideas apply to the current and future environments."[8] A detailed analysis of military tactics lies beyond the scope of this book.

In information strategy, the tactical use of communication is employed to implement a broader strategy. Tactics are used to drive a message. Joe Gaylord's dictum merits repeating: repetition = penetration = impact. Messages must be trumpeted and then driven home. "More important," Ayers adds, "words must be supported by action. One can make a compelling case that 70% of US government's strategic communication should consist of action."[9]

Critical to effective tactics in strategic communication is maintaining message discipline. The fastest way to shred credibility in an operation is to communicate inconsistent messages or policies. Effective information strategy requires coherent, cohesive messaging, especially in a 24/7 global media environment. Politics may be local, but information is global. What is said in one place can be communicated globally and used against the sender in minutes.[10]

Punches Can Hurt; Counterpunches Can Hurt More

Politics, as Senator Lloyd Bentsen once advised, is a contact sport. Competing interests define choices. Democracy is a chaotic conversation, but the same holds true for politics in nations that may not be free or are only partly free. People want their voices to be heard. Strategic communication and campaigns of influence trigger counterpunches, and anticipating them is vital.

The 2004 US presidential election offers a splendid example. Democratic nominee Senator John Kerry's team devised a strategy to brand the candidate as a war hero to inoculate him against Republican claims that Democrats are soft on national security. At the Democratic National Convention, veterans who served with Kerry in South Vietnam stood beside him on the podium. Delegates left the convention full of hope that George W. Bush could be toppled. They felt confident they had landed a tough blow on those who asserted that Democrats were weak on national security.

Incredibly, it seems never to have crossed the mind of Kerry or his key strategists that a group calling itself the Swift Boat Veterans for Truth would unleash a series of TV ads that the news media would quickly pick up that savaged Kerry, who served about four months in Vietnam. The ads, unveiled at a May 4, 2004, press conference, contended that he had exaggerated claims about his own service and unfairly attacked other Vietnam servicemen.[11] The issue here is not whether their attacks were unfair or misleading, and the attacks were eviscerated as unfair smear tactics.[12] What's relevant is that Kerry's campaign failed to grasp the potential impact of them in discrediting his narrative. Worse was the failure to anticipate them. It was a costly mistake. They did not materialize out of thin air; Kerry had been fighting a running gunboat battle with them for years over his criticism of America's engagement in the South Vietnam war. The debate knocked Kerry off stride and undercut an excellent opportunity to oust an incumbent president.

It pays to think ahead. President George W. Bush told Congress that in Iraq, "this crusade, this war on terrorism, is going to take a while."[13] As described in the next chapter, using the term *crusade* handed a sword to al-Qaeda, which it employed against the United States enthusiastically and effectively.

In Yemen, President Ali Abdullah Saleh operated what Robert Burrowes termed a kleptocracy—a government of, by, and for thieves.[14] Saleh once said that he didn't trust a man who didn't steal. In the minds of those living in the southern part of Yemen, his actions—including the failure to act—matched his rhetoric. Despite pleas for national unity, his strategic communication left him isolated in the capital of Sana'a and spurred the creation of the Southern Mobility Movement (SMM). This movement commenced when former southern military officials forced into compulsory retirement after the 1994 civil war between the country's north and south demanded higher pension payments. Saleh's obstinacy sent thousands of protestors into the streets where they chanted antigovernment slogans, cried out for an end to the northern occupation, and called for secession. Yemen's politics are complicated by rebellion from the al-Houthis in the north and a newly invigorated al-Qaeda. By 2011, matters had deteriorated to the point that a popular uprising was triggered that forced

Saleh to step down within months. There is a lesson here: Any political executive's language or actions *are* going to prompt a reaction.

Benazir Bhutto understood clearly that her opponents would try to discredit her as corrupt and would attack her two terms as prime minister of Pakistan as having achieved little. She anticipated these lines of attack, and her speeches prior to returning home in 2007 did an excellent job of inoculating her against them. Elections do not silence critics, but they afford a venue for neutralizing their charges and turning criticism back on their critics. Bhutto was effective in pushing the argument that it was President Musharraf whose flaws were holding Pakistan back.

Conversely, Afghanistan offers a dramatic example of actions that represent ill-judged strategic communication by a NATO partner. As the commander of British Forces at the time, Colonel Stephen Padgett, recalled:

> I attended a ceremony to mark the change of command from one NATO contingent to another from the same nation. The guest list included more than 25 Afghans. After the parade, the guests joined the incoming and outgoing troops, about 600 people in total, for a reception at which champagne (unsurprisingly, given the nation involved, it was the real thing), lobster, and an astonishing variety of other delicacies were served in a display of excess that had me, never mind the Afghans, stunned. I found it hard to imagine how, during a counterinsurgency campaign in an impoverished country, the message being sent by this grotesque display could possibly contribute to the achievement of NATO's mission.[15]

Rightly, Padgett was aghast at the failure to understand the realities of life in Afghanistan and the insensitivity of such displays of Western excess. The opportunities for the Taliban to capitalize on that for effective strategic communication are evident.

On a separate occasion, a very senior member of the Afghan government posed to Padgett the following question: "How could it be justifiable for people like me—soldiers—who come voluntarily to this country to do a job that is by its nature risky, to transfer our risks to innocent members of this population as a side effect of the measures we take to protect ourselves?"[16]

Padgett notes: "This seemed a particularly apposite query as, on my way to the meeting, my SUV had been forced off the road along with donkey carts, taxis, and many frightened pedestrians in a relatively safe area of central Kabul by a convoy of heavily armored NATO vehicles racing through the streets with all hatches battened down to minimize their occupants' exposure to attack by snipers or suicide bombers. Aside from civilian casualties caused, unintentionally, by air strikes during engagements with insurgents, casualties were caused routinely by coalition vehicles on roads across Afghanistan each year."[17]

Experiences like Padgett's underscore that strategic communication occurs through routine activity and not merely in the heat of battle. Gen. Stanley McChrystal and Gen. David Petraeus made protection of civilians a top priority. McChrystal's strategy (infused in what the Pentagon terms "Commander's Intent") is to ensure that this precept is implemented at the level of the strategic corporal. In February 2010, the International Security Assistance Force (ISAF) began publishing *Coin Common Sense*, which details the exceptional impact that protecting people, separating them from insurgents, and building relationships at the grassroots level can have. The step-by-step actions described may seem small, but they define strategic communication and cumulatively represent a giant leap forward.

Political communication opens up enough avenues at any time for counterpunching, and dealing with that while fighting a war makes life especially complicated. The actor Fess Parker who portrayed Davy Crockett uttered the phrase, "Look before you leap," and although it was movie talk, it was on point.

PART IV

Weapons of Strategic Communication

CHAPTER 15

Television as a Weapon

Television has powerfully shaped values, attitudes, and opinions, and is a powerful weapon for strategic communication. Ambassador Joseph Nye has remarked how American cinema in the postwar era provided a positive, hopeful, and energetic future of freedom, modernity, and youthfulness that had a tremendous impact on making society more democratic.[1] Sam Wasson's splendid not-to-be-missed book on the making of the film *Breakfast at Tiffany's* describes how Hubert de Givenchy's little black dress designed for Audrey Hepburn transformed attitudes toward fashion and how women saw themselves.[2] Victor Malarek has recorded the tragic impact of the film *Pretty Woman* has had in causing numerous victims of human trafficking to believe in the fairytale happy ending that awaits prostitutes.[3] Jack Shaheen has complained that it's movies that vilify Arabs, and that this has done as much to arouse hostility to the West as our policies.[4]

Still, one may draw a better sense of television's power by focusing on two examples: al-Qaeda's use of television and American political advertising. Examining how al-Qaeda has co-opted the medium and its use in political campaigns illustrates its power. Two outstanding examples for using television as a weapon are President Lyndon Johnson's reelection advertising in 1964 and, on a more extreme level, Osama bin Laden's attack on the World Trade Towers on September 11, 2001. In 1964, Lyndon Johnson's campaign aired the "Daisy" ad just one time, but it destroyed the campaign of his opponent, Senator Barry Goldwater. Planes may have destroyed the twin towers—but the weapon that provided global impact on that fateful September morning was television.[5] Bin Laden may or may not have contemplated the role television would play. But that was the medium through which the horrifying images were communicated, and the strong emotional responses evoked.

Al-Qaeda's Growing Sophistication

Al-Qaeda's grasp of the potential of new media technologies is impressive. Despite the expertise and sophistication of political communications and the exploitation of satellite television, the Internet, DVD technology, and cellular communications in the West, al-Qaeda is beating us at our own game. Their use of electronic media shows strategic sophistication. They know how to forge, project, and drive messages that strike a responsive chord. The tactics basic to any political campaign translate powerfully into tools for winning the war of ideas. Ironically, al-Qaeda has failed to employ them meaningfully in the new Arab revolts that characterized the 2011 Arab Spring.

The power of modern electronic media lies in its capacity to achieve resonance: It affords immediate, direct access to the mind of a listener or viewer, and it provides visual context for a message. It is hard to change fixed beliefs, and the best political communication rarely tries to do so. Tony Schwartz, who produced the "Daisy" ad campaign for Johnson, argues that effective media provides stimuli that evoke feelings an audience already has and provides a context for a viewer to express these feelings.[6] It takes what is unconscious in the mind, makes it conscious, and directs an individual to support a particular message and a narrative that gives meaning to the message. The challenge is less to get things "across to people as much as out of people."[7] Al-Qaeda has shown a clear grasp of this political truth in its use of the best techniques of Western political communication to promote its own narratives and drive its themes and messages.

That is merely the starting point in forging a media campaign. Campaigns aim to win public support for a candidate, group, policy, law, or political action by defining a credible rationale, and then using reason to persuade and emotion to motivate. They develop awareness, arouse support, and mobilize public opinion to act. In that sense, the struggle against information-age terror groups such as al-Qaeda is at heart a political campaign, not a military one, although it employs violence and military operations.

This flows from the nature of the opponent. Al-Qaeda has elements of both a vertical hierarchy and a horizontally dispersed network without being constrained by either. It is an innovative, open-source, interactive, participatory operation. It offers distinct agendas and publicizes its decisions in the public domain rather than by communicating secretly through compartments. Using the Internet, anyone can provide input into its strategy and tactics. New participants can easily enter this world. They may borrow or adopt from al-Qaeda's ideological pronouncements, but they can easily form new groups and undertake violent acts without contacting a central organization or securing permission to do so.

The media space in which the ideas and ideology of al-Qaeda or its like must be engaged and defeated starts at the grassroots, with one-to-one relationships, and reaches upward to include paid and earned media. All elements of this space may interact with the others. Al-Qaeda's words and actions aim for political impact in this space. Its violence is geared toward achieving political information effects, not winning tactical military engagements. What matters is how the target audiences perceive its actions. Al-Qaeda taps into the emotions and existing dispositions of intended audiences to forge support for its narratives and to motivate people to action. It operates throughout this media space, and defeating it requires engaging simultaneously at every level.

The Power of Video

In political communication, video provides context. It combines emotion and persuasion to shape the political environment. It has a unique power to turn attitudes into political will and to galvanize ideas into action. "Daisy," the seminal political TV ad for President Lyndon Johnson's 1964 reelection campaign, shows the impact that video can have. The ad fades up on a young girl standing in a meadow, picking flowers. Her expression is the soul of innocence. She removes petals from a daisy, counting each one as she does. As she reaches ten, the frame freezes. The camera zooms into her eye and her voice is replaced by an announcer counting backward from ten. As he says "zero," we are close in on the pupil of her eye. An atomic bomb detonates, mushroom clouds fill the screen, and Johnson proclaims: "These are the stakes: to make a world in which all of God's children can live or to go into the darkness. We must either love each other or we must die." The announcer enjoins the viewer to vote for the president: "The stakes are too high for you to stay home."[8]

Shown only once on national television, this may be the single most powerful television political ad in history. The images were startling and dramatic, yet the power of the ad lay in its political relevance and the underlying feelings that it evoked and channeled toward Johnson. In that election, two years after the Cuban Missile Crisis, the fear of a nuclear war occupied center stage. Although polling just before Kennedy's death in November 1963 had indicated a close race between him and Goldwater, by 1964, voters worried whether Goldwater had an itchy finger on the nuclear trigger.

"Daisy" reinforced those doubts, striking deep emotional chords while providing reasoned reassurance from the stolid Johnson that we could not afford to elect a president who would act irresponsibly. The spot shredded Goldwater's credibility and Johnson was reelected in a landslide. The ad demonstrates brilliantly the power of visual media in a battle of ideas. Truth had little to do with

Johnson's campaign. Goldwater was a measured conservative whose work on national security in the US Senate earned bipartisan respect. Yet, as Schwartz points out, reality in politics is a matter of perception and electronic media is uniquely powerful in its ability to shape that perception by striking a responsive chord among audiences.

Schwartz's analysis of what makes electronic media work applies directly to countering the ideas espoused by violent extremists and to strategic communication generally. Osama bin Laden's charisma as a political leader was not inherent, but was rather a smartly constructed image rooted in a well-devised narrative about a virtuous, humble man who worked hard, had ability and dreams and, moved by the grace of God, left his rich lifestyle to lead a jihad in harsh surroundings. He presented himself as a warrior-leader, a modern Saladin engaged in a historic struggle that is a part of divine destiny. Images reinforce this narrative: Jihadi propaganda depicts him in photographs in which he wears combat gear or a camouflage jacket while seated next to an AK-47.

Some photos show him seated before a map of Arabia, in a white keffiyeh, looking holy and political, or in a Caucasus hat, or on horseback. In his relatively rare media appearances, he was seen in a cave, not a villa. The image spun is that of a hero who embarked upon a mythical journey into the desert and who returned purified, a specific reference to Mohammed's journey from Mecca to Medina.[9] Other photos depict him in a heavenly light that implies divine sanction. In all photographs, bin Laden and al-Qaeda members are shown with fist-length beards, an homage to the prophet.

Bin Laden's rhetoric complemented the images. It was rooted in poetry and mystical literature. He invoked dreams and visions as messages from God. He presented himself within an ostensible religious framework. He quoted the Koran, projected himself as a man of God, and justified violence as divinely inspired. But no matter how tightly bin Laden wrapped himself in the rhetoric of religion, he remained a political player.

Al-Qaeda's sophisticated videos give global range and power to its rhetorical appeals to its target audiences. It uses a variety of distribution channels, including the Internet, cassettes, mobile phones, and DVDs. Some videos are picked up and shown as news items on Western broadcasts, providing new reach into mainstream audiences. Al-Qaeda's operatives are adept at uploading a video simultaneously to several websites and posting messages on numerous others to attract audiences throughout the Muslim world.[10] Many of the products are aimed at terrorist-cell leaders who can download them to create DVDs or cassettes that can be shown in appropriate venues. Responsibility for the production of these videos lies with an entirely different cell than those that do the fighting.

Al-Qaeda understands better than most of its Western adversaries that winning a political debate rests as much as anything on how the debate is framed. Although its messages are negative, it maintains impressive message discipline in casting its actions in terms and with images that drive a narrative about standing up for the dignity and integrity of Islam, battling injustice and repression at the hands of the West, fighting against foreign occupation, and rebuffing a modern Christian crusade to dominate Muslims. It also promotes anti-Zionism, nationalism, restoration of the Caliphate, and related themes.

These videos legitimize violent tactics. They arouse fear among adversaries through images of gross brutality such as beheadings. They espouse doctrine and ideas through speeches by leaders such as Ayman al-Zawahiri, and, until their deaths, bin Laden and Abu Musab al-Zarqawi. They glorify suicide attacks. They record sniper attacks and destruction using weapons such as improvised explosive devices to demonstrate the ability to achieve military success. They show how to use weapons and kill people.

The videos attack Americans as crusaders; abusers of women and prisoners; sponsors of violence who destroy cities, homes, and families; and as infidels who seek to destroy Islam, divide Iraq and Muslims, kill innocents while protecting their own troops, and spread injustice and repression. The videos also tout insurgent success stories, martyr biographies, and operational news. Most are short, but some are much longer. *The Wedding of Martyrs*, for example, is a thirty-minute documentary about the ambush of a US patrol in Iraq.

Al-Qaeda operatives steal footage from YouTube.com or other sources and edit it, or change the soundtrack to suit their narrative. In one notable example, in Mesopotamia al-Qaeda created a montage based on the HBO documentary "Baghdad ER," which dealt with emergency medical care for wounded coalition forces. The group substituted its own soundtrack and a new beginning and ending to communicate the message that US forces were crying, hurting, and being defeated day after day. Although produced after Zarqawi's death, the closing features an image of a smiling Zarqawi with an audio track from a speech by Zawahiri proclaiming that the group was defeating coalition forces in Iraq.

Three videos, detailed below, illustrate how Iraqi jihadists approach strategy.[11] They have established sophisticated production companies that produce high-quality videos that seem to be rigorously evaluated for quality control and employ cutting-edge techniques.[12] The content shows political savvy and an ability to capitalize on rapidly changing circumstances.

THE REEMERGENCE OF THE CRUSADERS

Produced by a group that calls itself The Flag of Truth (Raya ul-Bayinah), *The Reemergence of the Crusaders* is a fine example of visual and rhetorical carpet-bombing.[13] It employs a sledgehammer approach that portrays the American presence in Iraq as an effort to promote Christianity, divide and destroy Islam, and humiliate and undermine the faith of Muslims. It argues that to achieve these goals America will do or say anything to win, including murdering innocent Iraqi civilians.

The video opens with a still image of crusaders mounted on awesome stallions attacking Muslims, over which we hear President George W. Bush declare, "This Crusade, it's going to take a while."

A rousing musical chorus in Arabic replaces the voice of the president.

Cut to former presidential candidate, Christian Coalition leader, and television evangelist Pat Robertson, who intones gravely: "Adolf Hitler was bad, but what the Muslims want to do to the Jews is worse."

Cut to Christian evangelist Reverend Jerry Falwell: "I think Mohammed was a terrorist."

Cut to evangelist Jerry Vines: "Islam was founded by Mohammed, a demon-possessed pedophile who had twelve wives and his last one was a nine-year-old girl."

Cut to a fourth evangelist: "We ought to take every single Muslim student in every college in this nation and shoot them back to where they came from."

Cut to Bush, speaking to Congress: "I also want to speak tonight to Muslims throughout the world. We respect your faith."

Cut to Falwell: "I think Mohammed was a terrorist."

Cut to Bush: "Our war is against evil, not against Islam. We don't hold a religion accountable. We're fighting against evil."

Cut to Robertson: "When are we going to get over political correctness and call a spade a spade and recognize what these people are?"

Cut to very tight shots of the president's mouth: "This Crusade . . . this Crusade . . . it's going to take a while."

Thumping music comes up, punctuated by drumbeats to suggest the notion of shots being fired.

Dissolve into a rapid montage punctuated by musical beats: soldiers at a church service where the most prominent image is a cross; US soldiers firing M-4s; a soldier, his palms turned upward toward heaven at a church service; a soldier strumming a guitar beneath a cross at mass; a Christian chaplain blessing a soldier; a closeup of a bible; a cross hanging from the turret of a tank.

Cut to Bush standing on a podium beneath a painting that depicts Christ: "This Crusade, it's going to take a while."

Cut to a lecherously grinning soldier in dark sunglasses with devil's horns attached to his helmet.

Christian images permeate the rest of the video, but now they are intercut with a new motif: Americans bring with them death, suffering, and humiliation for Muslims. The images include a US soldier, gruffly escorting a detained child and handing the child off into the custody of another soldier, images of Christian services, a cross hanging from a tank turret; dead Iraqi civilian children lying on the sand before an American tank as US soldiers languidly ignore the carnage; photos of Bush, in church, over which we hear the familiar refrain: "This Crusade, it's going to take a while." US soldiers occupying Muslim buildings, standing armed guard over Muslims who rest on their knees as they pray; mosques destroyed or defaced with tank or artillery fire; and, in general, US forces exercising armed domain over Iraq. The video closes with the president's words again: "This Crusade, it's going to take a while."

The editing technique is what is called a mash-up, a montage of different images taken out of their original context and articulated to form a cohesive statement with a new meaning that supports the insurgent cause. Every statement and image is taken from an American broadcast and presumably captured over the Internet, yet edited to drive an insurgent message. The video is disseminated in several languages, including English. An emotionally resonant soundtrack bolsters the slick editing. The editing inverts the meaning and context of the original images into a powerful visual indictment of the American presence in Iraq. Its impact is underscored by repeating and putting center-stage a single, ill-advised statement by Bush, transforming a casual remark into a universal declaration of anti-Islamic philosophy to drive the message that the American presence represents a modern-day crusade against Muslims. The brutal impact is reinforced by excerpts from harsh statements that capture the real anti-Muslim attitude of some Christian evangelists. The final product is a brilliantly articulated denunciation of who Americans are, what they stand for, and what they are doing in Iraq. The video aims to discredit the coalition and justify the combat waged against it.

In a 24/7 global media environment, anything uttered by a public figure may be instantly disseminated around the world, archived, and made accessible on the Internet. It can be taken out of context and amplified. According to Patricia Kushlis, "that was done regularly by third world media, but we did not know about it because it was local."[14] Politics may be local, but information is global. Many Muslims, moreover, do not distinguish between the personal statements made by public figures and the position of the US government. This video was skillfully edited to convey the impression that the preachers are echoing the president's true sentiments, rendering the president both anti-Islam and a hypocrite. Political figures need to be culturally sensitive to what they say even in a domestic political environment because their statements resonate globally. The use of the word "crusade'" was an inadvertent mistake; it meant something quite different to the president than to many Muslims. Finally, the video shows that information effects are created and sustained by action as much as words and must be thought about in that context.

Information environments are rife with ambiguity, and the jihadists look for any opportunity to twist actions or words in order to support their narrative and discredit that of their adversaries. A Muslim may respect the desire of Americans to practice their own faiths, yet take grave offense if persuaded that they do so at the expense of Islam. There is no formula for surmounting such challenges. Dealing with them requires thinking ahead, anticipating flashpoints, and taking steps to inoculate against such attacks—and, hopefully, turning those attacks against adversaries.

The Reemergence of the Crusaders shows the initiative of Iraqi insurgents. Its reach and penetration are unclear, but it is effective propaganda that draws power from doubts already held about the American presence in Iraq. These doubts are well reflected in polling data, and there is no reason to presume that insurgents are unaware of them.[15]

Although edited to fit an insurgent narrative, the images presented echo what Iraqis see on the ground, and that reinforces other doubts. Strategically, the video offers a window through which Iraqis and other Muslims are invited to perceive Americans more generally. The political implication is that a nation that actively imposes its own Christian religion on Muslims and that treats Muslims harshly is bent on conquest and domination, represents a threat to Muslim identity and culture, and should be ejected. The video serves to legitimize violence and death and opposition to American presence. No other medium could articulate that case as concisely or powerfully.

THE REPUBLIC OF FALLUJAH

The Republic of Fallujah is a one-hour documentary produced by al-Arabiya Television that was aired in November 2005. It was posted in its entirety on a jihadi website in December 2005, an example of the insurgent tactic of using documentaries produced by third parties for their own purposes. A key segment features the family of Hajj Mahmood, a resident of the Iraqi city of Fallujah, who volunteered for the Red Crescent during the first battle for the city in April 2004, the coalition's Operation Vigilant Resolve. The Mahmoods cooked and delivered food to needy families and fighters. Coalition forces called off the operation after an agreement was reached with local residents to keep insurgents out of the city. After the second battle, Operation Phantom Fury, in November 2004, al-Arabiya went back to see what had happened to the Mahmoods. The segment is a powerful before-and-after look that jihadis used to advance the argument that they were fighting against a brutal and unjust foreign presence. The segment tells a simple, easily understood story that insurgents turned into a compelling message denouncing the arrogance of American power and the destructive consequences of American tactics in Iraq.

The first part presents a happy, middle-class family home in Fallujah prior to the first battle. Mahmood invites the TV crew into his home, and Umm Mustafa, his wife, greets the TV crew, proudly announcing that "we are serving the people of our city, and we have decided to stay and see how things will end."

Sad music comes up and under as we cut to Umm Mustafa in November. She is crying, and laments that "we have left our house out of fear. After [the US troops] destroyed our home, they burned it and left, there is nothing left for us in this house, I lost my son during the air bombing, I lost my son. Where are my children and where am I going to live? Do we live in the streets? There is no power to rely on—only God's power."

The battle has destroyed the home. Umm Mustafa explains what happened, as they look at the ruined kitchen: "The first bomb came thrown from here. We ran with fear to the neighbor's house." As she speaks, we see dramatic side-by-side images of the before and after. The film's narrator declares: "Hajj Mahmood did not have the opportunity to bury the bodies of two of his relatives, so he left them in the top of the roof of his burned house."

Mahmood's wife is inconsolable. She asks her husband: "What are we going to do here, Mahmood? What are we going to do? Our son was killed, we lost our house, and nothing is left for us here. Why should we stay here?"

Over other images, the narrator relates: "A few days later . . . the national guards captured Umm Mustafa for two days. After that the American forces arrest him." He goes on to state that Mahmood has been held in Boca prison in Basra under the number 67, and concludes: "More than eight months have passed since his arrest, and till now, he has not been charged with anything."

The video's impact turns, as did *The Reemergence of the Crusaders*, on the combination of words, music, and images that Iraqis saw on television. Indeed, so powerful are video images that as Marc Lynch has observed, al-Jazeera's media coverage of the first battle, where its crews were present, "contradicted the coalition's narrative so graphically and dramatically that it determined the outcome of that battle."[16]

It is not clear who actually destroyed the Mahmood home. Battle may have destroyed it, or insurgents may have destroyed it in order to create a photo-op to discredit American operations. The point is that the insurgents are ruthless in capitalizing on any battle to develop and drive the messages that support their rationale, and they show sophistication in comprehending what images help to achieve that goal.

THE TOP TEN

Undercutting coalition credibility in Iraq is one thing. But insurgents also face the challenge of showing that they can succeed in ways that appeal to specific demographic audiences who may provide active recruits. A video titled *The Top Ten*, later expanded to *The Top Twenty*, presents a montage of incidents that ostensibly document insurgent sniper and bomb attacks against coalition forces.[17] The title was consciously selected to echo television shows that appeal to younger people who comprise a target audience of potential recruits.

The structure of the video is simple. It opens with a snazzy, animated graphic from the Islamic Media Front studio that is a knockoff of the opening animation from 20th Century Fox pictures, followed by animation that announces the "Top Ten Attacks." These are followed by clips of attacks on coalition soldiers, vehicles, or installations.

The video is a form of reality television. It aims, first, to show that insurgent tactics produce success. Insurgents have grown adept at planning attacks and take special care to make video recordings to document them, sometimes using two to three cameramen to record the action. These are distributed to the news media and through other channels such as the Internet. Second, the video aims to demoralize the opposition by showing insurgent capacity to inflict casualties and damage. It is clever propaganda for demonstrating to a populace that the authorities are unable to protect themselves or the people, undermining confidence in the government and its stability. The video technique is direct, clear, and uncluttered.

THE TALIBAN

In Afghanistan, the Taliban have duplicated the tactic reflected by *The Top Ten*. DVD stalls in Kabul sell videos that portray Western troops wounded or killed, or US military vehicles exploding, and foreigners being dragged and mutiliated. As with the al-Qaeda videos in Iraq, the violent images are punctuated, produced by operations such as Quetta Jihadi Studios or Wardak Matyrdom Studios, and include soundtracks that feature gunfire and male voices that chant praise for their martyrs.[18]

Games People Play

Video games offer cutting-edge technology to communicate and influence values, attitudes, and opinions, to define themes and messages, and provide training. They are an innovative and unconventional way to influence mass audiences that would otherwise be difficult to reach. The interactive nature of such games and their hip image offer an opportunity to engage, on a one-to-one basis, targeted audiences that conventional means of communication have difficulty reaching. Games can reach a global audience through online distribution.

First-person shooter games portray the action from the player's point of view. The goal is to personally engage and defeat an adversary, although the games can also be played by multiple players. They can easily be modified to accommodate different cultures, and they can be played on mobile phones. "Kuma War" and "Battlefield 1942" are examples, as is "America's Army," an official game of the US army used to provide civilians with what it calls an "inside perspective and a virtual role in today's premier land force," as a recruiting tool, and to train soldiers for combat. Another game that the army commissioned for recruiting, "Future Force Company Commander," portrays the military in 2015 as an invulnerable high-tech machine.[19]

Real-time strategy games set the player up as a general commanding troops. These can be single player or multiplayer. "Command and Conquer: Generals" is a good example of this format. Role-playing games can be very sophisticated and have particular relevance to the war of ideas. "The Sims" and the Lucas Arts *Star Wars* game "Knights of the Old Republic" are familiar examples. A striking quality of this format is that the player may be forced to make moral choices. Such games can be designed to communicate strategic messages that support specific values.

Massive multiplayer online role-player games such as "Everquest" involve thousands of players at one time. The game play can be very realistic. "Second Life," developed by Linden Labs in 2003, which claims millions of players, is probably the best example.[20] A three-dimensional alternate world created by its residents and manifested by computer-generated avatars enables players almost literally to lead second lives.

Al-Qaeda has a first-person shooter game in which the objective is to kill the US president, the British prime minister, and other targets. Hezbollah has heavily marketed two sophisticated first-person shooter games, "Special Force" and "Special Force 2," available in several languages, including English. The first game posits a combat situation in which Hezbollah fighters engage and defeat Israeli attackers. The second recreates key events of the 2006 Israel-

Hezbollah war. The game is aimed at psychologically empowering young people (the average gamer is in his mid-twenties) with a sense that they can make a difference in fighting Israel.

According to Hezbollah media official Sheikh Ali Daher, the second game, sold in retail stores in Lebanon, presents the culture of the resistance to children: that occupation must be resisted, and that the land and the nation must be guarded. Through this game the child can build an idea of some of the most prominent battles and the idea that this enemy can be defeated.[21] Daher argues that the game forces players to think and use resources wisely.[22] It boasts first-rate graphics, a roaring soundtrack, and very competent action for the genre. Hezbollah has doubtless reached the same conclusion as American trainers about the ability of video games to effect a revolution in the art of warfare.[23]

Iran has come out with its own first-person shooter game produced by the Students Islamic Association, in which the player is an Iranian commando named Commander Bahman who must rescue two nuclear engineers, a husband-and-wife team kidnapped by the US military during a pilgrimage to the Shia holy site of Karbala and held in Iraq and Israel. Iran's red, white, and green flag flutters throughout the game. "We tried to promote the idea of defense, sacrifice, and martyrdom in this game," Mohammed Taqi Fakhrian, a leader of the group, stated.[24] The game was apparently designed in response to Kuma War's game "Assault on Iran," which depicts an attack on an Iranian nuclear facility. The same student group was previously responsible for an anti-Israeli game, "World without Zionism."[25]

Al-Qaeda's Information Strategy

Al-Qaeda's vision of the future is deeply rooted in a perception of the past thousand years, a point that resonates with an audience that grew up with and lives with the Koran as the central part of their lives. Bin Laden's vision of success involved ejecting the United States from Muslim lands, as he defined them. He sought to establish a global caliphate, although achievement of that goal in his mind necessarily lay down the road in the future, after infidels had been driven out of what he considered to be Muslim territory.[26] His demand was political, not religious, although he invoked religion to justify al-Qaeda's strategy and tactics of violence. Iraqi insurgents and the Taliban in Afghanistan similarly demand the expulsion of foreigners from their countries.

These political objectives are limited. Neither al-Qaeda nor any other Islamist terrorist group calling for overturning a state has defined a viable vision for an alternate society, a potentially lethal vulnerability that could be exploited.[27] But its definition of winning satisfies key information-campaign prerequisites for success. It sets forth a cause, defines stakes, and offers a narrative rooted in the claim that group members fight to right injustice, rectify humiliation, relieve suffering, and eject foreigners; it also offers a rationale that Islam justifies and indeed mandates extremist tactics. The organization's communication strategies and tactics aim to sustain that narrative. Al-Qaeda is about change and positions itself as a catalyst for change. Its actions and communication strategies reinforce that notion and provide a viable framework for political action. Forcing the United States to withdraw from Iraq or the Gulf, for example, would meet the group's definition of victory.

Al-Qaeda has a relatively straightforward strategy: Create chaos and instigate change by destabilizing and destroying any state that stands in its way. This strategy confronts, conceptually, an easier challenge than protecting an excising order. Al-Qaeda seeks to tear down, rather than protect or strengthen, a functioning government or society. In competing for control of populations or the power of a state, the primary goal of its tactics is to undermine trust and confidence in governments and officials, arouse hostility against any adversary, and create a sense of insecurity in a populace.[28] Religion, nationalism, and identity politics are invoked to justify violence, and the organization's communication tactics focus on enabling it to carry out this strategy. It is straight out of Marx and Lenin.

The capacity of violent extremist networks to use different aspects of the media space to give legitimacy to their actions and forge political support is impressive. Videos offered over the Internet or sent to news media are a uniquely powerful tool in their arsenal. They use the Internet and cyber-generated information differently than the United States does, because their decision-making process is streamlined. They are set up to move rapidly—often much more rapidly than Western governments do.[29]

Terrorist groups, especially in Iraq and Afghanistan, use videos to demonstrate success. A vital metric they employ is how quickly they get a video over the Internet and generate or influence news coverage. There can be a huge premium in getting to the news media first. Videos can generate coverage on satellite TV channels, which have the greatest reach for Arab viewers. Metrics are a complicated question and may differ from situation to situation, but it is critical to establish an information baseline from which to measure effects and to devise an approach that yields a concrete assessment of whether strategies, plans, and tactics succeed.

Al-Qaeda's assertion of injustice, suffering, humiliation, and the presence of foreigners in Muslim lands provides a core around which it has built a narrative, into which it has a clear definition of the stakes for each targeted audience. It roots the use of violence against civilians in religious justification and doctrines that emerged out of the Algerian civil war.[30] These include the doctrines of proportional response, which holds that when an infidel kills a Muslim, Muslims may attack infidel civilians in kind, and collective guilt, which holds that civilians who support an adversarial regime act as surrogates and representatives of the enemy and thus become legitimate targets.[31]

Central to al-Qaeda's operational thinking is the tenet that messages can be expressed through actions as well as through language and images. Military action has information effects; al-Qaeda's kinetic activity aims to achieve political impact and provides a foundation for the language and images that underlie its political communication.

Finally, hope and fear are the key motivators. Al-Qaeda's appeal to hope informs a strategy aimed at showing that it can succeed. Its appeal to fear, by showing that it can inflict destruction and death, is central to its images and videos.

Fighting Back

Balancing kinetic operations and information strategy is a challenge in countering insurgencies where the hearts and minds of the citizenry are the prize. The United States felt that it had important military reasons for attacking Fallujah, yet the information effects of the two battles had political consequences. The message that many Iraqis drew from the fighting was that coalition strategy and tactics placed firepower ahead of the safety and well-being of the civilians.

A key lesson of American political campaigns is that negative messages must be answered or risk audiences believing them. Failure to answer al-Qaeda messages bolsters their credibility and undermines that of Western forces. The Western forces also need to document what they do through their own videos and photographs and communicate these and their objectives to both the military and the media, so that reports of a battle support the narrative.

The recognition that information effects might shape the outcome of the battle as easily as traditional military action was not lost on coalition commanders when they moved in November. During the first battle, insurgents had taken over the hospital and transmitted false assertions of deaths and injuries to civilians. As the second battle began, American forces immediately seized control of the hospital, blocking insurgents from using it for propaganda. The coverage from the second battle was much more favorable to coalition activity.

The two battles drove home the necessity of laying a proper information foundation for military operations, providing a clear and credible explanation with documentation for an operation and doing this rapidly through credible channels. Beyond simply driving the message, an information strategy must anticipate what aspects of the operation can be used by the adversary to impeach one's credibility while building up its own. It is possible to inoculate against the damage that videos like *The Republic of Fallujah* may cause by driving the message that operations like those in Fallujah displace or destroy political fanatics who commit criminal acts of murder against innocent civilians, and that however difficult the fighting, the objective is to make a place better and more secure for the populace.

One asset that terrorist groups have for getting out their messages quickly is that they do not have to deal with a government bureaucracy. That challenge needs to be addressed. There is a need to move quickly to preempt efforts by adversaries to get out their story first. This means filling the media space from the ground up because every moment of attention that one's narrative attracts means less attention for that of one's adversaries. Equally, it has to be recognized that the goal of driving adversary communications off the air or shutting them down is a fantasy. They will have their say and they will get their message out. Those messages must be anticipated and beaten to the punch in order to undercut their credibility and keep driving the countermessage.

Political communication respects no formula, but a cardinal precept is that repetition equals penetration equals impact. Themes and messages need to be driven again and again. They need to be consistent and consistently articulated, and applied across the board in a theater of operations. One of the criticisms leveled against American efforts in Iraq, for example, was that for too long this principle was ignored.[32]

Exposing inconsistency is a good way to demonstrate hypocrisy and to discredit an opponent. People may agree or disagree with a rationale, but hypocrisy is a political turnoff as it goes to the core issues of trust and integrity. The United States cannot defeat terrorist ideas or ideology if its adversaries succeed in persuading audiences that it lacks either quality. But conversely, there needs to be focused effort to discredit videos that terrorist groups use. Truth is an ally in political television. Video responses to adversarial videos pointing out their fallacies and lies should be produced quickly, be uploaded to appropriate websites, and distributed to the news media.

There should be mash-ups of jihadi videos turning their images and rhetoric against them. Videos should employ humor and mock adversaries. Middle Eastern newspapers show a real sense of humor in their editorial cartoons. When the Lebanese weekly show *A Nation Smiles* broadcast a satire against Hezbollah leader Hassan Nasrullah, he responded by staging street demonstrations—a sure sign that mockery is an effective way to throw adversaries off their game and to force mistakes.

A series of videos that make a strong case supporting the Western narrative should also be produced and distributed, especially by uploading to YouTube and similar websites. The source of such videos needs to be host nations or local allies, who will be seen as more credible messengers, although the United States may provide technical or strategic assistance. These videos need not necessarily ask audiences to support the policy of the United States or other Western nations; they are helpful if they simply discredit terrorist ideas and ideology. Debates on talk shows carried by Arab satellite networks such as al-Jazeera, and internal al-Qaeda critiques found in publications by groups such as Egyptian Islamic Jihad, offer important material that can be used against the extremists.[33] The visibility of such critiques in the Muslim world should be promoted through public and private sources.

Clever media is not the same as effective political media. Clever videos can be turned back on their makers or be exploited to convey a different message. An example is the Senate race in Delaware in November 2010, where Christine O'Donnell had won an upset victory in the Republican primary to secure the nomination. Earlier in her career, she had confessed to dabbling in witchcraft, a statement that haunted her campaign. Her opening general-election spot presented her staring into the camera against a stark, black background. In a sweet, alluring tone, she stated: "I'm not a witch. I'm nothing you've heard. I'm you."[34] The ad aimed to refocus attention on her. It succeeded, but it also turned her into a laughingstock. The satiric television show *Saturday Night Live* led the way with a parody duplicating the look and feel of O'Donnell's ad and featuring an O'Donnell look-alike who stated: "Hi, I'm Christine O'Donnell and I'm not a witch. I'm nothing like you've heard. I'm you. And just like you, I have to constantly deny that I'm a witch. Isn't that what the people of Delaware deserve—a candidate who promises first and foremost that she is not a witch? That's the kind of candidate Delaware hasn't had since 1692."[35]

O'Donnell and her consultant did draw a lot of media attention, but not the kind they may have hoped for. She was never likely to win and, as most strategists predicted, got crushed in the election. But airing clever media that opened her up to ridicule squandered whatever opportunity she had. The failure defines a political trap to avoid: Creative media is not necessarily smart media.

A parody of the classic million-dollar 1984 television spot that introduced the Apple Macintosh computer, directed by Academy Award winner Ridley Scott, shows how easily a brilliantly produced video can be mashed up and used by another party to suit its own agenda. Justifiably famous, the Mac ad depicted a grey, Orwellian world destroyed by a vibrant, colorfully dressed female insurgent, with the tagline "you'll see that 1984 won't be like 1984."

In 2007, during the early stages of the US presidential election campaign, a mash-up of the video was produced independently in support of Barack Obama's candidacy, replacing the image of Big Brother with an image of Hillary Clinton, with the tagline "you'll see that 2008 won't be like 1984."[36] An impressed Brian Williams, the anchor of *NBC Nightly News*, commented on television that someone had obviously spent a lot of money on this video. In fact, it could have been produced using inexpensive and widely available software for a few hundred dollars. The mash-up drew over two million hits within a week and gave Barack Obama's campaign an injection of energy and freshness.

The best political communications do not require and often reject fancy production values. What matters is that the images and message be credible and resonate. Videos like *The Top Ten*, *The Republic of Fallujah*, and *The Reemergence of the Crusaders* are essentially products of image collection and editing. High production values do not necessarily equate to effective political media.

A case study is offered by an unidentified group that presented a magnificently produced ad to discourage suicide bombers.[37] Produced at a cost of a million dollars, it depicts a suicide bomber entering a crowded marketplace and blowing himself up, along with shoppers and children. The exceptional special effects consciously replicated the visual feeling and texture of the groundbreaking film *The Matrix*. But the Hollywood production house that handled the production issued a press release that bragged about its role in the production.[38] In a 24/7 global media environment, that boast helped discredit that ad as Western propaganda. The bomber, moreover, looked a lot like Jason Stratham, the handsome action star of *The Transporter*; two Middle Eastern focus groups asked to evaluate the ad produced severely negative responses. A West Bank group laughed it off as obviously a product of Hollywood, and pointed out that news coverage of suicide attacks showed more blood, gore, and despair. A group from Egyptian Islamic Jihad felt that it glamorized the attack and was more likely to encourage than discourage a suicide attack, given the spectacle. Beyond that, the quick editing that creates a kaleidoscopic portrait of the marketplace and the action makes this ad interesting to watch, but lends itself to simple mash-ups that could just as easily depict the destruction coming at the hands of American warplanes, Israeli tanks, or some other combination that discredits counterterrorist forces.

Conclusion

Media evolves with technology. The United States and its allies need to anticipate where and how these changes will occur in projecting strategic narratives, and stay ahead of the curve technically and substantively in engaging and prevailing against terrorist ideas and ideology in the media battlespace. But that space is too large, complex, and fluid for any one actor to dominate. Vision plays a pivotal role in any political dynamic, but it can never be presumed that one's own positive vision is clear, comprehensible, or understood by foreign audiences. Successful strategy requires that such perceptions are not left to chance.

CHAPTER 16

Radio as a Weapon

RADIO CAN BE USED AS A TOOL FOR STRATEGIC COMMUNICATION AND A WEAPON to kill. The Hutu campaign of genocide in 1994 that apparently exterminated 80 percent of the Tutsi in Rwanda offers a compelling case study. There is much excellent scholarship and reporting on this preventable tragedy.[1] Radio was a powerful weapon for killing, although it served as merely one of several elements in a killing machine that planned, mounted, supervised, and executed the genocide.

The International Criminal Tribunal for Rwanda

The remarkable books by Alison des Forges and Philip Gourevitch stand as landmarks in understanding the genocide.[2] In truly comprehending how radio was used as a weapon and the context in which it was used, the written judgments rendered by the International Criminal Tribunal for Rwanda (ICTR) offer particular insight.[3]

The Historical Context

In 1959, Rwanda gained independence from Belgium, to whom the League of Nations had granted a governing mandate. Modern Rwanda history has been marked by revolution and ethnic clashes between the Hutu and Tutsi peoples.[4] Rwanda was organized into eighteen clans defined along lines of kinship.[5] In the 1930s, Belgian authorities made ethnicity central to identity, dividing the population into three ethnic groups: the Hutu (who represented 84 percent of the population), the Tutsi (about 15 percent), and the Twa (about 1 percent). They also required people to carry identity cards, a decision that had ominous consequences. Like the Belgians, the Catholic Church treated the Tutsis as an elite.[6]

In 1956, Belgium organized elections for local bodies. That changed the nation's political dynamics. The Hutu majority voted along ethnic lines to give them a majority. Political parties formed in 1957. They organized along ethnic lines, not ideology.[7] In March 1957, Hutu intellectuals published *The Hutu Manifesto*, which argued that as the majority, Hutus should rule. Not surprisingly, that fueled ethnic tensions.

These tensions created violence that persisted after independence was declared in 1962. In 1963, Tutsi guerillas who had fled the country returned to make small incursions into southern Rwanda. The Hutu called the intruders *Inyenazi*, or cockroaches, a term that came to haunt the nation thirty years later. In July 1973, Army Chief of Staff Juvenal Habyarimana seized power in a coup, although some contend that his wife, Madame Agathe, exercised the real power from behind the scenes as part of a hardcore Hutu power bloc known as the *akazu* (little house).[8] He instituted a one-party system run by the Mouvement revolutionaire national pour le developpement (MRND). All citizens were required to become members.[9] Punitive action against the Tutsi followed, and a quota system enshrined ethnic discrimination.

The Tutsi refused to bow to Hutu rule. In October 1990, an exiled Tutsi group called the Rwandan Patriotic Front (RPF) launched an attack from Uganda. It met with superficial success. Habyarimana was forced to strike a compromise that accepted in principle a multiparty system. The compromise did nothing to dampen the ambitions of both sides for power.

The RPF was determined to overthrow Habyarimana. The Hutus understood that and reacted. Enraged mobs and militia massacred Tutsis in October 1990, in the early months of 1991, and in August 1992. Officials, the police, and the army in Rwanda encouraged or were complicit in these attacks.[10] These engagements set the stage for the genocide. Author Gerald Caplan argues that the lesson Hutu organizers drew was that "they could not only massacre large numbers of people quickly and efficiently, they could get away with it."[11]

In February 1993, the RPF launched a new attack that seriously undermined relations between the RPF and the Hutu opposition parties. Habyarimana supporters exploited the situation to call for Hutu unity. The country polarized into two camps: Hutu and Tutsi.[12]

In the meantime, a group of Hutu hard-liners had founded a new radical political party, the Coalition pour la defense de la republique (CDR). The CDR was even more extremist than Habyarimana.[13] An extremist youth militia, the Interahamwe, was formed in July 1993. It established Radio Television Libre des Mille Collines (RTLM), which wasted no time spreading anti-Tutsi hatred. In August 1993, the Hutu-dominated government of Rwanda and the RPF signed an agreement, the Arusha Accords, that provided for power-sharing between the Tutsi's Rwanda Patriotic Front and the Hutu government in a broad-based transitional government that included the RPF and four other political parties.[14] One feature called for the deployment of a United Nations peacekeeping force, the United Nations Assistance Mission for Rwanda (UN-AMIR), to monitor the peace agreement.[15]

The accords settled nothing, and soon after, the political situation began to disintegrate. In October 1993, Tutsi soldiers staging a coup assassinated the Hutu president of neighboring Burundi, Melchior Ndadaye. Tutsi massacres of Hutu followed. Many Rwandan Hutu argued that this proved the Tutsis could not be trusted. Hutu power emerged as an explicit and public organizing concept.[16]

On April 6, 1994, an aircraft carrying President Habyarimana and Ciyprien Ntaryamira, the new Hutu Burundian president, crashed near Kigali airport, killing all aboard. In Burundi, military and political leaders successfully maintained calm. In Rwanda, the assassinations unleashed the waiting forces of genocide. The United Nations commander, Lt. Gen. Romeo Dallaire, had earlier cabled his superiors in writing on January 11 that the Hutus were arming and putting in place a plan to exterminate the Tutsis that included drawing up lists of Tutsis whom they targeted for elimination. Dalliare got nowhere. Both Kofi Annan, then the head of African Peacekeeping operations for the UN, and Secretary-General Boutros Boutros-Ghali, ignored it.[17]

Whether intervention once the genocide got under way could have stopped most of the violence is an argument to be resolved in a different venue. There are competing views about the speed with which the genocide unfolded and who knew what and when.[18] By heeding Dallaire's request for 5,000 well-armed troops in advance, the UN might have prevented the tragedy. What could have been achieved had such a force arrived after it started centers more on the extent to which the killing might have been limited.

It wasn't a matter of whether troops could have been sent; they were sent. A thousand well-trained French, Belgian, and Italian forces arrived quickly as part of Operation Amaryllis. Another 1,500 Belgian, American, and French troops were on standby in the region.[19] There is a dispute as to whether this force might have stopped the violence. Scholars such as Alan J. Kuperman argue that this force was too small and too lightly armed to stop the quickly unfolding violence. He contends that the force already faced hostility from both Hutu militia and national police as well as Tutsi rebels who had access to surface-to-air missiles and were threatening to attack the evacuators if they extended their mission.[20] Others, like Alison des Forges, argue that "the evacuation force could have deterred the killings had they acted promptly."[21] Indeed, the Hutu leadership was identifiable, well integrated, and relatively easy for such a force to strike. The foreign troops could have stopped the genocide. But their mission was limited to evacuating Western residents of Rwanda.[22]

The United States and Britain refused to intervene—a decision for which Bill Clinton would later apologize. Samantha Power, today a special assistant to President Obama and a senior director on the National Security Council, has written a brilliant, searing indictment of Clinton's State Department and its decision making, his national security adviser Tony Lake, and Richard Clarke for their appalling performance.[23] There are many parties to blame. The Catholic and Anglican churches declined to exert their moral influence to prevent genocide. So did the French government, whom the Hutus viewed as their strong allies—not a surprising perception, given that the French had armed the Hutu and advised them.[24]

In the wake of Habyarimana's death, the presidential guard wasted no time in slaughtering Tutsi and political opposition leaders. Any Hutu who opposed the genocide was executed. Jean Kampanda, who was later given a life sentence by the International Criminal Tribunal, took over as prime minister. Instructions were given to Hutus to kill Tutsi: the killing was called "work," and machetes and firearms were described as "tools."[25] Roadblocks stopped fleeing Tutsis, and others were driven to churches, schools, or public places where they were then slaughtered. Much of this took place in April 1994, but the killings continued into the summer.

The Hutu Propaganda Campaign of Hate

Radio was a key weapon in the campaign of genocide. The Hutus drew upon the experience of experts: Lenin and Goebbels. Well before the genocide, a Hutu propagandist wrote a book that advocated the use of lies, exaggeration, ridicule, and innuendo. The book argued that the public had to be persuaded that the adversary "stands for war, death, slavery, repression, injustice, and sadistic cruelty." He stressed the importance of linking propaganda to events or creating them. He proposed the tactic of "accusation in a mirror," by which one's own intentions are imputed to the adversary. In other words, the party using terror should accuse the enemy of employing it. The communication strategy was to persuade honest people that any means necessary to defeat the enemy were legitimate.[26] A military commission defined the Tutsi as the "enemy" and ordered all units to draw up lists of enemy accomplices.[27]

In any conflict, control of the narrative is vital. The Hutus understood that and went out of their way to define and control one that placed them on the moral high ground. They relied upon radio and newspapers to drive themes and messages that characterized their killing as defensive. Radio was a weapon, although only one among several employed; newspapers played a role, notably *Kangura* ("Wake Up"), which molded attitudes and opinions of elites.

In December 1990, *Kangura* published the notorious "Appeal to the Conscience of the Hutu." The article contained "Ten Commandments" warning readers that the enemy—the Tutsi—was "still there, among us" and waiting "to decimate us."[28] The text "was an unequivocal call to take action against the Tutsi."[29] A call-to-arms for Hutu ideology, they portrayed the Tutsi "as the enemy, as evil, dishonest and ambitious." In the words of the International Criminal Tribunal, the text conveyed "contempt and hatred for the Tutsi ethnic group and for Tutsi women in particular as enemy agents." The text condemned Tutsis purely because of their ethnicity.[30]

The commandments merit review. They focused on the role of sex, money, business, and Hutu identity. The introduction declared: "Hutu, wherever you may be, wake up! Be firm and vigilant. Take all necessary measures to deter the enemy from launching a fresh attack." It described the Tutsi as "bloodthirsty" and committed to the "permanent dream of the Tutsi" to rule Rwanda. It accused the Tutsi of using money to dishonestly take over Hutu companies and the state. It warned against "the Tutsi woman," whom the Tutsis would sell or marry off to Hutus as spies. It charged that any Hutu who married a Tutsi woman, kept one as a concubine, or made one his secretary or protégée was a traitor.

The "Ten Commandments" was followed up by the "19 Commandments." Ostensibly a call for readers to follow Tutsi commandments, the actual intent of these—which included a commandment that Tutsi should subordinate the Hutu—was to fuel Hutu hatred. *Kangura* understood exactly how the Hutus would respond. Other articles portrayed the Tutsi as "wicked and ambitious, using women and money against the vulnerable Hutu."[31] Presenting Tutsi women as femmes fatales associated their sexuality with danger. This narrative articulated a framework that made the sexual attack of Tutsi women "a foreseeable consequence of the role attributed to them."[32]

RTLM RADIO

"Hello, good day, have you started to work yet?" RTLM Radio asked its listeners every morning.[33] RTLM radio began broadcasting in July 1993. Darryl Li characterizes its broadcasters as *animateurs*, contending that the English words "journalist," "broadcaster," "disc jockey," and "personality" "do not capture this dimension, nor does the Kinyarwanda word *umunyamakuru* (literally, 'one of the news' or 'newsman').[34] A half dozen or so individuals became renowned in this role: Kantano Habimana, Valerie Bemeriki, Noel Hitimana, Georges Ruggiu (a Belgian), Ananie Nkurunziza, Ferdinand Nahimana, and the gifted singer and composer Simon Bikindi, whose uplifting, spirited compositions served the darkest of purposes in inciting anti-Tutsi hatred and violence. Most are now in prison, dead, or missing.

Some might expect that the Hutus were inartful thugs, but in reality, those whom RTLM employed had enormous talent. In a culture that prized the oral tradition of communication, its animateurs had "distinctive on-air personalities and sought to implicate listeners in the genocide."[35] Des Forges explains: "RTLM brought the voice of ordinary people to the airwaves. Listeners could call in to request their favourite tunes or to exchange gossip with announcers and a wider audience. RTLM journalists went out into the streets and invited passers-by to comment on topics of the day. This populist approach allowed RTLM to claim a legitimacy different from that of Radio Rwanda," which had more staid programming and tended to broadcast statement. Citing one Rwandan, she noted that RTLM offered comments that sounded like "a conversation among Rwandans who knew each other well and were relaxing over some banana beer or a bottle of Primus in a bar."[36]

The animateurs had wit and street smarts, could establish a one-to-one bond with listeners, and attracted listeners with popular music from the Congo and, notably, eight Bikindi compositions.[37] Different personalities fulfilled different roles. Nkurunziza offered political analysis. Hitimana offered personal greetings to different regions and individuals. Gaspard Gahigi was a political pundit. Habimana had radio charisma. Ruggiu was apparently hired because he was white. According to Darryl Li, this gave RTLM "the appearance of strength.[38]

The Hutus employed RTLM and Radio Rwanda as integral tools for strategic communication and to facilitate genocide. RTLM's efforts were mounted in tandem with *Kangura*, whose editor appeared as a guest. Tutsis and opposition voices were accorded virtually no opportunity to be heard on these radio channels.[39] More typically, the broadcasts incited Hutu emotions by denouncing the Tutsis as *Inyenzi* (cockroaches) and *Inkotanyi* (enemy) who plan to attack and kill Hutu.[40] In a November 1993 broadcast, Noel Nahimana explained to Gaspard Gahigi the origin of the term *Inyenzi*: "There is no difference between the RPF and the *Inyenzi* because the *Inyenzi* are the refugees who fled Rwanda after the mass majority Revolution of 1959." They "are people who attack and kill."[41] Kantano Habimana, considered among the most able *animateurs*, and Noel Hitimana declared in a March 23, 1994, broadcast that Tutsi "still have the single objective: to take back the power that the Hutus seized from them . . . and keep it for as long as they want."[42] Not only, RTML broadcasters said, did the Tutsi want to regain power; they intended to seize it by force or trickery.[43] RTLM called upon Hutus to be vigilant.[44] Such statements laid a clear foundation for Hutus to be wary of and fear the Tutsi, and they were made with the conscious intent of inspiring that response.

In early April, RTML was broadcasting the names of individuals whom Hitimana identified as enemy accomplices, as well as where to find them.[45] In May and June, Habimana broadcast a call for the extermination of the Tutsi.[46] Rwandan scholar Scott Straus contends that much of the genocide had taken place by then, but there is little doubt that the murders continued into the summer.[47] Another scholar, Jean-Paul Christien, observed that broadcasts targeted Tutsi who were frightened and took refuge in churches.[48] What struck the International Criminal Tribunal as it reviewed transcripts of the broadcasts was "the striking indifference to these massacres evident in the broadcasts and the dehumanization of the victims."[49] Thus, the clubbing to death of a child was described in dispassionate, clinical language: "Last night, I saw a Tutsi child who had been wounded and thrown into a hole 15 meters deep. He managed to get out of the hole, after which he was finished with a club. Before he died he was interrogated. . . . We are more numerous than them. I believe they will be wiped out if they don't withdraw."[50]

One tribunal witness testified that RTLM "was constantly asking people to kill other people, to look for those who were in hiding, and to describe the hiding places of those who were described as being accomplices."[51] It broadcast "The Ten Commandments" to unite Hutus and sanction genocide. Husbands even received sanction to kill Tutsi wives, and children of mixed ethnic marriages were encouraged to kill their Tutsi mothers.[52]

Hate broadcasts were punctuated by Bikindi's music, with "I Hate the Hutu" and other songs being especially popular.[53] Nanga Abahutu preached hatred against Hutu who were friends with Tutsi, Hutu who forsook their Hutu identity by becoming Tutsi for employment or education advantages, Hutu who despised other Hutu, Hutu who were greedy and lived off bribes from Tutsi, Hutu who engaged in war with Tutsi without realizing what was at stake; and Hutu who failed to ensure the unity of the Hutu.[54] One verse stated: "As for me, I hate the Hutu, these Hutu who do not remember, who do not remember the saying you must deal with Ruhande by killing Mphandahande," reminding the Hutu of the evil deeds that the Tutsi carried out against the Hutu subchief Mpandahande of Ruhande.[55]

"Bene Sebahinzi" referenced a Tutsi king who wore the genital organs of defeated Hutu, thus reminding listeners of their killers. On May 17, 1994, RTLM journalist Habimana stated that "Bene Sebahinzi" predicted the future and that there would be no more cockroaches, as they would have been exterminated: "Please listen to Bikindi's advice to the *Inkotayani* (Tutsi)." The tribunal found that he was warning them they will all be wiped out.

Twasezereye, which is posted on YouTube, became a rallying call for Hutu unity by reminding them of past subservience to the Tutsi.[56] The first refrain translates to "we bade farewell to the monarchy," a reference to external Tutsi threats. It's a little unsettling. One might expect evil people to write bad music, but Bikindi did the opposite, disseminating pro-Hutu ideology and anti-Tutsi hatred with creative compositions.[57] RTML was highly successful in using music to attract cadres of listeners. Radio transcripts showed that journalists and speakers interpreted the lyrics as a message to kill.[58] They became integral as part of the campaign to "target the Tutsi enemy and to sensitize and incite the listening public to target and commit acts of violence against the Tutsi."[59] Many RTLM broadcasts "explicitly called for extermination."[60]

THE IMPACT OF RADIO

Rwanda's oral tradition amplified the impact of radio broadcasts, and Rwandans paid great heed to them. They provided a cloak of legitimacy to the campaign, as Scott Straus points out.[61] The tribunal found a direct causal link between broadcasting the names of victims and their murderers, and that RTLM broadcasts engaged in ethnic stereotyping and promoted contempt, hatred, and extermination.[62] Habimana spoke of exterminating them "from the surface of the earth . . . to make them disappear for good."[63] Nkurunziza expressed the hope in June that the extermination was under way and that "we continue exterminating them at the same pace."[64]

Radio was the medium of mass communication. People listened to RTLM at home, in bars, on the streets, and at roadblocks. They whipped up hatred that the militia used to encourage—and force—people to kill. The message was that "the Tutsi were the enemy and had to be eliminated once and for all."[65] It aired advertisements for *Kangura*, and the animateurs commented on every single issue that the newspaper published.[66] RTLM and *Kangura* functioned as partners in the Hutu coalition along with the CDR, with *Kangura* invoking the word "solidarity."[67]

The United States rejected suggestions to jam, destroy, or counter RTLM. Financially, the Department of Defense objected to the cost of jamming, estimating it to be $8,500 an hour.[68] One person engaged in the discussions was former Director of the US Information Agency Joseph Duffey, who is critical of US decision making in the Rwanda crisis. "DoD was flat wrong," he says. "In my judgment, we could have jammed RTLM for far less than that. We had portable jammers. They were available. They were not being used. We could have stationed them in Burundi." Duffey drafted an action plan but got nowhere. "Incredibly, I was met by objections from the broadcast people at the Voice of America, who thought that the United States should respect Rwandans' free speech. They reasoned that in other regions of the world, it was US broadcasting that was being jammed. They had protested and they wanted to be consistent. My feeling was that RTLM's hate broadcasting was costing lives. Stopping it was the priority. Unfortunately, the bureaucracy proved intransigent and prevailed."[69]

State Department lawyers were no help, either. Instead of seeking solutions, they worried about whether jamming might violate Rwandan sovereignty. One must not oversimplify. Different actions by the Hutu played vital roles in an organized campaign of genocide driven by the Hutu extremist leadership. Concludes Scott Straus: "Many who participated in the genocide did so only after authorities or groups of violent toughs demanded face-to-face that they do so. The elites and young toughs formed a core of violence. These people crisscrossed communities to recruit Hutu killers. They recruited by going house-to-house, at markets, rural commercial centers, rural bars or at meetings called by authorities. National elites fanned out to local areas to meet with local officials who then mobilized citizens in their areas to kill."[70]

Rwanda is a geographically compact nation. Its hierarchical structure of government facilitated the ability of a centralized leadership to exert influence on local authorities. Hutu leadership, military, police, and violent youth groups were able to overcome local resistance that emerged in different areas to enforce their will. Helping that was the fact that the genocide transpired in a chaotic political environment of suspicion, mistrust, and war, and the assassinations of the Hutu presidents of Rwanda and Burundi.[71] These events molded public opinion and attitudes and framed the context for the strategic communication undertaken by all sides. In this case radio was a vital weapon for murder as an integral part in a larger political and military killing machine.

PART V

More Effective Strategic Communication

CHAPTER 17

Change That Would Matter

Changing the way the US government does business ranks among the more challenging ambitions anyone can take on, but its approach to strategic communication would be more effective if a core set of reforms were adopted. These suggestions are focused on national security and foreign affairs.

Centralize Control of Strategic Communication

Centralizing control of strategic communication for the US government within the White House on key issues would help ensure consistency. Eisenhower recognized the value of this approach. It produced a unified government approach to strategic communication against the Soviets. Other presidents have reshaped the process to suit their tastes, with less appealing results. Many people have suggested placing strategic communication under White House control, and that is my suggestion as well. The White House has the authority and political responsibility to manage political agendas, define policies, and to forge and drive narratives, themes, and messages. Centralizing control would help cut through debates at high levels as to who has the lead for strategic communication. This is a very complicated and nuanced challenge; one cannot do a discussion justice in a few paragraphs, but the issue merits highlighting. *How* the White House exerts control over communication is as important as the effort to do so. That will vary from issue to issue, crisis to crisis, administration to administration. As National Security Council strategist Kevin McCarty explained above, the George W. Bush administration's effort in doing everything possible to ensure that the surge in Iraq was successful offers a key example of how that task can be done correctly.

Overgeneralizing is dangerous. Still, on selected issues, the White House communications director would seem well advised to require every assistant secretary of public affairs at the cabinet officer level to participate in a conference call twice a week to discuss narratives, themes, messages, and talking points, to receive reports on what they are doing to advance administration goals in their area, and to ensure consistent direction. That was done during the George W. Bush administration in regards to Iraq during the second term. Those conversations focused the high-level key players in a disciplined way on a consistent strategy, plan, and messages. It was a proactive effort and forward-looking, not reactive. It worked well. Each administration needs to decide how to accomplish this in a disciplined way on specific issues.

Doing this for all issues would prove overwhelming. Agencies like the Voice of America and Broadcasting Board of Governors that have forged clearly defined missions and strategic objectives may offer competing views to those held by the Department of State, and their views may differ from those held by the Defense Department or other stakeholders.[1] It's vital that the US government establish consistent narratives as to what, why, where, and how it does things in countering violent extremism or other issues.

Maximize Efforts at Strategic Communication

In 2012, the Office of the Coordinator for Counterterrorism in the Department of State was elevated to the status of a bureau and placed under the lead of an assistant secretary of state, who reports to the undersecretary of state for civil society, democracy, and human rights. The bureau's mission is to take the lead for the Department of State in developing counterterrorism strategies, policies, operations, and programs to defeat terrorism.[2] In 2011, the president established, as a temporary organization, a Center for Strategic Counterterrorism Communications (CSCC) under the direction of an eminent diplomat and under the purview of the undersecretary of state for public diplomacy and public affairs.[3] As noted earlier, such efforts to mount effective information strategies to counter adversaries abroad have been tried before. One wishes the latest efforts to be successful.

CSCC functions include monitoring and evaluating narratives, messages, and events abroad that are central to the US strategic narrative, and to counter violent extremism and terrorism that threaten the national security of the United States. It is tasked with developing narratives and strategies; identifying trends in extremist communications; employing digital technologies to fight violent extremism; sharing expertise among agencies; requiring agencies to provide intelligence, data, and analysis; identifying shortfalls in US capabilities; and working with other agencies to provide its expertise. There seems a better chance of success in countering the ideology of violent extremism by ensuring that the CSCC is permanently and robustly resourced.

Additional steps that would help maximize the effectiveness of such efforts by both the Bureau of Counterterrorism and the CSCC would be to coalesce them into a single organization, which I'll term "the center" here. The steps would include:

- Centralizing their functions within the White House, where the center would report to the president rather than the secretary of state or an interagency steering committee. The State Department has historically shown caution against engaging even in public diplomacy. Patricia Kushlis contends that "foreign service careers in public diplomacy are just not priorities for the Department. They rarely enhance careers. During the past decade, State has proven yet again that it cannot handle a robust public diplomacy or even public affairs presence, no matter which administration is in power."[4] Even after September 11, the State Department showed no interest in participating in a 2004 proposal embraced by the Defense Science Board that originated in the Department of Defense, and was pursued with its backing to help other nations shoulder the burden of responsibility for protecting their sovereignty within their borders by providing counsel on issue management campaigns to discredit or marginalize violent extremist ideas and actions.

- It bears noting that the most successful information warfare effort made by the US government arguably took place under President Dwight Eisenhower, who centralized those efforts in the White House through the Operations Coordinating Board and the National Security Council. Keen for expert input, he employed these institutions in tandem with a circle of close advisers whom he consulted informally.[5] Eisenhower was an extremely effective executive whose grandfatherly public face masked a steel-trap mind, a clear vision in national security, and tough-minded decisiveness, and he was unwilling to allow the Department of State or any other part of government to obstruct his foreign policy. Critics wondered whether his approach was too bureaucratic, whether a less experienced president could make it function, and that it did not adequately address the broad range of issues confronting a president. Eisenhower's son has written that his father relied more upon informal processes for decision making, but that is merely one opinion.[6] Others have disagreed. But it worked well for an experienced, informed president who understood national security. Eisenhower offered the right model for dealing with violent extremism.

- Eisenhower was focused on winning the Cold War by whatever means appropriate. Current efforts by CSCC aim at countering violent extremism through communication. The current structure is too diffuse, too narrow, and too separated from the center of power that resides in the Executive Office. Centralizing efforts to counter violent extremism in the White House would enable the government to leverage all of its tools in a "whole of government" approach to surmounting this challenge, including communication, military, law enforcement, and other resources.

- Here is the cold reality of government: People in one department or agency don't like spending their time, money, and resources on other people's ideas. This is true not just for the State Department, but across the whole of government; the "not invented here" syndrome is alive and well, especially where concerns arise that an idea may intrude on someone else's turf. It's important to remember that except among elected officials and political appointees, many of the key battles in government are not about philosophy. They're about the money: who controls it and who spends it. Efforts to co-opt funds from someone else's budget are greeted with the same enthusiasm as a sea captain repelling boarders from a pirate vessel. These fights are also about a bureaucrat's power and promotions within the organization.

- This approach will spur imagination and innovation. In government, the reward for offering or taking initiative in proposing new action plans or different ways to solve a problem is more likely to be forty lashes than a gold star. A center like this should strive to create interagency cooperation and coordination. It should expect resistance if its work intrudes onto another party's turf, requests personnel paid for by that party, or seeks funding support of any kind. Placing the center in the White House structure will ensure that it operates with the political clout and resources to cut through bureaucratic resistance to ideas or action that the White House can uniquely assure.

- The center's director (however titled) should report to the president. That director may require Senate confirmation.

- The center should have its own congressionally authorized budget and congressional oversight, and the legislative authority and financial resources to hire staff and support that would be drawn from outside and inside of government. It should tap into the best talent available to solve specific problems on an interdisciplinary basis. Diplomatic and military expertise is vital. The intelligence community should provide just that: intelligence and analysis of intelligence. But countering extremist ideas and articulating our own narratives, themes, and messages—which should emanate from the White House as the chief political and policymaking body in government—is about molding and influencing attitudes and opinions to shape behavior. At heart, that is a political campaign objective. An effective team requires experienced experts in politics and political campaigns as one component of the organization. Career government officials rightly resent unqualified political appointees, but they often resist outside expertise whose political expertise is helpful. The only place where it can be easily mobilized and deployed is the White House. The fact is, the organization should consist of an interdisciplinary team that utilizes the best talent for a project, whether that comes from inside or outside of the government.

- Empower the center with the authority in executing information strategies to operate covertly, so that communication needn't be attributed on a real-time or delayed basis. Title 50 of the United States Code imposes tight restraints on covert operations, and generally these are reserved for the intelligence community. That authority should be extended to the center.

- Provide it with robust funding and do so with an appropriations bill that avoids the need to operate with a continuing resolution. Continuing resolutions limit flexibility, adaptability, and the capacity to plan ahead. A single F-22 fighter costs $500 million. For half that amount you could lavishly fund a lot of very worthwhile projects for strategic communication that would advance national security interests for several years.

- As the center would most likely fall under the purview of the National Security Council, would that make the NSC operational? The answer is affirmative. It was under Eisenhower, in tandem with the Operations Coordinating Board. Again, in today's world, that would require ensuring that there is adequate congressional oversight. Thinking back on the Iran–Contra scandal as just one example, political reality requires inoculating the center against such concerns.

Rethink Definitions

The US government needs to rethink its definitions for psychological operations, military information support operations, propaganda, public diplomacy, and public affairs. As currently stated, they are inconsistent, and this undercuts the objective of strengthening the government's credibility and reputation for telling the truth. Some examples:

- One understands that people consider the term "propaganda" pejorative. Still, the literature treats most psychological operations as propaganda. Until recently, the US government understood that substantively the term is neutral, and that whether its connotation is positive or negative depended upon the use to which it is put. As it stands, the actions that the term propaganda connotes qualify as psychological operations or military information support operations. Pretending that they are different looks hypocritical—which is counterproductive. Labeling the actions as strategic communication is one solution to that problem. Deleting propaganda from the Department of Defense Dictionary of Military and Associated Terms (JP1-02) would be productive, given that the content of the current definition is identical to that of military information support operations, except that, in a move that is too cute by half, JP1-02 essentially says that propaganda is what the enemy does. This word game undercuts credibility.

- Most public affairs officers believe that they should inform but not influence. The chapter on public affairs uncovers why that doesn't work. The US government and those who deal with the media should stand up proudly for its policies. We should not flinch from developing narratives, themes, and messages that emanate from them—or from capitalizing on our talented public affairs people to drive them. Let's stick to the truth as we understand it. Too often public affairs officers seem fearful of the media. Patricia Kushlis notes that "this challenge has historically proven a problem at the Department of State, although it was not one for the US Information Agency officers assigned abroad as information officers."[7] Those fears should be set aside. The media will always judge individual US government public affairs officers and US government actions on their own merits, no matter what label is attached. The distinction between an information operations officer and a public affairs officer should be rooted in a delineation of their functions in dealing with the public and the news media, not whether they aim to influence foreign audiences. In stating that, one understands the proscriptions against US action that consciously targets domestic US audiences. But we must recognize that we live in a 24/7 global media environment, and American audiences may well read a public affairs communication addressed to a foreign audience. It may surprise some Americans, but the vast majority of federal employees work hard, are deeply committed to doing the best job possible, and are motivated by deep patriotism. If we don't trust someone, then they should be fired—but our people are entitled to a strong presumption of trust.

- Strategic communication is too often described by US government officials as a process. The official definitions place it mainly in that space. It is partly a process, but as this book has argued, we need to think of it more as an art of communication.

Improve Military Training in Information Operations

Information Operations expert Jack Guy has suggested that the military can do a better job of training officers and enlisted personnel in information operations. His excellent notions—which might well apply to the foreign affairs agencies across the board—include:

- Send all MISO officers and noncommissioned officers to the Defense Language Institute in Monterey, CA, where they can develop fluency in a foreign language.
- Provide them with the formal education required to complement language fluency with cultural expertise in a nation or region that we want them to work in.
- Set that up as a parallel to the cultural and language training that is entailed in the foreign area officer training provided in places like Garmisch, Germany, where officers are prepared to serve overseas as defense attachés.
- Early in their careers, place people in nations where they can use their developed language and cultural understanding.
- Forge stronger partnerships with US companies operating abroad. The companies have a wealth of expertise, and the synergy that the military can obtain from closer relationships with them would be beneficial.
- It is worth emphasizing that situational awareness is rooted in cultural understanding, political sensibility, and dependable, continuing intelligence from the local population—whose feeling of security is vital in securing their cooperation and willingness to provide information. Successful information strategies depend upon the ability to capitalize on all three of these factors. Only then can information strategies

become fully and properly integrated with military action to achieve a confluence of defined political, military, and diplomatic objectives.

Improve State Department Efficiency

Patricia Kushlis offers the following suggestions, which make plenty of sense. The concern that she addresses is that the State Department has traditionally relied upon its five-day-a-week noon media briefings conducted by the department spokesperson, and occasional ad hoc briefings by the secretary or designated spokespeople, to communicate US policy to Americans. This is a one-way street with gatekeepers in between. The journalists who cover these events are accredited by the department. They represent major American news outlets as well as some foreign media. When a secretary travels, there are normally spaces reserved for some of these journalists to go along as well. This gives them access to various briefings, from on-the-record to off, not only by the secretary but by other accompanying knowledgeable officials as well.

The problem, she observes, is that the communications world has changed since this model was developed, and it needs to be augmented. Fewer Americans watch the network news. Fewer news organizations will pay the price to send a reporter on these expensive overseas trips. Foreign news—especially which does not concern the US military—is not carried the way it once was when the media briefings were inaugurated during the Cold War, or perhaps even before.

In Kushlis's view, the State Department's presence in the United States is mostly confined to diplomats-in-residence at a few university campuses. They spend their time in student services, at job fairs, and on military bases recruiting new employees for the foreign service.

The department needs to reach beyond these approaches to educate and engage the American people about this country's multifaceted role in the world—a role that goes well beyond its military and clandestine aspects. This is not strategic communication, and should not be hampered by Smith-Mundt restrictions; it is simply public affairs done as it could and should be conducted. The Pentagon understands this all too well. Her proposals, which she believes would provide key improvements at minimal cost, consist of the following:

- The department needs to enhance the budget and schedule for knowledgeable senior diplomats to speak at American universities and nongovernmental foreign affairs organizations throughout the United States, as well as at US-based foreign affairs conferences beyond the beltway and the northeast corridor. Media interviews with qualified local journalists could also be included in the mix (or not). The department, not the local organizations, should cover the speakers' travel costs—unlike the reverse situation now—and the State Department officers who agree to participate should be given due credit in their annual efficiency reports. Local speaker programs could be designed along similar lines to the tried and true ones used for American speakers traveling abroad under State Department auspices. Furthermore, the department could work with the American Foreign Service Association (AFSA), the American Committees on Foreign Relations, and the World Affairs Councils of America, as well as unaffiliated local groups to help place and maximize use of its traveling officers.

- The department should reinstitute regular substantive briefings for US-based foreign affairs bloggers like those that James Glassman introduced during the brief time he was undersecretary for public diplomacy. Bloggers are important parts of the new media environment, some have influence, and the department likely knows who most of them are. Their input is important in ongoing, fast-moving foreign affairs discussion in this country, and it's important that they (we) get the facts right.

- The department should redesign its diplomat-in-residence program so that it is not simply a high-priced recruitment tool for human resources. Better to have strong substantive senior officers assigned to international studies and global affairs institutes to teach seminars and upper-division courses on US foreign policy, diplomatic practice, and area studies—this is where the strongest candidates for the foreign service will be found—and that includes members and former members of the military pursuing advanced degrees. These State Department senior officers could also be used to address local organizations, and possibly engage in media interviews and foreign affairs conferences throughout the region where they are located.

- The department could make far better use of its retirees, especially those who have relocated outside Washington, DC, to recruit for the foreign service at local and regional events. They should be paid for their work (which would be far less expensive than the upkeep for a diplomat in residence), and the workload could be spread out among several retirees. Furthermore, the department could assist AFSA in augmenting its retiree local speakers' offerings in a variety of ways.

Provide Training to Officers at the Strategic and Operational Levels

Specific training should be provided to officers at the strategic and operational levels so that they know how to use the Maxwell strategic message grid effectively (see figure 17.1). Created over three decades ago by John Maxwell, one of the country's most original and brilliant political consultants and strategists, it was first employed in the 1980 Iowa Senate race to overcome a double-digit lead and elect Chuck Grassley to the US Senate. It is a vital tool for clear strategic thinking that enables one to define and employ strategic messaging in powerful and effective ways. It translates well into national security challenges for operational planning in information warfare.

FIGURE 17.1 THE MAXWELL STRATEGIC MESSAGE/ACTION GRID

OUR WORDS AND ACTIONS	ADVERSARY WORDS AND ACTIONS
What we say to advance our narrative 1. 2. 3.	What they say to advance their narrative 1. 2. 3.
What we say to discredit their narrative 1. 2. 3.	What they say to discredit our narrative 1. 2. 3.
Actions we take to advance our narrative 1. 2. 3. 4. 5.	Actions they take to advance their narrative 1. 2. 3. 4. 5.
Actions we take to discredit their narrative 1. 2. 3. 4. 5.	Actions they take to discredit our narrative 1. 2. 3. 4. 5.

Used with permission from John Maxwell, Maxwell & Associates.

Measure Effectiveness Better

The US government needs to improve the way it handles measures of effectiveness. For starters, mall testing should be used to help forge, define, and test stories, narratives, themes, and messages. There is too much current emphasis upon focus or dial groups. The problem with these is that they are vulnerable to groupthink. Mall testing places individuals in a private setting in which responses to speeches, ads, news clips, or other items can be offered with those influences. Focus groups provide very useful qualitative analysis for understanding language and context, but their utility must be properly understood. Dial groups offer similar opportunity and are subject to similar constraints.

Integrate Information Strategies or Tactics with Other Operational Strategies or Tactics

Top-down guidance must be matched by bottom-up flexibility and a spirit of innovation so that units on the ground can adjust their own communications. Command guidance is vital to ensure that all operations—information, kinetic, and other activities—are properly integrated and aligned.

Hold People Accountable

Hold people accountable for what they say, but do so in a way that does not constrain their ability to operate. That requires training, clear policy guidance from commanders, and flexibility. But the argument of this book is that the government has every right to advocate for its policies and to employ information strategies and tactics to justify them. There is too much fear in government—and notably within the Pentagon—about whether "influence" is a dirty word. It's not. If individuals act irresponsibly, fire them and hire competent people who do their jobs well. That is what happens in the corporate and political worlds. It should be the approach that the US government—and, as this book centers largely on national security, the military and Department of State—adopts.

Adapt for Specific Audiences

We must train units to learn the nature of our opposition and their cause, and to try to deal with them on terms that a foreign audience will respond to. An example is Sovereign Challenge, an outreach program of the US Special Operations Command that engages in dialogue with foreign military attachés.

Sovereign Challenge learned that the US notion of terrorism differed from that held by many other countries who viewed activities we might consider to be purely criminal (such as narco-trafficking, counterfeiting, and smuggling) as fundamental threats to their internal stability and security.[8] Shibley Telhami has pointed out that not every enemy is a terrorist, and that the legitimacy of tactics may be influenced by the sense of whether a target audience believes they are "just."[9] Information strategies need to anticipate the basis for these arguments and use the facts and our moral authority to counter those raised by adversaries while driving our own messages.

Remember That Nothing Is Ever Settled

The operational design notion contemplates an end-state. That may suit a military operation, but information strategies affect political goals: support, loyalty, complicity of a populace, impact on an enemy, or some other defined objective. It is well to remember the insight of former Secretary of State George Schultz, who pointed out that in political processes, nothing is ever settled. We may achieve defined objectives, but the process will continue. Nothing in politics is static. It flows, changes, and evolves constantly, and pictures or definitions of success for any information strategy must keep that truth centrally in mind.

Coordinate with Allies

Strategic communication and information strategy need to be coordinated closely with coalition allies. Training our commands to ensure consistency with host nation strategy will help inoculate against any effort by adversaries to exploit inconsistencies or contradictions and maximize the impact of coalition efforts. We need to work closely with coalition allies in offering our technology and techniques to help train their forces in the fundamentals of information strategy so that as they forge their own strategies, rooted in their indigenous appreciation of their own culture, language, values, attitudes, and opinions, we can each better understand how both sides think and approach such strategy. They know their own country and what is more likely to resonate and reverberate at home, and how best to communicate with their audiences.

Understand Differing Rationales

Thought processes of foreign allies may be counterintuitive to ours. They may operate on the basis of entirely different rationales that are perfectly logical to their own culture and society. Training their forces, or training with them, requires knowing those rationales and how they may mesh or conflict with our own. Closely aligning our technology and techniques with local rationales, attitudes, and approaches is a key to effective information strategy on the ground in local situations.

Technology Isn't Everything

Some other nations may seem low-tech or unsophisticated by our standards. Yet modern battlefields from Mogadishu to Chechnya show that low tech doesn't necessarily lose to high tech. We must factor that in to how we coordinate with others so that we can maximize the effects of information strategy.

Strategic Communication Equals Military Strategy

Strategic communication and its confluent effects with kinetic action should stand on an equal footing with military strategy. Asymmetric actors realize they cannot go toe-to-toe with high-tech US forces; they employ actions to create information effects rather than to win tactical engagements on the battlefield. Their field of battle is political, and information strategy is their key weapon. Support of the populace is the key battlespace and politics is the key process.[10] In training or coordinating with foreign allies, it's vital that we communicate to them this pivotal principle and persuade them to respect it, even as our own military, as a learning organization, learns to respect it.

CHAPTER 18

Conclusion

Sᴛʀᴀᴛᴇɢɪᴄ ᴄᴏᴍᴍᴜɴɪᴄᴀᴛɪᴏɴ ɪs ᴍᴏʀᴇ ᴀʀᴛ ᴛʜᴀɴ sᴄɪᴇɴᴄᴇ, ᴀʟᴛʜᴏᴜɢʜ ɪᴛs results can sometimes—but not always—be measured quantitatively. It is not for the neophyte. Effective strategic communication requires a grounding in theory, history, and techniques, as well as the specialized knowledge that on-the-ground practice provides.

The principles that underlie the art of strategic communication date from ancient times. Technology has evolved, but the ways that people think about influencing audiences through communication contain striking echoes. In the US government, influence has become a dirty word in some circles—and propaganda even more so. Governments exist to serve their publics. They do so through political policies forged by political leaders. Explanations come not only from leaders, but from traditional and social media. Common sense mandates that leaders employ the tools of power to communicate what, how, and why they intend to do things. Arousing and mobilizing support requires the use of strategic communication to influence audiences so that they understand and support policies. Leaders throughout history have understood the necessity for strategic communication—it is indeed a key to leadership.

Strategic communication is an elastic notion. Political leaders tend to think more directly in terms of *political* communication, by which they mean every and all communication that can influence an audience. Their notion of it is consistent with the definition of the art of strategic communication that this book has embraced. It is how those who conceive and forge government policy think.

It seems odd that the US government hesitates to acknowledge that except for elected officials and political appointees, it engages in influence communication only within fairly narrow frameworks. This anomaly has produced ambiguous concepts and doctrines that make government more rigid and less effective in dealing with the challenges it faces in a 24/7 global media environment.

The constraints aim to bolster the credibility of government communications. Ironically, when taken literally, they produce the converse result. It's hard to reconcile the logic of assigning the term "propaganda" to adversaries and "military information support operations" or "psychological operations" to ourselves and our allies, when the substantive content of each set of definitions fits the other.

Considering public affairs or public diplomacy as merely informing and not influencing the public at home or abroad puts able, hardworking, honest officials at odds with the reality of communication. The selection of facts cited to communicate information is inherently a subjective act, and the imperatives of governing require making a case that supports certain actions and policies. Officials who prove unable to discharge their duties competently and explain them honestly should and will be replaced. What we should avoid is denying the nature or purpose of public affairs. Political leaders and corporations recognize that reality, and government should be no less realistic.

Strategic communication's modern incarnation may capitalize on the latest technology, and it must deal with the nature of the media environment as it exists today. Yet no tool offers more practical power on a day-to-day basis to advance interests, fulfill policies, attain objectives, and help create conditions that satisfy the requirements of a desired end-state.

Notes

Introduction

1. Mark U. Edwards, *Propaganda and Martin Luther* (Minneapolis: Fortress Press, 1994), 25.

2. Interview with Matt Armstrong. In 2011 and 2012 the author conducted a series of personal interviews with Armstrong, who reviewed key parts of the manuscript and offered many insights.

3. Henry Fairlie, *The Spoiled Child of the Western World* (New York: Doubleday, 1976), 62.

4. Ibid., 95.

5. Ibid., 70.

6. Jonathan R. Dull, *A Diplomatic History of the American Revolution* (New Haven, CT: Yale University Press, 1985), 52.

7. Dull, *A Diplomatic History of the American Revolution*, Part III; and James Breck Perkins, *France in the American Revolution* (Boston: Houghton Mifflin Company, 1911).

8. Perkins, *France in the American Revolution*, 1, 4.

9. Department of Defense Dictionary of Military and Associated Terms, Joint Publication JP 1–02, November 8, 2010 (as amended through January 31, 2011). Similar: *The 2006 Quadrennial Defense Review (QDR) Strategic Communication Executive Roadmap*, a planning document that Congress orders the Pentagon to produce every four years, defines strategic communication as "focused United States Government processes and efforts to understand and engage key audiences to create, strengthen or preserve conditions favorable to advance national interests and objectives through the use of coordinated information, themes, plans, programs and actions synchronized with other elements of national power." See Cyberspace and Information Operations Study Center, www.au.af.mil/info-ops/strategic.htm.

10. Interview with Ted Tzavellas, the vice president of S4, Inc. He is recognized in the public, private, and legal worlds as a foremost expert on strategic communication. Personal and telephone interviews with the author, 2011 and 2012.

11. Personal interviews with Al Bynum, 2011 and 2012.

12. Personal interviews with Rich Galen, 2011 and 2012.

13. Personal interviews with Kevin McCarty, 2011 and 2012.

14. See, e.g., Art of Design, School of Advanced Military Studies, 2.1: www.cgsc.edu /events/sams/ArtofDesign_v2.pdf; U.S. Field Manual 5-0, The Operations Process, Final Approved Draft (Washington, DC, Headquarters, Department of the Arm, 2010), 3–1.

15. Though few realize it, US political consultants handle most of the democratic election campaigns around the world.

16. Personal interviews with Ed Goeas, 2011 and 2012.

17. Rand Corporation expert Christopher Paul has written an informative book that examines the notion as doctrine within official and unofficial US government circles, and its

conceptual underpinnings. Christopher Paul, *Strategic Communication: Origins, Concepts and Current Debates.* (Santa Barbara, CA: Praeger, 2011).

18. Armstrong, interview.

Chapter 1

1. Joint Publication 1–102, 234; and Joint Publication 3–13.2. The definition goes on to state that "the specific purpose of psychological operations (PSYOP) is to influence foreign audience perceptions and subsequent behavior as part of approved programs in support of USG policy and military objectives" (ibid.). The use of the same substantive language for MISO caused sighs of relief. A change in the substantive definition may have affected the funding stream for such operations. Retired army colonel Glenn Ayers has suggested that many military people will continue to use the term "psychological operations." Telephone interview with Glen Ayers, 2011. He correctly observes that this term embraces actions that extend beyond purely military support. The US Special Operations Command defines PSYOP's mission as to "disseminate truthful information to foreign audiences in support of U.S. goals and objectives." The notion of "truthful" is powerful, but gives rise to varying interpretations of what satisfies that standard. As PSYOP was changed to MISO, the new mission description omits that notion. See also the description of MISO from the 4th Military Information Support Group, www.soc.mil/Assorted%20pages/4th%20Military%20Information%20Support%20Group.html. Note that MISO is considered a capability that provides primary support to information operations at SOCOM, but the definition of information operations does not yet reflect the name change from PSYOP to MISO.

2. "Psy Ops Now Called Military Information Support Operations—Conditioning the People," *Free Press International/AP*, July 2, 2010.

3. Possibly the Pentagon will accord MISO a new definition. Whether the content changes the substance of its definition of PSYOP remains to be seen.

4. Interview with Joe Meissner.

5. Ibid.

6. Interview with Cdr. Steve Tatham. The author exchanged emails with Tatham and conducted telephone interviews in 2011.

7. Ibid.

8. Joint Publication 3–13.2. The definition goes on to state that "the specific purpose of psychological operations (PSYOP) is to influence foreign audience perceptions and subsequent behavior as part of approved programs in support of USG policy and military objectives." The definition was formulated before PSYOP was rebranded as MISO (ibid.).

9. Some argue that in a counterinsurgency environment, the audience is the most important target. That reflects a change in policy embraced by Generals David Petraeus and Stanley McChrystal.

10. Interview with Chris Lamb. His views, obviously, are his own and do not necessarily represent those of the US government, Department of Defense, or National Defense University.

11. Interview with Joe Meissner. The author conducted a series of telephone interviews with Meissner in 2011, and exchanged various emails. Meissner reviewed this chapter and offered many helpful suggestions and insights.

12. Meissner, interview. He is the editor of *Perspectives* and the *Daily Frontpost*, publications that deal with issues of interest to the PSYOP community.

13. Christopher J. Lamb, "Confused Chickens Come Home to Roost," *Institute for Strategic Studies*, July 19, 2010.

14. Col. Alfred H. Paddock Jr., *Psychological and Unconventional Warfare, 1941–1952*, monograph for US Army College, 1982, 7.

15. Christopher Mauch, *The Shadow War against Hitler*, trans. J. Reimer (New York: Columbia University Press, 1999), 59.

16. Ibid. The distinction between "unattributable" and "unattributed" has relevance to special operations forces for whose activities attribution may, in certain circumstances, be delayed. A further distinction exists in the military that revolves around this issue. Covert activity, governed by Title 50 of the US Code, can conceal its sponsorship. Effectively, such activity is reserved to the Central Intelligence Agency. Clandestine operations refer to the secrecy of the activity, not disclosure of the sponsor. Special forces can and do conduct clandestine operations all the time.

17. Eugene Liptak, *Office of Strategic Services, 1942–45* (Botley, UK: Osprey Publishing, 2009). OSS was also ordered to coordinate its activities with the military; Kenneth Osgood, *Total Cold War: Eisenhower's Secret Propaganda Battle at Home and Abroad* (Lawrence: University of Kansas, 2006), 31. Osgood cites numerous sources that amplify on this.

18. Liptak, *Office of Strategic Services*, 8.

19. Interview with Doug Waller. See Douglas Waller, *Wild Bill Donovan: The Spymaster Who Created the OSS and Modern American Espionage* (New York: Free Press, 2011).

20. Kermit Roosevelt, *War Report of the OSS*, 99. PSYOP was defined as "the coordination and use of all means, including moral and physical, by which the end is attained—other than those of recognized military operations, but including the psychological exploitation of the result of those recognized military actions—which tend to destroy the will of the enemy to achieve victory and to damage his political or economic capacity to do so; which tend to deprive the enemy of the support, assistance, or sympathy of his allies or associates or of neutrals, or to prevent his acquisition of such support, assistance, or sympathy; or which tend to create, maintain, or increase the will to victory of our own people and allies and to acquire, maintain, or to increase the support, assistance, and sympathy of neutrals."

21. Liptak, *Office of Strategic Services*.

22. Paddock Jr., *Psychological and Unconventional Warfare*, 20, citing Historical Records Section, AGO, Reference Aid No. 7, "Records Pertaining to Psychological Warfare in Custody of Historical Records Section," November 8, 1949, 5, RG 319, P&O 091.412 (October 7, 1949), F/W 25/2, National Archives.

23. Walter L. Hixon, *Parting the Curtain: Propaganda, Culture and the Total Cold War, 1945–1961* (New York: St. Martin's Griffin, 1997), 19; also cited by Osgood, *Total Cold War*, 45.

24. A "lead agency" determines the agenda, ensures cohesion among the agencies, and is responsible for implementing decisions. See "Forging a New Shield," *Project for National Security Reform*, November 2008, 62, www.pnsr.org/data/files/pnsr_forging_a_new_shield_report.pdf. The report traces the history of decision-making processes on national security and offers reforms.

25. Shawn J. Parry-Giles. "The Eisenhower Administration's Conceptualization of the USIA: The Development of Overt and Covert Propaganda Strategies," *Presidential Studies Quarterly* 24, no. 2 (1994): 263.

26. R. R. Bowie and R. H. Immerman, *Waging Peace: How Eisenhower Shaped an Enduring Cold War Strategy* (New York: Oxford University Press, 1998), 77.

27. Parry-Giles, "Eisenhower Administration's Conceptualization."

28. Stephen E. Ambrose, *Eisenhower: Soldier and President* (New York: Simon & Schuster, 1990), 368–72, 377; Fred I. Greenstein, *The Hidden Hand Presidency: Eisenhower as Leader* (New York: Basic Books, 1982).

29. Osgood, *Total Cold War*, 78.

30. "Forging a New Shield," 64.

31. Osgood, *Total Cold War*, 78.

32. "Memorandum on Radio in Psychological Warfare," June 22, 1953. White House Central Files—Confidential File, Box 61, Dwight D. Eisenhower Library, 8–9. Cited by Parry-Giles, "Eisenhower Administration's Conceptualization."

33. Speech by C. D. Jackson before the National Security Commission and Committees of the American Legion, August 28, 1953. C. D. Jackson Papers: 1934–1967, Box 82, Dwight D. Eisenhower Library, 7–8. Cited by Parry-Giles, "Eisenhower Administration's Conceptualization."

34. See Osgood, *Total Cold War*.

35. The President's Committee on International Information Activities: Report to the President, June 30, 1953. U.S. President's Committee on International Information Activities: the Jackson Committee, Box 14, Dwight D. Eisenhower Library, 55–56. Cited by Parry-Giles, "Eisenhower Administration's Conceptualization."

36. Ibid.

37. John F. Kennedy dismantled the NSC system that Eisenhower employed and replaced it with a looser system of decision making that suited his own temperament and preferences. Ibid., 71.

38. Osgood, *Total Cold War*, 90.

39. Ibid., 92, 95.

40. Parry-Giles, "Eisenhower Administration's Conceptualization."

41. Yale Richmond, *Practicing Public Diplomacy* (New York: Berghahn Books, 2008), 45. By 1959, USIA had designed the first American National Exposition in Moscow where the infamous Nixon–Khrushchev Kitchen Debate took place. See Hans Tuch, *Communicating with the World: U.S. Public Diplomacy Overseas* (Washington: St. Martin's, 1990), 24.

42. See "Proposed Plan for a Psychological Warfare Offensive" 2, 5–6; and "The USIA Program for 1953," July 15, 1953. White House Central Files Institute for International–American Affairs, Box 909, Dwight D. Eisenhower Library, 2–5. Cited by Parry-Giles, "Eisenhower Administration's Conceptualization."

43. This conclusion is borne out by the Gallup World Poll. See John L. Esposito and Dalia Mogahed, *Who Speaks for Islam? What a Billion Muslims Really Think* (New York: Gallup Press, 2007), 96. The Pew Global Attitudes Project data has reflected skepticism about US intentions in fighting a "war on terror" and whether US policy considers the interests of other countries. See, e.g., Pew Global Attitudes Project, "Nine Nation Survey" (March 2004), and Pew Global Attitudes Project, "47-Nation Pew Global Attitudes Survey" (June 2004), and the analysis of Pew data between 2002–2005, Andrew Kohut and Bruce Stokes, *America against the World* (New York: Henry Holt & Co., 2006), 38, 95.

44. Osgood, *Total Cold War*, 102.

45. Christopher Paul, *Strategic Communication* (Washington: Prager, 2011), 76.

46. Stephen Johnson, Helle C. Dale, and Patrick Cronin, "Strengthening U.S. Public Diplomacy Requires Organization, Coordination and Strategy," *Heritage Foundation*, August 2, 2005, www.heritage.org/research/reports/2005/08/strengthening-us-public-diplomacy-requires-organization-coordination-and-strategy.

47. There is significant analysis as to operational issues governing PSYOP that fall outside the scope of this book. For a detailed, informed analysis, see Christopher Lamb with contribution from Paris Genalis, *Review of Psychological Operations: Lessons Learned from Recent Operational Experience* (Washington: National Defense University Press, 2005).

48. Ibid., 144.

49. See Sgt. Maj. Herbert Friedman (ret), "The American PSYOP Organization during the Korean War," www.psywarrior.com/KoreaPSYOPHist.html. The description of Korean War PSYOP tactics is drawn from his description.

50. Ibid.

51. Stanley Sandler, "Army Psywarriors—a History of U.S. Army Psychological Operations—Part I—Colonial America to Korea," in *Mindbenders*, vol. 8, no. 1 (1995).

52. Ibid.

53. Christopher Lamb with contribution from Paris Genalis, *Review of Psychological Operations*, 27–28, citing Department of Defense, "Psychological Warfare Fact Sheet," http://korea50.army.mil/index.html.

54. Stanley Sandler, *The Korean War: No Victors, No Vanquished* (Lexington: University of Kentucky, 1999), 207.

55. Ibid.

56. See Col. John T. Carney, Jr., *No Room for Error: The Covert Operations of America's Special Tactics Units from Iran to Afghanistan* (New York: Ballantine, 2002), 111–12. Carney quotes General H. Norman Schwarzkopf, who felt too many lives had been lost, and that there had been poor intelligence, communications, and disruptive interservice rivalry. Ibid., 164.

57. See Sgt. Maj. Herbert A. Friedman (Ret), "United States PSYOP in Grenada," 2, www.psywarrior.com/GrenadaHerb.html; and Stanley Sandler, *Cease Resistance: It's Good for You: A History of U.S. Army Combat Psychological Operations*, 2nd ed. (Ft. Bragg, NC: U.S. Army Civil Affairs and Psychological Operations Command, 1999).

58. Herbert A. Friedman, "U.S. PSYOP in Panama (Operation JUST CAUSE)," www.psywarrior.com/PanamaHerb.html.

59. Ibid.

60. "Operation Just Cause 1989–1990," www.specialoperations.com/Operations/Just_Cause/Operation_Profile4.htm.

61. Lt. Col. Thomas W. Collins, "Joint Efforts Prevent Humanitarian Disaster in Liberia," *Army Magazine*, February 2004.

62. Sgt. Maj. Herbert A. Friedman (Ret.), "Combined Task Force (CTF) Liberia PSYOP," www.psywarrior.com/LiberiaPsyop.html.

63. Ibid.

64. The description of activity is drawn from "Psychological Operation & Operation Allied Forces," www.psywarrior.com/kosovo.html; see also Christopher Lamb with contribution from Paris Genalis, *Review of Psychological Operations*, 65 and the after-action reports that comprise part of the bibliography.

65. Ibid., 27.

66. Ibid., 46.

67. Ibid., 47–48.

68. Herb Friedman, "PSYOP Mistakes," www.psywarrior.com/PSYOPMistakes.html.

69. Philip M. Taylor, *Munitions of the Mind: A History of Propaganda from the Ancient World to the Present Day*, 3rd ed. (Manchester: University of Manchester, 2003), 305.

70. Herb Friedman, "PSYOP Mistakes."

71. Ibid.

72. Ibid.

73. Interview with Pauletta Otis.

74. Herb Friedman, "PSYOP Mistakes."

75. Meissner, interview.

76. Jacob Sullum, "A Bright Shining Lie," *Reason*, July 1, 2011.

77. Meissner, interview.

78. Arturo Munoz, "U.S. Military Information Operations in Afghanistan: Effectiveness of Psychological Operations 2001–2010," RAND National Defense Research Institute 2012, 123–24.

79. Ibid., 125.

80. "Information Operations Roadmap," Department of Defense, October 30, 2003: www.gwu.edu/~nsarchiv/NSAEBB/NSAEBB177/info_ops_roadmap.pdf, 16, 24–27.

81. Ibid., 27.

82. See Munoz, "U.S. Military Information Operations in Afghanistan," supra, chapters 6 and 7, 119–41. Some of the other recommendations would be stronger if incorporated into a more strategic rather than tactical approach, but the report is well considered.

83. National Defense Authorization Act (2010), Pub. L. 111–84.

84. Secretary of Defense Robert Gates, "Strategic Communication and Information Operations in the DoD," January 25, 2011. www.carlisle.army.mil/dime/documents/Strategic%20Communication%20&%20IO%20Memo%2025%20Jan2011.pdf.

85. Ibid., paragraph 6.

86. Interview with Matt Armstrong, 2011.

87. Christopher Paul, *Strategic Communication: Origins, Concepts and Current Debates*, supra, 38.

88. Interview with Jack Guy. The author conducted a series of phone interviews with Guy in 2011. Guy also reviewed key sections of this manuscript and provided many helpful insights and suggestions.

89. See Christopher J. Lamb, "Information Operations as a Core Competency," *Joint Forces Quarterly*, issue 36: www.au.af.mil/au/awc/awcgate/jfq/1536.pdf.

Chapter 2

1. Garth S. Jowett and Victoria O'Donnell, *Propaganda and Persuasion*, 4th ed. (Thousand Oaks, CA: Sage Publications, 2005), 50, 53. Another 10,000 troopers were married to Persian concubines. Ibid.

2. Edward Bernays and Mark Crispin Miller, *Propaganda* (New York: Ig Publishing, 2004: Kindle Edition), 8–9; and Andras Szanto, *What Orwell Didn't Know: Propaganda and the New Face of American Politics* (New York: Public Affairs, 2007), xvii.

3. Bernays and Miller, *Propaganda,* Kindle edition, 10.

4. Harold Lasswell, *Politics: Who Gets What, When and How* (Peter Smith Publisher, 1990); see "Laswell's model in communication models," http://communicationtheory.org/lasswells-model/comment-page-1/. His formula is often referred to as the "transmission model of communication." Harold Lasswell, "The Theory of Political Propaganda," *The American Political Science Review*, vol. 21, no. 3 (Aug. 1927): 627.

5. Daniel Lerner, "The Psychological Warfare Campaign against Germany: D-Day to V-E Day," an essay in Anthony Rhodes, ed., *Propaganda: The Art of Persuasion: World War II*, 283–84.

6. Ibid., 283.

7. Philip M. Taylor, *Munitions of the Mind: War Propaganda from the Ancient World to the Nuclear Age* (Wellingborough: Patrick Stephens Ltd., 1990), 13.

8. Ibid.

9. Ibid., 13–14.

10. Jowett and O'Donnell, *Propaganda and Persuasion*, 16.

11. Bernays and Miller, *Propaganda*, Location 331–38.

12. Quoted by Steven Luckert and Susan Bachrach, *State of Deception*, 1, and citing C. Fleay and M. L. Sanders, "Looking into the Abysss: George Orwell at the BBC," *Journal of Contemporary History* 24 (1989): 503–18, at 512.

13. Oxford Dictionaries, "Propaganda," www.oxforddictionaries.com/view/entry/m_en_us1281135?rskey=jC3R03&result=1#m_en_us1281135.

14. Luckert and Bachrach, *State of Deception*, 2.

15. Randal Marlin, *Propaganda and the Ethics of Persuasion* (Peterborough, NH: Broadview Press, 2002), 22.

16. Joint Publication 1-02, 374; see also Joint Publication 3-13.2, "Psychological Operations," January 7, 2010: www.fas.org/irp/doddir/dod/jp3-13-2.pdf.

17. Robert Hastings, "Memorandum to the Office of Secretary of Defense," OSD Focal Point for Standardization of Military and Associated Technology (ESD/DD), March 10, 2009.

18. Robert Fyne, *The Hollywood Propaganda of World War II* (London: The Scarecrow Press, Inc., 1997), 1.

19. George Creel, *How We Advertised America* (BiblioLife reprint, 2009, Kindle Edition). Creel's book, a detailed report on what his Committee did, sold 7,000,000 copies, an indication of its appeal. The dryly written report revealed breadth and depth and a well-thought-through national campaign.

20. Ibid., Loc. 4260/8189.

21. John Whiteclay Chambers II and David Culbert, eds., *World War II Film and History* (New York: Oxford University Press, 1996), 3.

22. Kenneth Osgood, *Total Cold War: Eisenhower's Secret Propaganda Battle at Home and Abroad* (Lawrence: University of Kansas, 2006), 24.

23. George Creel, *How We Advertised America*, Location 206–20.

24. Ibid.

25. Bernays and Miller, *Propaganda*, Location 66–72.

26. Four that stand out are Clayton R. Koppes and Gregory D. Black, *Hollywood Goes to War* (London: I. B. Tauris & Co., 1986); Chambers and Culbert, *World War II: Film and History*; Robert Fyne, *The Hollywood Propaganda of World War II* (London: The Scarecrow Press, Inc., 1997); and Bernard F. Dick, *The Star-Spangled Screen: The American World War II Film* (Lexington: University of Kentucky Press, 1996).

27. The Nazis and British held the same opinion.

28. Dick, *The Star-Spangled Screen*, 265, citing Richard W. Steele, "The Greatest Gangster Film Ever Filmed: *Prelude to War*," *Prologue* 9 (Winter 1979), 232–33; and Taylor, *Munitions of the Mind*, 206.

29. Ibid., 59.

30. Ibid., 66.

31. Henry Luce, "The American Century," *Life* magazine, February 17, 1941. Text can be read at www.informationclearinghouse.info/article6139.htm.

32. Ibid.

33. The text can be read at www.winrock.org/wallace/wallacecenter/wallace/CCM.htm.

34. Koppes and Black, *Hollywood Goes to War*, 86. Their discussion of OSI's response to *Princess O'Rourke* and other movies contains piercing insights.

35. Taylor, *Munitions of the Mind*, 221.

36. Martin J. Medhurt, "Eisenhower and the Crusade for Freedom: The Rhetorical Origins of a Cold War Campaign," *Presidential Studies Quarterly* 27 (1997), www.questia .com/googleScholar.qst;jsessionid=80E851E0CEBBC2D60187859FC78D0C2C. inst1_1b?docId=5000546266.

37. Ibid.

38. Interview with Patricia Kushlis. The author conducted a series of phone interviews in 2011 with Kushlis, who also reviewed the manuscript and provided insights and suggestions.

39. George W. Bush, "The President's News Conference with Prime Minister Paul Martin of Canada," April 30, 2004, www.presidency.ucsb.edu/ws/index.php?pid=72613.

40. Ibid.

41. Mark Danner, "Words in a Time of War: On Rhetoric, Truth, and Power," in Szanto, *What Orwell Didn't Know*, 20–21.

42. The authors were Representative Karl Mundt and Senator H. Alexander Smith. This analysis draws heavily upon the scholarship of Matt Armstrong.

43. "Foreign Relations: The American Twang," *Time Magazine*, May 26, 1947, www.time. com/time/magazine/article/0,9171,793708,00.html.

44. Frank Ninkovich, *The Diplomacy of Ideas: U.S. Foreign Policy and Cultural Relations* (Cambridge: Cambridge University Press, 1981), 122.

45. The U.S. Information and Educational Exchange Act of 1948, 22 U.S.C.A. Section 1461, as amended (1972 and 1985). Congressmen Mac Thornberry and Adam Smith introduced "The Smith-Mundt Modernization Act of 2010" to update the Act, but it has not passed.

46. Kushlis, interview.

47. "The Report on the Smith-Mundt Symposium of January 13, 2009," sponsored by Armstrong Strategic Insights Group, LLC, 7, http://mountainrunner.us/files/s-m/Smith-Mundt_Symposium_Final_Report.pdf.

48. The amendment can be found in the Congressional Record, 99th Congress, 1st Session, 1984 (Legislative Day of June 3, 1985). See 22 U.S.C. 1461–1a.

49. Matt Armstrong, "Senator Edward Zorinsky and Banning Domestic Dissemination by USIA in 1985," *MountRunner.us*, May 28, 2009.

50. Joint Chiefs of Staff, *Public Affairs Support of Joint Operations*, Washington, DC, Joint Publication 3–61, III—21. See also John J. Garcia, "Working Together Downrange," *IO Sphere*, Winter 2009, 33.

51. See Joint Publication 1-02, 374; Joint Publication 3-13.2, "Psychological Operations," January 7, 2010, www.fas.org/irp/doddir/dod/jp3-13-2.pdf; see also "Doctrine for Joint Psychological Operations," JP-3-53, September 5, 2003.

52. Most Americans feel they can do whatever they please, unless the law prohibits them. The military operates on the converse principle: it requires authorization to conduct an action. Absent that, it may not and will not act. Give it a green light or it doesn't go.

53. Marc Lynch, *Voices of the New Arab Public* (New York: Columbia University Press, 2007); "Report on the Smith-Mundt Symposium," 14.

54. "Report on the Smith-Mundt Symposium," 10.

55. Armstrong, interview.

56. "Report on the Smith-Mundt Symposium," 10.

Chapter 3

1. Donald Rumsfeld, *Known and Unknown* (New York: Sentinel HC, 2011), 547.

2. Article 15-6, "Investigation of the 800th Military Police Brigade" (2004), www.npr.org/iraq/2004/prison_abuse_report.pdf. The investigation was conducted by Maj. Gen. Antonio M. Taguba after reports were received of detainee abuse, escapes, and lapses in accountability that suggested "a lack of clear standards, proficiency and leadership."

3. Carol A. Downing and Patricia A. Swann, "Situation: Abu Ghraib: A Comparative Study of Pedagogical Approaches to Faulty Communication," *Proceedings of the New York State Communication Association 2007,* www.nyscanet.org/pdf/07proceedings/swann.pdf.

4. Article 15-6, "Investigation of the 80th Military Police Brigade."

5. See Fred Hiatt, "Why Hawks Should Be Angry," *Washington Post,* May 31, 2004.

6. Downing and Swann, "Situation," 10–12.

7. Personal communication with Gen. Shiaron Naveh and Jim Schneider, May 2011.

8. President George W. Bush, "The President's News Conference with Prime Minister Paul Martin of Canada," April 30, 2004, www.presidency.ucsb.edu/ws/index.php?pid=72613.

9. Downing and Swann, "Situation," 7.

10. "Public Affairs Guidance Approved for Use Commencing 25 1500 AUG 04," www.aclu.org/files/projects/foiasearch/pdf/DOD045833.pdf.

11. Joint Chiefs of Staff, *Public Affairs Support of Joint Operations,* Washington, DC, Joint Publication 3-61, III–21. On September 27, 2004, Chairman of the Joint Chiefs of Staff Richard B. Meyers issued a dictum stating that public affairs should inform, not influence and that it was the function of IO to influence foreign audiences. When General Peter Pace became chairman, on June 14, 2007, he declared that Joint Publications 3-13 (February 13, 2006) and 3-61 (May 9, 2005) "superseded the policy on the Public Affairs relationship to Information Operations" and that General Meyers's memorandum was rescinded in favor of the revised joint doctrine. See also the discussion by Christopher Paul, *Strategic Communication: Origins, Concepts, and Current Debates*; and citing John M. Wilson, *The Hunting of the Snark: Organizing and Synchronizing of Informational Elements for Homeland Defense and Civil Support,* Thesis, Monterey, Calif.: Naval Postgraduate School, June 2009, 62; John J. Garcia, "Working Together Downrange," *IO Sphere,* Winter 2009, 33.

12. Helle Dale and Stephen Johnson, "Abu Ghraib Shows Limits of Carnival Barking," *Heritage.org,* July 2, 2004, www.heritage.org/research/commentary/2004/07/abu-ghraib-shows-limits-of-carnival-barking.

13. "Jessica Lynch Goes Home with Bronze Star," *Army News Service,* July 27, 2003, http://usmilitary.about.com/cs/army/a/jessicalynch.htm; David Gardner, "U.S. Soldier Hailed for Bravery in Iraq Says Pentagon Spin Doctors Made It All Up," *MailOnLine,* April 25, 2007, www.dailymail.co.uk/news/article-450509/U-S-soldier-hailed-bravery-Iraq-says-Pentagon-spin-doctors-up.html. See also the discussion by Paul Rutherford, *Weapons of Mass Persuasion: Marketing the War against Iraq* (Toronto: University of Toronto Press, 2004), 68–70.

14. Douglas J. Feith, *War and Decision* (New York: Harper, 2008), 171. Feith does an excellent job of laying out the battle lines and the underhanded tactics used to destroy OSI.

15. Observer's interview with the author was conducted off-the-record.

16. Indeed, Schmitt and this author have shared the same book editor, Jim Wade.

17. Eric Schmitt and Thom Shanker, *Counterstrike: The Untold Story of America's Secret Campaign against Al Qaeda* (New York: Times Books, 2011).

18. Interview with Patricia H. Kushlis.

19. Herb Schmetz with William Novak, *Good-bye to the Low Profile: The Art of Creative Confrontation* (New York: Little, Brown & Co., 1986), 20.

20. Ibid., 33.

21. Ibid., 77.

22. Interview with Virgil Scudder, founder and CEO of Virgil Scudder & Associates.

23. Scudder, interview.

24. Ibid.

25. Ibid.

26. Interview with Celinda Lake. Her firm, the Washington-based Lake Research Partners, has worked for a wide range of political and corporate clients, as well as NGOs, nationally and internationally.

27. Interview with Rich Galen. Galen is among the best and most experienced political and corporate communication experts in the world. He currently writes an online newsletter, *Mulllings.com.*

28. Telephone interview with Douglas Waller, 2011.

29. Garcia, "Working Together Downrange."

Chapter 4

1. See, e.g., "Hillary Clinton Egypt Trip Marks Highest Level Visit since Mubarak's Ouster," *Reuters*, March 15, 2011, and "Hillary Clinton Visits Egypt, Snubbed by Youth Activist Coalition," blog, Care2.com, www.care2.com/causes/politics/blog/hillary-clinton-visits-egypt-snubbed-by-youth-activist-coalition/.

2. On its website, the Public Diplomacy Alumni Association also cites the case of Armstrong and provides other examples. www.publicdiplomacy.org/1.htm.

3. Public Diplomacy Alumni Association, "What Is Public Diplomacy?" www.publicdi plomacy.org/1.htm.

4. Ibid.

5. Ibid.

6. US Department of State, www.state.gov/r/.

7. Public Diplomacy Council, "Professional Practice," http://publicdiplomacycouncil. org/professional-practice. Pamela Smith has also provided an excellent definition: "To understand, inform, and influence foreign publics in promotion of the national interest and to broaden the dialogue between Americans and US institutions and their counterparts abroad. To accomplish this, we explain and advocate US policies in terms that are credible and meaningful in foreign cultures; provide information about the United States, its people, values, and institutions; build lasting relationships and mutual understanding through the exchange of people and ideas; and advise U.S. decision-makers on foreign attitudes and their implications for U.S. policies." http://ics.leeds.ac.uk/papers/vp01.cfm?outfit=pmt&folder= 7&paper=1205.

8. Joint Publication 1-02, 377; Joint Publication 3-07.3 (74). See also Kennon H. Nakamura and Matthew C. Weed, *U.S. Public Diplomacy: Background and Current Issues*, Congressional Research Service Report for Congress, Washington, DC, December 18, 2009, in which

he discusses public diplomacy as "providing information to foreign publics," arts and music performances, and education and professional exchange programs.

9. US Department of State.

10. Interview with Brian Carlson, 2011.

11. Interview with Joseph L. Duffey, 2011.

12. Interview with Matt Armstrong, 2011.

13. The ads can be seen at www.archive.org/details/SharedValues.

14. Pew Research Center for the People and the Press, "Views of a Changing World 2003," http://people-press.org/report/185/views-of-a-changing-world-2003.

15. Alice Kendrick and Jami A. Fullerton, "Reactions to the Shared Values Initiative," July 2003. www.mountainrunner.us/2008/11 Reactions_to_Shared_Values/#.T8avxz1yu2s.

16. Email exchange with Doug Schoen.

17. PDD 68, April 30, 1999: www.fas.org/irp/offdocs/pdd/pdd-68.htm.

18. Interview with Patricia Kushlis.

19. Rachel Greenspan, "Public Diplomacy in Uniform," *AmericanDiplomacy.org*, March 2011. She quotes Title 22 as the key basis for her definition of "public diplomacy." www.unc .edu/depts/diplomat/item/2011/0104/comm/greenspan_pduniform.html.

20. Philip C. Habib, quoted in *The New York Times*, November 29, 1982.

21. Interview with Glenn Ayers.

22. "Forging a New Shield," Project for National Security Reform, December 3, 2008, Part V, www.pnsr.org.

Chapter 5

1. Nicholas J. Cull, David Culbert, and David Welch, *Propaganda and Mass Persuasion: A Historical Encyclopedia, 1500 to the Present* (Santa Barbara, CA: ABC CLIO, 2003).

2. See Greg Myre and Jennifer Griffin, *This Burning Land* (London: Wiley & Sons, Inc., 2010), 77, 81, 82, 83.

3. Ibid., 121.

4. Shaykh Anwar al-Awlaki, "A Message to the Media," *The NEFA Foundation*, February 13, 2011.

5. Ayman Zawahiri, "Message of Hope to Our People in Egypt," February 18, 2001 (OSC), www.opensource.gov/portal/server.pt/gateway/PTARGS_6_0_5295_746_1525_43/ content/Display/23707989.

6. Harold Maia and Sylvia Caras, "Words Matter," www.peoplewho.org/documents/ wordsmatter.htm.

7. See The Perseus Project, Tufts University (English Translation), www.perseus.tufts.edu/ hopper/text?doc=Perseus:text:1999.02.0151.

8. *The Arthashastra* discusses propaganda and endorses strategies and tactics that inspire comparison to Machiavelli's *The Prince*. Authorship is attributed to Chanakya (350–283 BC), a scholar who served as prime minister of the Maurya Empire. The text endorses deceit, trickery, torture, and other nefarious activities as legitimate means to gain and hold power. The text can be found at http://api.ning.com/files/eCyBsmRzuZTH3Xd8pq2Da5H2ilFG gn5ML4qYjQ3dtViNR5vOXqF-s1O4MeYYDM7tNMO7IdASXIA3qo1gAkoRkDT7tp gLqq17/Arthashastra_of_Chanakya__English.pdf.

9. Philip M. Taylor, *Munitions of the Mind: War Propaganda from the Ancient World to the Nuclear Age*, 26. The action would probably *not* qualify as military deception. JP1-02

defines that as "Actions executed to deliberately mislead adversary military decision makers as to *friendly military capabilities, intentions, and operations* [emphasis added], thereby causing the adversary to take specific actions (or inactions) that will contribute to the accomplishment of the friendly mission."

10. Thucydides, *History of the Peloponnesian War*, text and translation by Charles Martin Smith (London: Loeb, 1919–1923), 1:70.

11. The text of Pericles's speech in English can be found at www.wsu.edu/~dee/Greece/pericles.htm. One should note that the speech that has come down to us was reported by Thucydides in Book Two of his *History of the Peloponnesian War*, and may or may not be literal.

12. Donald Kagan, *Pericles of Athens and the Birth of Democracy* (New York: The Free Press, 1991). See also Kagan's other books, *The Peloponnesian War* (New York: Penguin, 2004); *The Outbreak of the Peloponnesian War* (Ithaca: Cornell University Press, 1969); *The Archidamian War* (Ithaca: Cornell University Press, 1974); *The Peace of Nicias and the Sicilian Expedition* (Ithaca: Cornell University Press, 1981); and *The Fall of the Athenian Empire* (Ithaca: Cornell University Press, 1987).

13. Kagan, *Pericles of Athens*, 9.

14. The Greeks' notion of what made people great does not reflect the tenets articulated during the Sermon on the Mount. The Greeks valued strength, courage, and excellence in achievement as the goal in living up to an individual's potential. They called it *arête*.

15. Kagan, *Pericles of Athens*, 9.

16. William J. Safire, ed., *Lend Me Your Ears: Great Speeches in History* (New York: The Cobbett Corporation, 1992).

17. For text, see www.fiftiesweb.com/usa/winston-churchill-fight-beaches.htm.

18. For text, see http://americancivilwar.com/north/lincoln.html.

19. For text, see www.americanrhetoric.com/speeches/fdrfirstinaugural.html.

20. For text, see www.americanrhetoric.com/speeches/jfkinaugural.htm.

21. See Robert Caro, *The Passage of Power: The Years of Lyndon Johnson* (New York: Knopf, 2012), the fourth in a magnificent series of biographies by Caro of Johnson. Caro well illuminates both Johnson's remarkable talent and his deeply felt insecurities.

22. In 1967, the author was a congressional intern for Congressman F. Edward Hebert. Writing a story for the *Tulane Hullabaloo*, he interviewed President Johnson's close confident and advisor, Jack Valenti. Valenti reversed the interview and disclosed his and Johnson's sentiments about Kennedy, the romanticism about his administration as "Camelot," and Johnson's frustration that his personal style—he was an extremely powerful figure in personal contact—did not project well on television or in photographs.

23. For text, see www.americanrhetoric.com/speeches/ronaldreaganddayaddress.html.

24. Interview with Celinda Lake.

25. Bob Woodward, *Obama's Wars* (New York: Simon & Schuster, 2010).

26. See www.youtube.com/watch?v=15D3ElV1Jzw.

27. Nia-Malika Henderson, "Gingrich: Sarah Palin Was Right on Death Panels," *Washington Post*, October 11, 2011, and "Palin: Obama's 'Death Panel' Could Kill My Down Syndrome Baby," *Huffington Post*, August 7, 2009.

28. Neil MacFarquhar, *The Media Relations Department of Hizbollah Wishes You a Happy Birthday: Unexpected Encounters in the Changing Middle East* (New York: Public Affairs, 2009), 80–81.

29. Henry Kissinger, *On China* (New York: Penguin Press, 2011), 92.

30. William Safire, *Lend Me Your Ears*, 378–82.

31. See Georgie Anne Geyer, *Guerilla Prince: The Untold Story of Fidel Castro* (New York: Little, Brown, 1991). Geyer exposes the savage brutality, paranoia, and ruthlessness of Castro. See also David Grann, "The Yankee Comandante," *The New Yorker*, May 28, 2012.

32. Safire, *Lend Me Your Ears*, 378–82.

33. Neil Faulkner, "The Official Truth: Propaganda in the Roman Empire," *BBC News*, February 2, 2011. www.bbc.co.uk/history/ancient/romans/romanpropaganda_article_01.shtml.

34. Interview with Adrian Goldsworthy.

35. Adrian Goldsworthy, *Caesar: Life of a Colossus* (New Haven, CT: Yale University Press, 2006), 186, 189.

36. Goldsworthy, interview.

37. Kenneth Scott, "The Political Propaganda of 44–30 B.C.," *Memoirs of the American Academy in Rome* (American Academy in Rome, 1933). www.jstor.org/pss/4238573.

38. It was a rowdy time for the Papacy. Pope Sixtus (1471–83) licensed brothels, taxed priests who kept mistresses, and sold indulgences to be applied to the dead. Pope Alexander VI (1492–1503) fathered seven children, including Lucrezia and Cesare Borgia, by mistresses. See David Wiley, "Fresco Fragment Revives Papal Scandal," *BBC News,* July 21, 2007, and Philipp Harper, "History's 10 Greatest Entrepreneurs," www.msnbc.msn.com/id/5519861.

39. Mark U. Edwards Jr., *Printing, Propaganda and Martin Luther* (Berkeley: University of California Press, 1st ed., 1994), 1. The Reformation produced various divisions and doctrinal differences between Luther, John Calvin, Ulrich Zwingli and others, which led to the establishment of rival Protestant denominations, including Lutherans, Presbyterians, Puritans, and Anglicans. A discussion of the Reformation lies well beyond the scope of this book.

40. Ibid., 2–4, 7.

41. See David Plouffe, *The Audacity to Win* (New York: Viking, 2009), chapter 3. This chapter describes what they did.

42. "Print: The Function of the New Media in Seventeenth-Century England," www.cyberartsweb.org/cpace/infotech/asg/ag14.html.

43. Ibid.

44. Jason Peacey, *Politicians and Pamphleteers: Propaganda during the English Civil Wars and Interregnum* (Aldershot: Ashgate Publishling Limited, 2004).

45. Carl Berger, *Broadsides and Bayonets: The Propaganda War of the American Revolution* (Philadelphia: University of Pennsylvania Press, 1961), 17–18.

46. James P. Farwell, "Countering Cyber Piracy and Cyber Vandalism: A New Perspective," Australian Security Research Center, Canberra, Australia (October 10, 2010), and Rafal Rohozinski, James P. Farwell, Elinor Buxton, and Natalie Ratcliffe, "Collusion and Collison: Search for Guidance in Chinese Cyberspace," SecDeve Group, Toronto (September 20, 2011). See also James Bamford, *The Shadow Factor* (New York: Doubleday, 2008).

47. "Gadhafi Forces Seek to Widen Grip," *Wall Street Journal*, March 5, 2011; "Journalists Barred from Leaving Hotel," *iol.co.na (IOL News)*, March 4, 2011; Peter Beaumont, "Libya Regime Treating Journalists Like Idiots—But Ones Who Are Useful to Them," *Guardian.co.uk*, March 8, 2011; and David Garner, "Qaddafi Forces Sexually Assault NYT Reporter: 'You'll Die Tonight,'" *nation.fox.news.com*, March 22, 2011.

48. Juan Cole, "Did Bush Plan to Bomb Al-Jazeera," *Salon.com*, November 30, 2005, www.salon.com/news/opinion/feature/2005/11/30/al_jazeera, and "On the Other Hand: Al Jazeerea Missing U.S. Cable T.V.," *Portland Spectator*, March 8, 2011.

49. Garth S. Jowett and Victoria O'Donnell, *Propaganda and Persuasion*, 4th ed. (Sage Publications, 2005), 57.

50. Eugene Liptak, *Office of Strategic Services: The World War II Origins of the CIA* (Oxford: Osprey Publishing, 2009), 12.

51. David A. Bell, *The First Total War* (New York: Houghton Mifflin Company, 2007), 202.

52. Philip Dwyer, *Napoleon: The Path to Power* (New Haven, CT: Yale University Press, 2007), 254.

53. Ibid., 256–57.

54. Ibid., 258.

55. Ibid., 196, 206–7.

56. Karl Marx and Friederich Engels, *The Communist Manifesto* (Chartwell Books, Inc., 2010) (in English).

57. Political Party Manifesto European Elections 2009, www.aontas.com/download/pdf/political_party_manifesto_european.pdf; and Manifestos of the European Political Groups, www.myopinionmyvote.eu/webdown/lo/english/online/euloistitutionEN/euloistitutionEN/manifestos_of_the_european_political_groups.html.

58. Arthur Schlesinger Jr., *Kennedy or Nixon: Does It Make Any Difference?* (New York: MacMillan, 1960), 2–3.

59. Interview with Ron Faucheux.

60. Steven McVeigh, *The American Western* (Edinburgh: Edinburgh University Press, 2007), 132.

61. Ibid., 13.

62. Ibid., 18–19.

63. Robert Caro, *The Passage of Power*, supra, 103–5.

64. See Tim Weiner, *Legacy of Ashes: The History of the CIA* (New York: Doubleday, 2007), 200–203.

65. Frederick Kempe, *Berlin 1961* (New York: Putnam, 2011), and Henry Fairlie, *The Kennedy Promise: The Politics of Expectation* (London: Methuen, 1973).

66. Gene Sharp, *From Dictatorship to Democracy* (Albert Einstein Institution, 1993), www.aeinstein.org/organizations98ce.html, and David D. Kirkpatrick and David E. Sanger, "A Tunisian-Egypt Link That Shook Arab History," *New York Times*, February 13, 2011.

67. Taylor, *Munitions of the Mind*, 145.

68. Robert B. Holtman, *Napoleonic Propaganda* (London: Greenwood Press, 1969).

69. Simon Burrows, "The Struggle for European Opinion in the Napoleonic Wars: British Francophone Propaganda, 1803–1814," *French History* 11, no. 1 (1997): 29–30.

70. Gill Merom, *How Democracies Lose Small Wars* (New York: Cambridge University Press, 2003), 103, 110–20. See also Alistair Horne, *A Savage Peace: Algieria 1954–1962* (New York: NYRB, 2006), ch. 11.

71. See John Arquilla, David Ronfeldt, Graham Fuller, and Melissa Fuller, *The Zapatista Social Netwar in Mexico* (Santa Monica: RAND, 1998). They provide an insightful analysis of Zapatista strategy and the success achieved.

72. Rafal Rohozinski and Ronald J. Deibert, "Controlling the Internet," 1, a draft article for the *Global Civil Society Yearbook*, privately provided and cited with permission.

73. Interview with Eric Michael, 2011.

74. Ibid.

75. See Margaret Thatcher, *Downing Street Years* (New York: HarperCollins, 1995); John Roy Major, *John Major* (New York: HarperCollins, 1999); Tony Blair, *A Journey: My Political Life* (New York: Knopf, 2010); Harold Macmillan, *Riding the Storm* (London: Macmillan, 1971) and *The Blast of War 1935–45* (London: Macmillan, 1967).

76. Barack Obama, *The Audacity of Hope: Thoughts on Reclaiming the American Dream* (New York: Crown, 2006) and *Dreams from My Father: A Story of Race and Inheritance* (New York: Crown, 2007); and Bob Dole, *One Soldier's Story: A Memoir* (New York: HarperCollins, 2005). See also Barack Obama, *Change We Can Believe In: Barack Obama's Plan to Renew America's Promise* (New York: Three Rivers Press, 2008); Mitt Romney, *No Apology: The Case for American Greatness* (New York: St. Martin's Press, 2010), and Tim Pawlenty, *Courage to Stand: An American Story* (Carol Stream, IL: Tyndale House Publishers, 2011). Pawlenty's book combines his life story with his political ideas.

77. Al Gore, *Our Choice: A Plan to Solve the Climate Crisis* (New York: Rodale Books, 2009).

78. Both were prolific authors who argued passionately for their respective viewpoints. Carter also has written various books about his personal life. See, e.g., Jimmy Carter, *White House Diary* (New York: Farrar, Straus and Giroux, 2010), *Palestine: Peace Not Apartheid* (New York: Simon & Schuster, 2006), and *An Hour before Daylight: Memoirs of a Rural Boyhood* (New York: Touchstone, 2001); Richard M. Nixon, *Memoirs of Richard Nixon* (Buccaneer Books, 1994), *Leaders* (New York: Grand Central Publishing, 1982), and *Beyond Peace* (New York: Random House, 1995).

79. Charles De Gaulle, *The Complete War Memoires of Charles De Gaulle, 1940–1946* (Da Capo Press, Inc., 1984). De Gaulle wrote a number of books, only some of which have been translated into English.

80. Few of their books are in English.

81. Nicolas Sarkozy, *Testimony: France, Europe and the World in the Twenty-First Century* (New York: Harper Perennial, 2007); Royal has written a handful of books in French, although excerpts in English can be found in Robert Harneis, *Segolene Royal: A Biography* (Harriman House, 2007).

82. Lin Bao, *Quotations from Chairman Mao-Tse Tung*. Text can be read at http://art-bin. com/art/omaotoc.html.

83. Michael Crichton, *State of Fear* (New York: HarperCollins, 2007).

84. John Steinbeck, *The Moon Is Down* (New York: Viking, 1942).

85. I. M. Buffaloed, "John Steinbeck's Propaganda Novel *The Moon Is Down*," *fairlee.wordpress.com*, September 27, 2009, http://fairlee.wordpress.com/2009/09/27/john-steinbecks%E2%80%99s-propaganda-novel-the-moon-is-down/.

86. Interview with Doug Waller.

87. See Anton Powell, *Roman Poetry and Propaganda in the Age of Augustus* (London: Duckworth Publishers, 2008).

88. Faulkner, "The Official Truth."

89. Brian Croke, "Poetry and Propaganda: Anastasius I as Pompey," *Greek, Romance and Byzantine Studies* 48 (2008): 447–66. www.duke.edu/web/classics/grbs/FTexts/48/croke.pdf.

90. Jowett and O'Donnell, *Propaganda and Persuasion*, 65. The poem—controversial in Spanish history—is about the slaughter by Basques of trapped soldiers serving in Char-

lemagne's rear guard as the main army withdrew from the Battle of Roncevaux Pass in 778. For text of the poem in English, see www.gutenberg.org/cache/epub/391/pg391.html.

91. The poem has two parts. Dryden wrote the first part. Nahum Tate wrote a portion of Part II, with Dryden apparently polishing it. The text can be seen at http://books.google.com/books?id=bTUG4Lic1dQC&printsec=frontcover&dq=%22Absalom+and+Achitophel%22&source=bl&ots=oDufIt5vSd&sig=pvI7pPOxWvPGmQNkXI3WRY48vKE&hl=en&ei=QTNQTderJ4fAgQfA8L0Y&sa=X&oi=book_result&ct=result&resnum=8&ved=0CFAQ6AEwBw#v=onepage&q&f=false.

92. Maud Newton, "Dryden's 17th Century Propaganda," *maudnewton.com*, May 14, 2007, http://maudnewton.com/blog/?p=7628.

93. See Geert Buelens lecture, *Library of Congress Webcast*, www.youtube.com/watch?v=VSIADtgAGdM.

94. Philip Hitti, *History of the Arabs, Revised: 10th Ed.* (Palgrave MacMillan, 2002), 90. See also MacFarquhar, *Media Relations Department*, 81.

95. See http://abcnews.go.com/international/story?id=814358page=1#.T8afdelyuzq.

96. See "BBCM: Afghan Taliban Use Songs, Poetry to Influence Opinion," *BBC Monitoring/OSC*, February 23, 2010. The story offers a detailed description of the Taliban's approach in using song and poetry.

97. Srinagar, "Taliban Add Song to the Armory," *Kashmir Monitor* (India), June 30, 2011.

98. Ibid.

99. Ibid.

100. "Tunisia's rappers provide soundtrack to a revolution," *CNN.com*, March 2, 2011, http://articles.cnn.com/2011-03-02/world/tunisia.rappers.balti_1_tunisian-people-rappers-sfax?_s=PM:WORLD.

101. Joseph S. Nye, Jr, *Soft Power: The Means to Success in World Politics* (New York: Public Affairs, 2004), 47.

102. See Fatma Muge Gocek, ed., *Political Cartoons in the Middle East: Culture Representations in the Middle East* (Markus Wiener Publishers, lst. ed., 1998).

103. J. G. Lewin and P. J. Huff, *Lines of Contention: Political Cartoons of the Civil War* (New York: Harper Collins, 2007). The cartoons cited are in their excellent book.

104. "A 'Smash' for Jeff," *Harper's Weekly*, November 2, 1861.

105. "Little Mac's Union Squeeze," *Harper's Weekly*, February 8, 1862.

106. "Lincoln's Two Difficulties," *Punch*, August 23, 1862.

107. "Lincoln—'I'm sorry to have to drop you, Sambo, but this concern won't carry us both,'" *Leslie's Illustrated*, October 12, 1861.

108. Allen Douglas and Fedwa Malti-Douglas, *Arab Comic Strips: Politics of an Emerging Mass Culture* (Indianapolis: Indiana University Press, 1994), 27. The Nasser comic is quite sophisticated. Their detailed analysis of its many dimensions is incisive and revealing.

109. Dr. Seuss, *The Cat in the Hat* (New York: Random House Books for Young Readers, 1957) and *How the Grinch Stole Christmas* (New York: Random House Books for Young Readers, 1957); see also Richard H. Minear (author), Art Spiegelman (author), and Dr. Seuss (illustrator), *Dr. Seuss Goes to War: The World War II Editorial Cartoons of Theodor Seuss Geisel* (New York: New Press, 2001).

110. Anthony Rhodes, *Propaganda: The Art of Persuasion: World War II* (London: Chelsea House, 1983), 189.

111. See, e.g., Pat Oliphant: *Oliphant's Presidents: Twenty-Five Years of Caricature* (Andrews McMeel Publishing, 1990).

112. Fredrick Stromberg, *Comic Art Propganda* (Lewes: ILEX, 2010), 9.

113. Tim Walker, "Iraq: How a Daring New Generation of Graphic Novelists View the Art of War," *The Independent*, June 23, 2008.

114. Mark Mazzetti and Borzou Daraghai, "U.S. Military Covertly Pays to Run Stories in Iraqi Press," *Los Angeles Times*, November 30, 2005; and Renai Merle, "Pentagon Funds Diplomacy Effort," *Washington Post*, June 11, 2005.

115. Lynne Duke, "Word at War. Propaganda? Nah, Here's the Scoop, Say the Guys Who Planted Stories in Iraqi Papers," *Washington Post*, March 26, 2006.

116. See, e.g., Patricia H. Kushlis, "When Fake Good News Fails, Send in Rummy's Personal Paramilitary," *Whirledview*, March 9, 2006, http://whirledview.typepad.com/whirledview/2006/03/when_fake_good_.html.

Chapter 6

1. Jutta Held, "How Do the Political Effects of Pictures Come About? The Case of Picasso's *Guernica*," *The Oxford Art Journal* 11, no. 1 (1988): 38.

2. Interviews with Joe Gaylord, 2010–2011.

3. Interview with Ron Faucheux, 2011.

4. Augustus imprinted his likeness on coins to bolster his visibility and presence. There isn't much written propaganda. In *History of Rome* (*Ab Urbe Condita*), Titus Livius wrote a history that glorifies the founding of Rome, beginning with the arrival into Italy of Aeneas, and the city's rise. The work appealed to Roman patriotism. See the Perseus Project, Tufts University (English Translation), www.perseus.tufts.edu/hopper/text?doc=Perseus: text:1999.02.0151. *The Arthashastra* discusses propaganda and endorses strategies and tactics that inspire comparison to Machiavelli's *The Prince*. Authorship is attributed to Chanakya (350–283 BC), a scholar who served as prime minister of the Maurya Empire. The text endorses deceit, trickery, torture, and other nefarious activities as legitimate means to gain and hold power. The text can be found at http://api.ning.com/files/eCyBsmRzuZTH3Xd8pq2Da 5H2ilFGgn5ML4qYjQ3dtViNR5vOXqF-s1O4MeYYDM7tNMO7IdASXIA3qo1gAkoRk DT7tpgLqq17/Arthashastra_of_Chanakya__English.pdf.

5. Paul Zanker, *The Power of Images in the Age of Augustus* (Ann Arbor: University of Michigan Press, 1990), 2–3.

6. Interview with Adrian Goldsworthy, 2011; see also Garth S. Jowett and Victoria O'Donnell, *Propaganda and Persuasion*, 4th ed. (Thousand Oaks, CA: Sage, 2005), 41.

7. The National Defense University of the United States devised the doctrine, which holds that the use of overwhelming power, dominant battlefield awareness, and spectacular displays of force can paralyze an adversary's perception on the battlefield and destroy its will to fight. Confounding the will to resist is a key objective of psychological operation. One can argue, of course, that "shock and awe" is a kinetic military action and not a psychological operation. It satisfies both notions. See Harlan K. Ullman and James P. Wade, "Shock and Awe: Achieving Rapid Dominance," *National Defense University*, 1996, www.dodccrp.org/files/Ullman_Shock.pdf.

8. Neil Faulkner, "The Official Truth: Propaganda in the Roman Empire," *bbc.co.uk*, October 15, 2010, www.bbc.co.uk/history/ancient/romans/romanpropaganda_article_01. shtml.

9. Akbar S. Ahmed, *Jinnah, Pakistan and Islamic Identity* (London: Routledge, 1997), 228. Ahmed writes: "The depiction of Jinnah in the national dress, consciously painted in dark hues, conveys a 'fundamentalist' Jinnah; he is portrayed as grim and unsmiling; he looks like a stern headmaster. This makes a point: discipline is required. The headmaster's cane is to be kept at hand, and people have to obey."

10. Interview with Ayesha Jalal, 2011. See also Ayesha Jalal, *The Sole Spokesman: Jinnah, The Muslim League and the Demand for Pakistan* (Cambridge: Cambridge University Press, 1985).

11. Interviews with Stephen Padgett, 2010–2011.

12. Ibid.

13. See, e.g., Joby Warrick and Colum Lynch, "Diplomats Condemn Syrian Slaughter But Lament Lack of Options," *Washington Post*, May 30, 2012. www.washingtonpost.com/world/national-security/diplomats-condemn-syrian-slaughter-but-lament-lack-of-options/2012/05/30/gJQAim5m2U_story.html.

14. Aram Nerguizian, "Assad's Hidden Strength in Syria," *Los Angeles Times*, March 5, 2012, www.sacbee.com/2012/03/05/4311987/assads-hidden-strength-in-syria.html; and Roger Cohen, "Arm Syria's Rebels," Op Ed, *New York Times*, February 27, 2012. www.nytimes.com/2012/02/28/opinion/cohen-arm-syrias-rebels.html.

15. Aram Nerguizian, "Assad's Hidden Strength in Syria."

16. Arild Moen, "EU: Russia Must Boost Syrian Role," *Wall Street Journal*, March 6, 2012. http://online.wsj.com/article/SB10001424052970203370604577265012233909018.html. See also Steven Erlander, "Syrian Conflict Poses the Risk of Wider Strife," *New York Times*, February 25, 2012, www.nytimes.com/2012/02/26/world/middleeast/syrian-conflict-poses-risk-of-regional-strife.html.

17. "Asma al-Assad: Syria's First Lady," ABC News. http://abcnews.go.com/International/slideshow/lady-alma-al-assad-mother-fashionable-intelligent-philanthropic-15089414. See also Joseph Weissman, "Why Do Bell Pottinger Lobbyists Work with Syria & Belarus, Not Zimbabwe or Uzbekistan?" *Huffington Post*, December 23, 2011. www.huffingtonpost.co.uk/joseph-weissman/bell-pottinger-lobbyists_b_1164850.html/. *The Guardian* revealed that he was also receiving media counsel from his London-based father-in-law, Fawaz Akhras, on how to mute criticism of regime brutality. See Jonathan Miller, "Syrian Defectors Accuse Assad Relatives of Ordering Crimes against Humanity," *Guardian.co.uk,* May 27, 2012, www.guardian.co.uk/world/2012/may/27/syrian-defectors-assad-relatives?INTCMP=SRCH.

18. Sana Seed, "Asma al-Assad as a Hope for Peace Because She Wears Louis Vuitton? Pah," *Guardian.co.uk,* April 20, 2012, www.guardian.co.uk/commentisfree/2012/apr/20/asma-al-assad-syria-petition?INTCMP=SRCH.

19. Nour Ali, "Syrian Regime Steps Up Propaganda War amid Bloody Crackdown on Protests," *Guardian.co.uk,* July 20, 2011, www.guardian.co.uk/world/2011/jul/20/syria-propaganda-protests-assad.

20. Jeremy Singer-Vine, "Orange, and Tulip Revolutions?" *Slate.com*, January 20, 2011, www.slate.com/id/2281845/.

21. Mia Couto, "Thirty Years Ago They Smiled," *Le Monde Diplomatique*, April 2004, mondediplo.com/2004/04/15mozambique.

22. See, e.g., www.afghansforafghans.org/learn.html.

23. Nick Paton Walsh, "Pink Revolution Rumbles On in Blood and Fury," *Guardian.co.uk.*, March 27, 2005, www.guardian.co.uk/world/2005/mar/27/nickpatonwalsh.theobserver.

The color yellow meant change, claimed one revolutionary leader. See Jeremy Page, "From West to East, Rolling Revolution Gathers Pace across the Former USSR," *The Times*, February 19, 2005, www.timesonline.co.uk/tol/news/world/article516189.ece. Ibid.

24. Vladimir Radyuhin, "Moscow and Multipolarity," *The Hindu*, December 30, 2004, www.hindu.com/2004/12/30/stories/2004123000391000.htm.

25. Walsh, "Pink Revolution Rumbles On."

26. Zaal Anjapardize, "Georgian Advisors Stepping Forward in Bishkek," *Jamestown Foundation, Eurasia Daily Monitor* 2, no. 59 (March 24, 2005), www.jamestown.org/single/?no_cache=1&tx_ttnews[tt_news]=30153.

27. Bryan Walsh, "Thailand after Thaksin," *Time.com*, April 16, 2006, www.time.com/time/asia/covers/501060417/story.html.

28. Charlotte Sector, "Belarusians Wear Jeans in Silent Protest," *ABCNews.go.com*, January 13, 2006, http://abcnews.go.com/International/story?id=1502762.

29. Interview with Steven Luckert. See also Steven Luckert and Susan Bachrach, *State of Deception: The Power of Nazi Propaganda* (Washington: US Holocaust Memorial Museum and W.W. Norton, 2009), published in conjunction with the exhibition.

30. For example, Rudyard Kipling adorned the cover of some of his books on India with a swastika. It had nothing in his mind to do with Nazis or fascism, but was an ancient symbol that he used as a link to India. The origin of the symbol is unclear, but appears to be of Sanskrit origin and a symbol of good luck or well being. See www.khandro.net/swastika.htm.

31. "How effective this type of propaganda was is most strikingly shown by the fact that after four years of war, it not only enabled the enemy to stick to its guns but even to nibble at our own people." Adolph Hitler, *Mein Kampf*, chapter VI, www.hitler.org/writings/Mein_Kampf/mkv1ch06.html.

32. Anthony Rhodes, *Propaganda: The Art of Persuasion: World War II*, 18–19.

33. Luckert, interview.

34. Except on ceremonial occasions, Hitler sat in the front seat of his car next to his driver, not in the back. He was also a vegetarian.

35. Richard Overy, *The Dictators* (New York: W. W. Norton, 2004), 99–100, 112, 113. See also Peter York, *Dictator Style: Lifestyles of the World's Most Colorful Despots* (San Francisco: Chronicle Books, 2006), 22.

36. Nicholas J. Cull, David Culbert, and David Welch, *Propaganda and Mass Persuasion: A Historical Encyclopedia, 1500 to the Present* (ABC-CLIO, 2003), 46.

37. Dominique Moisi, *The Geopolitics of Emotion* (New York: Doubleday, 2009), 6.

38. York, *Dictator Style*, 17.

39. Ibid.

40. Ibid., 87–89.

41. Victor T. Le Vine, *Politics in Francophone Africa* (Boulder: Lynne Rienner Publishers, 2004), 268; and "Africa: French Fiddling," *Time.com*, October 18, 1979, www.time.com/time/magazine/article/0,9171,916883,00.html.

42. Dominic Moisi, *The Geopolitics of Emotion* (New York: Doubleday, 2009), 6.

43. For photographs, see http://2008gamesbeijing.com/10-amazing-new-buildings-in-china/. Moisi has written cogently on the importance of confidence and optimism and the pitfalls of the converse attitudes for a nation.

44. Website, J. Paul Getty Museum, "Portrait of Louis XIV," www.getty.edu/art/gettyguide/artObjectDetails?artobj=582. The comments are drawn from the Getty's.

45. See www.louvre.fr/llv/oeuvres/detail_notice.jsp?CONTENT%3C%3Ecnt_id=101341 98673225718&CURRENT_LLV_NOTICE%3C%3Ecnt_id=10134198673225718&FOL DER%3C%3Efolder_id=9852723696500815&baseIndex=36&bmLocale=en.

46. Philip Dwyer, *Napoleon: The Path to Power* (New Haven, CT: Yale University Press, 2007), 221–22, 249–57.

47. Cull, Culbert, and Welch, *Propaganda and Mass Persuasion*, 47.

48. See James Voorhies, "Francisco de Goya (1746–1828) and the Spanish Enlightenment," Metropolitan Museum of Art, www.metmuseum.org/toah/hd/goya/hd_goya.htm.

49. Olivier Bernier, *Fireworks at Dusk* (New York: Little, Brown & Co., 1993), 192; and Jutta Held, "How Do the Political Effects of Pictures Come About? The Case of Picasso's *Guernica*," *The Oxford Art Journal* 11, no. 1 (1988): 34.

50. Olivier Bernier, *Fireworks at Dusk*, 8.

51. Held, "How Do the Political Effects of Pictures Come About?" 33.

52. Richard Cook, "Disaster of War," *Tate Magazine*, Issue 2, www.tate.org.uk/magazine/issue2/fougeron.htm. Cook was writing about *Martyred Spain*, a powerful piece of anti-fascist propaganda against Franco's callous barbarity.

53. Bernier, *Fireworks at Dusk*, 246–47, 254.

54. Antony Beevor, *The Battle for Spain: The Spanish Civil War, 1936–1939* (London: Weidenfeld & Nicolson, 2006). Beevor's detailed account reveals the complexities of this violent war.

55. Ibid., xxv–xxvi.

56. Peter Kafka, "Associated Press Settles Copyright Case with Obama Poster-Maker Shepard Fairey," *Media Memo*, January 12, 2011, http://mediamemo.allthingsd.com/20110112/associated-press-settles-copyright-case-with-obama-poster-maker-shepard-fairey/. See also David Itzkoff, "Associated Press Files Countersuit over Obama Poster," *New York Times/Associated Press*, March 11, 2009.

Chapter 7

1. British Army Field Manual, Vol. 1, Part 10, January 2010—Countering Insurgency.

2. Interview with Stephen Padgett, 2011.

3. See Douglas E. Farah and Stephen Braun, *Merchant of Death* (New York: Wiley, 2007). Their hair-raising account of Bout explains why Africa wound up as a killing ground for internecine slaughter while he aided the Taliban in Afghanistan and the United States in Iraq. When people ask how this can happen, the answer is, in no small measure, because the United States and others, who could have stopped Bout much earlier than they did, allowed him to carry on.

4. For a fuller report, see Maj. Gen. Jonathon P. Riley, "The U.K. in Sierre Leone: A Post-Conflict Operation Success?" *Heritage Lecture # 958, The Heritage Foundation*, June 15, 2006, www.heritage.org/research/africa/hl958.cfm.

5. Padgett, interview.

6. Ibid.

7. See Maj. Clifford E. Day, "Critical Analysis on the Defeat of Task Force Ranger," a brilliantly researched paper presented to the Research Department, Air Command and Staff College, March 1997, www.gwu.edu/~nsarchiv/NSAEBB/NSAEBB63/doc10.pdf. Major Day's detailed and incisive assessment is required reading for understanding the pitfalls of such operations.

8. Technically, the Deltas came from the US Army's 1st Special Forces Operational Detachment-Delta (Delta Force).

9. Mark Bowden, *Blackhawk Down: A Story of Modern Warfare* (New York: Atlantic Monthly Press, 1999). Director Ridley Scott turned the book into a fine film.

10. Day, "Critical Analysis," 16. Day lacerates the operation partly as a misguided effort to validate the use of highly specialized teams like Rangers and Deltas in Somalia. Other failures included not obtaining AC-130Hs, which can pepper a ground with bullets, or armor. Day and others lambast Secretary of Defense Les Aspin for failing to provide it, as well as Chairman of the Joint Chiefs of Staff Colin Powell and ground commanders for failing to forcefully insist upon the requirement.

11. Interview with Chris Stewart.

12. See Day, "Critical Analysis," chapter 2. Day offers important lessons on why the missions of UNOSOM II and the Task Force failed, starting with the failure to set clear objectives.

13. Richard H. Schultz Jr. and Andrea J. Dew, *Insurgents, Terrorists and Militias* (New York: Columbia University Press, 2006), 92–94. See also Jonathan Stevenson, *Losing Mogadishu: Testing U.S. Policy in Somalia* (US Naval Institute Press, 1995).

14. See Stevenson, *Losing Mogadishu*, 74.

15. "Turmoil in Liberia," *CNN.com/WORLD*, July 7, 2003.

16. Colonel Blair A. Ross, Jr., "The U.S. Joint Task Force Experience in Liberia," *Military Review*, May–June, 2005.

17. See, e.g., "The Evolving Modern Egyptian Republic: A Special Report," *Stratfor*, March 1, 2011, www.stratfor.com/analysis/20110224-evolving-modern-egyptian-republic-special-report.

18. Hamza Hendawi, "Analysis: Military Coup Was behind Mubarak's Exit," *Washington Post*, February 11, 2011.

19. "Mubarak and Sons Detained in Egypt," *Al Jazeera*, April 13, 2011.

20. Kristen Chick, "Court Order to Dissolve Egypt's NDP Deals Body Blow to Old Power Structure," *Christian Science Monitor*, April 17, 2011, www.csmonitor.com/world/middle_east/2011/0417/court-order-to-dissolve-egypt-s-NDP-deals-body-blow-to-old-power-structure.

21. David D. Kirkpatrick and David E. Sanger, "A Tunisian–Egyptian Link That Shook Arab History," *New York Times*, February 13, 2011.

22. See, e.g., Hendawi, "Analysis: Military Coup Was behind Mubarak's Exit," February 11, 2011.

23. See, e.g., "Egypt's Historic Election – Wednesday, May 23," *Guardian.co.uk*, May 23, 2012, www.guardian.co.uk/world/middle-east-live/2012/may/23/egypt-presidential-elections-live. On hand to help monitor the process, former President Jimmy Carter noted that constraints made it difficult to judge how truly fair the elections were, but called what he saw "encouraging." "Carter: Egypt Polls 'Encouraging' Despite Unprecedented Constraints on His Team," *Ahram OnLine*, May 26, 2012, http://english.ahram.org.eg/NewsContent/36/122/42954/Presidential-elections-/Presidential-elections-news/Carter-Egypt-polls-encouraging-despite-unprecedent.aspx. In postprimary, off-the-record discussions between the author and close observers of the election, some doubts have cropped up about Shafiq's finish, but given that he drew less than a quarter of the vote, the result does not undercut the credibility of the process. Charles Levinson's account of Shafiq's rise provides an informed explanation of his success: Charles Levinson, "Surprise Rise

of Mubarak Loyalist," *Wall Street Journal*, May 30, 2012, http://online.wsj.com/article/ SB10001424052702303674004577434562867892748.html?KEYWORDS=Egyptian+ Presidential+election.

24. Charles Levinson, "Surprise Rise of Mubarak Loyalist," *Wall Street Journal*, May 30, 2012, http://online.wsj.com/article/SB10001424052702303674004577434562867892748. html?KEYWORDS=Egyptian+Presidential+election.

25. Tania Branigan, "China Confirms Stealth Fighter Jet Tests," *Guardian.co.uk*, January 11, 2011, www.guardian.co.uk/world/2011/jan/11/china-stealth-fighter-jet-tests.

26. Stewart, interview. See also Rohozinski, "Bullets to Bytes: Reflections on ICTs and 'Local' Conflict," in *Bombs and Bandwith: The Emerging Relationship between IT and Security*, Robert Latham, ed., The New Press, 2003), 4–5.

27. In Iraq, where the media is present for most major engagements, different constraints apply. In Fallujah, al-Jazeera's coverage directly affected the first assault on the city.

28. Rohozinski, "Bullets to Bytes," 4–5.

29. See "1979: Millions Cheer as the Pope Comes Home," news.bbc.co., http://news.bbc. co.uk/onthisday/hi/dates/stories/june/2/newsid_3972000/3972361.stm.

30. Interview with Newt Gingrich, 2011.

31. Carl Berger, *Broadsides and Bayonets: The Propaganda War of the American Revolution* (Philadelphia: University of Pennsylvania Press, 1961), 191.

32. H. A. Drake, *Constantine and the Bishops: The Politics of Intolerance* (Baltimore: Johns Hopkins University Press, 2002); Michael Grant, *Constantine the Great: The Man and His Times* (New York: Scribner, 2009); D. G Kousoulas, *The Life and Times of Constantine the Great* (Book-Surge Publishing [Amazon], 2nd Ed., 2007); and Morgan Caillet and Robert Ludovic, "Constantine the Great and the Destiny of the Christian Church," *World Religion Watch*, February 1, 2008, www.world-religion-watch.org/index.php?option=com_content&view=article&id =108:constantine-the-great-and-the-destiny-of-the-christian-church&catid=48:Courts%20 Points%20for%20Trasversal%20Discussion&Itemid=102.

33. See Robert Kagan, *On the Origins of War and the Preservation of Peace* (New York: Doubleday/Anchor Books, 1995), 34–35. Kagan notes that Greece was then dominated by two great alliances: the Delian League, the name by which modern scholars call the Athenian Empire, and the Peloponnesian League, controlled by Sparta. Shifting alliances between these powers and other city-states created significant tensions. It was Sparta's ally Corinth who badgered Sparta into the series of wars that led to the fall of the Athenian empire. Ibid., at 19, 24.

34. Rumsfeld, *Known and Unknown*, 692.

35. See "Awakening Movement in Iraq," *New York Times*, October 19, 2010.

36. Rumsfeld, *Known and Unknown*, 716.

37. Fred W. Baker III, "Surge Troops Stabilized Iraq, Chairman Tells Troops," *Armed Forces Press Service*, June 19, 2008, quoting Chairman Mike Mullen; and Fareed Zakaria, "Don't Forget America's Other War," *Newsweek*, December 19, 2009.

38. See, e.g., Thomas E. Ricks, *The Gamble* (New York: Penguin, 2009); "June 17: Petraeus Hints Iraq 'Surge' May Be Needed Longer," *Washington Post*, June 6, 2007; and Rumsfeld, *Known and Unknown*.

39. Interview with Kevin McCarty.

40. Ibid.

41. Ibid.

42. "During Ramadan Dinner at White House, Obama Honors Muslim Survivors of Sept. 11 Attacks," *Associated Press*, August 10, 2011.

43. Col. Lawrence Dietz, "Small Article-Big Potential?" *PSYOP Regimental Blog*, August 11, 2011, http://psyopregiment.blogspot.com/.

44. The text of the speech can be found at www.oecd.org/document/10/0,3746, en_2649_201185_1876938_1_1_1_1,00.html.

45. George Kennan, "Top Secret Supplement to the Report of the Policy Planning Staff of July 23, 1947, titled Certain Aspects of the European Recovery Problem from the United States Standpoint." The memorandum can be seen at Matt Armstrong's blog: http://mountainrunner.us/2009/09/psychological_byproducts.html.

46. Ibid.

47. Matt Armstrong, "The Intended 'Psychological By-Products of Development,'" *MountainRunner.us*, September 1, 2009, http://mountainrunner.us/2009/09/psychological_byproducts.html

48. McCarty, interview.

Chapter 8

1. Interview with Julian Wheatley, 2011; and see David I. Steinberg, "'Legitimacy' in Burma/Myanmar: Concepts and Implications," in N. Ganesan and Kyaw Yin Hlaing, eds., *Myanmar, State, Society and Ethnicity* (Singapore: ISEAS, 2007).

2. Ibid.

3. Wheatley, interview. See also David I. Steinberg, "Myanmar in 2010: The Elections Year and Beyond," *Southeast Asian Affairs 2011* (Singapore: ISEAS, 2011).

4. Mary P. Callahan, *Making Enemies: War and State Building in Burma* (Ithaca: Cornell University Press, 2004), 3.

5. Robert H. Taylor, *The State in Myanmar* (Singapore: NUS Press, 2009), 471–72.

6. Wheatley, interview.

7. "Burma Leader Than Shwe Gives Election Warning," *BBC News*, January 4, 2010.

8. Wheatley, interview.

9. "Aung San Suu Kyi: Burma Election Not 'Free and Fair,'" *BBC News*, March 12, 2012, www.bbc.co.uk/news/world-asia-17558542. See also "Opposition Claims Historic Sweep in Myanmar Elections," *Christian Science Monitor*, April 1, 2012, www.csmonitor.com/World/Asia-Pacific/2012/0401/Opposition-claims-historic-sweep-in-Myanmar-elections; and Damien Gayle, "A Triumph of the People: Heroine of Burma Aung San Suu Kyi Hails a 'New Era' in the Country's Politics as Her Party Claims Victory in Every Seat Contested in Historic Election," *Daily Mail*, March 31, 2012, www.dailymail.co.uk/news/article-2123178/Myanmar-elections-2012-Aung-San-Suu-Kyi-claims-victory-hails-new-era-Burma.html.

10. Jocelyn Gecker, "Get the Camera, Here Comes Aung San Suu Kyi," *Associated Press/Timesunion.com*, May 31, 2012, www.timesunion.com/news/article/Get-the-camera-here-comes-Aung-San-Suu-Kyi-3597359.php.

11. Information on Saudi Arabia's campaign is drawn from an interview with Saud Alsati, political counselor to the Kingdom, and materials he provided. The Saudi program embraces over a dozen strategies that employ strategic communication, security force action, and tools of the law. Christopher Bourcek and Abdullah Ansary have well described the Saudi approach. See Christopher Boucek, "Saudi Arabia's 'Soft' Counterterrorism Strategy: Prevention, Rehabilitation, and Aftercare," *Carnegie Endowment*, Middle East Program, no. 97, September

2008, www.carnegieendowment.org/files/cp97_boucek_saudi_final_pdf; Abdullah F. Ansary, "Combating Extremism: A Brief Overview of Saudi Arabia's Approach," *Middle East Policy* 15, no. 2 (Summer 2008), www.mepc.org/journal/middle-east-policy-archives/combating-extremism-brief-overview-saudi-arabias-approach.

12. B. R. Meyers, *The Cleanest Race* (New York: Melville House, 2010), 15.

13. Ibid.

14. B. R. Meyers, "North Korea's Race Problem," *Foreign Policy*, March/April 2010, www.foreignpolicy.com/articles/2010/02/22/north_koreas_race_problem.

15. Meyers, *The Cleanest Race*, 17.

16. Choe Sang-Hun and Martin Fackler, "Kim Jong-un," *New York Times*, January 7, 2011.

17. "Kim Jong-un Stars in New North Korean TV Documentary," *The Telegraph*, January 8, 2012, www.telegraph.co.uk/news/worldnews/asia/northkorea/9000784/Kim-Jong-un-stars-in-new-North-Korean-TV-documentary.html.

18. Interview with Trita Parsi. He is the author of *Treacherous Alliance: The Secret Dealings of Israel, Iran and the United States* (New Haven, CT: Yale University Press, 2007), an important study of Iranian diplomacy.

19. So does the Turkish government.

20. "Report: Iran to Ban Google's Gmail," *EarthTimes*, February 2010; Ali Akbar Dareini, "YouTube Blocked in Iran, Watchdogs Say," *Associated Press*, December 6, 2006; and "Iran Protestors Defy Rally Ban," *BBC News*, June 15, 2009.

21. See Parisa Ghobben, quoting Asieh Mir's remarks to the United States Institute of Peace, "Iran Faces 'Legitimacy Crisis' Amid Election Aftermath," *niacouncil.com*, June 26, 2009, www.niacouncil.org/index.php?option=com_content&task=view&id=1457&Itemid=2.

22. Monavar Khalaj, "Mousavi Warns of Iran Losing 'Legitimacy,'" *Financial Times*, February 27, 2010.

23. "Reformists Question legitimacy of Iran's Government," *CNN.com*, July 2, 2009, www.cnn.com/2009/WORLD/meast/07/01/iran.election/index.html.

24. "Open Letter to the People" and "Reformists Question Legitimacy of Iran's Government," *CNN.com*, July 2, 2009, www.cnn.com/2009/WORLD/meast/07/01/iran.election/index.html.

25. Interview with Trita Parsi, 2011.

26. Mark Lander and Nazila Fathi, "President of Iran Defends His Legitimacy," *The New York Times*, September 23, 2009.

27. Thomas Erdbrink, "Ahmadinejad Says Egypt, Tunisia Were Inspired by Iran's Anti-Western Protests," *Washington Post*, February 12, 2011.

28. Ladane Nasseri, "Iran Cheers Egypt, Tunisia Revolts as Ahmadinejad Stifles Domestic Dissent," *Bloomberg*, February 14, 2011, www.bloomberg.com/news/2011-02-14/iran-cheers-egypt-tunisia-revolts-as-ahmadinejad-stifles-domestic-dissent.html.

29. "Ahmadinejad: Egypt Unrest Hails a Mideast without U.S., Israel," *Associated Press*, February 11, 2011.

30. Thomas Erdbrink and Liz Sly, "As Egypt Uprising Inspires Middle East, Iran Sees Biggest Protests in a Year," *Washington Post*, February 14, 2011.

Chapter 9

1. "Reports: Exiled Tunisian President in Coma after Stroke," *AOLNews*, February 18, 2011, www.aolnews.com/2011/02/18/reports-exiled-tunisian-president-zine-el-abidine-ben-ali-in-co/.

2. "Highlights: Egyptian President Hosni Mubarak's Speech," *Reuters*, January 29, 2011, www.reuters.com/article/2011/01/29/us-egypt-mubarak-speech-idUSTRE70S0SA20110129.

3. Jeffrey Fleishmann and Edmund Sanders, "Unease in Egypt as Police Replaced by Army, Neighbors Band against Looters," *Los Angeles Times*, January 29, 2011.

4. It took only four states to nominate a competitive choice for vice president. The McCain forces did not feel that they had control of the convention and, mistakenly in the judgment of this author—who served as executive director of the McCain Ad Council in the campaign—refused to fight. One of the campaign's imaginative media consultants, Mike Hudome, argued that the campaign should have nominated its choice, provoked a floor fight, filmed the battles, and used the fight to show voters that McCain was his own man. It was savvy politics. Too bad the McCain high command rejected the idea.

5. Frank Rich, "The Up-or-Down Vote on Obama's Presidency," *The New York Times*, March 7, 2010.

6. The speech can be viewed on YouTube.com, www.youtube.com/watch?v=tydfsfSQiYc. It bears noting that once Hillary Clinton got her act together after Texas, her talent, experience, and panache surfaced and she clobbered Obama in subsequent major primaries.

7. David Plouffe, *The Audacity to Win* (New York: Viking, 2009), 187–89.

8. James Fallows, "Obama Explained," *Atlantic* Magazine, March 2012, www.theatlantic.com/magazine/archive/2012/03/obama-explained/8874/.

9. Interview with John Maddox, 2011.

10. Rich, "The Up-or-Down Vote on Obama's Presidency," *The New York Times*, March 7, 2010.

11. Lori Montgomery, "Running in the Red: How the U.S., on the Road to Surplus, Detoured to Massive Debt," *Washington Post*, April 30, 2011.

12. The Gramm-Leach-Bliley Act of 1999, more formally, the Financial Modernization Act of 1999, http://banking.senate.gov/conf/.

13. The 1999 legislation opened up the market among banking, securities, and insurance companies. Glass-Steagall (the Banking Act of 1933) had prohibited any one institution from acting in any combination of an investment bank, insurance company, and commercial banks. Thus Citicorp merged with Travelers Group to form Citigroup. The bill opened up the floodgates to creative financial instruments backed by notes and other commercial paper. Banks responded by holding bundled mortgage-backed securities that were deemed safe by rating agencies but that ultimately failed the market test. The banks were already doing this, but needed legislation to sanction what they were up to. This deregulation helped cause the crisis by allowing the creating of giant supermarkets—huge banks—that were too big. There was a fundamental failure of regulation. While the Federal Reserve was enshrined as the top regulator for giant firms like Citigroup and Bank of America, it did not give any regulator sweeping powers over investment banks like Bears Stearns, Lehman Brothers, or AIG. Some who took advantage of the change to the grief of homeowners were mortgage-finance companies. Mortgage-finance companies were not banks, so no one oversaw their business. Commercial banks like Citigroup, though overseen by multiple federal agencies, were able to accumulate huge levels of exposure by housing risky assets in investment vehicles that were not part of their balance sheets. Assets held off from balance sheets proved to be a key blind spot. By spreading regulatory authority among different regulators, the banks could move products from entity to entity. Some entities were subject to regulation. Others were not. There was no single agency that had complete purview over all activities. It made the examination by all regulators less effective.

14. "TARP's Bank Bailout Program Nears Break-Even Point with Latest Repayment," *Los Angeles Times*, February 2, 2011, and "TARP Repayments Push US Bank Bailout into Profit," *Reuters*, March 30, 2011.

15. "Missile Defense Amendment to START II Treaty (December 2010," Voteview.spia. uga.edu/blog?p=623.

16. Pub.L. 111-203, H.R. 4173.

17. Steve Clemons, "Obama Moved at Warp Speed on Libya," *Huffington Post*, March 30, 2011. Clemons points out that while the Security Council took three years to move on an International Criminal Tribunal for former Yugoslavia, Obama persuaded it to move in nine days; that an asset freeze for Bosnia required a year, but Obama got that done in nine days; that it took a year after bombing civilians to impose a No Fly Zone over former Yugoslavia, and Obama managed that feat in thirty-one days.

18. See, e.g., Elliott Abrams, "Obama's Pathetic Response to Libya," *Weekly Standard.com*, February 23, 2011; Nicholas D. Kristof, "On the Line with Libya," *New York Times*, February 23, 2011; Oliver Tree, " 'I Saw Gaddafi's Troops Shoot Children': U.S. Citizens Describe Horror as They Dock in Malta," *MailOnLine*, February 25, 2011; Rick Moran, "Where's Obama on Libya?", *Americanthinker.com*, February 22, 2011.

19. Glen Thush, "Day after Saying No Second Term, a Big Win for Hillary Clinton," *Politico.com*, March 17, 2011.

20. Glenn Thrust and Matt Negrin, "Barack Obama on Libya: Mission Is 'Focused,'" *Politico.com*, March 18, 2011.

21. January 28, 1986, www.youtube.com/watch?v=gEjXjfxoNXM.

22. Chris Matthews, *Now Let Me Tell You What I Really Think* (New York: The Free Press, 2002).

23. *Stratfor* reported that "the very same property was raided in 2003 by Pakistani intelligence with American cooperation." "Who Was Hiding bin Laden in Abbottabad?," *Stratfor*, May 5, 2011.

24. "Taliban React to Report of bin Laden's Death with Suspicion, Demand Proof," *Associated Press*, May 3, 2011; Jeremy Pelofsky and Kamran Haider, "Obama Decides Not to Release Bin Laden Photos," *Reuters*, May 4, 2011.

25. Sometimes called Operation Evening Light or Operation Rice Bowl.

26. Lt. A. Chua Lu Fong, "Operation Eagle Claw, 1980: A Case Study in Crisis Management and Military Planning," *Journal of the Singapore Armed Forces* (April–June 2002).

27. Ibid.

28. Interview, Lt. Gen. Charles Pitman. In 1996, the author was engaged as a strategist and media consultant to Patrick Taylor, who planned to run for the United States Senate from Louisiana. General Pitman was advising him and related the story of his briefing at the White House to the author. In May 2011, he reconfirmed the account. It was a tragedy because they had identified the location of the hostages in Tehran and the operation very likely would have been successful had it gone forward with even five helicopters.

29. Ibid.

30. Ibid.

31. See Peter L. Bergen, *Manhunt: The Ten-Year Search for Bin Laden—from 9/11 to Abbottabad* (New York: Crown, 2012). Bergen provides a detailed account of the planning and execution of the attack.

32. Declan Walsh and Sam Jones, "Osama bin Laden Raid Team was Prepared to Fight Pakistani Forces," *Guardian.co.uk*, May 10, 2011, and "Bin Laden Assault Team was Prepared to Fight Pakistani Forces," *Boston.com*, May 10, 2011.

33. Anwar Iqbal, "US Lawmakers Threaten to Suspend Aid," *Dawn.com*, May 3, 2011; Karin Brulliard, "Pakistan Defends Role, Questions 'Unilateral' U.S. Action," *Washington Post*, May 3, 2011; Karin Brulliard, "Pakistan Questions Legality of U.S. Operation That Killed Bin Laden," *Washington Post*, May 5, 2011; and Jane Perlez, "Pakistan Pushes Back against U.S. Criticism on Bin Laden," *New York Times*, May 3, 2011.

34. Kamran Shafi, "Truth Will Out," *Dawn.com*, May 3, 2011. In Shafi's words: "Now that the Americans have done what they said they would do if they had the intelligence—go after who they consider their enemies no matter where they are holed up—it is much more important to ask why our much-vaunted Deep State didn't know Osama bin Laden was living in Abbottabad Cantonment all these years? And to ask why everyone and Charlie's aunt in the security establishment went blue and red with anger when told that Osama and his close advisers were hiding in Pakistan?" Ibid.

35. Karin Brulliard and Shaiq Hussain, "Pakistani Spy Chief Offers to Resign," *Washington Post*, May 12, 2011; and "Pakistan: ISI Paralyzed Al Qaeda, Should Not Be Criticized—Agency Head," *Stratfor*, May 13, 2011.

36. "Army, Agencies' Budget Be Presented in Assembly: Nawaz," *The News*, May 14, 2011.

37. "More Abbottabad-like Raids Not to Be Tolerated: COAS," *The News*, May 10, 2011; and Jane Perlez, "Pakistani Army Chief Warns U.S. on Another Raid," *New York Times*, May 5, 2011.

38. Greg Miller and Joby Warrick, "Osama Bin Laden 'Resisted' Assault But Was Unarmed, U.S. Officials Say," *Washington Post*, May 3, 2011.

39. Michael D. Shear, "White House Corrects Bin Laden Narrative," *New York Times*, May 3, 2011; and "Contradictions, Misstatements from White House in Telling Story of Bin Laden Raid," *Washington Post*, May 3, 2011.

40. "White House: Bin Laden Unarmed during Assault," *Associated Press*, May 3, 2011.

41. David Martin, "Bin Laden Intel Revealing New Leads Every Hour," *CBSnews.com*, May 10, 2011.

42. See, e.g., B. Raman, "Abbottabad Raid: A Reconstruction through Tweets," *International Terrorism Monitor,* Paper 715, Institute for Topical Studies, Chennai, South Asia Analysis Group, May 5, 2011; Simon Mann, "Daughter, 12, Saw Killing of Unarmed Bin Laden," *Sydney Morning Herald*, May 5, 2011; and Elisabeth Bumiller, "Raid Account, Hastily Told, Proves Fluid," *New York Times*, May 6, 2011.

43. See Pew Global Attitudes Project, "Osama bin Laden Largely Discredited among Muslim Publics in Recent Years," May 2, 2011, http://pewglobal.org/2011/05/02/osama-bin-laden-largely-discredited-among-muslim-publics-in-recent-years/.

44. "Anger over Leaks on bin Laden Raid in US," *Dawn.com*, May 14, 2011.

45. See, e.g., Maria Cardona, "GOP's 'Faux Anger' Is All the Rage," *CNN.com,* May 2, 2012 (Cardona is a Democratic strategist arguing that the GOP is just envious): www.cnn.com/2012/05/02/opinion/cardona-faux-gop-anger/index.html; Peter Baker and Michael D. Shear, "Obama Trumpets Killing of bin Laden, and Critics Pounce," *New York Times*, April 27, 2012, www.nytimes.com/2012/04/28/us/politics/critics-pounce-on-obamas-trumpeting-of-bin-laden-death.html; and Karl Rove, "Obama's Campaign Is Off to a Rocky Start," *Wall*

Street Journal, May 16, 2012, http://online.wsj.com/article/SB100014240527023034484045
77408101945994054.html.

46. Husain Haqqani, *Pakistan: Between Mosque and Military* (Washington: Carnegie Endowment for International Peace, 2005), 6. Currently Pakistan's Ambassador to the United State, Haqqani has earned a strong reputation as a diplomat, political activist, and scholar.

47. Stephen Philip Cohen, *The Idea of Pakistan* (Washington: Brookings Institution, 2004), 33. Cohen's lucid history and concise analysis illuminate splendidly the Muslim League vision, Pakistan's birth pangs, its culture, and challenges.

48. Interview with Ayesha Jalal.

49. Rahmat Ali (Choudhary), "NOW OR NEVER: Are We to Live or Perish Forever," published by G. Allana, *Pakistan Movement Historical Documents* (Karachi: Department of International Relations, University of Karachi, 1969), www.columbia.edu/itc/mealac/pritchett/00islamlinks/txt_rahmatali_1933.html.

50. Cohen, *The Idea of Pakistan*, 35.

51. Ibid., 36. Cohen records that the Pakistani movement identified themselves as culturally Indian, although in opposition to Hindu Indians; an extension of South Asia Islamic empires; a legatee of the Raj tradition; a boundary between India and Central Asia; and as part of the Islamic world, a place destined to share in the *ummah*'s destiny. Ibid., 37–38.

52. Jalal, interview. The statement also appears in her excellent book, *The State of Martial Rule* (Cambridge: Cambridge University Press, 1990), 16–18. In *The Sole Spokesman: Jinnah, the Muslim League and the Demand for Pakistan* (Cambridge: Cambridge University Press, 1985), she explores "the political aims of Jinna and the All-India Muslim League in the final decade of the British raj in India" and moved to establish himself as "the sole spokesman of all Indian Muslims." Ibid., xv.

53. Jalal, interview.

54. Haqqani, *Pakistan*, 2. This book's point about the use of Islam for strategic communication is based upon Haqqani's excellent and penetrating history of events.

55. Ibid., 3. Haqqani provides an incisive, clear analysis of the politics that underlay the founding of Pakistan and some comments in this section draw upon that.

56. Amir Mir, "Was Jinnah a Secularist?," *Cobrapost.com*, www.cobrapost.com/documents/JinnahSecularist.htm

57. Ibid.

58. Ibid.

59. Ibid.

60. Ibid.

61. *Quaid-i-Azam Mohammed Ali Jinnah's Speeches as Governor General of Pakistan, 1947–48* (Karachi: Government of Pakistan, 1964).

62. Haqqani, *Pakistan*, 13. The complete text of the speech can be seen at www.pakistani.org/pakistan/legislation/constituent_address_11aug1947.html.

63. Official website, Government of Pakistan, "A Call to Duty," www.pakistan.gov.pk/Quaid/speech09.htm.

64. Official website, Government of Paksitan, "Selfless Devoting to Duty," www.pakistan.gov.pk/Quaid/speech24.htm.

65. "Celebrating Quaid-e-Azam M.A. Jinnah's Birthday," *Haq's Musings*, December 25, 2009.

66. Ibid.

67. Haqqani, *Pakistan*, 14.

68. Juan Forero, "'Alo Presidente,' Are You Still Talking?" *Washington Post*, May 30, 2009, and "What Chavez Thinks of Bush," excerpt from *Alo Presidente*, www.youtube.com/watch?v=RNvG7IAyTK4.

69. "The Hugo Chavez Show," *Frontline*, PBS, www.pbs.org/wgbh/pages/frontline/hugo chavez/interviews/.

70. Jon Lee Anderson, "Fidel's Heir," *New Yorker*, April 23, 2008, www.newyorker.com/reporting/2008/06/23/080623fa_fact_anderson?printable=true.

71. Christopher Toothaker, "Chavez Hires 200 to Manage His Twitter Account," *Associated Press*, May 8, 2010; and Evgeny Morozov, *The Net Delusion* (New York: Public Affairs, 2011), 114.

72. Bart Jones, *Hugo: The Hugo Chavez Story from Mud Hut to Perpetual Revolution* (Hanover: Steerforth Press, 2007), 235.

73. Jones, *Hugo*, 22.

74. Moises Naim, *Introduction to Hugo Chavez* (New York: Random House, 2004), xix. Naim is the editor in chief of *Foreign Policy* magazine.

75. Interview with Alberto Barrera Tyszka (identified as Alberto Barrera), *pbs.org*, www.pbs.org/wgbh/pages/frontline/hugochavez/interviews/barrera.html.

76. Jones, *Hugo*, 148.

77. Ibid., 158. Jones's book contains an excellent account of the failed coup. This description of events draws partly upon it.

78. Ibid., 156.

79. Politics is characterized by impermanence. In 2006, Arias Cardenas and Chavez made up. Chavez appointed him ambassador to the United Nations.

80. Gregory Wilpert, "Collision in Venezuela," *New Left Review*, May–June 2003, http://newleftreview.org/?view=2451.

81. Quoted by Rory Carroll, "Hugo Chavez's Twitter Habit Proves a Popular Success," *Guardian.co.uk*, August 20, 2010, www.guardian.co.uk/world/2010/aug/10/hugo-chavez-twitter-venezuela.

82. Gerhard Masur, *Simon Bolivar* (Albuquerque: University of New Mexico Press, 1948), 185.

83. Ibid., 411.

84. Robert Harvey, *Liberators: Latin America's Struggle for Independence* (Woodstock: Overlook, 2000), 124. Jones also cites this source.

85. "IACHR Publishes Report on Venezuela," *Organization of American States*, February 24, 2010, www.cidh.oas.org/Comunicados/English/2010/20V-10eng.htm. The report, however, severely criticized human rights abuses and limitations on press freedoms.

86. Raquel C. Barreiro, "Mercal Is 34% Cheaper," *El Universal.com*, March 4, 2006 (Google Translation) and "Housing Bank Transferred 66 Billion for subsidies," *El Universal.com*, November 10, 2006 (Google Translation).

87. Interview with Alberto Barrera, *pbs.org*.

88. See CIA World Factbook: Venezuela, updated March 8, 2011, www.cia.gov/library/publications/the-world-factbook/geos/ve.html; Press Freedom: Venezuela, *Freedom House* (2010): www.freedomhouse.org/template.cfm?page=251&year=2010. Freedom House considers the press not free, the only nation in Latin or Central American to receive that characterization. Most of Central and South America is considered partly free.

89. Ibid.; see also "Controversial Media-Law Changes Approved in Venezuela," *CNN.com*, December 21, 2010.

90. Jones, *Hugo.*

91. Christina Marcano and Alberto Barrera Tyszra, *Hugo Chavez*, 197; and Franklin Foer, "The Talented Mr. Chavez," *Atlantic*, May 2006.

92. Press Freedom: Venezuela, *Freedom House* (2010). The government uses 38 television channels 238 radio stations, 340 publications, and 125 websites to get out its messages.

93. Ibid.

94. See Alistair Horne, *How Far from Austerlitz: Napoleon 1805–1815* (New York: St. Martin's Press, 1996), and David A. Bell, *The First Total War* (New York: Houghton Mifflin Company, 2007).

95. Enrique Andres Pretel, "Chavez Defends His Record on Crime in Venezuela," *Reuters*, September 2, 2010, www.reuters.com/article/2010/09/03/us-venezuela-crime-id USTRE68201520100903.

96. James Bosworth, "What a Comparison of Chavez's and Calderon's Wars on Crime Can Teach," *Christian Science Monitor*, August 15, 2011.

97. Alex Kennedy and Theresa Bradley, "Chavez May Seize Supermarkets as Food Prices Surge," *Bloomberg*, February 14, 2007, www.bloomberg.com/apps/news?pid=newsarchive&sid =aeyf53XK1MQ0.

98. "Country Report: Venezuela," *Economist Intelligence Unit*, April 2011, 7, www.open source.gov/providers/eiu/report_dl.asp?issue_id=1717931556&mode=pdf.

99. Ray Walser, "Venezuela's Legislative Elections: Democratic Opposition Makes Major Gains," *Heritage.org*, September 27, 2010.

100. "Country Report: Venezuela,", 4–5, 10–11.

101. Dan Rather, "Chavez's Cancer Has 'Entered the End Stage,'" Yahoo News, May 30, 2012, http://news.yahoo.com/report--chavez-s-cancer-has--entered-the-end-stage-.html.

Chapter 10

1. Interview with John Maddox, 2011.

2. James Bradley, *Imperial Cruise* (New York: Little, Brown & Co., 2009), 5–58, 81–83. Bradley's provocative book illustrates as well a different lesson about strategic communication. Today's actions can have consequences tomorrow. Roosevelt spurred the appalling American occupation of the Philippines that triggered a bloody insurgency that cost the lives of over 4,000 Americans and 300,000 Filipinos. The bitterness persists, an object lesson for members of the Special Operations Task Force–Philippines (SOTF-P) working to help quell extremist insurgency in the southern Philippines. Americans tend to have short memories in politics, but that's not necessarily true for other cultures or nations.

3. "U.S. Image in Pakistan Falls No Further following bin Laden Killing," *Pew Research Center*, June 21, 2011, www.pewglobal.org/2011/06/21/u-s-image-in-pakistan-falls-no-further-following-bin-laden-killing/.

4. Omar Warailch, "Anatomy of a Deadly NATO Air Strike: The Pakistani Version," *Time.com*, November 30, 2011, www.time.com/time/world/article/0,8599,2100869,00.html.

Chapter 11

1. Interview with Sophie Meunier, 2011.

2. This article is based on ideas presented to Special Operations-Low-Intensity Conflict division (SOLIC) in late 2001 and developed at the Army War College in 2005, with input

from a distinguished team of military and civilian experts, and updated since then with input from Col. (Ret.) Al Bynum, Daniel Devlin, and Rafal Rohozinski.

3. Not *all* conflicts fit one model. War is characterized by fast change, variants, and surprise. Every major war in the last hundred years surprised political leaders and presumably commanders—partly in that they occurred, partly in their conduct, and partly in what achieved victory. The author comes from the perspective of political and corporate communications, where there is no formula for winning.

4. See Thomas Ricks, *The Gamble* (New York: Penguin Press, 2008). This chapter is oriented to what the military might think about in forging and executing information strategies, but strategic success requires a cross-government approach. The suggestions offered here aim to support and reinforce information strategies and plans that the State Department is separately sponsoring. The Defense and State Departments need to collaborate on a cross-government basis to maximize information operations and strategic information planning. The infrastructure to maximize these efforts already exists.

5. Roger Trinquier, *Modern Warfare: A French View of Counterinsurgency* (Westport, CT: Praeger Security International, 1964). Trinquier ignited deep controversy over his views on interrogation and is often ignored. His argument that defeating an insurgency requires providing security to a population is well recognized. See also Daniel Galula, *Counterinsurgency Warfare* (Westport, CT: Praeger Security International, 1964). Galula's book heavily influenced the current US Army manual on counterinsurgency.

6. See *Encyclopedia Britannica*, 14th edition (1929) and Lawrence's commentary on guerilla warfare specially commissioned for that edition.

7. See Jack Weatherford, *Genghis Kahn and the Making of the Modern World* (New York: Three Rivers Press, 2004), 142–59.

8. Thomas X. Hammes has written insightfully on the impact of strategies and tactics in the Middle East in *The Sling and the Arrow* (St. Paul, MN: Zenith Press, 2004).

9. Controversies such as Abu Ghraib in Iraq show how military actions can have second- and third-order effects on American voters. Civilian leadership approves information strategy, but the military must ensure that civilian policy is clear and that military strategies and tactics reflect those policies, not just the commander's intent.

Chapter 12

1. "Morocco to Put New Constitution to Public Vote," *Agence France Presse*, March 10, 2011, and "Morocco's King Promises Elected PM, Revised Constitution," *thestar.com*, March 10, 2011.

2. Hassan Alaoui, "Morocco Constitution to Be Revised, Says King," *Huffington Post*, March 22, 2011.

3. "Fraud Claims Taint Musharraf Win," *CNN.com*, May 2, 2002.

4. NATO Strategic Concept, "Core Tasks and Principles," November 19, 2010, No. 1.

5. Interview with Stephen Padgett. Various interviews with Col. Padgett (one of the colonels to whom this book is dedicated) have been previously noted.

6. Ibid.; W. Murray and M. Grimsley, "Introduction: On Strategy," *The Making of Strategy: Rulers, States, and War*, ed. Williamson Murray and Alvin Bernstein (Cambridge: Cambridge University Press, 1994), 12.

7. See Hedrick Smith, *The Power Game: How Washington Works* (New York: Ballantine Books, 1996).

8. See Robert Fisk, *The Great War for Civilisation* (New York: Knopf, 2005), 201–4, 256–58; and Kenneth M. Pollack, *The Persian Puzzle: The Conflict between Iran and America* (New York: Random House, 2004), chapter 7.

9. Goeffrey Park, "Making of Strategy in Habsburg Spain," in *The Making of Strategy: Rulers, States, and War,* 127 and 129.

10. "Russian Orthodox Church Sets Out to Be 'First among Equals,' *Radio Free Europe,* March 21, 2010.

Chapter 13

1. Williamson Murray and Mark Grimsley, "Introduction: On Strategy," *The Making of Strategy: Rulers, States, and War,* ed. Williamson Murray and Alvin Bernstein (Cambridge: Cambridge University Press, 1994), 1.

2. See Donald Kagan, "Athenian Strategy in the Peloponnesian War," in *The Making of Strategy,* chapter 2. Kagan's biography of Pericles is a classic case study in political/military strategy. See Donald Kagan, *Pericles of Athens and the Birth of Democracy* (New York: The Free Press, 1991).

3. Richard H. Schultz and Andrew J. Dew, *Insurgents, Terrorists and Militias* (New York: Columbia University Press, 2006).

4. Interview with Joe Gaylord, 2011. For over two decades, Joe has been my partner and colleague on many political and corporate campaigns and has greatly influenced my thinking about strategic communication. His election campaign books, including his latest, *Campaign Solutions,* describe in detail precepts that govern election campaigns. See www.americansolutions.com/solutionsacademy/wiki/index.php/Candidate_Trainingd.

5. Interview with Ron Faucheux, 2011. Faucheux and I have worked together for forty years on various political campaigns, commencing in a 1969 New Orleans mayoral campaign, and we share a common approach on strategy. He has quantified some of the best precepts that top political consultants employ in one of the three best books written about winning election to public office on US politics, *Running for Office* (New York: M. Evans & Company, 2002). Joe Gaylord, *Flying Upside Down,* a challenger's playbook originally written for the Republican National Committee, and its sequel for incumbents, *Flying Rightside Up,* are very insightful.

6. Lou Cannon, *Role of a Lifetime* (New York: Simon & Schuster, 1991), 496.

7. Lori Montgomery, "Running in the Red: How the U.S., on the Road to Surplus, Detoured to Massive Debt," *Washington Post,* April 30, 2011.

8. "CIDE Presents the Survey Results, 'Mexico, the Americas and the World,'" *Protocolo.*

9. Douglas Farah and Stephen Braun, *Merchant of Death* (Hoboken: John Wiley & Sons, 2007).

10. Ibid.

11. See William Booth and Steve Fainaru, "New Strategy Urged in Mexico: Calderon's U.S.-Backed War against Drug Cartels Losing Support," *Washington Post,* July 28, 2009.

12. The military's notion of operational design employs narrative in a slightly different context. Design treats narrative as a way to connect data and meaning through story and plot that describe an evolving strategic situation and the logic of a mission to overcome obstacles and achieve objectives or a desired end-state. It communicates the design team's explanation of the environment, the problem, and the solution. It helps understand the logic of what is observed. For the military, discourse is the means by which narrative is articulated.

13. Mark J. Penn with E. Kinney Zalesore, *Microtrends* (New York: Twelve, 2007), and personal discussions with Penn.

14. Sarah Palin's impact has been debated. She fired up the Republican base, although independent voters reacted less favorably.

15. Charles Moore, "The Invincible Mrs. Thatcher," *Vanity Fair*, December 2011, www.vanityfair.com/politics/features/2011/12/margaret-thatcher-201112. See also Charles Moore, *The Life of Margaret Thatcher* (London: Allen Lane, 2009). The best and most insightful—though biting—biography of Thatcher came from Hugo Young, who well understood her strengths and weaknesses. See Hugo Young, *The Iron Lady* (London: Noonday Press, 1989).

16. Will Stewart, "Revealed: Red Army Colonel Who Dubbed Maggie the Iron Lady . . . and Changed History," *Mail Online*, February 24, 2007, www.dailymail.co.uk/news/article-438281/Revealed-Red-Army-colonel-dubbed-Maggie-Iron-Lady---changed-history.html. See also Margaret Thatcher, *The Downing Street Years* (New York: Harper Collins, 1993), 65.

17. Thatcher, *Downing Street Years*, 10.

18. Young, *Iron Lady*, 135.

19. Thatcher, *Downing Street Years*, 122.

20. Ibid. See also "Thatcher 'Not for Turning,'" *BBC News*, http://news.bbc.co.uk/onthis day/hi/dates/stories/october/10/newsid_2541000/2541071.stm.

21. Neville Bolt, *The Violent Image: Insurgent Propaganda and the New Revolutionaries* (London: C. Hurst & Co., 2012), 32, citing James Harding, *Alpha Dogs: How Political Spin Became a Global Business* (London: Atlantic Books, 2008).

22. Interview with Scott Miller, 2012.

23. Margaret Thatcher, "Gulf War: Bush-Thatcher Phone Conversation (No Time to Go Wobbly [memoires extract]," August 26, 1990, Margaret Thatcher Foundation, www.margaret thatcher.org/document/110711.

24. "The Miners Strike," BBC News, August 15, 2008, www.bbc.co.uk/wales/history/sites/themes/society/industry_coal06.shtml.

25. Moore, *Life of Margaret Thatcher*.

26. Paul Treckel, "Forging the Thunderbolts: Elizabeth Cady Stanton and American Feminism," Chautauqua Institution, July 28, 1995, http://gos.sbc.edu/t/treckel.html.

27. Alma Lutz, *Susan B. Anthony: Rebel, Crusader, Humanitarian* (Washington: Zenger Publishing Co., 1959), Kindle location 859/6981.

28. Geoffrey C. Ward and Ken Burns, *Not for Ourselves Alone* (New York: Knopf, 1999), 38–41, 58–61 sets out the wording of the Declaration in full.

29. Ibid., 38–41. See also Declaration of Independence, paragraph 2, www.ushistory.org/declaration/document/.

30. Ward and Burns, *Not for Ourselves Alone*, 52.

31. "Declaration of Sentiments," published in full in Ward and Burns, *Not for Ourselves Alone*, 58–61. See also Douglas M. Rife, *Seneca Falls Declaration of Sentiments and Resolutions* (Dayton, OH: Teaching & Learning Company, 2002).

32. Elinor Rice Hays, *Morning Star: A Biography of Lucy Stone* (New York: Harcourt, Brace, 1961), 88.

33. Ward and Burns, *Not for Ourselves Alone*, 95.

34. Lori D. Ginzberg, *Elizabeth Cady Stanton: An American Life* (New York: MacMillan, 2010), 42.

35. Passed in 1972 by both houses of Congress, the Equal Rights Amendment (ERA) states that "equality of rights under the law shall not be denied or abridged by the United States or by any State on account of sex." Submitted to the states for ratification, which had to occur by March 22, 1979, thirty states moved rapidly to pass it. Only five of the required thirty-five states ultimately did so, and four rescinded their ratification. The tragedy for proponents was that the ERA failed because its political leadership failed, allowing themselves to be painted as goofy, extreme, and, in light of modern interpretations of the Fourteenth Amendment, pursuing a new amendment that substantively failed to expand constitutional rights that were already assured.

36. Ann Gordon, "Taking Possession of the Country," in Ward and Burns, *Not for Ourselves Alone*, 163.

37. In 1875, the US Supreme Court rejected that view, holding that citizenship referred to "membership in a nation and nothing more." *Minor v. Happersett*, 88 U.S. 162, 167 (1875). The case upheld Missouri state court decisions that denied women the right to vote because state laws permitted only men to vote. See www.law.cornell.edu/supct/html/historics/USSC_CR_0088_0162_ZS.html.

38. Stanton declined to follow suit, causing Anthony great angst. See Lutz, *Susan B. Anthony*, Kindle location 3292/6981.

39. Ibid.

40. Ibid., Kindle locations 3307–3455.

41. Ibid., Kindle location 3357.

42. The fatwa was first published in *Al Quds Al Arabi*, a London-based newspaper in August of 1996, and titled "Declaration of War against the Americans Occupying the Land of the Two Holy Places." See www.pbs.org/newshour/terrorism/international/fatwa_1996.html.

43. See Fawaz Gerges, *Journey of the Jihadist* (New York: Harcourt, 2005).

44. Establishing a seventh-century society may resonate rhetorically with some people, but it's hardly a political agenda on which to rest a real revolution.

45. "Osama bin Laden Largely Discredited among Muslim Publics in Recent Years," *Pew Global Attitudes Project*, May 2, 2011, http://pewglobal.org/2011/05/02/osama-bin-laden-largely-discredited-among-muslim-publics-in-recent-years/.

46. See, e.g., the Global World Poll, April 24, 2007, surveying Morocco, Egypt, Pakistan, and Indonesia, which shows that large majorities in those nations agree that a key strategic US goal is to protect its access to oil. A separate question elicited the majority view that "America pretends to be helpful to Muslim countries, but in fact everything it does is really part of a scheme to take advantage of the people in the Middle East and steal their oil." Pew's 2007 poll reached a similar conclusion. An April 20, 2007, Global World Opinion poll of Morocco, Pakistan, Egypt, and Indonesia shows that high percentages oppose al-Qaeda attacks *and* the United States. But many support al-Qaeda's views of the United States, and majorities endorsed their objectives.

47. Louise Richardson, *What Terrorists Want* (New York: Random House, 2006), 85–87.

48. Ibid.

49. Gil Mirom, *How Democracies Lose Small Wars* (New York: Cambridge University Press, 2003) wonders if democracies are capable of winning asymmetric wars—what he terms "small wars." He argues that winning requires the brutal tactics and a cost we won't bear. He's dead wrong about the need for brutality. The danger of that—as McChrystal and Petraeus have recognized—is evident in the blowback caused by civilian casualties.

50. Interagency coordination between the Department of Defense and the Department of State; academia, corporations, and other coalitions and global partners may prove a make or break in achieving that. Quantitative and qualitative research through polling, focus groups, and even mall intercepts can be crucially helpful—to confirm judgments and instincts, not as a substitute for them.

51. Royal Navy Lt. Commander Steve Tatham, "Hearts and Minds—Time to Get Smarter," May 2007; private paper, 2. See also Andrew Mackay and Steve Tatham, *Behavioral Conflict* (Saffron Walden: Military Press, 2011).

52. See John A. Nagl, *Learning to Eat Soup with a Knife* (Chicago: University of Chicago Press, 2002), part II.

53. See www.youtube.com/watch?v=esUTn6L0UDU; Karl Rove, interview, *Fox News Sunday:* November 8, 2004, www.foxnews.com/story/0,2933,137853,00.html.

54. Interview, Ron Faucheux.

55. Interview with Martin Hamburger, 2011.

56. The 2004 presidential election opened a new era, as for the first time bloggers were accredited as part of the presidential press corps. See Shirley Biagi, *Media/Impact: An Introduction to Mass Media* (Florence, KY: Wadsworth Publishing, 2006), 187.

57. "In Russia, Bloggers Report on Election Fraud," *Ground Report,* October 19, 2009, www.groundreport.com/World/In-Russia-Bloggers-Report-on-Election-Fraud/2909571.

58. Ibid.

59. Joshua Goldstein and Juliana Rotich, "Digitally Networked Technology in Kenya's 2007–2008 Post-Election Crisis," Berkman Center for Internet and Society at Harvard University, September 2008, 2, 8, http://cyber.law.harvard.edu/sites/cyber.law.harvard.edu/files/Goldstein&Rotich_Digitally_Networked_Technology_Kenyas_Crisis.pdf.pdf.

60. The National Accord and Reconciliation Act, Februay 28, 2008, signed by both Kibaki and Odinga. See "Key Points: Kenya Power-Sharing Deal," *BBC News*, February 28, 2008, http://news.bbc.co.uk/2/hi/africa/7269476.stm.

61. Michael Weiss, "Obladi, Obrador, Life Goes On," *Slate.com*, July 7, 2006.

62. Interview with Joe Gaylord.

63. Interview with Glen Bolger, 2011.

64. Garrett M. Graff, "The First Campaign: Globalization, the Web, and the Race for the White House," *Carnegiecouncil.org*, December 6, 2007; Hamburger, interview.

65. Interview with Patricia H. Kushlis, 2011.

66. Bolger, interview.

67. Massachusetts voters are networked online. Fewer than 5 percent of Kenyans have regular Internet access. But, Goldstein and Retich report, their "influence ballooned further when radio broadcasters began to read influential bloggers over the airwaves, helping them reach not 5%, but 95 percent of the Kenya population." Joshua Goldstein and Juliana Rotich, "Digitally Networked Technology in Kenya's 2007–2008 Post-Election Crisis," 8.

68. "Bloggers Offer No Apologies over Impact on News," *Associated Press/MSNBC.com*, November 14, 2004.

69. See George Packer, *Assassin's Gate*.

70. Mark Perry, *Talking to Terrorists* (New York: Basic Books, 2010), 54–55. Packard recounts how a group of US officers had effectively laid the groundwork for reconstituting the army, although on a smaller scale.

71. Interview with Ron Faucheux, 2011.

72. The author has discussed with Maxwell this concept on many occasions, and employed it with him in campaigns.

73. "Somalia: Sheik Hassan Dahir Aweys Dismisses Washington's Accusation," *AfricaFiles. org*, September 11, 2007; older quote but included as it sets a foundation for his posture. "Somalia: Hizbul Islam Chief Accuses Senior Rebel of 'Joining Govt,'" *Garoweonline*, April 28, 2010.

74. "Somalia's Shabaab Pledges to Help Yemen's Qaeda," *alarabiya.net*, January 1, 2010, and Mohammaed Omar Hussein, "Somalia: Al-Shabab Claims to Have Damaged a Drone," *somaliweyn.org*, March 30, 2010.

75. "Al-Qaeda Linked Al-Shabaab Bans Prayer Beads," *The Jawa Report/mypetjawa.mu.nu*, May 23, 2010.

76. "Somalia: Al-Shabab Outlaws Cutting Down of Trees," *somaliweyn.org*, May 10, 2010.

77. "Al-Shabab Imposes Curfew over Stronghold," *Hiiraan OnLine*, February 7, 2010.

78. Abdi Sheikh, "Somalia Islamists Pull Teeth from 'Sinners,'—Residents," *Reuters*, August 12, 2009.

79. Abdulkarim Jimale, "Al-Shabab Bans Bell Rings for Schools," *beforeitsnews.com*, cited on *shabelle.net*, April 15, 2010.

80. "Valentines Day Al Shabab Style (Beheading)," *mypetjaw.mu.nu/shabelle.net*, February 14, 2009.

81. Katherine Houreld, "Somali Militants Increasing Use of Child Soldiers," *GaroweOnLine*, May 1, 2010.

82. "Stop Terror Sheikhs, Muslim Academics Demand," *Arab News*, October 30, 2004, cited by Robin Wright, *Dreams and Shadows* (New York: Penguin Press, 2008).

83. Wright, *Dreams and Shadows*, 5.

84. See www.ammammessage.com/.

85. Peter Carlson, "Embedded with the Resistance: Iraqi 'Terrorists' Tell Their Story in Harpers," *Washington Post*, June 1, 2004.

Chapter 14

1. See *Encyclopedia Britannica*, 14th ed. (1929), and Lawrence's commentary on guerilla warfare specially commissioned for that edition.

2. T. E. Lawrence, *The Seven Pillars of Wisdom* (New York: Anchor Books, 1991), chapter 33.

3. "Bahrain King Declares Martial Law over Protests," *Associated Press*, March 15, 2011, www.msnbc.com/id/42087238/ns/world_news-mideast-n-africa/t/bahrain-/tng-declares-martial-law-over-protests/.

4. Steven Erlanger, "Sarkozy Reshuffles Cabinet Once Again," *New York Times*, February 27, 2011, www.nytimes.com/2011/02/28/world/europe/28france-sarkozy-cabinet.html ?ref=alainjuppe.

5. Katrin Bennhold, "Sarkozy Reshuffles Cabinet after an Election Setback," *New York Times*, June 20, 2007, www.nytimes.com/2007/06/20/world/europe/20france.html?ref=alainjuppe.

6. "Brown Continues Cabinet Reshuffle," *BBC.co.uk*, October 4, 2008; "Britain's Cabinet Reshuffle Revealed," *English.people.com*, June 6, 2009; and "Britain's Cabinet Reshuffle: Blair's Own Goal," *Economist*, June 19, 2003.

7. Carl von Clausewitz, *On War*, Kindle location 1414–22.

8. Interview with Glenn Ayers, 2011.

9. Ibid.

10. Different cultures utilize different channels of communication to transmit information, but do so quickly. For example, in the Middle East, text messaging on cellphones seems an especially popular way to instantly communicate information. In this country, text messaging seems popular among younger audiences, but it hardly ranks as more common compared to e-mail.

11. The Swift Boat Veterans for Truth website is www.swiftvets.com.

12. See, e.g., Maria I. La Ganga and Stephen Braun, "Veterans Battle over the Truth," *Los Angeles Times,* August 17, 2007; and Maria Newman, "Campaigns Continue to Focus on Kerry's War Record," *The New York Times,* August 25, 2004.

13. Peter Ford, "Europe Cringes at Bush 'Crusade' against Terrorists," *Christian Science Monitor*, September 19, 2001, quoting from the president's address to Congress.

14. Robert D. Burrowes, "Political Economy and the Effort against Terrorism," in *Battling Terrorism in the Horn of Africa*, R. I. Rotberg, ed. (Washington, DC: Brookings Institution Press, 2005), 146.

15. Interview with Stephen Padgett.

16. Ibid.

17. Ibid.

Chapter 15

1. Joseph Nye, *Soft Power* (New York: Public Affairs, 2004), 48–49.

2. Sam Wasson, *Fifth Avenue, 5 A.M.: Audrey Hepburn, Breakfast at Tiffany's, and the Dawn of the Modern Woman* (New York: Harper, 2010).

3. Victor Malarek, *The Natashas: Inside the New Global Sex Trade* (New York: Arcade Publishing, 2004).

4. Jack G. Shaheen, *Reel Bad Arabs: How Hollywood Vilifies a People* (New York: Olive Branch Press, 2001), and Shaheen, *Guilty: Hollywood's Verdict on Arabs after 9/11* (New York: Olive Branch Press, 2008).

5. Mark Danner also noticed this. See "Words in a Time of War: On Rhetoric, Truth, and Power," *What Orwell Didn't Know: Propaganda and the New Face of Politics* (New York: Public Affairs, 2007), 25.

6. Tony Schwartz, *The Responsive Chord* (New York: Anchor Press, 1973), 93.

7. Ibid., 96.

8. The ad can be viewed at www.lbjlib.utexas.edu/johnson/media/daisyspot/.

9. Michael Vlahos, "Terror's Mask: Insurgency within Islam," paper, Johns Hopkins University Applied Physics Laboratory, May 2002, 18–19, www.jhuapl.edu/POW/library/terror mask.htm.

10. The BBC documentary "Jihad_TV.avi" available at http://video.google.ca/videoplay ?docid=6652279024382177865&total=31&start=o&num=10&so=o&type=search&plin dex=9, explores this pattern in detail.

11. The jihadi videos discussed in this essay were captured by the center for International Issues Research. Ala Fa'ik of the center was especially helpful in providing videos, translations, and other assistance.

12. For a discussion of insurgent communication tactics in Iraq, see Daniel Kimmage and Kathleen Ridolfo, "Iraqi Insurgent Media: The War of Ideas and Images" (Washington, DC: Radio Free Europe/Radio Liberty, 2007), www.rferl.org/content/article/1077316.html.

13. The center for International Issues Research identified versions of this video on Arabic, Chechen, and Indonesian websites in a variety of languages. See netislam.magnify.net/video/the re-emergence-of-the-crusader-theater.

14. Interview with Patricia Kushlis, 2011.

15. See, for example, "Global Unease with Major World Powers," Pew Global Attitudes Project, June 2007, available at http://pewglobal.org/2007/06/27/global-unease-with-major-world-powers/. Pew's polling since the 2003 Iraq War has consistently shown hostile attitudes among most Muslims towards the American presence. See also Anthony Cordesman, "Iraqi Perceptions of the War: Public Opinion by City and Region" (Washington, DC: Center for Strategical International Studies, 2007), http://csis.org/files/media/csis/pubs/070502_burke iraq_perceptions.pdf.

16. Marc Lynch, *Voices of the New Arab Public* (New York: Columbia University Press, 2006), 6.

17. Versions of *The Top Ten* were produced in 2004, 2005, and 2006, and *The Top Twenty* in 2007.

18. Pamela Constable, "In Kabul, Taliban Videos Hold Allure," *Washington Post*, July 3, 2011.

19. www.goarmy.com/download/games.jsp. See Marty Graham, "Army Game Proves U.S. Can't Lose," *Wired*, November 27, 2006. Clerk Boyd, "US Army Cuts Teeth on Video Game," *BBC News*, November 25, 2005.

20. See http://secondlife.com/.

21. Tom Perry, "Hezbollah Brings Israel War to Computer Screen," *Reuters*, August 16, 2007.

22. Ibid. Trailers for the two Special Force games can be viewed at www.youtube.com/watch?v-Y4ktvNztwsY and www.youtube.com/watch?v-OUux6nxN5CI.

23. Jose Antonio Vargas, "Virtual Reality Prepares Soldiers for Real War," *Washington Post*, February 14, 2006.

24. Ali Akbar Dareini, "Iranian Video Game Rescues Nuke Scientist," *MSNBC*, July 16, 2007, www.msnbc.msn.com/id/19792794/.

25. Ibid.; Zach Whalen, "Iran vs. America, the Video Game," Gameology, www.game-ology.org/node/1051; see also the gaming site Firing Squad at www.firingsquad.com/news/newsarticle.asp?asearchid=10469.

26. Private conversation with Farhad Cacard at the USSOCOM/USSTRATCOM Foreign Military Attaché Conference, Tampa, Florida, November 8, 2007; see also Walid Phares, *The War of Ideas* (New York: Palgrave Macmillan, 2007).

27. See Louise Richardson, *What Terrorists Want* (New York: Random House, 2006), 85–87. Olivier Roy argues that the inability of Islamists to define a viable vision for a society to replace that which they would overturn leads to inevitable failure. See Olivier Roy, *The Failure of Political Islam*, trans. Carol Volk (Cambridge, MA: Harvard University Press, 1994).

28. See John Rob, *Brave New War* (Hoboken, NJ: John Wiley, 2007), 20.

29. See Timothy L. Thomas, "Cyber Mobilization: A Growing Counterinsurgency Campaign," *IOSphere*, Summer 2006, 23–28, www.av.af.mil/info-ops/iosphere summer 06-thomas.pdf.

30. See Bruce Hoffman, *Inside Terrorism* (New York: Columbia University Press, 2006), 96–97; Jason Burke, *Al-Qaeda* (London: I.B. Tauris, 2003), 32–33; and Peter Bergin, *The Osama Bin Laden I Know* (New York: The Free Press, 2006), 196, 205–8.

31. See Quintan Wiktorowicz, "A Genealogy of Radical Islam," *Studies in Conflict and Terrorism* 28, no. 2 (March–April 2005): 75–97.

32. See, for example, Thomas Ricks, *Fiasco* (New York: Penguin, 2006).

33. See Fawaz Gerges, *Journey of the Jihadist* (New York: Harcourt Books, 2006).

34. See www.youtube.com/watch?v=uxJyPsmEask.

35. See www.youtube.com/watch?v=2mUn2c_PKho&NR=1.

36. See www.youtube.com/watch?v=OYecfV3ubP8 (1984) and www.youtube.com/watch ?v=6h3G-IMZxjo (Vote Different).

37. See www.youtube.com/watch?v=YilPdQ2tVIE.

38. The Los Angeles production company 900 Frames and Lebanon's EFXFilms claimed credit, but the funding source has not been disclosed. See "Television War: Big-Budget Ad Battles Suicide Bombing," Salon.com, www.salon.com/ent/video_dog/ads/2006/08/22/iraq_psa/; and Lorraine Ali, "This Is Your Street Mid-Bombing," *Newsweek*, June 20, 2006. 900 Frames bragged that it was imitating the film *The Matrix* in its use of a 120-camera setup for special effects.

Chapter 16

1. The best-known research was conducted by Alison des Forge of Human Rights Watch, who testified before the International Criminal Tribunal for Rwanda as a Prosecution Expert. She authored what is considered the most authoritative work on the genocide. See Alison Des Forges, *Leave None to Tell the Story* (London: Human Rights Watch, 1999). In addition to the Judgments of the International Criminal Tribunal for Rwanda, other important sources reviewed include Scott Straus, "What Is the Relationship between Hate Radio and Violence? Rethinking Rwanda's 'Radio Machete,'" *Politics and Society* 35, no. 4, December 2007 (note: the author also interviewed Straus); Romeo Dallaire, *Shake Hands with the Devil* (New York: Carroll & Graf, 2003); *The Media and the Rwanda Genocide*, ed. Allan Thompson (London: Pluto Press, 2007); Jean-Pierre Chretien and Marcel Kabanda commentaries in *The Media and the Rwanda Genocide* (Chretien is considered a notably important scholar of the genocide); Darryl Li, "Echoes of Violence: Considerations On Radio and Genocide in Rwanda," *Journal of Genocide Research* (March 2004), www.harvard. academic.edu/DarrylLi/papers/329115/echoes-of-violence+consideration-on-radio-and-genocide-in-rwanda; Mary Kimani, "RTLM: The Medium That Became a Tool for Mass Murder," *International Development Research Centre*, www.idrc.ca/en/ev-108190-201-1-DO_TOPIC.html; B. Jones, "The Arusha Peace Process," *The Path of Genocide: The Rwanda Crisis from Uganda to Zaire*, eds. H. Adelman and A. Suhkre (New Brunswick: Transaction Publishers, 1999); Charles Mironko, "The Effect of RTLM's Rhetoric of Ethnic Hatred in Rwanda," *International Development Research Centre*, www.idrc.ca/cp/ev-108192-201-1-DO_TOPIC.html; Linda Malvern, *A People Betrayed: The Role of the West in Rwanda's Genocide*, 2nd. ed. (London: Zed Books, 2009); Philip Gourevitch, *We Wish to Inform You That Tomorrow We Will Be Killed with Our Families: Stories from Rwanda* (New York: Farrar, Straus and Giroux, 1998); Jean Hatzfeld, *Machete Season: The Killers in Rwanda Speak* (New York: Farrar, Straus, and Giroux, 2005); and Samantha Power, "Bystanders to Genocide," *Atlantic*, September 2001, www.theatlantic.com/magazine/archive/2001/09/bystanders-to-genocide/4571/.

2. Des Forges's book is expensive, but the most authoritative history. Gourevitch is elegant, concise, insightful, and well merited the National Book Critics Circle Award for his work.

3. The statement of facts here is largely drawn from the findings of fact determined by the International Criminal Tribunal for Rwanda in the prosecutions against Simon Bikindi, Ferdinand Jean-Bosco Barayagwiza, and Hassan Ngeze. Its nuanced, detailed examination and assessment of the evidence is impressive. See *The Prosecutor v Ferdinand Nahimana, Jean-Bosco Barayagwiza and Hassan Ngeze*, Case No. ICTR-99-52-T, www.rwandainitiative.ca/resources/pdfs/judgment.pdf; and the *Prosecutor v Simon Bikindi*, Case No. ICTR-01-72-T, www.unhcr.org/cgi-bin/texis/vtx/refworld/rwmain/opendocpdf.pdf?reldoc=y&docid=4935248c2.

4. *The Prosecutor v Ferdinand Nahimana*, 29.

5. Ibid.

6. Ibid., 30.

7. Ibid.

8. Ibid., 76–77. After the assassination, she was evacuated from the country on a French plane to French exile. She was arrested in 2010 on a warrant issued by the Rwandan government. See also Philip Gourevitch, "The Arrest of Madame Agathe," *New Yorker*, March 2, 2010, www.newyorker.com/online/blogs/newsdesk/2010/03/the-arrest-of-madame-agathe.html.

9. *The Prosecutor v Ferdinand Nahimana*, 32.

10. Gerald Caplan, "Rwanda: Walking the Road to Genocide," in *The Media and the Rwanda Genocide*, 24.

11. Ibid.

12. Ibid., 33.

13. Ibid.

14. Parti Social Democrate, Parti Liberal, Parti Democrate Chretien, and the Mouvement Democratique Republicain.

15. *The Prosecutor v Ferdinand Nahimana*, 34, and United Nations Security Council Resolution 872 (1993).

16. Caplan, "Rwanda," 25.

17. Dallaire, *Shake Hands with the Devil*, 141–47.

18. See Alison L. Des Forges and Alan J. Kuperman, "Shame Rationalizing Western Apathy on Rwanda," *Foreign Affairs*, May–June 2000, www.foreignaffairs.com/articles/56063/Alison-1-des-forges-and-alan-j-kuperman/shame-rationalizing-western-apathy-on-rwanda. Des Forges is viewed by many as the leading authority on the genocide. She and Kuperman hold conflicting views on critical aspects of the tragedy and the options available for preventing or stopping it.

19. Gerald Caplan, comment on *Shake Hands with the Devil*, *New York Review of Books*, May 26, 2005, www.nybooks.com/articles/archives/2005/dec/01/shake-hands-with-the-devil/. Caplan's view is supported by Daillaire, Alison des Forges, Samantha Power, and others. The United States had 300 marines in Burundi.

20. Alan J. Kuperman, "Rwanda in Retrospect," *Foreign Affairs*, January–February 2000, www.forgeignaffairs.com/articles/55636/alan-j-kuperman/rwanda-in-retrospect.

21. Des Forges and Kuperman, "Shame Rationalizing Western Apathy."

22. It's worth noting that Tutsi leader Paul Kagame opposed outside intervention on grounds that it might interfere with his own ambitions.

23. See Power, "Bystanders to Genocide." After September 11, Clarke would earn his living complaining that the George W. Bush administration was insufficiently focused on protecting the world from terrorism, which targets innocent civilians for violence.

24. This is a point Philip Gourevitch stresses in *We Wish to Inform*, 89.

25. *The Prosecutor v Ferdinand Nahimana*, 37.

26. Ibid., 36.

27. Ibid., 36–37.

28. Ibid., 45–47.

29. Ibid., 51.

30. Ibid.

31. Ibid., 62.

32. Ibid., 62–63.

33. Quoted by Li, "Echoes of Violence," 15.

34. *The Prosecutor v Ferdinand Nahimana*, 63.

35. Li, "Echoes of Violence," 12–15.

36. Des Forges, "Call to Genocide," 44.

37. *The Prosecutor v Ferdinand Nahimana*, 146; *The Prosecutor v Simon Bikindi*, 48.

38. Li, "Echoes of Violence."

39. *The Prosecutor v Ferdinand Nahimana,* 121.

40. *The Prosecutor v Simon Bikindi*, 26. The tribunal explains the use of these two loaded terms to denigrate the Tutsi.

41. *The Prosecutor v Ferdinand Nahimana*, 121.

42. Ibid., 123.

43. Ibid., 126.

44. Ibid., 127–28.

45. Ibid., 130.

46. Ibid., 135.

47. Straus, interview; see also Straus, "What Is the Relationship between Hate Radio and Violence?"

48. *The Prosecutor v Ferdinand Nahimana*, 140.

49. Ibid., 141.

50. Ibid., 141–42.

51. Ibid., 147.

52. Ibid., 148.

53. Ibid.; *The Prosecutor v Simon Bikindi*, 48–56.

54. *The Prosecutor v Simon Bikindi,* 52.

55. Ibid.

56. See www.youtube.com/watch?v=ZR0ZsEFypoo.

57. *The Prosecutor v Simon Bikindi,* 61.

58. Ibid., 62.

59. Ibid.

60. *The Prosecutor v Ferdinand Nahimana*, 164.

61. Straus, interview.

62. *The Prosecutor v Ferdinand Nahimana,* 164–65.

63. Ibid., 164.

64. Ibid., 164–66.

65. Ibid., 166.

66. Ibid., 313.

67. Ibid., 316.

68. Declassified Memorandum from Under Secretary of Defense Frank G. Wisner to national security advisor Sandy Berger, May 5, 1994, www.gwu.edu/~nsarchiv/NSAEBB /NSAEBB53/rw050594.pdf.

69. Interview with Joseph D. Duffey.

70. Straus, interview.

71. Philip Gourevitch offers excellent insights on this issue in chapter 12 of his book.

Chapter 17

1. Interview with Ken Berman, director, Information and Technology, Broadcasting Board of Governors, 2011.

2. See www.state.gov/r/pa/prs/ps/2012/01/180136.htm.

3. Presidential Executive Order, March 17, 2011.

4. Interview with Patricia Kushlis, 2011. See also Christopher Paul, *Strategic Communication*, 39, 87.

5. See "Forging a New Shield," *Project for National Security Reform*, November 2008, 56–62, http://pnsr.org/data/files/pnsr%20forging%20a%20new%20shield.pdf; Kenneth Osgood, *Total Cold War*, 85–86; and Fred I. Greenstein, *The Hidden Hand Presidency: Eisenhower as Leader*, 132–36.

6. "Forging a New Shield," 62; and Douglas Kinnard (quoting John D. Eisenhower), *President Eisenhower and Strategy Management: A Study in Defense Politics* (Washington: International Defense Publishers, 1989), 133–34.

7. Kushlis, interview.

8. We think of criminal activity as aimed at profit, while terrorist activity is aimed at achieving political objectives. Some other countries view any activity that threatens their stability or integrity as terrorist.

9. Shibley Telhami, *The Stakes* (Cambridge: Westview Press 2002), 8. Louise Richardson rightly points out that the asserted justness of a cause is a key to the rationale of terrorists like Osama bin Laden in their self-branding as "revolutionaries." Richardson, *What Terrorists Want*, 8.

10. While that view has proven characteristic of most insurgency and terrorist actions, our own strategic approach to countering them has tended to put military action first. There are stirrings—led by Generals Petraeus and McChrystal—to give more and, indeed, equal emphasis to information effects, but that has not been characteristic of US strategy in the past.

About the Author

James P. Farwell is an author, defense consultant, and an internationally recognized expert in strategic communication and cyber warfare who has advised the US Department of Defense, US Strategic Command (STRATCOM), US Special Operations Command (SOCOM), the Office of Undersecretary for Defense (Policy), and the Office of Undersecretary of Defense (Intelligence). For SOCOM he was a coarchitect of Sovereign Challenge, a flagship program of the COCOM entailing outreach to foreign military attachés and senior military officers.

He is a senior research scholar in strategic studies at the Canada Centre for Global Security Studies (Canada Centre), Munk School of Global Affairs, University of Toronto. He writes widely on national security affairs. Farwell is the author of *The Pakistan Cauldron: Conspiracy, Assassination and Instability* (Washington, DC: Potomac Books, 2011). His commentaries have appeared in *The National Interest, Christian Science Monitor, Huffington Post, Survival,* and numerous other publications.

He is a longtime political consultant with international experience in handling campaigns at the presidential level in South Korea, Greece, Bermuda, and other nations. *Campaigns & Elections* named him among its "rising stars," and *Roll Call* cited him as one of the top political consultants in the United States.

Farwell is also an attorney who has a J.D. from Tulane University and a D.C.L.S. in Comparative Law from the University of Cambridge (Trinity College), UK. He has served as an arbitrator for the New York Stock Exchange and the American Arbitration Association.

Index